Contents at a Glance

About the Author. . .

Herbert Schildt is the world's leading programming author. He is an authority on the C and C++ languages, a master Windows programmer, and an expert on Java. His programming books have sold nearly two million copies worldwide and have been translated into all major foreign languages. He is the author of numerous best-sellers, including *C: The Complete Reference*, *C++: The Complete Reference*, *C++ from the Ground Up*, *Expert C++*, *MFC Programming from the Ground Up*, *Windows 95 Programming in C and C++*, *Windows NT 4 Programming from the Ground Up*, and many others. Schildt is the president of Universal Computing Laboratories, a software consulting firm in Mahomet, Illinois. He is also a member of both the ANSI C and C++ standardization committees. He holds a master's degree in computer science from the University of Illinois.

Teach

Yourself C++,

Third Edition

Herbert Schildt

Osborne **McGraw-Hill**

Berkeley New York St. Louis San Francisco Auckland Bogotá Hamburg London Madrid Mexico City
Milan Montreal New Delhi Panama City Paris São Paulo Singapore Sydney Tokyo Toronto

PUBLISHER
Brandon A. Nordin

EDITOR-IN-CHIEF
Scott Rogers

ACQUISITIONS EDITOR
Megg Bonar

PROJECT EDITOR
Janet Walden

EDITORIAL ASSISTANT
Gordon Hurd

TECHNICAL EDITOR
Greg Guntle

COPY EDITOR
Katherine Krause

PROOFREADERS
Pat Mannion
Emily Wolman

INDEXER
Sheryl Schildt

COMPUTER DESIGNER
Jani Beckwith

ILLUSTRATOR
Roberta Steele

SERIES DESIGN
Roberta Steele

COVER DESIGN
Arlette Crosland

Osborne/McGraw-Hill
2600 Tenth Street
Berkeley, California 94710
U.S.A.

For information on translations or book distributors outside the U.S.A., or to arrange bulk purchase discounts for sales promotions, premiums, or fund-raisers, please contact Osborne/**McGraw-Hill** at the above address.

Teach Yourself C++, Third Edition

1234567890 DOC DOC 901987654321098

ISBN 0-07-882392-7

Contents

Acknowledgments

I wish to say special thanks to

Bjarne Stroustrup
Steve Clamage
P. J. Plauger
Al Stevens

for sharing their knowledge, advice, and expertise during the preparation of this book. It was much appreciated.

Introduction

If you already know C and are moving up to C++, this book is for you.

C++ is the C programmer's answer to Object-Oriented Programming (OOP). Built upon the solid foundation of C, C++ adds support for OOP (and many other new features) without sacrificing any of C's power, elegance, or flexibility. C++ has become the universal language of programmers around the world and is the language that will create the next generation of high-performance software. It is the single most important language that a professional programmer must know.

C++ was invented in 1979 by Bjarne Stroustrup at Bell Laboratories in Murray Hill, New Jersey. Initially it was called "C with classes." The name was changed to C++ in 1983. Since then, C++ has undergone three major revisions, the first in 1985 and the second in 1990. The third occurred during the C++ standardization process. Several years ago, work began on a standard for C++. Towards that end, a joint ANSI (American National Standards Institute) and ISO (International Standards Organization) standardization committee was formed. The first draft of the proposed standard was created on January 25, 1994. In that draft, the ANSI/ISO C++ committee (of which I am a member) kept the features first defined by Stroustrup and added some new ones as well. But, in general, this initial draft reflected the state of C++ at the time.

Soon after the completion of the first draft of the standard an event occurred that caused the standard to be greatly expanded: the creation of the Standard Template Library (STL) by Alexander Stepanov. As you will learn, the STL is a set of generic routines that you can use to manipulate data. It is both powerful and elegant. But it is also quite large. Subsequent to the first draft, the committee voted to include the STL in the specification for C++. The addition of the STL expanded the scope of C++ well beyond its original definition. While important, the inclusion of the STL, among other things, slowed the standardization of C++.

It is fair to say that the standardization of C++ took far longer than any one had expected when it began. However, it is now nearly complete. The final draft has been prepared and passed out of committee. It now awaits only formal approval. In a practical sense, a standard for C++ is now a reality. Compilers already are beginning to support all of the new features.

The material in this book describes Standard C++. This is the version of C++ created by the ANSI/ISO standardization committee and it is the one that is currently accepted by all major compilers. Therefore, using this book, you can be confident that what you learn today will also apply tomorrow.

What Is New in the Third Edition

This is the third edition of *Teach Yourself C++*. It includes all of the material contained in the first two editions and adds two new chapters and many new topics. The first new chapter covers Run-Time Type ID (RTTI) and the new casting operators. The second covers the Standard Template Library (STL). Both of these topics are major features added to the C++ language since the previous edition was published. New topics include namespaces, the new-style headers, and coverage of the modern-style I/O system. In all, the third edition of *Teach Yourself C++* is substantially larger than its preceding two editions.

If You're Using Windows

If your computer uses Windows and your goal is to write Windows-based programs, then you have chosen the right language to learn. C++ is completely at home with Windows programming. However, none of the programs in this book are Windows programs. Instead, they are console-based programs. The reason for this is easy to understand: Windows programs are, by their nature, large and complex. The overhead required to create even a minimal Windows skeletal program is 50 to 70 lines of code. To write Windows programs that demonstrate the features of C++ would require hundreds of lines of code each. Put simply, Windows is not an appropriate environment in which to learn programming. However, you can still use a Windows-based compiler to compile the programs in this book because the compiler will automatically create a console session in which to execute your program.

Once you have mastered C++, you will be able to apply your knowledge to Windows programming. In fact, Windows programming

using C++ allows the use of class libraries such as MFC, that can
greatly simplify the development of a Windows program.

How This Book Is Organized

This book is unique because it teaches you the C++ language by
applying mastery learning. It presents one idea at a time, followed
by numerous examples and exercises to help you master each topic.
This approach ensures that you fully understand each topic before
moving on.

The material is presented sequentially. Therefore, be sure to work
carefully through the chapters. Each one assumes that you know the
material presented in all preceding chapters. At the start of every
chapter (except Chapter 1) there is a Review Skills Check that tests
your knowledge of the preceding chapter. At the end of each chapter
you will find a Mastery Skills Check that checks your knowledge of the
material present in the chapter. Finally, each chapter concludes with a
Cumulative Skills Check which tests how well you are integrating new
material with that presented in earlier chapters. The answers to the
book's many exercises are found in Appendix B.

This book assumes that you are already an accomplished C
programmer. Put simply, you can't learn to program in C++ until you
can program in C. If you can't program in C, take some time to learn it
before attempting to use this book. A good way to learn C is to read my
book *Teach Yourself C, Third Edition* (Osborne/McGraw-Hill, Berkeley
CA, 1997). It uses the same presentation style as this book.

Don't Forget: Code on the Web

Remember, the source code for all of the programs in this book is
available free-of-charge on the Web at **http://www.osborne.com**.
Downloading this code prevents you from having to type in
the examples.

For Further Study

Teach Yourself C++, Third Edition is your gateway into the "Herb Schildt" series of programming books. Here is a partial list of Schildt's other books.

If you want to learn more about C++, then you will find these books especially helpful.

C++: The Complete Reference
C++ From the Ground Up
Expert C++

If you want to learn more about C, the foundation of C++, we recommend

Teach Yourself C
C: The Complete Reference
The Annotated ANSI C Standard

If you will be developing programs for the Web, you will want to read

Java: The Complete Reference

co-authored by Herbert Schildt and Patrick Naughton.

Finally, if you want to program for Windows, we recommend

Schildt's Windows 95 Programming in C and C++
Schildt's Advanced Windows 95 Programming in C and C++
Windows NT 4 From the Ground Up
MFC Programming From the Ground Up

When you need solid answers, fast, turn to **Herbert Schildt,** the recognized authority on programming.

1

An Overview of C++

C++ is an enhanced version of the C language. C++ includes everything that is part of C and adds support for object-oriented programming (OOP for short). In addition, C++ contains many improvements and features that simply make it a "better C," independent of object-oriented programming. With very few, very minor exceptions, C++ is a superset of C. While everything that you know about the C language is fully applicable to C++, understanding its enhanced features will still require a significant investment of time and effort on your part. However, the rewards of programming in C++ will more than justify the effort you put forth.

The purpose of this chapter is to introduce you to several of the most important features of C++. As you know, the elements of a computer language do not exist in a void, separate from one another. Instead, they work together to form the complete language. This interrelatedness is especially pronounced in C++. In fact, it is difficult to discuss one aspect of C++ in isolation because the features of C++ are highly integrated. To help overcome this problem, this chapter provides a brief overview of several C++ features. This overview will enable you to understand the examples discussed later in this book. Keep in mind that most topics will be more thoroughly explored in later chapters.

Since C++ was invented to support object-oriented programming, this chapter begins with a description of OOP. As you will see, many features of C++ are related to OOP in one way or another. In fact, the theory of OOP permeates C++. However, it is important to understand that C++ can be used to write programs that are and are *not* object oriented. How you use C++ is completely up to you.

At the time of this writing, the standardization of C++ is being finalized. For this reason, this chapter describes some important differences between versions of C++ that have been in common use during the past several years and the new Standard C++. Since this book teaches Standard C++, this material is especially important if you are using an older compiler.

In addition to introducing several important C++ features, this chapter also discusses some differences between C and C++ programming styles. There are several aspects of C++ that allow greater flexibility in the way that you write programs. While some of these features have little or nothing to do with object-oriented programming, they are found in most C++ programs, so it is appropriate to discuss them early in this book.

Before you begin, a few general comments about the nature and form of C++ are in order. First, for the most part, C++ programs physically look like C programs. Like a C program, a C++ program begins execution at **main( )**. To include command-line arguments, C++ uses the same **argc, argv** convention that C uses. Although C++ defines its own, object-oriented library, it also supports all the functions in the C standard library. C++ uses the same control structures as C. C++ includes all of the built-in data types defined by C.

This book assumes that you already know the C programming language. In other words, you must be able to program in C before you can learn to program in C++ by using this book. If you don't know C, a good starting place is my book *Teach Yourself C, Third Edition* (Berkeley: Osborne/McGraw-Hill, 1997). It applies the same systematic approach used in this book and thoroughly covers the entire C language.

Note

This book assumes that you know how to compile and execute a program using your C++ compiler. If you don't, you will need to refer to your compiler's instructions. (Because of the differences between compilers, it is impossible to give compilation instructions for each in this book.) Since programming is best learned by doing, you are strongly urged to enter, compile, and run the examples in the book in the order in which they are presented.

1.1 *W*HAT IS OBJECT-ORIENTED PROGRAMMING?

Object-oriented programming is a powerful way to approach the task of programming. Since its early beginnings, programming has been governed by various methodologies. At each critical point in the evolution of programming, a new approach was created to help the programmer handle increasingly complex programs. The first programs were created by toggling switches on the front panel of the computer. Obviously, this approach is suitable for only the smallest programs. Next, assembly language was invented, which allowed longer programs to be written. The next advance happened in the 1950s when the first high-level language (FORTRAN) was invented.

By using a high-level language, a programmer was able to write programs that were several thousand lines long. However, the method of programming used early on was an ad hoc, anything-goes approach. While this is fine for relatively short programs, it yields unreadable (and unmanageable) "spaghetti code" when applied to larger programs. The elimination of spaghetti code became feasible with the invention of *structured programming languages* in the 1960s. These languages include Algol and Pascal. In loose terms, C is a structured language, and most likely the type of programming you have been doing would be called structured programming. Structured programming relies on well-defined control structures, code blocks, the absence (or at least minimal use) of the GOTO, and stand-alone subroutines that support recursion and local variables. The essence of structured programming is the reduction of a program into its constituent elements. Using structured programming, the average programmer can create and maintain programs that are up to 50,000 lines long.

Although structured programming has yielded excellent results when applied to moderately complex programs, even it fails at some point, after a program reaches a certain size. To allow more complex programs to be written, a new approach to the job of programming was needed. Towards this end, object-oriented programming was invented. OOP takes the best of the ideas embodied in structured programming and combines them with powerful new concepts that allow you to organize your programs more effectively. Object-oriented programming encourages you to decompose a problem into its constituent parts. Each component becomes a self-contained object that contains its own instructions and data that relate to that object. In this way, complexity is reduced and the programmer can manage larger programs.

All OOP languages, including C++, share three common defining traits: encapsulation, polymorphism, and inheritance. Let's look at these concepts now.

ENCAPSULATION

Encapsulation is the mechanism that binds together code and the data it manipulates, and keeps both safe from outside interference and misuse. In an object-oriented language, code and data can be combined in such a way that a self-contained "black box" is created. When code and data are linked together in this fashion, an *object* is created. In other words, an object is the device that supports encapsulation.

Within an object, code, data, or both may be *private* to that object or *public*. Private code or data is known to and accessible only by another part of the object. That is, private code or data cannot be accessed by a piece of the program that exists outside the object. When code or data is public, other parts of your program can access it even though it is defined within an object. Typically, the public parts of an object are used to provide a controlled interface to the private elements of the object.

For all intents and purposes, an object is a variable of a user-defined type. It may seem strange that an object that links both code and data can be thought of as a variable. However, in object-oriented programming, this is precisely the case. Each time you define a new type of object, you are creating a new data type. Each specific instance of this data type is a compound variable.

POLYMORPHISM

Polymorphism (from the Greek, meaning "many forms") is the quality that allows one name to be used for two or more related but technically different purposes. As it relates to OOP, polymorphism allows one name to specify a general class of actions. Within a general class of actions, the specific action to be applied is determined by the type of data. For example, in C, which does not significantly support polymorphism, the absolute value action requires three distinct function names: **abs( )**, **labs( )**, and **fabs( )**. These functions compute and return the absolute value of an integer, a long integer, and a floating-point value, respectively. However, in C++, which supports polymorphism, each function can be called by the same name, such as **abs( )**. (One way this can be accomplished is shown later in this chapter.) The type of data used to call the function determines which specific version of the function is actually executed. As you will see, in C++, it is possible to use one function name for many different purposes. This is called *function overloading*.

More generally, the concept of polymorphism is characterized by the idea of "one interface, multiple methods," which means using a generic interface for a group of related activities. The advantage of polymorphism is that it helps to reduce complexity by allowing one interface to specify a *general class of action*. It is the compiler's job to select the *specific action* as it applies to each situation. You, the programmer, don't need to do this selection manually. You need only remember and utilize the general interface. As the example in the preceding paragraph illustrates, having three names for the absolute value function instead of just one makes the general activity of obtaining the absolute value of a number more complex than it actually is.

Polymorphism can be applied to operators, too. Virtually all programming languages contain a limited application of polymorphism as it relates to the arithmetic operators. For example, in C, the **+** sign is used to add integers, long integers, characters, and floating-point values. In these cases, the compiler automatically knows which type of arithmetic to apply. In C++, you can extend this concept to other types of data that you define. This type of polymorphism is called *operator overloading.*

The key point to remember about polymorphism is that it allows you to handle greater complexity by allowing the creation of standard interfaces to related activities.

INHERITANCE

Inheritance is the process by which one object can acquire the properties of another. More specifically, an object can inherit a general set of properties to which it can add those features that are specific only to itself. Inheritance is important because it allows an object to support the concept of *hierarchical classification.* Most information is made manageable by hierarchical classification. For example, think about the description of a house. A house is part of the general class called **building**. In turn, **building** is part of the more general class **structure**, which is part of the even more general class of objects that we call **man-made**. In each case, the child class inherits all those qualities associated with the parent and adds to them its own defining characteristics. Without the use of ordered classifications, each object would have to define all characteristics that relate to it explicitly. However, through inheritance, it is possible to describe an object by stating what general class (or classes) it belongs to along with those specific traits that make it unique. As you will see, inheritance plays a very important role in OOP.

EXAMPLES

1. Encapsulation is not entirely new to OOP. To a degree, encapsulation can be achieved when using the C language. For example, when you use a library function, you are, in effect, using a black-box routine, the internals of which you cannot alter or affect (except, perhaps, through malicious actions). Consider the **fopen( )** function. When it is used to open a file, several internal variables are created and initialized. As far as your program is concerned, these variables are hidden and not accessible. However, C++ provides a much more secure approach to encapsulation.

2. In the real world, examples of polymorphism are quite common. For example, consider the steering wheel on your car. It works the same whether your car uses power steering, rack-and-pinion steering, or standard, manual steering. The point is that the interface (the steering wheel) is the same no matter what type of actual steering mechanism (method) is used.

3. Inheritance of properties and the more general concept of classification are fundamental to the way knowledge is organized. For example, celery is a member of the **vegetable** class, which is part of the **plant** class. In turn, plants are living organisms, and so forth. Without hierarchical classification, systems of knowledge would not be possible.

EXERCISE

1. Think about the way that classification and polymorphism play an important role in our day-to-day lives.

1.2 **T**WO VERSIONS OF C++

At the time of this writing, C++ is in the midst of a transformation. As explained in the preface to this book, C++ has been undergoing the process of standardization for the past several years. The goal has been to create a stable, standardized, feature-rich language that will suit the needs of programmers well into the next century. As a result, there are really two versions of C++. The first is the traditional version that is based upon Bjarne Stroustrup's original designs. This is the version of C++ that has been used by programmers for the past decade. The second is the new Standard C++, which was created by Stroustrup and the ANSI/ISO standardization committee. While these two versions of C++ are very similar at their core, Standard C++ contains several enhancements not found in traditional C++. Thus, Standard C++ is essentially a superset of traditional C++.

This book teaches Standard C++. This is the version of C++ defined by the ANSI/ISO standardization committee, and it is the version implemented by all modern C++ compilers. The code in this book reflects the contemporary coding style and practices as encouraged by Standard C++. This means that what you learn in this book will be applicable today as well as tomorrow. Put directly, Standard C++ is the future. And, since Standard C++ encompasses all features found in earlier versions of C++, what you learn in this book will enable you to work in all C++ programming environments.

However, if you are using an older compiler, it might not accept all of the programs in this book. Here's why: During the process of standardization, the ANSI/ISO committee added many new features to the language. As these features were defined, they were implemented by compiler developers. Of course, there is always a lag time between the addition of a new feature to the language and the availability of the feature in commercial compilers. Since features were added to C++ over a period of years, an older compiler might not support one or more of them. This is important because two recent additions to the C++ language affect every program that you will write—even the simplest. If you are using an older compiler that does not accept these new features, don't worry. There is an easy workaround, which is described in the following paragraphs.

The differences between old-style and modern code involve two new features: new-style headers and the **namespace** statement. To demonstrate these differences we will begin by looking at two versions of a minimal, do-nothing C++ program. The first version, shown here, reflects the way C++ programs were written until recently. (That is, it uses old-style coding.)

```
/*
   A traditional-style C++ program.
*/

#include <iostream.h>

int main()
{
  /* program code */
  return 0;
}
```

Since C++ is built on C, this skeleton should be largely familiar, but pay special attention to the **#include** statement. This statement includes the file **iostream.h**, which provides support for C++'s I/O system. (It is to C++ what **stdio.h** is to C.)

Here is the second version of the skeleton, which uses the modern style:

```
/*
   A modern-style C++ program that uses
   the new-style headers and a namespace.
*/
#include <iostream>
using namespace std;

int main()
{
  /* program code */
  return 0;
}
```

Notice the two lines in this program immediately after the first comment; this is where the changes occur. First, in the **#include** statement, there is no **.h** after the name **iostream**. And second, the next line, specifying a namespace, is new. Although both the new-style headers and namespaces will be examined in detail later in this book, a brief overview is in order now.

THE NEW C++ HEADERS

As you know from your C programming experience, when you use a library function in a program, you must include its header file. This is done using the **#include** statement. For example, in C, to include the header file for the I/O functions, you include **stdio.h** with a statement like this:

```
#include <stdio.h>
```

Here **stdio.h** is the name of the file used by the I/O functions, and the preceding statement causes that file to be included in your program. The key point is that the **#include** statement *includes a file*.

When C++ was first invented and for several years after that, it used the same style of headers as did C. In fact, Standard C++ still supports C-style headers for header files that you create and for backward compatibility. However, Standard C++ has introduced a new kind of header that is used by the Standard C++ library. The new-style headers *do not* specify filenames. Instead, they simply specify standard identifiers that might be mapped to files by the compiler, but they need not be. The new-style C++ headers are abstractions that simply guarantee that the appropriate prototypes and definitions required by the C++ library have been declared.

Since the new-style header is not a filename, it does not have a **.h** extension. Such a header consists solely of the header name contained between angle brackets. For example, here are some of the new-style headers supported by Standard C++:

<iostream>
<fstream>
<vector>
<string>

The new-style headers are included using the **#include** statement. The only difference is that the new-style headers do not necessarily represent filenames.

Because C++ includes the entire C function library, it still supports the standard C-style header files associated with that library. That is, header files such as **stdio.h** and **ctype.h** are still available. However, Standard C++ also defines new-style headers that you can use in place of these header files. The C++ versions of the standard C headers simply add a **c** prefix to the filename and drop the **.h**. For example, the new-style C++ header for **math.h** is **< cmath >**, and the one for **string.h** is **< cstring >**. Although it is currently permissible to include a C-style header file when using C library functions, this approach is deprecated by Standard C++. (That is, it is not recommended.) For this reason, this book will use new-style C++ headers in all **#include** statements. If your compiler does not support new-style headers for the C function library, simply substitute the old-style, C-like headers.

Since the new-style header is a recent addition to C++, you will still find many, many older programs that don't use it. These programs instead use C-style headers, in which a filename is specified. As the old-style skeletal program shows, the traditional way to include the I/O header is as shown here:

```
#include <iostream.h>
```

This causes the file **iostream.h** to be included in your program. In general, an old-style header will use the same name as its corresponding new-style header with a **.h** appended.

As of this writing, all C++ compilers support the old-style headers. However, the old style headers have been declared obsolete, and their use in new programs is not recommended. This is why they are not used in this book.

While still common in existing C++ code, old-style headers are obsolete.

NAMESPACES

When you include a new-style header in your program, the contents of that header are contained in the **std** namespace. A *namespace* is simply a declarative region. The purpose of a namespace is to localize the names of identifiers to avoid name collisions. Traditionally, the names of library functions and other such items were simply placed into the global namespace (as they are in C). However, the contents of new-style headers are placed in the **std** namespace. We will look closely at namespaces later in this book. For now, you don't need to worry about them because you can use the statement

```
using namespace std;
```

to bring the **std** namespace into visibility (i.e., to put **std** into the global namespace). After this statement has been compiled, there is no difference between working with an old-style header and a new-style one.

WORKING WITH AN OLD COMPILER

As mentioned, both namespaces and the new-style headers are recent additions to the C++ language. While virtually all new C++ compilers support these features, older compilers might not. If you have one of these older compilers, it will report one or more errors when it tries to compile the first two lines of the sample programs in this book. If this is the case, there is an easy workaround: simply use an old-style header and delete the **namespace** statement. That is, just replace

```
#include <iostream>
using namespace std;
```

with

```
#include <iostream.h>
```

This change transforms a modern program into a traditional-style one. Since the old-style header reads all of its contents into the global namespace, there is no need for a **namespace** statement.

One other point: For now and for the next few years, you will see many C++ programs that use the old-style headers and that do not include a **namespace** statement. Your C++ compiler will be able to compile them just fine. For new programs, however, you should use the modern style because it is the only style of program that complies with Standard C++. While old-style programs will continue to be supported for many years, they are technically noncompliant.

EXERCISE

1. Before proceeding, try compiling the new-style skeleton program shown above. Although it does nothing, compiling it will tell you if your compiler supports the modern C++ syntax. If it does not accept the new-style headers or the **namespace** statement, substitute the old-style header as described. Remember, if your compiler does not accept new-style code, you must make this change for each program in this book.

1.3   *C++ CONSOLE I/O*

Since C++ is a superset of C, all elements of the C language are also contained in the C++ language. This implies that all C programs are also C++ programs by default. (Actually, there are some very minor exceptions to this rule, which are discussed later in this book.) Therefore, it is possible to write C++ programs that look just like C programs. While there is nothing wrong with this per se, it does mean that you will not be taking full advantage of C++. To get the maximum benefit from C++, you must write C++-style programs. This means using a coding style and features that are unique to C++.

Perhaps the most common C++-specific feature used by C++ programmers is its approach to console I/O. While you may still use functions such as **printf( )** and **scanf( )**, C++ provides a new, and better, way to perform these types of I/O operations. In C++, I/O is performed using *I/O operators* instead of I/O functions. The output operator is << and the input operator is >>. As you know, in C, these are the left and right shift operators, respectively. In C++, they still retain their original meanings (left and right shift) but they also take on the expanded role of performing input and output. Consider this C++ statement:

```
cout << "This string is output to the screen.\n";
```

This statement causes the string to be displayed on the computer's screen. **cout** is a predefined stream that is automatically linked to the console when a C++ program begins execution. It is similar to C's **stdout**. As in C, C++ console I/O may be redirected, but for the rest of this discussion, it is assumed that the console is being used.

By using the << output operator, it is possible to output any of C++'s basic types. For example, this statement outputs the value 100.99:

```
cout << 100.99;
```

In general, to output to the console, use this form of the << operator:

cout << *expression;*

Here *expression* can be any valid C++ expression—including another output expression.

To input a value from the keyboard, use the >> input operator. For example, this fragment inputs an integer value into **num**:

```
int num;
cin >> num;
```

Notice that **num** is *not* preceded by an **&**. As you know, when you use C's **scanf( )** function to input values, variables must have their addresses passed to the function so they can receive the values entered by the user. This is not the case when you are using C++'s input operator. (The reason for this will become clear as you learn more about C++.)

In general, to input values from the keyboard, use this form of >>:

cin >> *variable*;

The expanded roles of << *and* >> *are examples of operator overloading.*

In order to use the C++ I/O operators, you must include the header **< iostream >** in your program. As explained earlier, this is one of C++'s standard headers and is supplied by your C++ compiler.

EXAMPLES

1. This program outputs a string, two integer values, and a double floating-point value:

```
#include <iostream>
using namespace std;

int main()
{
  int i, j;
  double d;

  i = 10;
  j = 20;
  d = 99.101;
```

```
cout << "Here are some values: ";
cout << i;
cout << ' ';
cout << j;
cout << ' ';
cout << d;

return 0;
}
```

The output of this program is shown here.

```
Here are some values: 10 20 99.101
```

*If you are working with an older compiler, it might not accept the new-style headers and the **namespace** statements used by this and other programs in this book. If this is the case, substitute the old-style code described in the preceding section.*

2. It is possible to output more than one value in a single I/O expression. For example, this version of the program described in Example 1 shows a more efficient way to code the I/O statements:

```
#include <iostream>
using namespace std;

int main()
{
  int i, j;
  double d;

  i = 10;
  j = 20;
  d = 99.101;

  cout << "Here are some values: ";
  cout << i << ' ' << j << ' ' << d;

  return 0;
}
```

Here the line

```
cout << i << ' '<< j << ' ' << d;
```

outputs several items in one expression. In general, you can use a single statement to output as many items as you like. If this seems confusing, simply remember that the **<<** output operator behaves like any other C++ operator and can be part of an arbitrarily long expression.

Notice that you must explicitly include spaces between items when needed. If the spaces are left out, the data will run together when displayed on the screen.

3. This program prompts the user for an integer value:

```
#include <iostream>
using namespace std;

int main()
{
  int i;

  cout << "Enter a value: ";
  cin >> i;
  cout << "Here's your number: " << i << "\n";

  return 0;
}
```

Here is a sample run:

```
Enter a value: 100
Here's your number: 100
```

As you can see, the value entered by the user is put into **i**.

4. The next program prompts the user for an integer value, a floating-point value, and a string. It then uses one input statement to read all three.

```
#include <iostream>
using namespace std;

int main()
{
  int i;
```

```
    float f;
    char s[80];

    cout << "Enter an integer, float, and string: ";
    cin >> i >> f >> s;
    cout << "Here's your data: ";
    cout << i << ' ' << f << ' ' << s;

    return 0;
}
```

As this example illustrates, you can input as many items as you like in one input statement. As in C, individual data items must be separated by whitespace characters (spaces, tabs, or newlines).

When a string is read, input will stop when the first whitespace character is encountered. For example, if you enter the following into the preceding program

```
10 100.12 This is a test
```

the program will display this:

```
10 100.12 This
```

The string is incomplete because the reading of the string stopped with the space after **This.** The remainder of the string is left in the input buffer, awaiting a subsequent input operation. (This is similar to inputting a string by using **scanf( )** with the **%s** format.)

5. By default, when you use **>>**, all input is line buffered. This means that no information is passed to your C++ program until you press ENTER. (In C, the **scanf( )** function is line buffered, so this style of input should not be new to you.) To see the effect of line-buffered input, try this program:

```
#include <iostream>
using namespace std;

int main()
{
    char ch;

    cout << "Enter keys, x to stop.\n";
```

```
do {
  cout << ": ";
  cin >> ch;
} while (ch != 'x');

return 0;
}
```

When you test this program, you will have to press ENTER after each key you type in order for the corresponding character to be sent to the program.

EXERCISES

1. Write a program that inputs the number of hours that an employee works and the employee's wage. Then display the employee's gross pay. (Be sure to prompt for input.)

2. Write a program that converts feet to inches. Prompt the user for feet and display the equivalent number of inches. Have your program repeat this process until the user enters 0 for the number of feet.

3. Here is a C program. Rewrite it so it uses C++-style I/O statements.

```
/* Convert this C program into C++ style.
   This program computes the lowest common
   denominator.
*/
#include <stdio.h>

int main(void)
{
  int a, b, d, min;

  printf("Enter two numbers: ");
  scanf("%d%d", &a, &b);
  min = a > b ? b : a;
  for(d = 2; d<min; d++)
    if(((a%d)==0) && ((b%d)==0)) break;
```

```
if(d==min) {
  printf("No common denominators\n");
  return 0;
}
printf("The lowest common denominator is %d\n", d);
return 0;
}
```

C++ COMMENTS

In C++, you can include comments in your program two different ways. First, you can use the standard, C-like comment mechanism. That is, begin a comment with /* and end it with */. As with C, this type of comment cannot be nested in C++.

The second way that you can add a remark to your C++ program is to use the *single-line comment.* A single-line comment begins with a // and stops at the end of the line. Other than the physical end of the line (that is, a carriage-return/linefeed combination), a single-line comment uses no comment terminator symbol.

Typically, C++ programmers use C-like comments for multiline commentaries and reserve C++-style single-line comments for short remarks.

EXAMPLES

1. Here is a program that contains both C and C++-style comments:

```
/*
   This is a C-like comment.

   This program determines whether
   an integer is odd or even.
*/

#include <iostream>
using namespace std;
```

```
int main()
{
  int num;   // this is a C++ single-line comment

  // read the number
  cout << "Enter number to be tested: ";
  cin >> num;

  // see if even or odd
  if((num%2)==0) cout << "Number is even\n";
  else cout << "Number is odd\n";

  return 0;
}
```

2. While multiline comments cannot be nested, it is possible to nest a single-line comment within a multiline comment. For example, this is perfectly valid:

```
/* This is a multiline comment
   inside of which // is nested a single-line comment.
   Here is the end of the multiline comment.
*/
```

The fact that single-line comments can be nested within multiline comments makes it easier for you to "comment out" several lines of code for debugging purposes.

EXERCISES

1. As an experiment, determine whether this comment (which nests a C-like comment within a C++-style, single-line comment) is valid:

```
// This is a strange /* way to do a comment */
```

2. On your own, add comments to the answers to the exercises in Section 1.3.

1.5 C*LASSES: A FIRST LOOK*

Perhaps the single most important feature of C++ is the *class*. The class is the mechanism that is used to create objects. As such, the class is at the heart of many C++ features. Although the subject of classes is covered in great detail throughout this book, classes are so fundamental to C++ programming that a brief overview is necessary here.

A class is declared using the **class** keyword. The syntax of a **class** declaration is similar to that of a structure. Its general form is shown here:

```
class class-name {
    // private functions and variables
public:
    // public functions and variables
}  object-list;
```

In a class declaration, the *object-list* is optional. As with a structure, you can declare class objects later, as needed. While the *class-name* is also technically optional, from a practical point of view it is virtually always needed. The reason for this is that the *class-name* becomes a new type name that is used to declare objects of the class.

Functions and variables declared inside a class declaration are said to be *members* of that class. By default, all functions and variables declared inside a class are private to that class. This means that they are accessible only by other members of that class. To declare public class members, the **public** keyword is used, followed by a colon. All functions and variables declared after the **public** specifier are accessible both by other members of the class and by any other part of the program that contains the class.

Here is a simple class declaration:

```
class myclass {
  // private to myclass
  int a;
public:
  void set_a(int num);
  int get_a();
};
```

This class has one private variable, called **a**, and two public functions, **set_a( )** and **get_a( )**. Notice that functions are declared within a class using their prototype forms. Functions that are declared to be part of a class are called _member functions._

Since **a** is private, it is not accessible by any code outside **myclass**. However, since **set_a( )** and **get_a( )** are members of **myclass**, they can access **a**. Further, **get_a( )** and **set_a( )** are declared as public members of **myclass** and can be called by any other part of the program that contains **myclass**.

Although the functions **get_a( )** and **set_a( )** are declared by **myclass**, they are not yet defined. To define a member function, you must link the type name of the class with the name of the function. You do this by preceding the function name with the class name followed by two colons. The two colons are called the _scope resolution operator._ For example, here is the way the member functions **set_a( )** and **get_a( )** are defined:

```
void myclass::set_a(int num)
{
  a = num;
}

int myclass::get_a()
{
   return a;
}
```

Notice that both **set_a( )** and **get_a( )** have access to **a**, which is private to **myclass**. Because **set_a( )** and **get_a( )** are members of **myclass**, they can directly access its private data.

In general, to define a member function you must use this form:

ret-type class-name::func-name(parameter-list)
_{_
  // body of function
_}_

Here _class-name_ is the name of the class to which the function belongs.

The declaration of **myclass** did not define any objects of type **myclass**—it only defines the type of object that will be created when one is actually declared. To create an object, use the class name as a type specifier. For example, this line declares two objects of type **myclass**:

```
myclass ob1, ob2; // these are objects of type myclass
```

A class declaration is a logical abstraction that defines a new type. It determines what an object of that type will look like. An object declaration creates a physical entity of that type. That is, an object occupies memory space, but a type definition does not.

Once an object of a class has been created, your program can reference its public members by using the dot (period) operator in much the same way that structure members are accessed. Assuming the preceding object declaration, the following statement calls **set_a( )** for objects **ob1** and **ob2**:

```
ob1.set_a(10); // sets ob1's version of a to 10
ob2.set_a(99); // sets ob2's version of a to 99
```

As the comments indicate, these statements set **ob1**'s copy of **a** to 10 and **ob2**'s copy to 99. Each object contains its own copy of all data declared within the class. This means that **ob1**'s **a** is distinct and different from the **a** linked to **ob2**.

Each object of a class has its own copy of every variable declared within the class.

EXAMPLES

1. As a simple first example, this program demonstrates **myclass**, described in the text. It sets the value of **a** for **ob1** and **ob2** and then displays **a**'s value for each object:

```
#include <iostream>
using namespace std;

class myclass {
  // private to myclass
  int a;
```

```
public:
  void set_a(int num);
  int get_a();
};

void myclass::set_a(int num)
{
  a = num;
}

int myclass::get_a()
{
  return a;
}

int main()
{
  myclass ob1, ob2;

  ob1.set_a(10);
  ob2.set_a(99);

  cout << ob1.get_a() << "\n";
  cout << ob2.get_a() << "\n";
  return 0;
}
```

As you should expect, this program displays the values 10 and 99 on the screen.

2. In **myclass** from the preceding example, **a** is private. This means that only member functions of **myclass** can access it directly. (This is one reason why the public function **get_a( )** is required.) If you try to access a private member of a class from some part of your program that is not a member of that class, a compile-time error will result. For example, assuming that **myclass** is defined as shown in the preceding example, the following **main( )** function will cause an error:

```
// This fragment contains an error.
#include <iostream>
using namespace std;

int main()
{
```

```
  myclass ob1, ob2;

  ob1.a = 10; // ERROR! cannot access private member
  ob2.a = 99; // by non-member functions.

  cout << ob1.get_a() << "\n";
  cout << ob2.get_a() << "\n";

  return 0;
}
```

3. Just as there can be public member functions, there can be public member variables as well. For example, if **a** were declared in the public section of **myclass**, **a** could be referenced by any part of the program, as shown here:

```
#include <iostream>
using namespace std;

class myclass {
public:
  // now a is public
  int a;
  // and there is no need for set_a() or get_a()
};

int main()
{
  myclass ob1, ob2;

  // here a is accessed directly
  ob1.a = 10;
  ob2.a = 99;

  cout << ob1.a << "\n";
  cout << ob2.a << "\n";

  return 0;
}
```

In this example, since **a** is declared as a public member of **myclass**, it is directly accessible from **main( )**. Notice how the dot operator is used to access **a**. In general, when you are calling a member function or accessing a member variable from outside its class, the object's name followed by the dot operator followed by the member's name is required to fully specify which object's member you are referring to.

4. To get a taste of the power of objects, let's look at a more practical example. This program creates a class called **stack** that implements a stack that can be used to store characters:

```cpp
#include <iostream>
using namespace std;

#define SIZE 10

// Declare a stack class for characters
class stack {
  char stck[SIZE]; // holds the stack
  int tos; // index of top of stack

public:
  void init(); // initialize stack
  void push(char ch); // push character on stack
  char pop(); // pop character from stack
};

// Initialize the stack
void stack::init()
{
  tos = 0;
}

// Push a character.
void stack::push(char ch)
{
  if(tos==SIZE) {
    cout << "Stack is full";
    return;
  }
  stck[tos] = ch;
  tos++;
}

// Pop a character.
char stack::pop()
{
  if(tos==0) {
```

```
        cout << "Stack is empty";
        return 0; // return null on empty stack
    }
    tos--;
    return stck[tos];
}

int main()
{
    stack s1, s2;   // create two stacks
    int i;
    // initialize the stacks
    s1.init();
    s2.init();

    s1.push('a');
    s2.push('x');
    s1.push('b');
    s2.push('y');
    s1.push('c');
    s2.push('z');

    for(i=0; i<3; i++) cout << "Pop s1: " << s1.pop() << "\n";
    for(i=0; i<3; i++) cout << "Pop s2: " << s2.pop() << "\n";

    return 0;
}
```

This program displays the following output:

```
Pop s1: c
Pop s1: b
Pop s1: a
Pop s2: z
Pop s2: y
Pop s2: x
```

Let's take a close look at this program now. The class **stack** contains two private variables: **stck** and **tos**. The array **stck** actually holds the characters pushed onto the stack, and **tos** contains the index to the top of the stack. The public stack functions are **init( )**, **push( )**, and **pop( )**, which initialize the stack, push a value, and pop a value, respectively.

Inside **main( )**, two stacks, **s1** and **s2**, are created, and three characters are pushed onto each stack. It is important to understand that each stack object is separate from the other. That is, the characters pushed onto **s1** *in no way* affect the characters pushed onto **s2**. Each object contains its own copy of **stck** and **tos**. This concept is fundamental to understanding objects. Although all objects of a class share their member functions, each object creates and maintains *its own data*.

EXERCISES

1. If you have not done so, enter and run the programs shown in the examples for this section.

2. Create a class called **card** that maintains a library card catalog entry. Have the class store a book's title, author, and number of copies on hand. Store the title and author as strings and the number on hand as an integer. Use a public member function called **store( )** to store a book's information and a public member function called **show( )** to display the information. Include a short **main( )** function to demonstrate the class.

3. Create a queue class that maintains a circular queue of integers. Make the queue size 100 integers long. Include a short **main( )** function that demonstrates its operation.

1.6 S**OME DIFFERENCES BETWEEN C AND**
$C++$

Although C++ is a superset of C, there are some small differences between the two, and a few are worth knowing from the start. Before proceeding, let's take time to examine them.

First, in C, when a function takes no parameters, its prototype has the word **void** inside its function parameter list. For example, in C, if a function called **f1( )** takes no parameters (and returns a **char**), its prototype will look like this:

```
char f1(void);
```

However, in C++, the **void** is optional. Therefore, in C++, the prototype for **f1( )** is usually written like this:

```
char f1();
```

C++ differs from C in the way that an empty parameter list is specified. If the preceding prototype had occurred in a C program, it would simply mean that *nothing is said about* the parameters to the function. In C++, it means that the function *has no parameters.* This is the reason that the preceding examples did not explicitly use **void** to declare an empty parameters list. (The use of **void** to declare an empty parameter list is not illegal; it is just redundant. Since most C++ programmers pursue efficiency with a nearly religious zeal, you will almost never see **void** used in this way.) Remember, in C++, these two declarations are equivalent:

```
char f1();
char f1(void);
```

Another subtle difference between C and C++ is that in a C++ program, all functions must be prototyped. Remember, in C, prototypes are recommended but technically optional. In C++, they are required. As the examples from the previous section show, a member function's prototype contained in a class also serves as its general prototype, and no other separate prototype is required.

A third difference between C and C++ is that in C++, if a function is declared as returning a value, it must return a value. That is, if a function has a return type other than **void,** any **return** statement within that function must contain a value. In C, a non-**void** function is not required to actually return a value. If it doesn't, a garbage value is "returned."

In C, if you don't explicitly specify the return type of a function, an integer return type is assumed. C++ has dropped the "default-to-int" rule. Thus, you must explicitly declare the return type of all functions.

One other difference between C and C++ that you will commonly encounter in C++ programs has to do with where local variables can be declared. In C, local variables can be declared only at the start of a block, prior to any "action" statements. In C++, local variables can be declared anywhere. One advantage of this approach is that local variables can be declared close to where they are first used, thus helping to prevent unwanted side effects.

Finally, C++ defines the **bool** data type, which is used to store Boolean (i.e., true/false) values. C++ also defines the keywords **true** and **false,** which are the only values that a value of type **bool** can have. In C++, the outcome of the relational and logical operators is a value of type **bool,** and all conditional statements must evaluate to a **bool** value. Although this might at first seem to be a big change from C, it isn't. In fact, it is virtually transparent. Here's why: As you know, in C, **true** is any nonzero value and **false** is 0. This still holds in C++ because any nonzero value is automatically converted into **true** and any 0 value is automatically converted into **false** when used in a Boolean expression. The reverse also occurs: **true** is converted to 1 and **false** is converted to 0 when a **bool** value is used in an integer expression. The addition of **bool** allows more thorough type checking and gives you a way to differentiate between Boolean and integer types. Of course, its use is optional; **bool** is mostly a convenience.

EXAMPLES

1. In a C program, it is common practice to declare **main( )** as shown here if it takes no command-line arguments:

```
int main(void)
```

However, in C++, the use of **void** is redundant and unnecessary.

2. This short C++ program will not compile because the function **sum( )** is not prototyped:

```
// This program will not compile.
#include <iostream>
using namespace std;

int main()
{
  int a, b, c;

  cout << "Enter two numbers: ";
```

```
  cin >> a >> b;
  c = sum(a, b);
  cout << "Sum is: " << c;

  return 0;
}


// This function needs a prototype.
sum(int a, int b)
{
  return a+b;
}
```

3. Here is a short program that illustrates how local variables can be declared anywhere within a block:

```
#include <iostream>
using namespace std;

int main()
{
  int i; // local var declared at start of block

  cout << "Enter number: ";
  cin >> i;

  // compute factorial
  int j, fact=1; // vars declared after action statements

  for(j=i; j>=1; j--) fact = fact * j;

  cout << "Factorial is " << fact;

  return 0;
}
```

The declaration of **j** and **fact** near the point of first use is of little value in this short example; however, in large functions, the ability to declare variables close to the point of their first use can help clarify your code and prevent unintentional side effects.

4. The following program creates a Boolean variable called **outcome** and assigns it the value **false**. It then uses this variable in an **if** statement.

```cpp
#include <iostream>
using namespace std;

int main()
{
  bool outcome;

  outcome = false;

  if(outcome) cout << "true";
  else cout << "false";

  return 0;
}
```

As you should expect, the program displays **false**.

EXERCISES

1. The following program will not compile as a C++ program. Why not?

```cpp
// This program has an error.
#include <iostream>
using namespace std;

int main()
{
  f();

  return 0;
}
```

```
void f()
{
  cout << "this won't work";
}
```

2. On your own, try declaring local variables at various points in a C++ program. Try the same in a C program, paying attention to which declarations generate errors.

1.7 INTRODUCING FUNCTION OVERLOADING

After classes, perhaps the next most important and pervasive C++ feature is *function overloading.* Not only does function overloading provide the mechanism by which C++ achieves one type of polymorphism, it also forms the basis by which the C++ programming environment can be dynamically extended. Because of the importance of overloading, a brief introduction is given here.

In C++, two or more functions can share the same name as long as either the type of their arguments differs or the number of their arguments differs—or both. When two or more functions share the same name, they are said to be *overloaded.* Overloaded functions can help reduce the complexity of a program by allowing related operations to be referred to by the same name.

It is very easy to overload a function: simply declare and define all required versions. The compiler will automatically select the correct version based upon the number and/or type of the arguments used to call the function.

Note

It is also possible in C++ to overload operators. However, before you can fully understand operator overloading, you will need to know more about C++.

1. One of the main uses for function overloading is to achieve compile-time polymorphism, which embodies the philosophy of one interface, many methods. As you know, in C programming, it is common to have a number of related functions that differ only by the type of data on which they operate. The classic example of this situation is found in the C standard library. As mentioned earlier in this chapter, the library contains the functions **abs( )**, **labs( )**, and **fabs( )**, which return the absolute value of an integer, a long integer, and a floating-point value, respectively.

   However, because three different names are needed due to the three different data types, the situation is more complicated than it needs to be. In all three cases, the absolute value is being returned; only the type of the data differs. In C++, you can correct this situation by overloading one name for the three types of data, as this example illustrates:

```cpp
#include <iostream>
using namespace std;

// Overload abs() three ways
int abs(int n);
long abs(long n);
double abs(double n);

int main()
{
  cout << "Absolute value of -10: " << abs(-10) << "\n\n";
  cout << "Absolute value of -10L: " << abs(-10L) << "\n\n";
  cout << "Absolute value of -10.01: " << abs(-10.01) << "\n\n";

  return 0;
}

// abs() for ints
int abs(int n)
{
  cout << "In integer abs()\n";
```

```
  return n<0 ? -n : n;
}

// abs() for longs
long abs(long n)
{
  cout << "In long abs()\n";
  return n<0 ? -n : n;
}

// abs() for doubles
double abs(double n)
{
  cout << "In double abs()\n";
  return n<0 ? -n : n;
}
```

As you can see, this program defines three functions called **abs( )**—one for each data type. Inside **main( )**, **abs( )** is called using three different types of arguments. The compiler automatically calls the correct version of **abs( )** based upon the type of data used as an argument. The program produces the following output:

```
In integer abs()
Absolute value of -10: 10

In long abs()
Absolute value of -10L: 10

In double abs()
Absolute value of -10.01: 10.01
```

Although this example is quite simple, it still illustrates the value of function overloading. Because a single name can be used to describe a general class of action, the artificial complexity caused by three slightly different names—in this case, **abs( )**, **fabs( )**, and **labs( )**—is eliminated. You now must remember only one name—the one that describes the *general* action. It is left to the compiler to choose the appropriate *specific* version of the function (that is, the method) to call. This has the net effect of reducing complexity. Thus, through the use of polymorphism, three names have been reduced to one.

While the use of polymorphism in this example is fairly trivial, you should be able to see how in a very large program, the "one interface, multiple methods" approach can be quite effective.

2. Here is another example of function overloading. In this case, the function **date( )** is overloaded to accept the date either as a string or as three integers. In both cases, the function displays the date passed to it.

```cpp
#include <iostream>
using namespace std;

void date(char *date); // date as a string
void date(int month, int day, int year); // date as numbers

int main()
{
  date("8/23/99");
  date(8, 23, 99);

  return 0;
}

// Date as string.
void date(char *date)
{
  cout << "Date: " << date << "\n";
}

// Date as integers.
void date(int month, int day, int year)
{
  cout << "Date: " << month << "/";
  cout << day << "/" << year << "\n";
}
```

This example illustrates how function overloading can provide the most natural interface to a function. Since it is very common for the date to be represented as either a string or as three integers containing the month, day, and year, you are free to select the most convenient form relative to the situation at hand.

3. So far, you have seen overloaded functions that differ in the data types of their arguments. However, overloaded functions can also differ in the number of arguments, as this example illustrates:

```
#include <iostream>
using namespace std;

void f1(int a);
void f1(int a, int b);

int main()
{
  f1(10);
  f1(10, 20);

  return 0;
}

void f1(int a)
{
  cout << "In f1(int a)\n";
}

void f1(int a, int b)
{
  cout << "In f1(int a, int b)\n";
}
```

4. It is important to understand that the return type alone is not a sufficient difference to allow function overloading. If two functions differ only in the type of data they return, the compiler will not always be able to select the proper one to call. For example, this fragment is incorrect because it is inherently ambiguous:

```
// This is incorrect and will not compile.
int f1(int a);
double f1(int a);
  .
  .
  .
f1(10); // which function does the compiler call???
```

As the comment indicates, the compiler has no way of knowing which version of **f1( )** to call.

EXERCISES

1. Create a function called **sroot( )** that returns the square root of its argument. Overload **sroot( )** three ways: have it return the square root of an integer, a long integer, and a **double**. (To actually compute the square root, you can use the standard library function **sqrt( )**.)

2. The C++ standard library contains these three functions:

   ```
   double atof(const char *s);
   int atoi(const char *s);
   long atol(const char *s);
   ```

   These functions return the numeric value contained in the string pointed to by **s**. Specifically, **atof( )** returns a **double**, **atoi( )** returns an integer, and **atol( )** returns a **long**. Why is it not possible to overload these functions?

3. Create a function called **min( )** that returns the smaller of the two numeric arguments used to call the function. Overload **min( )** so it accepts characters, integers, and **double**s as arguments.

4. Create a function called **sleep( )** that pauses the computer for the number of seconds specified by its single argument. Overload **sleep( )** so it can be called with either an integer or a string representation of an integer. For example, both of these calls to **sleep( )** will cause the computer to pause for 10 seconds:

   ```
   sleep(10);
   sleep("10");
   ```

   Demonstrate that your functions work by including them in a short program. (Feel free to use a delay loop to pause the computer.)

1.8 *C*++ *KEYWORDS*

C++ supports all of the keywords defined by C and adds 30 of its own. The entire set of keywords defined by C++ is shown in Table 1-1. Also, early versions of C++ defined the **overload** keyword, but it is now obsolete.

*S*KILLS CHECK

Mastery
Skills Check

At this point you should be able to perform the following exercises and answer the questions.

1. Give brief descriptions of polymorphism, encapsulation, and inheritance.

2. How can comments be included in a C++ program?

3. Write a program that uses C++-style I/O to input two integers from the keyboard and then displays the result of raising the first to the power of the second. (For example, if the user enters 2 and 4, the result is 2^4, or 16.)

asm	const_cast	explicit	int	register	switch	union
auto	continue	extern	long	reinterpret_cast	template	unsigned
bool	default	false	mutable	return	this	using
break	delete	float	namespace	short	throw	virtual
case	do	for	new	signed	true	void
catch	double	friend	operator	sizeof	try	volatile
char	dynamic_cast	goto	private	static	typedef	wchar_t
class	else	if	protected	static_cast	typeid	while
const	enum	inline	public	struct	typename	

TABLE 1-2   *The C++ Keywords* ▼

4. Create a function called **rev_str( )** that reverses a string. Overload **rev_str( )** so it can be called with either one character array or two. When it is called with one string, have that one string contain the reversal. When it is called with two strings, return the reversed string in the second argument. For example:

```
char s1[80], s2[80];
strcpy(s1, "hello");
rev_str(s1, s2); // reversed string goes in s2, s1 untouched
rev_str(s1); // reversed string is returned in s1
```

5. Given the following new-style C++ program, show how to change it into its old-style form.

```
#include <iostream>
using namespace std;

int f(int a);

int main()
{
  cout << f(10);

  return 0;
}

int f(int a)
{
  return a * 3.1416;
}
```

6. What is the **bool** data type?

2

Introducing Classes

chapter objectives

T HIS chapter introduces classes and objects. Several important topics are covered that relate to virtually all aspects of C++ programming, so a careful reading is advised.

Review
Skills Check

Before proceeding, you should be able to correctly answer the following questions and do the exercises.

1. Write a program that uses C++-style I/O to prompt the user for a string and then display its length.

2. Create a class that holds name and address information. Store all the information in character strings that are private members of the class. Include a public function that stores the name and address. Also include a public function that displays the name and address. (Call these functions **store( )** and **display( )**.)

3. Create an overloaded **rotate( )** function that left-rotates the bits in its argument and returns the result. Overload it so it accepts **int**s and **long**s. (A rotate is similar to a shift except that the bit shifted off one end is shifted onto the other end.)

4. What is wrong with the following fragment?

```
#include <iostream>
using namespace std;

class myclass {
   int i;
public:
   .
   .
   .
};

int main()
{
```

```
myclass ob;
ob.i = 10;
  .
  .
  .
}
```

*C*ONSTRUCTOR AND DESTRUCTOR *FUNCTIONS*

If you have been writing programs for very long, you know that it is common for parts of your program to require initialization. The need for initialization is even more common when you are working with objects. In fact, when applied to real problems, virtually every object you create will require some sort of initialization. To address this situation, C++ allows a *constructor function* to be included in a class declaration. A class's constructor is called each time an object of that class is created. Thus, any initializations that need to be performed on an object can be done automatically by the constructor function.

A constructor function has the same name as the class of which it is a part and has no return type. For example, here is a short class that contains a constructor function:

```
#include <iostream>
using namespace std;

class myclass {
  int a;
public:
  myclass(); // constructor
  void show();
};

myclass::myclass()
{
  cout << "In constructor\n";
  a = 10;
}

void myclass::show()
{
```

```
   cout << a;
}

int main()
{
  myclass ob;

  ob.show();

  return 0;
}
```

In this simple example, the value of **a** is initialized by the constructor **myclass( )**. The constructor is called when the object **ob** is created. An object is created when that object's declaration statement is executed. It is important to understand that in C++, a variable declaration statement is an "action statement." When you are programming in C, it is easy to think of declaration statements as simply establishing variables. However, in C++, because an object might have a constructor, a variable declaration statement may, in fact, cause a considerable number of actions to occur.

Notice how **myclass( )** is defined. As stated, it has no return type. According to the C++ formal syntax rules, it is illegal for a constructor to have a return type.

For global objects, an object's constructor is called once, when the program first begins execution. For local objects, the constructor is called each time the declaration statement is executed.

The complement of a constructor is the *destructor*. This function is called when an object is destroyed. When you are working with objects, it is common to have to perform some actions when an object is destroyed. For example, an object that allocates memory when it is created will want to free that memory when it is destroyed. The name of a destructor is the name of its class, preceded by a ~. For example, this class contains a destructor function:

```
#include <iostream>
using namespace std;

class myclass {
   int a;
public:
```

```
  myclass(); // constructor
  ~myclass(); // destructor
  void show();
};

myclass::myclass()
{
  cout << "In constructor\n";
  a = 10;
}
myclass::~myclass()
{
  cout << "Destructing...\n";
}

void myclass::show()
{
  cout << a << "\n";
}

int main()
{
  myclass ob;

  ob.show();

  return 0;
}
```

A class's destructor is called when an object is destroyed. Local objects are destroyed when they go out of scope. Global objects are destroyed when the program ends.

It is not possible to take the address of either a constructor or a destructor.

Technically, a constructor or a destructor can perform any type of operation. The code within these functions does not have to initialize or reset anything related to the class for which they are defined. For example, a constructor for the preceding examples could have computed pi to 100 places. However, having a constructor or destructor perform actions not directly related to the initialization or orderly destruction of an object makes for very poor programming style and should be avoided.

1. You should recall that the **stack** class created in Chapter 1 required an initialization function to set the stack index variable. This is precisely the sort of operation that a constructor function was designed to perform. Here is an improved version of the **stack** class that uses a constructor to automatically initialize a stack object when it is created:

```cpp
#include <iostream>
using namespace std;

#define SIZE 10

// Declare a stack class for characters.
class stack {
  char stck[SIZE]; // holds the stack
  int tos; // index of top of stack
public:
  stack(); // constructor
  void push(char ch); // push character on stack
  char pop(); // pop character from stack
};

// Initialize the stack.
stack::stack()
{
  cout << "Constructing a stack\n";
  tos = 0;
}

// Push a character.
void stack::push(char ch)
{
  if(tos==SIZE) {
    cout << "Stack is full\n";
    return;
  }
  stck[tos] = ch;
  tos++;
}
```

```cpp
// Pop a character.
char stack::pop()
{
  if(tos==0) {
    cout << "Stack is empty\n";
    return 0; // return null on empty stack
  }
  tos--;
  return stck[tos];
}

int main()
{
  // Create two stacks that are automatically initialized.
  stack s1, s2;
  int i;

  s1.push('a');
  s2.push('x');
  s1.push('b');
  s2.push('y');
  s1.push('c');
  s2.push('z');

  for(i=0; i<3; i++) cout << "Pop s1: " << s1.pop() << "\n";
  for(i=0; i<3; i++) cout << "Pop s2: " << s2.pop() << "\n";

  return 0;
}
```

As you can see, now the initialization task is performed automatically by the constructor function rather than by a separate function that must be explicitly called by the program. This is an important point. When an initialization is performed automatically when an object is created, it eliminates any prospect that, by error, the initialization will not be performed. This is another way that objects help reduce program complexity. You, as the programmer, don't need to worry about initialization— it is performed automatically when the object is brought into existence.

2. Here is an example that shows the need for both a constructor and a destructor function. It creates a simple string class, called **strtype**, that contains a string and its length. When a **strtype** object is created, memory is allocated to hold the string and its initial length is set to 0. When a **strtype** object is destroyed, that memory is released.

```cpp
#include <iostream>
#include <cstring>
#include <cstdlib>
using namespace std;

#define SIZE 255

class strtype {
  char *p;
  int len;
public:
  strtype(); // constructor
  ~strtype(); //destructor
  void set(char *ptr);
  void show();
};

// Initialize a string object.
strtype::strtype()
{
  p = (char *) malloc(SIZE);
  if(!p) {
    cout << "Allocation error\n";
    exit(1);
  }
  *p = '\0';
  len = 0;
}

// Free memory when destroying string object.
strtype::~strtype()
{
  cout << "Freeing p\n";
  free(p);
}
```

```
void strtype::set(char *ptr)
{
  if(strlen(p) >= SIZE) {
    cout << "String too big\n";
    return;
  }
  strcpy(p, ptr);
  len = strlen(p);
}

void strtype::show()
{
  cout << p << " - length: " << len;
  cout << "\n";
}

int main()
{
  strtype s1, s2;

  s1.set("This is a test.");
  s2.set("I like C++.");

  s1.show();
  s2.show();

  return 0;
}
```

This program uses **malloc( )** and **free( )** to allocate and free memory. While this is perfectly valid, C++ does provide another way to dynamically manage memory, as you will see later in this book.

The preceding program uses the new-style headers for the C library functions used by the program. As mentioned in Chapter 1, if your compiler does not support these headers, simply substitute the standard C header files. This applies to other programs in this book in which C library functions are used.

3. Here is an interesting way to use an object's constructor and destructor. This program uses an object of the **timer** class to time the interval between when an object of type **timer** is created and when it is destroyed. When the object's destructor is called, the elapsed time is displayed. You could use an object like this to time the duration of a program or the length of time a function spends within a block. Just make sure that the object goes out of scope at the point at which you want the timing interval to end.

```cpp
#include <iostream>
#include <ctime>
using namespace std;

class timer {
  clock_t start;
public:
  timer(); // constructor
  ~timer(); // destructor
};

timer::timer()
{
  start = clock();
}

timer::~timer()
{
  clock_t end;

  end = clock();
  cout << "Elapsed time: " << (end-start) /
                            CLOCKS_PER_SEC << "\n";
}

int main()
{
  timer ob;
  char c;

  // delay ...
```

```
cout << "Press a key followed by ENTER: ";
cin >> c;

return 0;
}
```

This program uses the standard library function **clock( )**, which returns the number of clock cycles that have taken place since the program started running. Dividing this value by **CLOCKS_PER_SEC** converts the value to seconds.

EXERCISES

1. Rework the **queue** class that you developed as an exercise in Chapter 1 by replacing its initialization function with a constructor.

2. Create a class called **stopwatch** that emulates a stopwatch that keeps track of elapsed time. Use a constructor to initially set the elapsed time to 0. Provide two member functions called **start( )** and **stop( )** that turn on and off the timer, respectively. Include a member function called **show( )** that displays the elapsed time. Also, have the destructor function automatically display elapsed time when a **stopwatch** object is destroyed. (To simplify, report the time in seconds.)

3. What is wrong with the constructor shown in the following fragment?

```
class sample {
  double a, b, c;
public:
  double sample();  // error, why?
};
```

CONSTRUCTORS THAT TAKE PARAMETERS

It is possible to pass arguments to a constructor function. To allow this, simply add the appropriate parameters to the constructor function's declaration and definition. Then, when you declare an object, specify the arguments. To see how this is accomplished, let's begin with the short example shown here:

```cpp
#include <iostream>
using namespace std;

class myclass {
  int a;
public:
  myclass(int x); // constructor
  void show();
};

myclass::myclass(int x)
{
  cout << "In constructor\n";
  a = x;
}

void myclass::show()
{
  cout << a << "\n";
}

int main()
{
  myclass ob(4);

  ob.show();

  return 0;
}
```

Here the constructor for **myclass** takes one parameter. The value passed to **myclass( )** is used to initialize **a**. Pay special attention to how **ob** is declared in **main( )**. The value 4, specified in the parentheses following **ob**, is the argument that is passed to **myclass( )**'s parameter **x**, which is used to initialize **a**.

Actually, the syntax for passing an argument to a parameterized constructor is shorthand for this longer form:

```
myclass ob = myclass(4);
```

However, most C++ programmers use the short form. Actually, there is a slight technical difference between the two forms that relates to copy constructors, which are discussed later in this book. But you don't need to worry about this distinction now.

Note

Unlike constructor functions, destructor functions cannot have parameters. The reason for this is simple enough to understand: there exists no mechanism by which to pass arguments to an object that is being destroyed.

EXAMPLES

1. It is possible—in fact, quite common—to pass a constructor more than one argument. Here **myclass( )** is passed two arguments:

```cpp
#include <iostream>
using namespace std;

class myclass {
  int a, b;
public:
  myclass(int x, int y); // constructor
  void show();
};

myclass::myclass(int x, int y)
{
  cout << "In constructor\n";
  a = x;
  b = y;
}

void myclass::show()
{
  cout << a << ' ' << b << "\n";
}
```

```
int main()
{
  myclass ob(4, 7);

  ob.show();

  return 0;
}
```

Here 4 is passed to **x** and 7 is passed to **y**. This same general approach is used to pass any number of arguments you like (up to the limit set by the compiler, of course).

2. Here is another version of the **stack** class that uses a parameterized constructor to pass a "name" to a stack. This single-character name is used to identify the stack that is being referred to when an error occurs.

```
#include <iostream>
using namespace std;

#define SIZE 10

// Declare a stack class for characters.
class stack {
  char stck[SIZE]; // holds the stack
  int tos; // index of top of stack
  char who; // identifies stack
public:
  stack(char c); // constructor
  void push(char ch); // push character on stack
  char pop(); // pop character from stack
};

// Initialize the stack.
stack::stack(char c)
{
  tos = 0;
  who = c;
  cout << "Constructing stack " << who << "\n";
}

// Push a character.
void stack::push(char ch)
{
```

```
      if(tos==SIZE) {
        cout << "Stack " << who << " is full\n";
        return;
      }
      stck[tos] = ch;
      tos++;
    }

    // Pop a character.
    char stack::pop()
    {
      if(tos==0) {
        cout << "Stack " << who << " is empty\n";
        return 0; // return null on empty stack
      }
      tos--;
      return stck[tos];
    }

    int main()
    {
      // Create two stacks that are automatically initialized.
      stack s1('A'), s2('B');
      int i;

      s1.push('a');
      s2.push('x');
      s1.push('b');
      s2.push('y');
      s1.push('c');
      s2.push('z');

      // This will generate some error messages.

      for(i=0; i<5; i++) cout << "Pop s1: " << s1.pop() << "\n";
      for(i=0; i<5; i++) cout << "Pop s2: " << s2.pop() << "\n";

      return 0;
    }
```

Giving objects a "name," as shown in this example, is especially
useful during debugging, when it is important to know which
object generates an error.

3. Here is a different way to implement the **strtype** class (developed earlier) that uses a parameterized constructor function:

```cpp
#include <iostream>
#include <cstring>
#include <cstdlib>
using namespace std;

class strtype {
  char *p;
  int len;
public:
  strtype(char *ptr);
  ~strtype();
  void show();
};

strtype::strtype(char *ptr)
{
  len = strlen(ptr);
  p = (char *) malloc(len+1);
  if(!p) {
    cout << "Allocation error\n";
    exit(1);
  }
  strcpy(p, ptr);
}

strtype::~strtype()
{
  cout << "Freeing p\n";
  free(p);
}

void strtype::show()
{
  cout << p << " - length: " << len;
  cout << "\n";
}

int main()
{
  strtype s1("This is a test."), s2("I like C++.");
```

```
    s1.show();
    s2.show();
    return 0;
}
```

In this version of **strtype**, a string is given an initial value using the constructor function.

4. Although the previous examples have used constants, you can pass an object's constructor any valid expression, including variables. For example, this program uses user input to construct an object:

```
#include <iostream>
using namespace std;

class myclass {
  int i, j;
public:
  myclass(int a, int b);
  void show();
};

myclass::myclass(int a, int b)
{
  i = a;
  j = b;
}

void myclass::show()
{
  cout << i << ' ' << j << "\n";
}

int main()
{
  int x, y;

  cout << "Enter two integers: ";
  cin >> x >> y;

  // use variables to construct ob
  myclass ob(x, y);
```

```
    ob.show();

    return 0;
}
```

This program illustrates an important point about objects. They can be constructed as needed to fit the exact situation at the time of their creation. As you learn more about C++, you will see how useful constructing objects "on the fly" is.

EXERCISES

1. Change the **stack** class so it dynamically allocates memory for the stack. Have the size of the stack specified by a parameter to the constructor function. (Don't forget to free this memory with a destructor function.)

2. Create a class called **t_and_d** that is passed the current system time and date as a parameter to its constructor when it is created. Have the class include a member function that displays this time and date on the screen. (Hint: Use the standard time and date functions found in the standard library to find and display the time and date.)

3. Create a class called **box** whose constructor function is passed three **double** values, each of which represents the length of one side of a box. Have the **box** class compute the volume of the box and store the result in a **double** variable. Include a member function called **vol( )** that displays the volume of each **box** object.

2.3 ∎NTRODUCING INHERITANCE

Although inheritance is discussed more fully in Chapter 7, it needs to be introduced at this time. As it applies to C++, inheritance is the mechanism by which one class can inherit the properties of another. Inheritance allows a hierarchy of classes to be built, moving from the most general to the most specific.

To begin, it is necessary to define two terms commonly used when discussing inheritance. When one class is inherited by another, the class that is inherited is called the *base class*. The inheriting class is called the *derived class*. In general, the process of inheritance begins with the definition of a base class. The base class defines all qualities that will be common to any derived classes. In essence, the base class represents the most general description of a set of traits. A derived class inherits those general traits and adds properties that are specific to that class.

To understand how one class can inherit another, let's first begin with an example that, although simple, illustrates many key features of inheritance.

To start, here is the declaration for the base class:

```
// Define base class.
class B {
   int i;
public:
   void set_i(int n);
   int get_i();
};
```

Using this base class, here is a derived class that inherits it:

```
// Define derived class.
class D : public B {
   int j;
public:
   void set_j(int n);
   int mul();
};
```

Look closely at this declaration. Notice that after the class name **D** there is a colon followed by the keyword **public** and the class name **B**. This tells the compiler that class **D** will inherit all components of class **B**. The keyword **public** tells the compiler that **B** will be inherited such that all public elements of the base class will also be public elements of the derived class. However, all private elements of the base class remain private to it and are not directly accessible by the derived class.

Here is an entire program that uses the **B** and **D** classes:

```cpp
// A simple example of inheritance.
#include <iostream>
using namespace std;

// Define base class.
class B {
  int i;
public:
  void set_i(int n);
  int get_i();
};

// Define derived class.
class D : public B {
  int j;
public:
  void set_j(int n);
  int mul();
};

// Set value i in base.
void B::set_i(int n)
{
  i = n;
}

// Return value of i in base.
int B::get_i()
{
  return i;
}

// Set value of j in derived.
```

```
void D::set_j(int n)
{
  j = n;
}

// Return value of base's i times derived's j.
int D::mul()
{
  // derived class can call base class public member functions
  return j * get_i();
}

int main()
{
  D ob;

  ob.set_i(10); // load i in base
  ob.set_j(4);  // load j in derived

  cout << ob.mul();  // displays 40

  return 0;
}
```

Look at the definition of **mul( )**. Notice that it calls **get_i( )**, which is a member of the base class **B**, not of **D**, without linking it to any specific object. This is possible because the public members of **B** become public members of **D**. However, the reason that **mul( )** must call **get_i( )** instead of accessing **i** directly is that the private members of a base class (in this case, **i**) remain private to it and not accessible by any derived class. The reason that private members of a class are not accessible to derived classes is to maintain encapsulation. If the private members of a class could be made public simply by inheriting the class, encapsulation could be easily circumvented.

The general form used to inherit a base class is shown here:

class *derived-class-name* : *access-specifier base-class-name* {

 .

 .

 .

};

Here *access-specifier* is one of the following three keywords: **public**, **private**, or **protected**. For now, just use **public** when inheriting a class. A complete description of the access specifiers will be given later in this book.

1. Here is a program that defines a generic base class called **fruit** that describes certain characteristics of fruit. This class is inherited by two derived classes called **Apple** and **Orange**. These classes supply specific information to **fruit** that are related to these types of fruit.

```cpp
// An example of class inheritance.
#include <iostream>
#include <cstring>
using namespace std;

enum yn {no, yes};
enum color {red, yellow, green, orange};

void out(enum yn x);

char *c[] = {
  "red", "yellow", "green", "orange"};

// Generic fruit class.
class fruit {
// in this base, all elements are public
public:
  enum yn annual;
  enum yn perennial;
  enum yn tree;
  enum yn tropical;
  enum color clr;
  char name[40];
};

// Derive Apple class.
class Apple : public fruit {
  enum yn cooking;
  enum yn crunchy;
```

```
  enum yn eating;
public:
  void seta(char *n, enum color c, enum yn ck, enum yn crchy,
          enum yn e);
  void show();
};

// Derive orange class.
class Orange : public fruit {
  enum yn juice;
  enum yn sour;
  enum yn eating;
public:
  void seto(char *n, enum color c, enum yn j, enum yn sr,
          enum yn e);
  void show();
};

void Apple::seta(char *n, enum color c, enum yn ck,
                enum yn crchy, enum yn e)
{
  strcpy(name, n);
  annual = no;
  perennial = yes;

  tree = yes;
  tropical = no;
  clr = c;
  cooking = ck;
  crunchy = crchy;
  eating = e;
}

void Orange::seto(char *n, enum color c, enum yn j,
                enum yn sr, enum yn e)
{
  strcpy(name, n);
  annual = no;
  perennial = yes;
  tree = yes;
  tropical = yes;
  clr = c;
  juice = j;
  sour = sr;
```

```
    eating = e;
}

void Apple::show()
{
  cout << name << " apple is: " << "\n";
  cout << "Annual: ";  out(annual);
  cout << "Perennial: ";  out(perennial);
  cout << "Tree: "; out(tree);
  cout << "Tropical: "; out(tropical);
  cout << "Color: " << c[clr] << "\n";
  cout << "Good for cooking: "; out(cooking);
  cout << "Crunchy: ";  out(crunchy);
  cout << "Good for eating: ";  out(eating);
  cout << "\n";
}

void Orange::show()
{
  cout << name << " orange is: " << "\n";
  cout << "Annual: ";  out(annual);
  cout << "Perennial: ";  out(perennial);
  cout << "Tree: ";  out(tree);
  cout << "Tropical: ";  out(tropical);
  cout << "Color: " << c[clr] << "\n";
  cout << "Good for juice: ";  out(juice);
  cout << "Sour: ";  out(sour);
  cout << "Good for eating: ";  out(eating);
  cout << "\n";
}

void out(enum yn x)
{
  if(x==no) cout << "no\n";
  else cout << "yes\n";
}

int main()
{
  Apple a1, a2;
  Orange o1, o2;

  a1.seta("Red Delicious", red, no, yes, yes);
```

```
a2.seta("Jonathan", red, yes, no, yes);

o1.seto("Navel", orange, no, no, yes);
o2.seto("Valencia", orange, yes, yes, no);

a1.show();
a2.show();

o1.show();
o2.show();

  return 0;
}
```

As you can see, the base class **fruit** defines several characteristics that are common to all types of fruit. (Of course, in order to keep this example short enough to fit conveniently in a book, the **fruit** class is somewhat simplified.) For example, all fruit grows on either annual or perennial plants. All fruit grows either on trees or on other types of plants, such as vines or bushes. All fruit has a color and a name. This base class is then inherited by the **Apple** and **Orange** classes. Each of these classes supplies information specific to its type of fruit.

This example illustrates the basic reason for inheritance. Here, a base class is created that defines the general traits associated with *all* fruit. It is left to the derived classes to supply those traits that are specific to each *individual* case.

This program illustrates another important fact about inheritance: A base class is not exclusively "owned" by a derived class. A base class can be inherited by any number of classes.

EXERCISE

1. Given the following base class,

```
class area_cl {
public:
  double height;
```

```
  double width;
};
```

create two derived classes called **rectangle** and **isosceles** that inherit **area_cl**. Have each class include a function called **area( )** that returns the area of a rectangle or isosceles triangle, as appropriate. Use parameterized constructors to initialize **height** and **width**.

***O**BJECT POINTERS*

So far, you have been accessing members of an object by using the dot operator. This is the correct method when you are working with an object. However, it is also possible to access a member of an object via a pointer to that object. When a pointer is used, the arrow operator (**->**) rather than the dot operator is employed. (This is exactly the same way the arrow operator is used when given a pointer to a structure.)

You declare an object pointer just like you declare a pointer to any other type of variable. Specify its class name, and then precede the variable name with an asterisk. To obtain the address of an object, precede the object with the **&** operator, just as you do when taking the address of any other type of variable.

Just like pointers to other types, an object pointer, when incremented, will point to the next object of its type.

EXAMPLE

1. Here is a simple example that uses an object pointer:

```
#include <iostream>
using namespace std;

class myclass {
  int a;
public:
  myclass(int x); // constructor
```

```
    int get();
};

myclass::myclass(int x)
{
  a = x;
}

int myclass::get()
{
  return a;
}

int main()
{
  myclass ob(120);  // create object
  myclass *p;  // create pointer to object

  p = &ob; // put address of ob into p

  cout << "Value using object: " << ob.get();
  cout << "\n";

  cout << "Value using pointer: " << p->get();

  return 0;
}
```

Notice how the declaration

```
myclass *p;
```

creates a pointer to an object of **myclass**. It is important to understand that creation of an object pointer does *not* create an object—it creates just a pointer to one. The address of **ob** is put into **p** by using this statement:

```
p = &ob;
```

Finally, the program shows how the members of an object can be accessed through a pointer.

We will come back to the subject of object pointers in Chapter 4, once you know more about C++. There are several special features that relate to them.

2.5   *C*LASSES, STRUCTURES, AND UNIONS ARE RELATED

As you have seen, the class is syntactically similar to the structure. You might be surprised to learn, however, that the class and the structure have virtually identical capabilities. In C++, the definition of a structure has been expanded so that it can also include member functions, including constructor and destructor functions, in just the same way that a class can. In fact, the only difference between a structure and a class is that, by default, the members of a class are private but the members of a structure are public. The expanded syntax of a structure is shown here:

```
struct type-name {
    // public function and data members
private:
    // private function and data members
} object-list;
```

In fact, according to the formal C++ syntax, both **struct** and **class** create new class types. Notice that a new keyword is introduced. It is **private**, and it tells the compiler that the members that follow are private to that class.

On the surface, there is a seeming redundancy in the fact that structures and classes have virtually identical capabilities. Many newcomers to C++ wonder why this apparent duplication exists. In fact, it is not uncommon to hear the suggestion that the **class** keyword is unnecessary.

The answer to this line of reasoning has both a "strong" and "weak" form. The "strong" (or compelling) reason concerns maintaining upward compatibility from C. In C++, a C-style structure is also perfectly acceptable in a C++ program. Since in C all structure members are public by default, this convention is also maintained in C++. Further, because **class** is a syntactically separate entity from **struct**, the definition of a class is free to evolve in a way that will not be compatible with a C-like structure definition. Since the two are separated, the future direction of C++ is not restricted by compatibility concerns.

The "weak" reason for having two similar constructs is that there is no disadvantage to expanding the definition of a structure in C++ to include member functions.

Although structures have the same capabilities as classes, most programmers restrict their use of structures to adhere to their C-like form and do not use them to include function members. Most programmers use the **class** keyword when defining objects that contain both data and code. However, this is a stylistic matter and is subject to your own preference. (After this section, this book reserves the use of **struct** for objects that have no function members.)

If you find the connection between classes and structures interesting, so will you find this next revelation about C++: unions and classes are also related. In C++, a union defines a class type that can contain both functions and data as members. A union is like a structure in that, by default, all members are public until the **private** specifier is used. In a union, however, all data members share the same memory location (just as in C). Unions can contain constructor and destructor functions. Fortunately, C unions are upwardly compatible with C++ unions.

Although structures and classes seem on the surface to be redundant, this is not the case with unions. In an object-oriented language, it is important to preserve encapsulation. Thus, the union's ability to link code and data allows you to create class types in which all data uses a shared location. This is something that you cannot do using a class.

There are several restrictions that apply to unions as they relate to C++. First, they cannot inherit any other class and they cannot be used as a base class for any other type. Unions must not have any **static** members. They also must not contain any object that has a constructor or destructor. The union, itself, *can* have a constructor and destructor, though. Finally, unions cannot have virtual member functions. (Virtual functions are described later in this book.)

There is a special type of union in C++ called an *anonymous union*. An anonymous union does not have a type name, and no variables can be declared for this sort of union. Instead, an anonymous union tells the compiler that its members will share the same memory location. However, in all other respects, the members act and are treated like normal variables. That is, the members are accessed directly, without the dot operator syntax. For example, examine this fragment:

```
union { // an anonymous union
  int i;
  char ch[4];
} ;
```

```
i = 10; // access i and ch directly
ch[0] = 'X';
```

As you can see, **i** and **ch** are accessed directly because they are not part of any object. They do, however, share the same memory space.

The reason for the anonymous union is that it gives you a simple way to tell the compiler that you want two or more variables to share the same memory location. Aside from this special attribute, members of an anonymous union behave like other variables.

Anonymous unions have all of the restrictions that apply to normal unions, plus these additions. A global anonymous union must be declared **static**. An anonymous union cannot contain private members. The names of the members of an anonymous union must not conflict with other identifiers within the same scope.

EXAMPLES

1. Here is a short program that uses **struct** to create a class:

```cpp
#include <iostream>
#include <cstring>
using namespace std;

// use struct to define a class type
struct st_type {
  st_type(double b, char *n);
  void show();
private:
  double balance;
  char name[40];
} ;

st_type::st_type(double b, char *n)
{
  balance = b;
  strcpy(name, n);
}

void st_type::show()
{
  cout << "Name: " << name;
  cout << ": $" << balance;
  if(balance<0.0) cout << "***";
  cout << "\n";
```

```
}

int main()
{
  st_type acc1(100.12, "Johnson");
  st_type acc2(-12.34, "Hedricks");

  acc1.show();
  acc2.show();
  return 0;
}
```

Notice that, as stated, the members of a structure are public by default. The **private** keyword must be used to declare private members.

Also, notice one difference between C-like structures and C++-like structures. In C++, the structure tag-name also becomes a complete type name that can be used to declare objects. In C, the tag-name requires that the keyword **struct** precede it before it becomes a complete type.

Here is the same program, rewritten using a class:

```
#include <iostream>
#include <cstring>
using namespace std;

class cl_type {
  double balance;
  char name[40];
public:
  cl_type(double b, char *n);
  void show();
} ;

cl_type::cl_type(double b, char *n)
{
  balance = b;
  strcpy(name, n);
}

void cl_type::show()
{
  cout << "Name: " << name;
  cout << ": $" << balance;
```

```
    if(balance<0.0) cout << "***";
    cout << "\n";
}

int main()
{
  cl_type acc1(100.12, "Johnson");
  cl_type acc2(-12.34, "Hedricks");

  acc1.show();
  acc2.show();

  return 0;
}
```

2. Here is an example that uses a union to display the binary bit pattern, byte by byte, contained within a **double** value.

```
#include <iostream>
using namespace std;

union bits {
  bits(double n);
  void show_bits();
  double d;
  unsigned char c[sizeof(double)];
};

bits::bits(double n)
{
  d = n;
}

void bits::show_bits()
{
  int i, j;

  for(j = sizeof(double)-1; j>=0; j--) {
    cout << "Bit pattern in byte " << j << ": ";
    for(i = 128; i; i >>= 1)
      if(i & c[j]) cout << "1";
      else cout << "0";
    cout << "\n";
  }
```

```
}

int main()
{
  bits ob(1991.829);

  ob.show_bits();

  return 0;
}
```

The output of this program is

```
Bit pattern in byte 7: 01000000
Bit pattern in byte 6: 10011111
Bit pattern in byte 5: 00011111
Bit pattern in byte 4: 01010000
Bit pattern in byte 3: 11100101
Bit pattern in byte 2: 01100000
Bit pattern in byte 1: 01000001
Bit pattern in byte 0: 10001001
```

3. Both structures and unions can have constructors and destructors. The following example shows the **strtype** class reworked as a structure. It contains both a constructor and a destructor function.

```
#include <iostream>
#include <cstring>
#include <cstdlib>
using namespace std;

struct strtype {
  strtype(char *ptr);
  ~strtype();
  void show();
private:
  char *p;
  int len;
};

strtype::strtype(char *ptr)
{
  len = strlen(ptr);
  p = (char *) malloc(len+1);
```

```
  if(!p) {
    cout << "Allocation error\n";
    exit(1);
  }
  strcpy(p, ptr);
}

strtype::~strtype()
{
  cout << "Freeing p\n";
  free(p);
}

void strtype::show()
{
  cout << p << " - length: " << len;
  cout << "\n";
}

int main()
{
  strtype s1("This is a test."), s2("I like C++.");

  s1.show();
  s2.show();

  return 0;
}
```

4. This program uses an anonymous union to display the individual bytes that comprise a **double**. (This program assumes that **double**s are 8 bytes long.)

```
// Using an anonymous union.
#include <iostream>
using namespace std;

int main()
{
  union {
    unsigned char bytes[8];
    double value;
  };
  int i;
```

```
    value = 859345.324;

    // display the bytes within a double
    for(i=0; i<8; i++)
      cout << (int) bytes[i] << " ";

    return 0;
}
```

As you can see, both **value** and **bytes** are accessed as if they were normal variables and not part of a union. Even though they are declared as being part of an anonymous union, their names are at the same scope level as any other local variable declared at the same point. This is why a member of an anonymous union cannot have the same name as any other variable known to its scope.

EXERCISES

1. Rewrite the **stack** class presented in Section 2.1 so it uses a structure rather than a class.

2. Use a **union** class to swap the low- and high-order bytes of an integer (assuming 16-bit integers; if your computer uses 32-bit integers, swap the bytes of a **short int**).

3. Explain what an anonymous union is and how it differs from a normal union.

2.6 **IN-LINE FUNCTIONS**

Before we continue this examination of classes, a short but related digression is needed. In C++, it is possible to define functions that are not actually called but, rather, are expanded in line, at the point of each call. This is much the same way that a C-like parameterized macro works. The advantage of *in-line functions* is that they have no overhead associated with the function call and return mechanism. This means that in-line functions can be executed much faster than normal functions. (Remember, the machine instructions that generate the function call and return take time each time a function is called. If there are parameters, even more time overhead is generated.)

The disadvantage of in-line functions is that if they are too large and called too often, your program grows larger. For this reason, in general only short functions are declared as in-line functions.

To declare an in-line function, simply precede the function's definition with the **inline** specifier. For example, this short program shows how to declare an in-line function:

```
// Example of an in-line function
#include <iostream>
using namespace std;

inline int even(int x)
{
  return !(x%2);
}

int main()
{
  if(even(10)) cout << "10 is even\n";
  if(even(11)) cout << "11 is even\n";

  return 0;
}
```

In this example, the function **even( )**, which returns **true** if its argument is even, is declared as being in-line. This means that the line

```
if(even(10))  cout << "10 is even\n";
```

is functionally equivalent to

```
if(!(10%2)) cout << "10 is even\n";
```

This example also points out another important feature of using **inline**: an in-line function must be defined *before* it is first called. If it isn't, the compiler has no way to know that it is supposed to be expanded in-line. This is why **even( )** was defined before **main( )**.

The advantage of using **inline** rather than parameterized macros is twofold. First, it provides a more structured way to expand short functions in line. For example, when you are creating a parameterized macro, it is easy to forget that extra parentheses are often needed to ensure proper in-line expansion in every case. Using in-line functions prevents such problems.

Second, an in-line function might be able to be optimized more thoroughly by the compiler than a macro expansion. In any event, C++ programmers virtually never use parameterized macros, instead relying on **inline** to avoid the overhead of a function call associated with a short function.

It is important to understand that the **inline** specifier is a *request,* not a command, to the compiler. If, for various reasons, the compiler is unable to fulfill the request, the function is compiled as a normal function and the **inline** request is ignored.

Depending upon your compiler, several restrictions to in-line functions may apply. For example, some compilers will not in-line a function if it contains a **static** variable, a loop statement, a **switch** or a **goto**, or if the function is recursive. You should check your compiler's user manual for specific restrictions to in-line functions that might affect you.

Remember   *If any in-line restriction is violated, the compiler is free to generate a normal function.*

EXAMPLES

1. Any type of function can be in-lined, including functions that are members of classes. For example, here the member function **divisible( )** is in-lined for fast execution. (The function returns **true** if its first argument can be evenly divided by its second.)

```
// Demonstrate in-lining a member function.
#include <iostream>
using namespace std;

class samp {
  int i, j;
```

```
public:
  samp(int a, int b);
  int divisible(); // in-lined in its definition
};

samp::samp(int a, int b)
{
  i = a;
  j = b;
}

/* Return 1 if i is evenly divisible by j.
   This member function is expanded in line.
*/
inline int samp::divisible()
{
  return !(i%j);
}

int main()
{
  samp ob1(10, 2), ob2(10, 3);

  // this is true
  if(ob1.divisible()) cout << "10 divisible by 2\n";

  // this is false
  if(ob2.divisible()) cout << "10 divisible by 3\n";

  return 0;
}
```

2. It is perfectly permissible to in-line an overloaded function. For example, this program overloads **min( )** three ways. Each way is also declared as **inline**.

```
#include <iostream>
using namespace std;

// Overload min() three ways.

// integers
inline int min(int a, int b)
{
  return a<b ? a : b;
```

```
}

// longs
inline long min(long a, long b)
{
  return a<b ? a : b;
}

// doubles
inline double min(double a, double b)
{
  return a<b ? a : b;
}

int main()
{
  cout << min(-10, 10) << "\n";
  cout << min(-10.01, 100.002) << "\n";
  cout << min(-10L, 12L) << "\n";

  return 0;
}
```

EXERCISES

1. In Chapter 1 you overloaded the **abs( )** function so that it could find the absolute value of integers, long integers, and **double**s. Modify that program so that those functions are expanded in line.

2. Why might the following function not be in-lined by your compiler?

```
void f1()
{
  int i;

  for(i=0; i<10; i++) cout << i;
}
```

AUTOMATIC IN-LINING

If a member function's definition is short enough, the definition can be included inside the class declaration. Doing so causes the function to automatically become an in-line function, if possible. When a function is defined within a class declaration, the **inline** keyword is no longer necessary. (However, it is not an error to use it in this situation.) For example, the **divisible( )** function from the preceding section can be automatically in-lined as shown here:

```cpp
#include <iostream>
using namespace std;

class samp {
  int i, j;
public:
  samp(int a, int b);

  /* divisible() is defined here and automatically
     in-lined. */
  int divisible() { return !(i%j); }
};

samp::samp(int a, int b)
{
  i = a;
  j = b;
}

int main()
{
  samp ob1(10, 2), ob2(10, 3);

  // this is true
  if(ob1.divisible()) cout << "10 divisible by 2\n";

  // this is false
  if(ob2.divisible()) cout << "10 divisible by 3\n";

  return 0;
}
```

As you can see, the code associated with **divisible( )** occurs inside the declaration for the class **samp**. Further notice that no other definition of **divisible( )** is needed—or permitted. Defining **divisible( )** inside **samp** causes it to be made into an in-line function automatically.

When a function defined inside a class declaration cannot be made into an in-line function (because a restriction has been violated), it is automatically made into a regular function.

Notice how **divisible( )** is defined within **samp**, paying particular attention to the body. It occurs all on one line. This format is very common in C++ programs when a function is declared within a class declaration. It allows the declaration to be more compact. However, the **samp** class could have been written like this:

```
class samp {
  int i, j;
public:
  samp(int a, int b);

  /* divisible() is defined here and automatically
     in-lined. */
  int divisible()
  {
    return !(i%j);
  }
};
```

In this version, the layout of **divisible( )** uses the more-or-less standard indentation style. From the compiler's point of view, there is no difference between the compact style and the standard style. However, the compact style is commonly found in C++ programs when short functions are defined inside a class definition.

The same restrictions that apply to "normal" in-line functions apply to automatic in-line functions within a class declaration.

EXAMPLES

1. Perhaps the most common use of in-line functions defined within a class is to define constructor and destructor functions. For example, the **samp** class can more efficiently be defined like this:

```
#include <iostream>
using namespace std;
```

```
class samp {
  int i, j;
public:
  // inline constructor
  samp(int a, int b) { i = a; j = b; }
  int divisible() { return !(i%j); }
};
```

The definition of **samp( )** within the class **samp** is sufficient, and no other definition of **samp( )** is needed.

2. Sometimes a short function will be included in a class declaration even though the automatic in-lining feature is of little or no value. Consider this class declaration:

```
class myclass {
  int i;
public:
  myclass(int n) { i = n; }
  void show() { cout << i; }
};
```

Here the function **show( )** is made into an in-line function automatically. However, as you should know, I/O operations are (generally) so slow relative to CPU/memory operations that any effect of eliminating the function call overhead is essentially lost. Even so, in C++ programs, it is still common to see small functions of this type declared within a class simply for the sake of convenience, and because no harm is caused.

EXERCISES

1. Convert the **stack** class from Section 2.1, Example 1, so that it uses automatic in-line functions where appropriate.

2. Convert the **strtype** class from Section 2.2, Example 3, so that it uses automatic in-line functions.

S*KILLS CHECK*

At this point you should be able to perform the following exercises and answer the questions.

1. What is a constructor? What is a destructor? When are they executed?

2. Create a class called **line** that draws a line on the screen. Store the line length in a private integer variable called **len**. Have **line**'s constructor take one parameter: the line length. Have the constructor store the length and actually draw the line. If your system does not support graphics, display the line by using *. Optional: Give **line** a destructor that erases the line.

3. What does the following program display?

```
#include <iostream>
using namespace std;

int main()
{
  int i = 10;
  long l = 1000000;
  double d = -0.0009;

  cout << i << ' ' << l << ' ' << d;
  cout << "\n";

  return 0;
}
```

4. Add another derived class that inherits **area_cl** from Section 2.3, Exercise 1. Call this class **cylinder** and have it compute the surface area of a cylinder. Hint: The surface area of a cylinder is $2 * pi * R^2 + pi * D * height$.

5. What is an in-line function? What are its advantages and disadvantages?

6. Modify the following program so that all member functions are automatically in-lined:

```cpp
#include <iostream>
using namespace std;

class myclass {
  int i, j;
public:
  myclass(int x, int y);
  void show();
};

myclass::myclass(int x, int y)
{
  i = x;
  j = y;
}

void myclass::show()
{
  cout << i << " " << j << "\n";
}

int main()
{
  myclass count(2, 3);

  count.show();

  return 0;
}
```

7. What is the difference between a class and a structure?

8. Is the following fragment valid?

```cpp
union {
  float f;
  unsigned int bits;
} ;
```

**Cumulative
Skills Check**

This section checks how well you have integrated material in this chapter with that from the preceding chapter.

1. Create a class called **prompt**. Pass its constructor function a prompting string of your own choosing. Have the constructor display the string and then input an integer. Store this value in a private variable called **count**. When an object of type **prompt** is destroyed, ring the bell on the terminal as many times as the user entered.

2. In Chapter 1 you created a program that converted feet to inches. Now create a class that does the same thing. Have the class store the number of feet and its equivalent number of inches. Pass to the class's constructor the number of feet and have the constructor display the number of inches.

3. Create a class called **dice** that contains one private integer variable. Create a function called **roll( )** that uses the standard random number generator, **rand( )**, to generate a number between 1 and 6. Then have **roll( )** display that value.

3

A Closer Look at Classes

chapter objectives

3.1 Assigning objects

3.2 Passing objects to functions

3.3 Returning objects from functions

3.4 An Introduction to friend functions

N this chapter you continue to explore the class. You will learn about assigning objects, passing objects to functions, and returning objects from functions. You will also learn about an important new type of function: the friend.

Review
Skills Check

Before proceeding, you should be able to correctly answer the following questions and do the exercises.

1. Given the following class, what are the names of its constructor and destructor functions?

```
class widgit {
  int x, y;
public:
  // ... fill in constructor and destructor functions
};
```

2. When is a constructor function called? When is a destructor function called?

3. Given the following base class, show how it can be inherited by a derived class called **Mars**.

```
class planet {
  int moons;
  double dist_from_sun;
  double diameter;
  double mass;
public:
  // ...
};
```

4. There are two ways to cause a function to be expanded in line. What are they?

5. Give two possible restrictions to in-line functions.

6. Given the following class, show how an object called **ob** that passes the value 100 to **a** and X to **c** would be declared.

```
class sample {
  int a;
  char c;
public:
  sample(int x, char ch) { a = x; c = ch; }
  // ...
};
```

3.1 *A*SSIGNING OBJECTS

One object can be assigned to another provided that both objects are of the same type. By default, when one object is assigned to another, a bitwise copy of all the data members is made. For example, when an object called **o1** is assigned to another object called **o2**, the contents of all of **o1**'s data are copied into the equivalent members of **o2**. This is illustrated by the following program:

```
// An example of object assignment.
#include <iostream>
using namespace std;

class myclass {
  int a, b;
public:
  void set(int i, int j) { a = i; b = j; }
  void show() { cout << a << ' ' << b << "\n"; }
};

int main()
{
  myclass o1, o2;

  o1.set(10, 4);

  // assign o1 to o2
  o2 = o1;

  o1.show();
  o2.show();

  return 0;
}
```

Here, object **o1** has its member variables **a** and **b** set to the values 10 and 4, respectively. Next, **o1** is assigned to **o2**. This causes the current value of **o1.a** to be assigned to **o2.a** and **o1.b** to be assigned to **o2.b**. Thus, when run, this program displays

```
10 4
10 4
```

Keep in mind that an assignment between two objects simply makes the data in those objects identical. The two objects are still completely separate. For example, after the assignment, calling **o1.set( )** to set the value of **o1.a** has no effect on **o2** or its **a** value.

EXAMPLES

1. Only objects of the same type can be used in an assignment statement. If the objects are not of the same type, a compile-time error is reported. Further, it is not sufficient that the types just be physically similar—their type names must be the same. For example, this is not a valid program:

```cpp
// This program has an error.
#include <iostream>
using namespace std;

class myclass {
  int a, b;
public:
  void set(int i, int j) { a = i; b = j; }
  void show() { cout << a << ' ' << b << "\n"; }
};

/* This class is similar to myclass but uses a
   different class name and thus appears as a different
   type to the compiler.
*/
class yourclass {
  int a, b;
public:
  void set(int i, int j) { a = i; b = j; }
  void show() { cout << a << ' ' << b << "\n"; }
};
```

```
int main()
{
  myclass o1;
  yourclass o2;

  o1.set(10, 4);

  o2 = o1; // ERROR, objects not of same type

  o1.show();
  o2.show();

  return 0;
}
```

In this case, even though **myclass** and **yourclass** are physically the same, because they have different type names, they are treated as differing types by the compiler.

2. It is important to understand that all data members of one object are assigned to another when an assignment is performed. This includes compound data such as arrays. For example, in the following version of the **stack** example, only **s1** has any characters actually pushed onto it. However, because of the assignment, **s2**'s **stck** array will also contain the characters **a**, **b**, and **c**.

```
#include <iostream>
using namespace std;

#define SIZE 10

// Declare a stack class for characters.
class stack {
  char stck[SIZE]; // holds the stack
  int tos; // index of top of stack
public:
  stack(); // constructor
  void push(char ch); // push character on stack
  char pop(); // pop character from stack
};

// Initialize the stack.
stack::stack()
{
```

```
    cout << "Constructing a stack\n";
    tos = 0;
}

// Push a character.
void stack::push(char ch)
{
  if(tos==SIZE) {
    cout << "Stack is full\n";
    return;
  }
  stck[tos] = ch;
  tos++;
}

// Pop a character.
char stack::pop()
{
  if(tos==0) {
    cout << "Stack is empty\n";
    return 0; // return null on empty stack
  }
  tos--;
  return stck[tos];
}

int main()
{
  // Create two stacks that are automatically initialized.
  stack s1, s2;
  int i;

  s1.push('a');
  s1.push('b');
  s1.push('c');

  // clone s1
  s2 = s1;  // now s1 and s2 are identical

  for(i=0; i<3; i++) cout << "Pop s1: " << s1.pop() << "\n";
```

```
    for(i=0; i<3; i++) cout << "Pop s2: " << s2.pop() << "\n";

    return 0;
}
```

3. You must exercise some care when assigning one object to
   another. For example, here is the **strtype** class developed in
   Chapter 2, along with a short **main( )**. See if you can find an
   error in this program.

```
// This program contains an error.

#include <iostream>
#include <cstring>
#include <cstdlib>
using namespace std;

class strtype {
  char *p;
  int len;
public:
  strtype(char *ptr);
  ~strtype();
  void show();
};

strtype::strtype(char *ptr)
{
  len = strlen(ptr);
  p = (char *) malloc(len+1);
  if(!p) {
    cout << "Allocation error\n";
    exit(1);
  }
  strcpy(p, ptr);
}

strtype::~strtype()
{
  cout << "Freeing p\n";
  free(p);
```

```
        }

        void strtype::show()
        {
          cout << p << " - length: " << len;
          cout << "\n";
        }

        int main()
        {
          strtype s1("This is a test."), s2("I like C++.");

          s1.show();
          s2.show();

          // assign s1 to s2 - - this generates an error
          s2 = s1;

          s1.show();
          s2.show();

          return 0;
        }
```

The trouble with this program is quite insidious. When **s1** and **s2** are created, both allocate memory to hold their respective strings. A pointer to each object's allocated memory is stored in **p**. When a **strtype** object is destroyed, this memory is released. However, when **s1** is assigned to **s2**, **s2**'s **p** now points to the same memory as **s1**'s **p**. Thus, when these objects are destroyed, the memory pointed to by **s1**'s **p** is freed *twice* and the memory originally pointed to by **s2**'s **p** is not freed *at all*.

While benign in this context, this sort of problem occurring in a real program will cause the dynamic allocation system to fail, and possibly even cause a program crash. As you can see from the preceding example, when assigning one object to another, you must make sure you are not destroying information that may be needed later.

EXERCISES

1. What is wrong with the following fragment?

```cpp
// This program has an error.
#include <iostream>
using namespace std;

class cl1 {
  int i, j;
public:
  cl1(int a, int b) { i = a; j = b; }
  // ...
};

class cl2 {
  int i, j;
public:
  cl2(int a, int b) { i = a; j = b; }
  // ...
};

int main()
{
  cl1 x(10, 20);
  cl2 y(0, 0);
  x = y;

  // ...
}
```

2. Using the **queue** class that you created for Chapter 2, Section 2.1, Exercise 1, show how one queue can be assigned to another.

3. If the **queue** class from the preceding question dynamically allocates memory to hold the queue, why, in this situation, can one queue not be assigned to another?

PASSING OBJECTS TO FUNCTIONS

Objects can be passed to functions as arguments in just the same way that other types of data are passed. Simply declare the function's parameter as a class type and then use an object of that class as an argument when calling the function. As with other types of data, by default all objects are passed by value to a function.

EXAMPLES

1. Here is a short example that passes an object to a function:

```
#include <iostream>
using namespace std;

class samp {
  int i;
public:
  samp(int n) { i = n; }
  int get_i() { return i; }
};

// Return square of o.i.
int sqr_it(samp o)
{
  return o.get_i() * o.get_i();
}

int main()
{
  samp a(10), b(2);

  cout << sqr_it(a) << "\n";
  cout << sqr_it(b) << "\n";

  return 0;
}
```

This program creates a class called **samp** that contains one integer variable called **i**. The function **sqr_it( )** takes an argument of type **samp** and returns the square of that object's **i** value. The output from this program is 100 followed by 4.

2. As stated, the default method of parameter passing in C++, including objects, is by value. This means that a bitwise copy of the argument is made and it is this copy that is used by the function. Therefore, changes to the object inside the function do not affect the calling object. This is illustrated by the following example:

```
/*
   Remember, objects, like other parameters, are passed
   by value. Thus changes to the parameter inside a
   function have no effect on the object used in the call.
*/
#include <iostream>
using namespace std;

class samp {
  int i;
public:
  samp(int n) { i = n; }
  void set_i(int n) { i = n; }
  int get_i() { return i; }
};

/* Set o.i to its square. This has no effect on the
   object used to call sqr_it(), however.
*/
void sqr_it(samp o)
{
   o.set_i(o.get_i() * o.get_i());

  cout << "Copy of a has i value of " << o.get_i();
  cout << "\n";
}

int main()
{
  samp a(10);

  sqr_it(a); // a passed by value

  cout << "But, a.i is unchanged in main: ";
  cout << a.get_i();  // displays 10

  return 0;
}
```

The output displayed by this program is

```
Copy of a has i value of 100
But, a.i is unchanged in main: 10
```

3. As with other types of variables, the address of an object can be passed to a function so that the argument used in the call can be modified by the function. For example, the following version of the program in the preceding example does, indeed, modify the value of the object whose address is used in the call to **sqr_it( )**.

```
/*
   Now that the address of an object is passed to sqr_it(),
   the function can modify the value of the argument whose
   address is used in the call.
*/
#include <iostream>
using namespace std;

class samp {
   int i;
public:
   samp(int n) { i = n; }
   void set_i(int n) { i = n; }
   int get_i() { return i; }
};

/* Set o.i to its square. This affects the calling
   argument.
*/
void sqr_it(samp *o)
{
   o->set_i(o->get_i() * o->get_i());

   cout << "Copy of a has i value of " << o->get_i();
   cout << "\n";
}

int main()
{
   samp a(10);

   sqr_it(&a); // pass a's address to sqr_it()

   cout << "Now, a in main() has been changed: ";
   cout << a.get_i();   // displays 100
```

```
  return 0;
}
```

This program now displays the following output:

```
Copy of a has i value of 100
Now, a in main() has been changed: 100
```

4. When a copy of an object is made when being passed to a function, it means that a new object comes into existence. Also, when the function that the object was passed to terminates, the copy of the argument is destroyed. This raises two questions. First, is the object's constructor called when the copy is made? Second, is the object's destructor called when the copy is destroyed? The answer may, at first, seem surprising.

   When a copy of an object is made to be used in a function call, the constructor function is *not* called. The reason for this is simple to understand if you think about it. Since a constructor function is generally used to initialize some aspect of an object, it must not be called when making a copy of an already existing object passed to a function. Doing so would alter the contents of the object. When passing an object to a function, you want the current state of the object, not its initial state.

   However, when the function terminates and the copy is destroyed, the destructor function *is* called. This is because the object might perform some operation that must be undone when it goes out of scope. For example, the copy may allocate memory that must be released.

   To summarize, when a copy of an object is created because it is used as an argument to a function, the constructor function is not called. However, when the copy is destroyed (usually by going out of scope when the function returns), the destructor function is called.

   The following program illustrates the preceding discussion:

```cpp
#include <iostream>
using namespace std;

class samp {
  int i;
public:
  samp(int n) {
    i = n;
```

```
      cout << "Constructing\n";
   }
   ~samp() { cout << "Destructing\n"; }
   int get_i() { return i; }
};

// Return square of o.i.
int sqr_it(samp o)
{
   return o.get_i() * o.get_i();
}

int main()
{
   samp a(10);

   cout << sqr_it(a) << "\n";

   return 0;
}
```

This function displays the following:

```
Constructing
Destructing
100
Destructing
```

As you can see, only one call to the constructor function is made. This occurs when **a** is created. However, two calls to the destructor are made. One is for the copy created when **a** is passed to **sqr_it( )**. The other is for **a** itself.

The fact that the destructor for the object that is the copy of the argument is executed when the function terminates can be a source of problems. For example, if the object used as the argument allocates dynamic memory and frees that memory when destroyed, its copy will free the same memory when its destructor is called. This will leave the original object damaged and effectively useless. (See Exercise 2, just ahead in this section, for an example.) It is important to guard against this type of error and to make sure that the destructor function of the copy of an object used in an argument does not cause side effects that alter the original argument.

As you might guess, one way around the problem of a parameter's destructor function destroying data needed by the calling argument is to pass the address of the object and not the object itself. When an address is passed, no new object is created, and therefore, no destructor is called when the function returns. (As you will see in the next chapter, C++ provides a variation on this theme that offers a very elegant alternative.) However, an even better solution exists, which you can use after you have learned about a special type of constructor called a *copy constructor*. A copy constructor lets you define precisely how copies of objects are made. (Copy constructors are discussed in Chapter 5.)

EXERCISES

1. Using the **stack** example from Section 3.1, Example 2, add a function called **showstack( )** that is passed an object of type **stack**. Have this function display the contents of a stack.

2. As you know, when an object is passed to a function, a copy of that object is made. Further, when that function returns, the copy's destructor function is called. Keeping this in mind, what is wrong with the following program?

```
// This program contains an error.
#include <iostream>
#include <cstdlib>
using namespace std;

class dyna {
  int *p;
public:
  dyna(int i);
  ~dyna() { free(p); cout << "freeing \n"; }
  int get() { return *p; }
};

dyna::dyna(int i)
{
  p = (int *) malloc(sizeof(int));
  if(!p) {
```

```
        cout << "Allocation failure\n";
        exit(1);
      }

      *p = i;
    }

    // Return negative value of *ob.p
    int neg(dyna ob)
    {
      return -ob.get();
    }

    int main()
    {
      dyna o(-10);

      cout << o.get() << "\n";
      cout << neg(o) << "\n";

      dyna o2(20);
      cout << o2.get() << "\n";
      cout << neg(o2) << "\n";

      cout << o.get() << "\n";
      cout << neg(o) << "\n";

      return 0;
    }
```

3.3 RETURNING OBJECTS FROM FUNCTIONS

Just as you can pass objects to functions, functions can return objects. To do so, first declare the function as returning a class type. Second, return an object of that type using the normal **return** statement.

There is one important point to understand about returning objects from functions, however: When an object is returned by a function, a temporary object is automatically created which holds the return value. It is this object that is actually returned by the function. After the value has been returned, this object is destroyed. The destruction of this temporary object might cause unexpected side effects in some situations, as is illustrated in Example 2 below.

EXAMPLES

1. Here is an example of a function that returns an object:

```cpp
// Returning an object
#include <iostream>
#include <cstring>
using namespace std;

class samp {
  char s[80];
public:
  void show() { cout << s << "\n"; }
  void set(char *str) { strcpy(s, str); }
};

// Return an object of type samp
samp input()
{
  char s[80];
  samp str;

  cout << "Enter a string: ";
  cin >> s;

  str.set(s);

  return str;
}

int main()
{
  samp ob;

  // assign returned object to ob
  ob = input();
  ob.show();

  return 0;
}
```

In this example, **input( )** creates a local object called **str** and then reads a string from the keyboard. This string is copied into **str.s**, and then **str** is returned by the function. This object is then assigned to **ob** inside **main( )** when it is returned by the call to **input( )**.

2. You must be careful about returning objects from functions if those objects contain destructor functions because the returned object goes out of scope as soon as the value is returned to the calling routine. For example, if the object returned by the function has a destructor that frees dynamically allocated memory, that memory will be freed even though the object that is assigned the return value is still using it. For example, consider this incorrect version of the preceding program:

```
// An error generated by returning an object.
#include <iostream>
#include <cstring>
#include <cstdlib>
using namespace std;

class samp {
  char *s;
public:
  samp() { s = '\0'; }
  ~samp() { if(s) free(s); cout << "Freeing s\n"; }
  void show() { cout << s << "\n"; }
  void set(char *str);
};

// Load a string.
void samp::set(char *str)
{
  s = (char *) malloc(strlen(str)+1);
  if(!s) {
    cout << "Allocation error\n";
    exit(1);
  }

  strcpy(s, str);
}

// Return an object of type samp.
samp input()
```

```
{
  char s[80];
  samp str;

  cout << "Enter a string: ";
  cin >> s;

  str.set(s);
  return str;
}

int main()
{
  samp ob;

  // assign returned object to ob
  ob = input();  // This causes an error!!!!
  ob.show();

  return 0;
}
```

The output from this program is shown here:

```
Enter a string: Hello
Freeing s
Freeing s
Hello
Freeing s
Null pointer assignment
```

Notice that **samp**'s destructor function is called three times. First, it is called when the local object **str** goes out of scope when **input( )** returns. The second time ~**samp( )** is called is when the temporary object returned by **input( )** is destroyed. Remember, when an object is returned from a function, an invisible (to you) temporary object is automatically generated which holds the return value. In this case, this object is simply a copy of **str**, which is the return value of the function. Therefore, after the function has returned, the temporary object's destructor is executed. Finally, the destructor for object **ob**, inside **main( )**, is called when the program terminates.

The trouble is that in this situation, the first time the destructor executes, the memory allocated to hold the string input by **input( )** is freed. Thus, not only do the other two calls to **samp**'s destructor try to free an already released piece of dynamic memory, but they destroy the dynamic allocation system in the process, as evidenced by the run-time message "Null pointer assignment." (Depending upon your compiler, the memory model used for compilation, and the like, you may or may not see this message if you try this program.)

The key point to be understood from this example is that when an object is returned from a function, the temporary object used to effect the return will have its destructor function called. Thus, you should avoid returning objects in which this situation is harmful. (As you will learn in Chapter 5, it is possible to use a copy constructor to manage this situation.)

EXERCISES

1. To illustrate exactly when an object is constructed and destructed when returned from a function, create a class called **who**. Have **who**'s constructor take one character argument that will be used to identify an object. Have the constructor display a message similar to this when constructing an object:

```
Constructing who #x
```

where **x** is the identifying character associated with each object. When an object is destroyed, have a message similar to this displayed:

```
Destroying who #x
```

where, again, **x** is the identifying character. Finally, create a function called **make_who( )** that returns a **who** object. Give each object a unique name. Note the output displayed by the program.

2. Other than the incorrect freeing of dynamically allocated memory, think of a situation in which it would be improper to return an object from a function.

3.4 *A*N INTRODUCTION TO FRIEND FUNCTIONS

There will be times when you want a function to have access to the private members of a class without that function actually being a member of that class. Towards this end, C++ supports friend functions. A friend is not a member of a class but still has access to its private elements.

Two reasons that friend functions are useful have to do with operator overloading and the creation of certain types of I/O functions. You will have to wait until later to see these uses of a friend in action. However, a third reason for friend functions is that there will be times when you want one function to have access to the private members of *two or more* different classes. It is this use that is examined here.

A friend function is defined as a regular, nonmember function. However, inside the class declaration for which it will be a friend, its prototype is also included, prefaced by the keyword **friend**. To understand how this works, examine this short program:

```
// An example of a friend function.
#include <iostream>
using namespace std;

class myclass {
  int n, d;
public:
  myclass(int i, int j) { n = i; d = j; }
  // declare a friend of myclass
  friend int isfactor(myclass ob);
};

/* Here is friend function definition. It returns true
   if d is a factor of n. Notice that the keyword
   friend is not used in the definition of isfactor().
*/
int isfactor(myclass ob)
{
  if(!(ob.n % ob.d)) return 1;
  else return 0;
}
```

```
int main()
{
  myclass ob1(10, 2), ob2(13, 3);

  if(isfactor(ob1)) cout << "2 is a factor of 10\n";
  else cout << "2 is not a factor of 10\n";

  if(isfactor(ob2)) cout << "3 is a factor of 13\n";
  else cout << "3 is not a factor of 13\n";

  return 0;
}
```

In this example, **myclass** declares its constructor function and the friend **isfactor( )** inside its class declaration. Because **isfactor( )** is a friend of **myclass**, **isfactor( )** has access to its private members. This is why, within **isfactor( )**, it is possible to directly refer to **ob.n** and **ob.d**.

It is important to understand that a friend function is not a member of the class for which it is a friend. Thus, it is not possible to call a friend function by using an object name and a class member access operator (a dot or an arrow). For example, given the preceding example, this statement is wrong:

```
ob1.isfactor(); // wrong; isfactor() is not a member function
```

Instead, friends are called just like regular functions.

Although a friend function has knowledge of the private elements of the class for which it is a friend, it can only access them through an object of the class. That is, unlike a member function of **myclass**, which can refer to **n** or **d** directly, a friend can access these variables only in conjunction with an object that is declared within or passed to the friend function.

The preceding paragraph brings up an important side issue. When a member function refers to a private element, it does so directly because a member function is executed only in conjunction with an object of that class. Thus, when a member function refers to a private element, the compiler knows which object that private element belongs to by the object that is linked to the function when that member function is called. However, a friend function is not linked to any object. It simply is granted access to the private elements of a class. Thus, inside the friend function, it is meaningless to refer to a private member without reference to a specific object.

Because friends are not members of a class, they will typically be passed one or more objects of the class for which they are friends. This is the case with **isfactor( )**. It is passed an object of **myclass**, called **ob**. However, because **isfactor( )** is a friend of **myclass**, it can access **ob**'s private elements. If **isfactor( )** had not been made a friend of **myclass**, it would not be able to access **ob.d** or **ob.n** since **n** and **d** are private members of **myclass**.

A friend function is not a member and cannot be qualified by an object name. It must be called just like a normal function.

A friend function is not inherited. That is, when a base class includes a friend function, that friend function is not a friend of a derived class.

One other important point about friend functions is that a friend function can be friends with more than one class.

EXAMPLES

1. One common (and good) use of a friend function occurs when two different types of classes have some quantity in common that needs to be compared. For example, consider the following program, which creates a class called **car** and a class called **truck**, each containing, as a private variable, the speed of the vehicle it represents:

```
#include <iostream>
using namespace std;

class truck; // a forward declaration

class car {
  int passengers;
  int speed;
public:
  car(int p, int s) { passengers = p; speed = s; }
  friend int sp_greater(car c, truck t);
};

class truck {
  int weight;
```

```
      int speed;
public:
    truck(int w, int s) { weight = w, speed = s; }
    friend int sp_greater(car c, truck t);
};

/* Return positive if car speed faster than truck.
   Return 0 if speeds are the same.
   Return negative if truck speed faster than car.
*/
int sp_greater(car c, truck t)
{
  return c.speed - t.speed;
}

int main()
{
  int t;
  car c1(6, 55), c2(2, 120);
  truck t1(10000, 55), t2(20000, 72);

  cout << "Comparing c1 and t1:\n";
  t = sp_greater(c1, t1);
  if(t<0) cout << "Truck is faster.\n";
  else if(t==0) cout << "Car and truck speed is the same.\n";
  else cout << "Car is faster.\n";

  cout << "\nComparing c2 and t2:\n";
  t = sp_greater(c2, t2);
  if(t<0) cout << "Truck is faster.\n";
  else if(t==0) cout << "Car and truck speed is the same.\n";
  else cout << "Car is faster.\n";

  return 0;
}
```

This program contains the function **sp_ greater( )**, which is a friend function of both the **car** and **truck** classes. (As stated, a function can be a friend of two or more classes.) This function returns positive if the **car** object is going faster than the **truck** object, 0 if their speeds are the same, and negative if the **truck** is going faster.

This program illustrates one important C++ syntax element: the *forward declaration* (also called a *forward reference*). Because

sp_ greater( ) takes parameters of both the **car** and the **truck** classes, it is logically impossible to declare both before including **sp_ greater( )** in either. Therefore, there needs to be some way to tell the compiler about a class name without actually declaring it. This is called a forward declaration. In C++, to tell the compiler that an identifier is the name of a class, use a line like this before the class name is first used:

class *class-name*;

For example, in the preceding program, the forward declaration is

```
class truck;
```

Now **truck** can be used in the friend declaration of **sp_greater( )** without generating a compile-time error.

2. A function can be a member of one class and a friend of another. For example, here is the preceding example rewritten so that **sp_greater( )** is a member of **car** and a friend of **truck**:

```
#include <iostream>
using namespace std;

class truck; // a forward declaration

class car {
  int passengers;
  int speed;
public:
  car(int p, int s) { passengers = p; speed = s; }
  int sp_greater(truck t);
};

class truck {
  int weight;
  int speed;
public:
  truck(int w, int s) { weight = w, speed = s; }

  // note new use of the scope resolution operator
  friend int car::sp_greater(truck t);
};
```

```
/* Return positive if car speed faster than truck.
   Return 0 if speeds are the same.
   Return negative if truck speed faster than car.
*/
int car::sp_greater(truck t)
{
  /* Since sp_greater() is member of car, only a
     truck object must be passed to it. */

  return speed-t.speed;
}

int main()
{
  int t;
  car c1(6, 55), c2(2, 120);
  truck t1(10000, 55), t2(20000, 72);

  cout << "Comparing c1 and t1:\n";
  t = c1.sp_greater(t1);  // evoke as member function of car
  if(t<0) cout << "Truck is faster.\n";
  else if(t==0) cout << "Car and truck speed is the same.\n";
  else cout << "Car is faster.\n";

  cout << "\nComparing c2 and t2:\n";
  t = c2.sp_greater(t2); // evoke as member function of car
  if(t<0) cout << "Truck is faster.\n";
  else if(t==0) cout << "Car and truck speed is the same.\n";
  else cout << "Car is faster.\n";

  return 0;
}
```

Notice the new use of the scope resolution operator as it occurs
in the friend declaration within the **truck** class declaration. In
this case, it is used to tell the compiler that the function
sp_greater( ) is a member of the **car** class.

One easy way to remember how to use the scope resolution
operator is that the class name followed by the scope resolution
operator followed by the member name fully specifies a
class member.

In fact, when referring to a member of a class, it is never
wrong to fully specify its name. However, when an object is

used to call a member function or access a member variable, the full name is redundant and seldom used. For example,

```
t = c1.sp_greater(t1);
```

can be written using the (redundant) scope resolution operator and the class name **car** like this:

```
t = c1.car::sp_greater(t1);
```

However, since **c1** is an object of type **car**, the compiler already knows that **sp_greater( )** is a member of the **car** class, making the full class specification unnecessary.

EXERCISE

---

1. Imagine a situation in which two classes, called **pr1** and **pr2**, shown here, share one printer. Further, imagine that other parts of your program need to know when the printer is in use by an object of either of these two classes. Create a function called **inuse( )** that returns **true** when the printer is being used by either and **false** otherwise. Make this function a friend of both **pr1** and **pr2**.

```
class pr1 {
  int printing;
  // ...
public:
  pr1() { printing = 0; }
  void set_print(int status) { printing = status; }
  // ...
};

class pr2 {
  int printing;
  // ...
public:
  pr2() { printing = 0; }
  void set_print(int status) { printing = status; }
  // ...
};
```

SKILLS CHECK

Mastery
Skills Check

Before proceeding, you should be able to answer the following questions and perform the exercises.

1. What single prerequisite must be met in order for one object to be assigned to another?

2. Given this class fragment,

```cpp
class samp {
  double *p;
public:
  samp(double d) {
    p = (double *) malloc(sizeof(double));
    if(!p) exit(1);  // allocation error
    *p = d;
  }
  ~samp() { free(p); }
  // ...
};


// ...
samp ob1(123.09), ob2(0.0);
// ...
ob2 = ob1;
```

what problem is caused by the assignment of **ob1** to **ob2**?

3. Given this class,

```cpp
class planet {
  int moons;
  double dist_from_sun; // in miles
  double diameter;
  double mass;
public:
  //...
  double get_miles() { return dist_from_sun; }
};
```

create a function called **light( )** that takes as an argument an object of type **planet** and returns the number of seconds that it takes light from the sun to reach the planet. (Assume that light travels at 186,000 miles per second and that **dist_from_sun** is specified in miles.)

4. Can the address of an object be passed to a function as an argument?

5. Using the **stack** class, write a function called **loadstack( )** that returns a stack that is already loaded with the letters of the alphabet (a-z). Assign this stack to another object in the calling routine and prove that it contains the alphabet. Be sure to change the stack size so it is large enough to hold the alphabet.

6. Explain why you must be careful when passing objects to a function or returning objects from a function.

7. What is a friend function?

Cumulative Skills Check

This section checks how well you have integrated the material in this chapter with that from earlier chapters.

1. Functions can be overloaded as long as the number or type of their parameters differs. Overload **loadstack( )** from Exercise 5 of the Mastery Skills Check so that it takes an integer, called **upper**, as a parameter. In the overloaded version, if **upper** is 1, load the stack with the uppercase alphabet. Otherwise, load it with the lowercase alphabet.

2. Using the **strtype** class shown in Section 3.1, Example 3, add a friend function that takes as an argument a pointer to an object of type **strtype** and returns a pointer to the string pointed to by that object. (That is, have the function return **p**.) Call this function **get_string( )**.

3. Experiment: When an object of a derived class is assigned to another object of the same derived class, is the data associated with the base class also copied? To find out, use the following two classes and write a program that demonstrates what happens.

```
class base {
  int a;
public:
  void load_a(int n) { a = n; }
  int get_a() { return a; }
};

class derived : public base {
  int b;
public:
  void load_b(int n) { b = n; }
  int get_b() { return b; }
};
```

4

Arrays, Pointers, and References

THIS chapter examines several important issues involving arrays of objects and pointers to objects. It concludes with a discussion of one of C++'s most important innovations: the reference. The reference is crucial to many C++ features, so a careful reading is advised.

Review
Skills Check

Before proceeding, you should be able to correctly answer the following questions and do the exercises.

1. When one object is assigned to another, what precisely takes place?

2. Can any troubles or side effects occur when one object is assigned to another? (Give an example.)

3. When an object is passed as an argument to a function, a copy of that object is made. Is the copy's constructor function called? Is its destructor called?

4. By default, objects are passed to functions by value, which means that what occurs to the copy inside the function is not supposed to affect the argument used in the call. Can there be a violation of this principle? If so, give an example.

5. Given the following class, create a function called **make_sum( )** that returns an object of type **summation**. Have this function prompt the user for a number and then construct an object having this value and return it to the calling procedure. Demonstrate that the function works.

```
class summation {
  int num;
  long sum; // summation of num
public:
  void set_sum(int n);
  void show_sum() {
    cout << num << " summed is " << sum << "\n";
  }
```

```
};

void summation::set_sum(int n)
{
  int i;
  num = n;

  sum = 0;
  for(i=1; i<=n; i++)
    sum += i;
}
```

6. In the preceding question, the function **set_sum( )** was not defined in line within the **summation** class declaration. Give a reason why this might be necessary for some compilers.

7. Given the following class, show how to add a friend function called **isneg( )** that takes one parameter of type **myclass** and returns true if **num** is negative and false otherwise.

```
class myclass {
  int num;
public:
  myclass(int x) { num = x; }
};
```

8. Can a friend function be friends with more than one class?

4.1 ARRAYS OF OBJECTS

As has been stated several times, objects are variables and have the same capabilities and attributes as any other type of variable. Therefore, it is perfectly acceptable for objects to be arrayed. The syntax for declaring an array of objects is exactly like that used to declare an array of any other type of variable. Further, arrays of objects are accessed just like arrays of other types of variables.

EXAMPLES

1. Here is an example of an array of objects:

```
#include <iostream>
using namespace std;
```

```
class samp {
  int a;
public:
  void set_a(int n) { a = n; }
  int get_a() { return a; }
};

int main()
{
  samp ob[4];
  int i;

  for(i=0; i<4; i++) ob[i].set_a(i);

  for(i=0; i<4; i++) cout << ob[i].get_a( );

  cout << "\n";

  return 0;
}
```

This program creates a four-element array of objects of type **samp** and then loads each element's **a** with a value between 0 and 3. Notice how member functions are called relative to each array element. The array name, in this case **ob**, is indexed; then the member access operator is applied, followed by the name of the member function to be called.

2. If a class type includes a constructor, an array of objects can be initialized. For example, here **ob** is an initialized array:

```
// Initialize an array.
#include <iostream>
using namespace std;

class samp {
  int a;
public:
  samp(int n) { a = n; }
  int get_a() { return a; }
};

int main()
{
  samp ob[4] = { -1, -2, -3, -4 };
```

```
    int i;

    for(i=0; i<4; i++) cout << ob[i].get_a() << ' ';

    cout << "\n";

    return 0;
}
```

This program displays **-1 -2 -3 -4** on the screen. In this example, the values -1 through -4 are passed to the **ob** constructor function.

Actually, the syntax shown in the initialization list is shorthand for this longer form (first shown in Chapter 2):

```
samp ob[4] = { samp(-1), samp(- 2),
               samp(-3), samp(- 4) };
```

However, the form used in the program is more common (although, as you will see, this form will work only with arrays whose constructors take only one argument).

3. You can also have multidimensional arrays of objects. For example, here is a program that creates a two-dimensional array of objects and initializes them:

```
// Create a two-dimensional array of objects.
#include <iostream>
using namespace std;

class samp {
  int a;
public:
  samp(int n) { a = n; }
  int get_a() { return a; }
};

int main()
{
  samp ob[4][2] = {
    1, 2,
    3, 4,
    5, 6,
    7, 8
  };
```

```
    int i;

    for(i=0; i<4; i++) {
      cout << ob[i][0].get_a() << ' ';
      cout << ob[i][1].get_a() << "\n";
    }

    cout << "\n";

    return 0;
}
```

This program displays

```
1 2
3 4
5 6
7 8
```

4. As you know, a constructor can take more than one argument.
   When initializing an array of objects whose constructor takes
   more than one argument, you must use the alternative form of
   initialization mentioned earlier. Let's begin with an example:

```
#include <iostream>
using namespace std;

class samp {
  int a, b;
public:
  samp(int n, int m) { a = n; b = m; }
  int get_a() { return a; }
  int get_b() { return b; }
};

int main()
{
  samp ob[4][2] = {
    samp(1, 2), samp(3, 4),
    samp(5, 6), samp(7, 8),
    samp(9, 10), samp(11, 12),
    samp(13, 14), samp(15, 16)
  };
```

```
int i;

for(i=0; i<4; i++) {
  cout << ob[i][0].get_a() << ' ';
  cout << ob[i][0].get_b() << "\n";
  cout << ob[i][1].get_a() << ' ';
  cout << ob[i][1].get_b() << "\n";
}

cout << "\n";

return 0;
}
```

In this example, **samp**'s constructor takes two arguments. Here, the array **ob** is declared and initialized in **main( )** by using direct calls to **samp**'s constructor. This is necessary because the formal C++ syntax allows only one argument at a time in a comma-separated list. There is no way, for example, to specify two (or more) arguments per entry in the list. Therefore, when you initialize arrays of objects that have constructors that take more than one argument, you must use the "long form" initialization syntax rather than the "shorthand form."

Note   *You can always use the long form of initialization even if the object takes only one argument. It's just that the short form is more convenient in this case.*

The preceding program displays

```
1  2
3  4
5  6
7  8
9  10
11 12
13 14
15 16
```

EXERCISES

1. Using the following class declaration, create a ten-element array and initialize the **ch** element with the values A through J. Demonstrate that the array does, indeed, contain these values.

```
#include <iostream>
using namespace std;

class letters {
  char ch;
public:
  letters(char c) { ch = c; }
  char get_ch() { return ch; }
};
```

2. Using the following class declaration, create a ten-element array, initialize **num** to the values 1 through 10, and initialize **sqr** to **num**'s square.

```
#include <iostream>
using namespace std;

class squares {
  int num, sqr;
public:
  squares(int a, int b) { num = a; sqr = b; }
  void show() {cout << num << ' ' << sqr << "\n"; }
};
```

3. Change the initialization in Exercise 1 so it uses the long form. (That is, invoke **letters'** constructor explicitly in the initialization list.)

4.2 *U*SING POINTERS TO OBJECTS

As discussed in Chapter 2, objects can be accessed via pointers. As you know, when a pointer to an object is used, the object's members are referenced using the arrow (**->**) operator instead of the dot (**.**) operator.

Pointer arithmetic using an object pointer is the same as it is for any other data type: it is performed relative to the type of the object. For example, when an object pointer is incremented, it points to the next object. When an object pointer is decremented, it points to the previous object.

EXAMPLE

1. Here is an example of object pointer arithmetic:

```cpp
// Pointers to objects.
#include <iostream>
using namespace std;

class samp {
  int a, b;
public:
  samp(int n, int m) { a = n; b = m; }
  int get_a() { return a; }
  int get_b() { return b; }
};

int main()
{
  samp ob[4] = {
    samp(1, 2),
    samp(3, 4),
    samp(5, 6),
    samp(7, 8)
  };
  int i;

  samp *p;
  p = ob; // get starting address of array

  for(i=0; i<4; i++) {
    cout << p->get_a() << ' ';
    cout << p->get_b() << "\n";
    p++;  // advance to next object
  }

  cout << "\n";
```

```
    return 0;
}
```

This program displays

```
1 2
3 4
5 6
7 8
```

As evidenced by the output, each time **p** is incremented, it points to the next object in the array.

EXERCISES

---

1. Rewrite Example 1 so it displays the contents of the **ob** array in reverse order.

2. Change Section 4.1, Example 3 so the two-dimensional array is accessed via a pointer. Hint: In C++, as in C, all arrays are stored contiguously, left to right, low to high.

4.3   **T**HE this POINTER

C++ contains a special pointer that is called **this**. **this** is a pointer that is automatically passed to any member function when it is called, and it is a pointer to the object that generates the call. For example, given this statement,

```
ob.f1();  // assume that ob is an object
```

the function **f1( )** is automatically passed a pointer to **ob**—which is the object that invokes the call. This pointer is referred to as **this**.

It is important to understand that only member functions are passed a **this** pointer. For example, a friend does not have a **this** pointer.

EXAMPLE

1. As you have seen, when a member function refers to another member of a class, it does so directly, without qualifying the member with either a class or an object specification. For example, examine this short program, which creates a simple inventory class:

```cpp
// Demonstrate the this pointer.
#include <iostream>
#include <cstring>
using namespace std;

class inventory {
  char item[20];
  double cost;
  int on_hand;
public:
  inventory(char *i, double c, int o)
  {
    strcpy(item, i);
    cost = c;
    on_hand = o;
  }
  void show();
};

void inventory::show()
{
  cout << item;
  cout << ": $" << cost;
  cout << "  On hand: " << on_hand << "\n";
}

int main()
{
  inventory ob("wrench", 4.95, 4);

  ob.show();

  return 0;
}
```

As you can see, within the constructor **inventory( )** and the member function **show( )**, the member variables **item**, **cost**, and **on_hand** are referred to directly. This is because a member function can be called only in conjunction with an object. Therefore, the compiler knows which object's data is being referred to.

However, there is an even more subtle explanation. When a member function is called, it is automatically passed a **this** pointer to the object that invoked the call. Thus, the preceding program could be rewritten as shown here:

```
// Demonstrate the this pointer.
#include <iostream>
#include <cstring>
using namespace std;

class inventory {
  char item[20];
  double cost;
  int on_hand;
public:
  inventory(char *i, double c, int o)
  {
    strcpy(this->item, i); // access members
    this->cost = c;  // through the this
    this->on_hand = o; // pointer
  }
  void show();
};

void inventory::show()
{
  cout << this->item; // use this to access members
  cout << ": $" << this->cost;
  cout << "  On hand: " << this->on_hand << "\n";
}

int main()
{
  inventory ob("wrench", 4.95, 4);

  ob.show();

  return 0;
}
```

Here the member variables are accessed explicitly through the **this** pointer. Thus, within **show( )**, these two statements are equivalent:

```
cost = 123.23;
this->cost = 123.23;
```

In fact, the first form is, loosely speaking, a shorthand for the second.

While no C++ programmer would use the **this** pointer to access a class member as just shown, because the shorthand form is much easier, it is important to understand what the shorthand implies.

The **this** pointer has several uses, including aiding in overloading operators. This use will be detailed in Chapter 6. For now, the important thing to understand is that by default, all member functions are automatically passed a pointer to the invoking object.

EXERCISE

1. Given the following program, convert all appropriate references to class members to explicit **this** pointer references.

```
#include <iostream>
using namespace std;

class myclass {
  int a, b;
public:
  myclass(int n, int m) { a = n; b = m; }
  int add() { return a+b; }
  void show();
};

void myclass::show()
{
  int t;

  t = add(); // call member function
  cout << t << "\n";
}
```

```
int main()
{
  myclass ob(10, 14);

  ob.show();

  return 0;
}
```

*U*SING *new* AND *delete*

Up to now, when memory needed to be allocated, you have been using **malloc( )**, and you have been freeing allocated memory by using **free( )**. These are, of course, the standard C dynamic allocation functions. While these functions are available in C++, C++ provides a safer and more convenient way to allocate and free memory. In C++, you can allocate memory using **new** and release it using **delete**. These operators take these general forms:

p-var = new *type*;
delete *p-var*;

Here *type* is the type specifier of the object for which you want to allocate memory and *p-var* is a pointer to that type. **new** is an operator that returns a pointer to dynamically allocated memory that is large enough to hold an object of type *type*. **delete** releases that memory when it is no longer needed. **delete** can be called only with a pointer previously allocated with **new**. If you call **delete** with an invalid pointer, the allocation system will be destroyed, possibly crashing your program.

If there is insufficient available memory to fill an allocation request, one of two actions will occur. Either **new** will return a null pointer or it will generate an exception. (Exceptions and exception handling are described later in this book; loosely, an exception is a run-time error that can be managed in a structured fashion.) In Standard C++, the default behavior of **new** is to generate an exception when it cannot satisfy an allocation request. If this exception is not handled by your program, your program will be terminated. The trouble is that the precise action that **new** takes on failure has been changed several times over the past few years. Thus, it is possible that your compiler will not implement **new** as defined by Standard C++.

When C++ was first invented, **new** returned null on failure. Later this was changed such that **new** caused an exception on failure. Finally, it was decided that a **new** failure will generate an exception by default, but that a null pointer could be returned instead, as an option. Thus, **new** has been implemented differently at different times by compiler manufacturers. For example, at the time of this writing, Microsoft's Visual C++ returns a null pointer when **new** fails. Borland C++ generates an exception. Although all compilers will eventually implement **new** in compliance with Standard C++, currently the only way to know the precise action of **new** on failure is to check your compiler's documentation.

Since there are two possible ways that **new** can indicate allocation failure, and since different compilers might do so differently, the code in this book will be written in such a way that both contingencies are accommodated. All code in this book will test the pointer returned by **new** for null. This handles compilers that implement **new** by returning null on failure, while causing no harm for those compilers for which **new** throws an exception. If your compiler generates an exception when **new** fails, the program will simply be terminated. Later, when exception handling is described, **new** will be re-examined and you will learn how to better handle an allocation failure. You will also learn about an alternative form of **new** that always returns a null pointer when an error occurs.

One last point: none of the examples in this book should cause **new** to fail, since only a handful of bytes are being allocated by any single program.

Although **new** and **delete** perform functions similar to **malloc( )** and **free( )**, they have several advantages. First, **new** automatically allocates enough memory to hold an object of the specified type. You do not need to use **sizeof**, for example, to compute the number of bytes required. This reduces the possibility for error. Second, **new** automatically returns a pointer of the specified type. You do not need to use an explicit type cast the way you did when you allocated memory by using **malloc( )** (see the following note). Third, both **new** and **delete** can be overloaded, enabling you to easily implement your own custom allocation system. Fourth, it is possible to initialize a dynamically allocated object. Finally, you no longer need to include < **cstdlib** > with your programs.

In C, no type cast is required when you are assigning the return value of **malloc( )** *to a pointer because the* **void *** *returned by* **malloc( )** *is automatically converted into a pointer compatible with the type of pointer on the left side of the assignment. However, this is not the case in C++, which requires an explicit type cast when you use* **malloc( )**. *The reason for this difference is that it allows C++ to enforce more rigorous type checking.*

Now that **new** and **delete** have been introduced, they will be used instead of **malloc( )** and **free( )**.

EXAMPLES

1. As a short first example, this program allocates memory to hold an integer:

    ```cpp
    // A simple example of new and delete.
    #include <iostream>
    using namespace std;

    int main()
    {
      int *p;

      p = new int; // allocate room for an integer
      if(!p) {
        cout << "Allocation error\n";
        return 1;
      }

      *p = 1000;

      cout << "Here is integer at p: " << *p << "\n";

      delete p;   // release memory

      return 0;
    }
    ```

Notice that the value returned by **new** is checked before it is used. As explained earlier, this check is meaningful only if your compiler implements **new** in such a way that it returns null on failure.

2. Here is an example that allocates an object dynamically:

```cpp
// Allocating dynamic objects.
#include <iostream>
using namespace std;

class samp {
  int i, j;
public:
  void set_ij(int a, int b) { i=a; j=b; }
  int get_product() { return i*j; }
};

int main()
{
  samp *p;

  p = new samp; // allocate object
  if(!p) {
    cout << "Allocation error\n";
    return 1;
  }

  p->set_ij(4, 5);

  cout << "Product is: " << p->get_product() << "\n";

  return 0;
}
```

EXERCISES

1. Write a program that uses **new** to dynamically allocate a **float**, a **long**, and a **char**. Give these dynamic variables values and display their values. Finally, release all dynamically allocated memory by using **delete**.

2. Create a class that contains a person's name and telephone number. Using **new**, dynamically allocate an object of this class and put your name and phone number into these fields within this object.

3. What are the two ways that **new** might indicate an allocation failure?

*M*ORE ABOUT new AND delete

This section discusses two additional features of **new** and **delete**. First, dynamically allocated objects can be given initial values. Second, dynamically allocated arrays can be created.

You can give a dynamically allocated object an initial value by using this form of the **new** statement:

p-var = new *type* (*initial-value*);

To dynamically allocate a one-dimensional array, use this form of **new**:

p-var = new *type* [*size*];

After this statement has executed, *p-var* will point to the start of an array of *size* elements of the type specified. For various technical reasons, it is not possible to initialize an array that is dynamically allocated.

To delete a dynamically allocated array, use this form of **delete**:

delete [ ] *p-var*;

This syntax causes the compiler to call the destructor function for each element in the array. It does *not* cause *p-var* to be freed multiple times. *p-var* is still freed only once.

*For older compilers, you might need to specify the size of the array that you are deleting between the square brackets of the **delete** statement. This was required by the original definition of C++. However, the size specification is not needed by modern compilers.*

1. This program allocates memory for an integer and initializes that memory:

```
// An example of initializing a dynamic variable.
#include <iostream>
using namespace std;

int main()
{
  int *p;

  p = new int(9); // give initial value of 9

  if(!p) {
    cout << "Allocation error\n";
    return 1;
  }

  cout << "Here is integer at p: " << *p << "\n";

  delete p;  // release memory

  return 0;
}
```

As you should expect, this program displays the value 9, which is the initial value given to the memory pointed to by **p**.

2. The following program passes initial values to a dynamically allocated object:

```
// Allocating dynamic objects.
#include <iostream>
using namespace std;

class samp {
  int i, j;
public:
  samp(int a, int b) { i=a; j=b; }
  int get_product() { return i*j; }
};

int main()
{
```

```
samp *p;

p = new samp(6, 5); // allocate object with initialization
if(!p) {
  cout << "Allocation error\n";
  return 1;
}

cout << "Product is: " << p->get_product() << "\n";

delete p;

return 0;
}
```

When the **samp** object is allocated, its constructor is
automatically called and is passed the values 6 and 5.

3. The following program allocates an array of integers:

```
// A simple example of new and delete.
#include <iostream>
using namespace std;

int main()
{
  int *p;

  p = new int [5]; // allocate room for 5 integers

  // always make sure that allocation succeeded
  if(!p) {
    cout << "Allocation error\n";
    return 1;
  }

  int i;

  for(i=0; i<5; i++) p[i] = i;

  for(i=0; i<5; i++) {
    cout << "Here is integer at p[" << i << "]: ";
    cout << p[i] << "\n";
  }
```

```
    delete [] p;   // release memory

    return 0;
}
```

This program displays the following:

```
Here is integer at p[0]: 0
Here is integer at p[1]: 1
Here is integer at p[2]: 2
Here is integer at p[3]: 3
Here is integer at p[4]: 4
```

4. The following program creates a dynamic array of objects:

```
// Allocating dynamic objects.
#include <iostream>
using namespace std;

class samp {
  int i, j;
public:
  void set_ij(int a, int b) { i=a; j=b; }
  int get_product() { return i*j; }
};

int main()
{
  samp *p;
  int i;

  p = new samp [10]; // allocate object array
  if(!p) {
    cout << "Allocation error\n";
    return 1;
  }

  for(i=0; i<10; i++)
    p[i].set_ij(i, i);

  for(i=0; i<10; i++) {
    cout << "Product [" << i << "] is: ";
    cout << p[i].get_product() << "\n";
  }
  delete [] p;
```

```
  return 0;
}
```

This program displays the following:

```
Product [0] is: 0
Product [1] is: 1
Product [2] is: 4
Product [3] is: 9
Product [4] is: 16
Product [5] is: 25
Product [6] is: 36
Product [7] is: 49
Product [8] is: 64
Product [9] is: 81
```

5. The following version of the preceding program gives **samp** a destructor, and now when **p** is freed, each element's destructor is called:

```
// Allocating dynamic objects.
#include <iostream>
using namespace std;

class samp {
  int i, j;
public:
  void set_ij(int a, int b) { i=a; j=b; }
  ~samp() { cout << "Destroying...\n"; }
  int get_product() { return i*j; }
};

int main()
{
  samp *p;
  int i;

  p = new samp [10]; // allocate object array
  if(!p) {
    cout << "Allocation error\n";
    return 1;
  }

  for(i=0; i<10; i++)
    p[i].set_ij(i, i);
```

```
for(i=0; i<10; i++) {
  cout << "Product [" << i << "] is: ";
  cout << p[i].get_product() << "\n";
}

delete [] p;
return 0;
}
```

This program displays the following:

```
Product [0] is: 0
Product [1] is: 1
Product [2] is: 4
Product [3] is: 9
Product [4] is: 16
Product [5] is: 25
Product [6] is: 36
Product [7] is: 49
Product [8] is: 64
Product [9] is: 81
Destroying...
Destroying...
Destroying...
Destroying...
Destroying...
Destroying...
Destroying...
Destroying...
Destroying...
Destroying...
```

As you can see, **samp**'s destructor is called ten times—once for each element in the array.

EXERCISES

1. Show how to convert the following code into its equivalent that uses **new**.

```
char *p;

p = (char *) malloc(100);
```

```
// ...
strcpy(p, "This is a test");
```

Hint: A string is simply an array of characters.

2. Using **new**, show how to allocate a **double** and give it an initial value of -123.0987.

---

*R*EFERENCES

C++ contains a feature that is related to the pointer: the *reference*. A reference is an implicit pointer that for all intents and purposes acts like another name for a variable. There are three ways that a reference can be used. First, a reference can be passed to a function. Second, a reference can be returned by a function. Finally, an independent reference can be created. Each of these applications of the reference is examined, beginning with reference parameters.

Without a doubt, the most important use of a reference is as a parameter to a function. To help you understand what a reference parameter is and how it works, let's first start with a program that uses a pointer (not a reference) as a parameter:

```
#include <iostream>
using namespace std;

void f(int *n);  // use a pointer parameter

int main()
{
  int i = 0;

  f(&i);

  cout << "Here is i's new value: " << i << '\n';
```

```
  return 0;
}

void f(int *n)
{
  *n = 100; // put 100 into the argument pointed to by n
}
```

Here **f( )** loads the value 100 into the integer pointed to by **n**. In this program, **f( )** is called with the address of **i** in **main( )**. Thus, after **f( )** returns, **i** contains the value 100.

This program demonstrates how a pointer is used as a parameter to manually create a call-by-reference parameter-passing mechanism. In a C program, this is the only way to achieve a call-by-reference. However, in C++, you can completely automate this process by using a reference parameter. To see how, let's rework the previous program. Here is a version that uses a reference parameter:

```
#include <iostream>
using namespace std;

void f(int &n); // declare a reference parameter

int main()
{
  int i = 0;

  f(i);

  cout << "Here is i's new value: " << i << '\n';

  return 0;
}

// f() now uses a reference parameter
void f(int &n)
{
  // notice that no * is needed in the following statement
  n = 100; // put 100 into the argument used to call f()
}
```

Examine this program carefully. First, to declare a reference variable or parameter, you precede the variable's name with the **&**. This is how **n** is declared as a parameter to **f( )**. Now that **n** is a

reference, it is no longer necessary—or even legal—to apply the *
operator. Instead, each time **n** is used within **f( )**, it is automatically
treated as a pointer to the argument used to call **f( )**. This means that
the statement

```
n = 100;
```

actually puts the value 100 into the variable used to call **f( )**, which, in
this case, is **i**. Further, when **f( )** is called, there is no need to precede
the argument with the **&**. Instead, because **f( )** is declared as taking a
reference parameter, the address to the argument is *automatically*
passed to **f( )**.

To review, when you use a reference parameter, the compiler
automatically passes the address of the variable used as the argument.
There is no need to manually generate the address of the argument by
preceding it with an **&** (in fact, it is not allowed). Further, within the
function, the compiler automatically uses the variable pointed to by
the reference parameter. There is no need to employ the * (and
again, it is not allowed). Thus, a reference parameter fully automates
the call-by-reference parameter-passing mechanism.

It is important to understand that you cannot change what a
reference is pointing to. For example, if the statement

```
n++;
```

were put inside **f( )** in the preceding program, **n** would still be
pointing to **i** in **main( )**. Instead of incrementing **n**, this statement
increments the value of the variable being referenced (in this case, **i**).

Reference parameters offer several advantages over their (more or
less) equivalent pointer alternatives. First, from a practical point of
view, you no longer need to remember to pass the address of an
argument. When a reference parameter is used, the address is
automatically passed. Second, in the opinion of many programmers,
reference parameters offer a cleaner, more elegant interface than the
rather clumsy explicit pointer mechanism. Third, as you will see in
the next section, when an object is passed to a function as a reference,
no copy is made. This is one way to eliminate the troubles associated
with the copy of an argument damaging something needed elsewhere
in
the
prog
ram

when its destructor function is called.

EXAMPLES

1. The classic example of passing arguments by reference is a function that exchanges the values of the two arguments with which it is called. Here is an example called **swapargs( )** that uses references to swap its two integer arguments:

```
#include <iostream>
using namespace std;

void swapargs(int &x, int &y);

int main()
{
  int i, j;

  i = 10;
  j = 19;

  cout << "i: " << i << ", ";
  cout << "j: " << j << "\n";

  swapargs(i, j);

  cout << "After swapping: ";
  cout << "i: " << i << ", ";
  cout << "j: " << j << "\n";

  return 0;
}

void swapargs(int &x, int &y)
{
  int t;

  t = x;
  x = y;
  y = t;
}
```

If **swapargs( )** had been written using pointers instead of references, it would have looked like this:

```
void swapargs(int *x, int *y)
{
  int t;

  t = *x;
  *x = *y;
  *y = t;
}
```

As you can see, by using the reference version of **swapargs( )**, the need for the * operator is eliminated.

2. Here is a program that uses the **round( )** function to round a **double** value. The value to be rounded is passed by reference.

```
#include <iostream>
#include <cmath>
using namespace std;

void round(double &num);

int main()
{
  double i = 100.4;

  cout << i << " rounded is ";
  round(i);
  cout << i << "\n";

  i = 10.9;
  cout << i << " rounded is ";
  round(i);
  cout << i << "\n";

  return 0;
}

void round(double &num)
{
  double frac;
  double val;

  // decompose num into whole and fractional parts
  frac = modf(num, &val);

  if(frac < 0.5) num = val;
```

```
  else num = val+1.0;
}
```

round( ) uses a relatively obscure standard library function called **modf( )** to decompose a number into its whole number and fractional parts. The fractional part is returned; the whole number is put into the variable pointed to by **modf()**'s second parameter.

EXERCISES

1. Write a function called **neg( )** that reverses the sign of its integer parameter. Write the function two ways—first by using a pointer parameter and then by using a reference parameter. Include a short program to demonstrate their operation.

2. What is wrong with the following program?

```
// This program has an error.
#include <iostream>
using namespace std;

void triple(double &num);

int main()
{
  double d = 7.0;

  triple(&d);

  cout << d;

  return 0;
}

// Triple num's value.
void triple(double &num)
{
  num = 3 * num;
}
```

3. Give some advantages of reference parameters.

PASSING REFERENCES TO OBJECTS

As you learned in Chapter 3, when an object is passed to a function by use of the default call-by-value parameter-passing mechanism, a copy of that object is made. Although the parameter's constructor function is not called, its destructor function is called when the function returns. As you should recall, this can cause serious problems in some instances—when the destructor frees dynamic memory, for example.

One solution to this problem is to pass an object by reference. (The other solution involves the use of copy constructors, which are discussed in Chapter 5.) When you pass the object by reference, no copy is made, and therefore its destructor function is not called when the function returns. Remember, however, that changes made to the object inside the function affect the object used as the argument.

Note

It is critical to understand that a reference is not a pointer. Therefore, when an object is passed by reference, the member access operator remains the dot (.), not the arrow (->).

EXAMPLE

1. The following is an example that demonstrates the usefulness of passing an object by reference. First, here is a version of a program that passes an object of **myclass** by value to a function called **f( )**:

```cpp
#include <iostream>
using namespace std;

class myclass {
  int who;
public:
  myclass(int n) {
    who = n;
    cout << "Constructing " << who << "\n";
  }
```

```
  ~myclass() { cout << "Destructing " << who << "\n"; }
  int id() { return who; }
};

// o is passed by value.
void f(myclass o)
{
  cout << "Received " << o.id() << "\n";
}

int main()
{
  myclass  x(1);

  f(x);

  return 0;
}
```

This function displays the following:

```
Constructing 1
Received 1
Destructing 1
Destructing 1
```

As you can see, the destructor function is called twice—first when the copy of object 1 is destroyed when **f( )** terminates and again when the program finishes.

However, if the program is changed so that **f( )** uses a reference parameter, no copy is made and, therefore, no destructor is called when **f( )** returns:

```
#include <iostream>
using namespace std;

class myclass {
  int who;
public:
  myclass(int n) {
    who = n;
    cout << "Constructing " << who << "\n";
  }
  ~myclass() { cout << "Destructing " << who << "\n"; }
  int id() { return who; }
```

```
};

// Now o is passed by reference.
void f(myclass &o)
{
  // note that . operator is still used!!!
  cout << "Received " << o.id() << "\n";
}

int main()
{
  myclass  x(1);

  f(x);

  return 0;
}
```

This version displays the following output:

```
Constructing 1
Received 1
Destructing 1
```

 Remember *When accessing members of an object by using a reference, use the dot operator, not the arrow.*

EXERCISE

1. What is wrong with the following program? Show how it can be fixed by using a reference parameter.

```
// This program has an error.
#include <iostream>
#include <cstring>
#include <cstdlib>
using namespace std;

class strtype {
  char *p;
public:
  strtype(char *s);
```

```
  ~strtype() { delete [] p; }
  char *get() { return p; }
};

strtype::strtype(char *s)
{
  int l;

  l = strlen(s)+1;

  p = new char [l];
  if(!p) {
    cout << "Allocation error\n";
    exit(1);
  }

  strcpy(p, s);
}

void show(strtype x)
{
  char *s;

  s = x.get();
  cout << s << "\n";
}

int main()
{
  strtype a("Hello"), b("There");

  show(a);
  show(b);

  return 0;
}
```

<hr>

4.8 *RETURNING REFERENCES*

A function can return a reference. As you will see in Chapter 6,
returning a reference can be very useful when you are overloading

certain types of operators. However, it also can be employed to allow a function to be used on the left side of an assignment statement. The effect of this is both powerful and startling.

EXAMPLES

1. To begin, here is a very simple program that contains a function that returns a reference:

```
// A simple example of a function returning a reference.
#include <iostream>
using namespace std;

int &f(); // return a reference
int x;

int main()
{
  f() = 100; // assign 100 to reference returned by f()

  cout << x << "\n";

  return 0;
}

// Return an int reference.
int &f()
{
  return x;  // returns a reference to x
}
```

Here function **f( )** is declared as returning a reference to an integer. Inside the body of the function, the statement

```
return x;
```

does *not* return the value of the global variable **x**, but rather, it automatically returns **x**'s address (in the form of a reference). Thus, inside **main( )**, the statement

```
f() = 100;
```

puts the value 100 into **x** because **f( )** has returned a reference to it.

To review, function **f( )** returns a reference. Thus, when **f( )** is used on the left side of the assignment statement, it is this reference, returned by **f( )**, that is being assigned to. Since **f( )** returns a reference to **x** (in this example), it is **x** that receives the value 100.

2. You must be careful when returning a reference that the object you refer to does not go out of scope. For example, consider this slight reworking of function **f( )**:

```
// Return an int reference.
int &f()
{
  int x; // x is now a local variable
  return x;  // returns a reference to x
}
```

In this case, **x** is now local to **f( )** and will go out of scope when **f( )** returns. This effectively means that the reference returned by **f( )** is useless.

Note — *Some C++ compilers will not allow you to return a reference to a local variable. However, this type of problem can manifest itself in other ways, such as when objects are allocated dynamically.*

3. One very good use of returning a reference is found when a bounded array type is created. As you know, in C and C++, no array boundary checking occurs. It is therefore possible to overflow or underflow an array. However, in C++, you can create an array class that performs automatic bounds checking. An array class contains two core functions—one that stores information into the array and one that retrieves information. These functions can check, at run time, that the array boundaries are not overrun.

The following program implements a bounds-checking array for characters:

```
// A simple bounded array example.
#include <iostream>
#include <cstdlib>
using namespace std;

class array {
  int size;
```

```
    char *p;
public:
    array(int num);
    ~array() { delete [] p; }
    char &put(int i);
    char get(int i);
};

array::array(int num)
{
    p = new char [num];
    if(!p) {
        cout << "Allocation error\n";
        exit(1);
    }
    size = num;
}

// Put something into the array.
char &array::put(int i)
{
    if(i<0 || i>=size) {
        cout << "Bounds error!!!\n";
        exit(1);
    }
    return p[i];  // return reference to p[i]
}

// Get something from the array.
char array::get(int i)
{
    if(i<0 || i>=size) {
        cout << "Bounds error!!!\n";
        exit(1);
    }
    return p[i]; // return character
}

int main()
{
    array a(10);
```

```
a.put(3) = 'X';
a.put(2) = 'R';

cout << a.get(3) << a.get(2);
cout << "\n";

// now generate run-time boundary error
a.put(11) = '!';

return 0;
}
```

This example is a practical use of functions returning references, and you should examine it closely. Notice that the **put( )** function returns a reference to the array element specified by parameter **i**. This reference can then be used on the left side of an assignment statement to store something in the array—if the index specified by **i** is not out of bounds. The reverse is **get( )**, which returns the value stored at the specified index if that index is within range. This approach to maintaining an array is sometimes referred to as a *safe array*. (You will see a better way to create a safe array later on, in Chapter 6.)

One other thing to notice about the preceding program is that the array is allocated dynamically by the use of **new**. This allows arrays of differing lengths to be declared.

As mentioned, the way that bounds checking is performed in this program is a practical application of C++. If you need to have array boundaries verified at run time, this is one way to do it. However, remember that bounds checking slows access to the array. Therefore, it is best to include bounds checking only when there is a real likelihood that an array boundary will be violated.

EXERCISES

1. Write a program that creates a two-by-three two-dimensional safe array of integers. Demonstrate that it works.

2. Is the following fragment valid? If not, why not?

```
int &f();
.
.
.
int *x;

x = f();
```

4.9 *INDEPENDENT REFERENCES AND RESTRICTIONS*

Although not commonly used, the *independent reference* is another type of reference that is available in C++. An independent reference is a reference variable that in all effects is simply another name for another variable. Because references cannot be assigned new values, an independent reference must be initialized when it is declared.

Note

Because independent references are sometimes used, it is important that you know about them. However, most programmers feel that there is no need for them and that they can add confusion to a program. Further, independent references exist in C++ largely because there was no compelling reason to disallow them. But for the most part, their use should be avoided.

There are a number of restrictions that apply to all types of references. You cannot reference another reference. You cannot obtain the address of a reference. You cannot create arrays of references, and you cannot reference a bit-field. References must be initialized unless they are members of a class, are return values, or are function parameters.

Remember   *References are similar to pointers, but they are not pointers.*

EXAMPLES

1. Here is a program that contains an independent reference:

```
#include <iostream>
using namespace std;

int main()
{
  int x;
  int &ref = x; // create an independent reference

  x = 10;  // these two statements
  ref = 10;  // are functionally equivalent

  ref = 100;
  // this prints the number 100 twice
  cout << x << ' ' << ref << "\n";

  return 0;
}
```

In this program, the independent reference **ref** serves as a different name for **x**. From a practical point of view, **x** and **ref** are equivalent.

2. An independent reference can refer to a constant. For example, this is valid:

```
const int &ref = 10;
```

Again, there is little benefit in this type of reference, but you may see it from time to time in other programs.

1. On your own, try to think of a good use for an independent reference.

S*KILLS CHECK*

Mastery
Skills Check

At this point, you should be able to perform the following exercises and answer the questions.

1. Given the following class, create a two-by-five two-dimensional array and give each object in the array an initial value of your own choosing. Then display the contents of the array.

```
class a_type {
  double a, b;
public:
  a_type(double x, double y) {
    a = x;
    b = y;
  }
  void show() { cout << a << ' ' << b << "\n"; }
};
```

2. Modify your solution to the preceding problem so it accesses the array by using a pointer.

3. What is the **this** pointer?

4. Show the general forms for **new** and **delete**. What are some advantages of using them instead of **malloc( )** and **free( )**?

5. What is a reference? What is one advantage of using a reference parameter?

6. Create a function called **recip( )** that takes one **double** reference parameter. Have the function change the value of that parameter into its reciprocal. Write a program to demonstrate that it works.

Cumulative Skills Check

This section checks how well you have integrated material in this chapter with that from the preceding chapters.

1. Given a pointer to an object, what operator is used to access a member of that object?

2. In Chapter 2, a **strtype** class was created that dynamically allocated space for a string. Rework the **strtype** class (shown here for your convenience) so it uses **new** and **delete**.

```cpp
#include <iostream>
#include <cstring>
#include <cstdlib>
using namespace std;

class strtype {
  char *p;
  int len;
public:
  strtype(char *ptr);
  ~strtype();
  void show();
};

strtype::strtype(char *ptr)
{
  len = strlen(ptr);
  p = (char *) malloc(len+1);
  if(!p) {
    cout << "Allocation error\n";
    exit(1);
  }
  strcpy(p, ptr);
}
```

```
strtype::~strtype()
{
  cout << "Freeing p\n";
  free(p);
}

void strtype::show()
{
  cout << p << " - length: " << len;
  cout << "\n";
}

int main()
{
  strtype s1("This is a test."), s2("I like C++.");

  s1.show();
  s2.show();

  return 0;
}
```

3. On your own, rework any program from the preceding chapter so that it uses a reference.

5

Function Overloading

chapter objectives

5.1 Overloading constructor functions

5.2 Creating and using a copy constructor

5.3 The **overload** anachronism

5.4 Using default arguments

5.5 Overloading and ambiguity

5.6 Finding the address of an overloaded function

159
▼

N this chapter you will learn more about overloading functions. Although this topic was introduced early in this book, there are several further aspects of it that need to be covered. Among the topics included are how to overload constructor functions, how to create a copy constructor, how to give functions default arguments, and how to avoid ambiguity when overloading.

Review
Skills Check

Before proceeding, you should be able to correctly answer the following questions and do the exercises.

1. What is a reference? Give two important uses.

2. Show how to allocate a **float** and an **int** by using **new**. Also, show how to free them by using **delete**.

3. What is the general form of **new** that is used to initialize a dynamic variable? Give a concrete example.

4. Given the following class, show how to initialize a ten-element array so that **x** has the values 1 through 10.

```
class samp {
  int x;
public:
  samp(int n) { x = n; }
  int getx() { return x; }
};
```

5. Give one advantage of reference parameters. Give one disadvantage.

6. Can dynamically allocated arrays be initialized?

7. Create a function called **mag( )** using the following prototype that raises **num** to the order of magnitude specified by **order**:

```
void mag(long &num, long order);
```

For example, if **num** is 4 and order is 2, when **mag( )** returns, **num** will be 400. Demonstrate in a program that the function works.

5.1 *O*VERLOADING CONSTRUCTOR FUNCTIONS

It is possible—indeed, common—to overload a class's constructor function. (It is not possible to overload a destructor, however.) There are three main reasons why you will want to overload a constructor function: to gain flexibility, to support arrays, and to create copy constructors. The first two of these are discussed in this section. Copy constructors are discussed in the next section.

One thing to keep in mind as you study the examples is that there must be a constructor function for each way that an object of a class will be created. If a program attempts to create an object for which no matching constructor is found, a compile-time error occurs. This is why overloaded constructor functions are so common to C++ programs.

EXAMPLES

1. Perhaps the most frequent use of overloaded constructor functions is to provide the option of either giving an object an initialization or not giving it one. For example, in the following program, **o1** is given an initial value, but **o2** is not. If you remove the constructor that has the empty argument list, the program will not compile because there is no constructor that matches a noninitialized object of type **samp**. The reverse is also true: If you remove the parameterized constructor, the program will not compile because there is no match for an initialized object. Both are needed for this program to compile correctly.

```
#include <iostream>
using namespace std;

class myclass {
  int x;
public:
  // overload constructor two ways
  myclass() { x = 0; } // no initializer
  myclass(int n) { x = n; } // initializer
  int getx() { return x; }
};

int main()
{
  myclass o1(10); // declare with initial value
  myclass o2; // declare without initializer

  cout << "o1: " << o1.getx() << '\n';
  cout << "o2: " << o2.getx() << '\n';

  return 0;
}
```

2. Another common reason constructor functions are overloaded is to allow both individual objects and arrays of objects to occur within a program. As you probably know from your own programming experience, it is fairly common to initialize a single variable, but it is not as common to initialize an array. (Quite often array values are assigned using information known only when the program is executing.) Thus, to allow noninitialized arrays of objects along with initialized objects, you must include a constructor that supports initialization and one that does not.

   For instance, assuming the class **myclass** from Example 1, both of these declarations are valid:

```
myclass ob(10);
myclass ob[5];
```

By providing both a parameterized and a parameterless constructor, your program allows the creation of objects that are either initialized or not as needed.

   Of course, once you have defined both parameterized and parameterless constructors you can use them to create initialized and noninitialized arrays. For example, the following program declares two arrays of type **myclass**; one is initialized and the other is not:

```
#include <iostream>
using namespace std;

class myclass {
  int x;
public:
  // overload constructor two ways
  myclass() { x = 0; } // no initializer
  myclass(int n) { x = n; } // initializer
  int getx() { return x; }
};

int main()
{
  myclass o1[10]; // declare array without initializers

  // declare with initializers
  myclass o2[10] = {1, 2, 3, 4, 5, 6, 7, 8, 9, 10};

  int i;

  for(i=0; i<10; i++) {
    cout << "o1[" << i << "]: " << o1[i].getx();
    cout << '\n';
    cout << "o2[" << i << "]: " << o2[i].getx();
    cout << '\n';
  }

  return 0;
}
```

In this example, all elements of **o1** are set to 0 by the constructor function. The elements of **o2** are initialized as shown in the program.

3. Another reason for overloading constructor functions is to allow the programmer to select the most convenient method of initializing an object. To see how, first examine the next example, which creates a class that holds a calendar date. It overloads the **date( )** constructor two ways. One form accepts

the date as a character string. In the other form, the date is passed as three integers.

```cpp
#include <iostream>
#include <cstdio> // included for sscanf()
using namespace std;

class date {
  int day, month, year;
public:
  date(char *str);
  date (int m, int d, int y) {
    day = d;
    month = m;
    year = y;
  }
  void show() {
    cout << month << '/' << day << '/';
    cout << year << '\n';
  }
};

date::date(char *str)
{
  sscanf(str, "%d%*c%d%*c%d", &month, &day, &year);
}

int main()
{
  // construct date object using string
  date sdate("12/31/99");

  // construct date object using integers
  date idate(12, 31, 99);

  sdate.show();
  idate.show();
  return 0;
}
```

The advantage of overloading the **date( )** constructor, as shown in this program, is that you are free to use whichever version most conveniently fits the situation in which it is being used. For example, if a **date** object is being created from user input, the string version is the easiest to use. However, if the **date** object is being constructed through some sort of internal computation, the three-integer parameter version probably makes more sense.

Although it is possible to overload a constructor as many times as you want, doing so excessively has a destructuring effect on the class. From a stylistic point of view, it is best to overload a constructor to accommodate only those situations that are likely to occur frequently. For example, overloading **date( )** a third time so the date can be entered in terms of milliseconds makes little sense. However, overloading it to accept an object of type **time_t** (a type that stores the system date and time) could be very valuable. (See the Mastery Skills Check exercises at the end of this chapter for an example that does just this.)

4. There is one other situation in which you will need to overload a class's constructor function: when a dynamic array of that class will be allocated. As you should recall from the preceding chapter, a dynamic array cannot be initialized. Thus, if the class contains a constructor that takes an initializer, you must include an overloaded version that takes no initializer. For example, here is a program that allocates an object array dynamically:

```cpp
#include <iostream>
using namespace std;

class myclass {
  int x;
public:
  // overload constructor two ways
  myclass() { x = 0; } // no initializer
  myclass(int n) { x = n; } // initializer
  int getx() { return x; }
  void setx(int n) { x = n; }
};

int main()
{
  myclass *p;
  myclass ob(10);  // initialize single variable

  p = new myclass[10]; // can't use initializers here
  if(!p) {
```

```
      cout << "Allocation error\n";
      return 1;
   }

   int i;

   // initialize all elements to ob
   for(i=0; i<10; i++) p[i] = ob;

   for(i=0; i<10; i++) {
      cout << "p[" << i << "]: " << p[i].getx();
      cout << '\n';
   }

   return 0;
}
```

Without the overloaded version of **myclass( )** that has
no initializer, the **new** statement would have generated
a compile-time error and the program would not have
been compiled.

EXERCISES

---

1. Given this partially defined class

```
class strtype {
   char *p;
   int len;
public:
   char *getstring() { return p; }
   int getlength() { return len; }
};
```

   add two constructor functions. Have the first one take no
   parameters. Have this one allocate 255 bytes of memory (using
   new), initialize that memory as a null string, and give **len** a
   value of 255. Have the other constructor take two parameters.
   The first is the string to use for initialization and the other is the
   number of bytes to allocate. Have this version allocate the
   specified amount of memory and copy the string to that

memory. Perform all necessary boundary checks and demonstrate that your constructors work by including a short program.

2. In Exercise 2 of Chapter 2, Section 2.1, you created a stopwatch emulation. Expand your solution so that the **stopwatch** class provides both a parameterless constructor (as it does already) and an overloaded version that accepts the system time in the form returned by the standard function **clock( )**. Demonstrate that your improvement works.

3. On your own, think about ways in which an overloaded constructor function can be beneficial to your own programming tasks.

5.2 *CREATING AND USING A COPY CONSTRUCTOR*

One of the more important forms of an overloaded constructor is the *copy constructor*. As numerous examples from the preceding chapters have shown, problems can occur when an object is passed to or returned from a function. As you will learn in this section, one way to avoid these problems is to define a copy constructor.

To begin, let's restate the problem that a copy constructor is designed to solve. When an object is passed to a function, a bitwise (i.e., exact) copy of that object is made and given to the function parameter that receives the object. However, there are cases in which this identical copy is not desirable. For example, if the object contains a pointer to allocated memory, the copy will point to the *same* memory as does the original object. Therefore, if the copy makes a change to the contents of this memory, it will be changed for the original object too! Also, when the function terminates, the copy will be destroyed, causing its destructor to be called. This might lead to undesired side effects that further affect the original object.

A similar situation occurs when an object is returned by a function. The compiler will commonly generate a temporary object that holds a copy of the value returned by the function. (This is done automatically and is beyond your control.) This temporary object goes out of scope once the value is returned to the calling routine, causing the temporary object's destructor to be called. However, if the destructor destroys something needed by the calling routine (for example, if it frees dynamically allocated memory), trouble will follow.

At the core of these problems is the fact that a bitwise copy of the object is being made. To prevent these problems, you, the programmer, need to define precisely what occurs when a copy of an object is made so that you can avoid undesired side effects. The way you accomplish this is by creating a copy constructor. By defining a copy constructor, you can fully specify exactly what occurs when a copy of an object is made.

It is important for you to understand that C++ defines two distinct types of situations in which the value of one object is given to another. The first situation is assignment. The second situation is initialization, which can occur three ways:

▼ when an object is used to initialize another in a declaration statement,

▼ when an object is passed as a parameter to a function, and

▼ when a temporary object is created for use as a return value by a function.

The copy constructor only applies to initializations. It does not apply to assignments.

By default, when an initialization occurs, the compiler will automatically provide a bitwise copy. (That is, C++ automatically provides a default copy constructor that simply duplicates the object.) However, it is possible to specify precisely how one object will initialize another by defining a copy constructor. Once defined, the copy constructor is called whenever an object is used to initialize another.

Copy constructors do not affect assignment operations.

The most common form of copy constructor is shown here:

classname (const *classname* &*obj*) {
  // *body of constructor*
}

Here *obj* is a reference to an object that is being used to initialize another object. For example, assuming a class called **myclass**, and that **y** is an object of type **myclass**, the following statements would invoke the **myclass** copy constructor:

```
myclass x = y; // y explicitly initializing x
func1(y);      // y passed as a parameter
y = func2();   // y receiving a returned object
```

In the first two cases, a reference to **y** would be passed to the copy constructor. In the third, a reference to the object returned by **func2( )** is passed to the copy constructor.

1. Here is an example that illustrates why an explicit copy constructor function is needed. This program creates a very limited "safe" integer array type that prevents array boundaries from being overrun. Storage for each array is allocated using **new**, and a pointer to the memory is maintained within each array object.

```
/* This program creates a "safe" array class. Since space
   for the array is dynamically allocated, a copy constructor
   is provided to allocate memory when one array object is
   used to initialize another.
*/
#include <iostream>
#include <cstdlib>
using namespace std;

class array {
  int *p;
  int size;
public:
  array(int sz) { // constructor
```

```
      p = new int[sz];
      if(!p) exit(1);
      size = sz;
      cout << "Using 'normal' constructor\n";
    }
    ~array() {delete [] p;}

    // copy constructor
    array(const array &a);

    void put(int i, int j) {
      if(i>=0 && i<size) p[i] = j;
    }
    int get(int i) {
      return p[i];
    }
};

/* Copy constructor.

In the following, memory is allocated specifically
for the copy, and the address of this memory is assigned
to p. Therefore, p is not pointing to the same
dynamically allocated memory as the original object.
*/
array::array(const array &a) {
  int i;

  size = a.size;
  p = new int[a.size];  // allocate memory for copy
  if(!p) exit(1);
  for(i=0; i<a.size; i++) p[i] = a.p[i]; // copy contents
  cout << "Using copy constructor\n";
}

int main()
{
  array num(10);  // this calls "normal" constructor
  int i;

  // put some values into the array
  for(i=0; i<10; i++) num.put(i, i);
```

```
// display num
for(i=9; i>=0; i--) cout << num.get(i);
cout << "\n";

// create another array and initialize with num
array x = num;  // this invokes copy constructor

// display x
for(i=0; i<10; i++) cout << x.get(i);

return 0;
}
```

When **num** is used to initialize **x**, the copy constructor is called, memory for the new array is allocated and stored in **x.p**, and the contents of **num** are copied to **x**'s array. In this way, **x** and **num** have arrays that have the same values, but each array is separate and distinct. (That is, **num.p** and **x.p** do not point to the same piece of memory.) If the copy constructor had not been created, the bitwise initialization **array x = num** would have resulted in **x** and **num** sharing the same memory for their arrays! (That is, **num.p** and **x.p** would have, indeed, pointed to the same location.)

The copy constructor is called only for initializations. For example, the following sequence does not call the copy constructor defined in the preceding program:

```
array a(10);
array b(10);

b = a; // does not call copy constructor
```

In this case, **b = a** performs the assignment operation.

2. To see how the copy constructor helps prevent some of the problems associated with passing certain types of objects to functions, consider this (incorrect) program:

```
// This program has an error.
#include <iostream>
#include <cstring>
#include <cstdlib>
using namespace std;
```

```
class strtype {
  char *p;
public:
  strtype(char *s);
  ~strtype() { delete [] p; }
  char *get() { return p; }
};

strtype::strtype(char *s)
{
  int l;

  l = strlen(s)+1;

  p = new char [l];
  if(!p) {
    cout << "Allocation error\n";
    exit(1);
  }

  strcpy(p, s);
}

void show(strtype x)
{
  char *s;

  s = x.get();
  cout << s << "\n";
}

int main()
{
  strtype a("Hello"), b("There");

  show(a);
  show(b);

  return 0;
}
```

In this program, when a **strtype** object is passed to **show( )**, a bitwise copy is made (since no copy constructor has been defined) and put into parameter **x**. Thus, when the function returns, **x** goes out of scope and is destroyed. This, of course, causes **x**'s destructor to be called, which frees **x.p**. However, the memory being freed is the same memory that is still being used by the object used to call the function. This results in an error.

The solution to the preceding problem is to define a copy constructor for the **strtype** class that allocates memory for the copy when the copy is created. This approach is used by the following, corrected, program:

```cpp
/* This program uses a copy constructor to allow strtype objects
   to be passed to functions. */
#include <iostream>
#include <cstring>
#include <cstdlib>
using namespace std;

class strtype {
  char *p;
public:
  strtype(char *s); // constructor
  strtype(const strtype &o); // copy constructor
  ~strtype() { delete [] p; } // destructor
  char *get() { return p; }
};

// "Normal" constructor
strtype::strtype(char *s)
{
  int l;

  l = strlen(s)+1;

  p = new char [l];
  if(!p) {
    cout << "Allocation error\n";
    exit(1);
  }

  strcpy(p, s);
}

// Copy constructor
strtype::strtype(const strtype &o)
{
```

```
    int l;

    l = strlen(o.p)+1;

    p = new char [l]; // allocate memory for new copy
    if(!p) {
      cout << "Allocation error\n";
      exit(1);
    }

    strcpy(p, o.p); // copy string into copy
}

void show(strtype x)
{
  char *s;

  s = x.get();
  cout << s << "\n";
}

int main()
{
  strtype a("Hello"), b("There");

  show(a);
  show(b);

  return 0;
}
```

Now when **show( )** terminates and **x** goes out of scope, the
memory pointed to by **x.p** (which will be freed) is not the same
as the memory still in use by the object passed to the function.

EXERCISES

1. The copy constructor is also invoked when a function generates
   the temporary object that is used as the function's return value
   (for those functions that return objects). With this in mind,
   consider the following output:

```
Constructing normally
Constructing normally
Constructing copy
```

This output was created by the following program. Explain why, and describe precisely what is occurring.

```cpp
#include <iostream>
using namespace std;

class myclass {
public:
  myclass();
  myclass(const myclass &o);
  myclass f();
};

// Normal constructor
myclass::myclass()
{
  cout << "Constructing normally\n";
}

// Copy constructor
myclass::myclass(const myclass &o)
{
  cout << "Constructing copy\n";
}

// Return an object.
myclass myclass::f()
{
  myclass temp;

  return temp;
}

int main()
{
  myclass obj;

  obj = obj.f();

  return 0;
}
```

2. Explain what is wrong with the following program and then fix it.

```cpp
// This program contains an error.
#include <iostream>
#include <cstdlib>
using namespace std;

class myclass {
  int *p;
public:
  myclass(int i);
  ~myclass() { delete p; }
  friend int getval(myclass o);
};

myclass::myclass(int i)
{
  p = new int;

  if(!p) {
    cout << "Allocation error\n";
    exit(1);
  }
  *p = i;
}

int getval(myclass o)
{
  return *o.p; // get value
}

int main()
{
  myclass a(1), b(2);

  cout << getval(a) << " " << getval(b);
  cout << "\n";
  cout << getval(a) << " " << getval(b);

  return 0;
}
```

3. In your own words, explain the purpose of a copy constructor and how it differs from a normal constructor.

5.3 ▰ *THE OVERLOAD ANACHRONISM*

When C++ was first invented, the keyword **overload** was required to create an overloaded function. Although **overload** is now obsolete and no longer supported by modern C++ compilers, you may still see **overload** used in old programs, so it is a good idea to understand how it was applied.

The general form of **overload** is shown here,

overload *func-name*;

where *func-name* is the name of the function to be overloaded. This statement must precede the overloaded function declarations. For example, this tells the compiler that you will be overloading a function called **timer( )**:

```
overload timer;
```

overload *is obsolete and no longer supported by modern C++ compilers.*

5.4 ▰ *USING DEFAULT ARGUMENTS*

There is a feature of C++ that is related to function overloading. This feature is called the *default argument,* and it allows you to give a parameter a default value when no corresponding argument is specified when the function is called. As you will see, using default arguments is essentially a shorthand form of function overloading.

To give a parameter a default argument, simply follow that parameter with an equal sign and the value you want it to default to if no corresponding argument is present when the function is called. For example, this function gives its two parameters default values of 0:

```
void f(int a=0, int b=0);
```

Notice that this syntax is similar to variable initialization. This function can now be called three different ways. First, it can be called with both arguments specified. Second, it can be called with only the first argument specified. In this case, **b** will default to 0. Finally, **f( )** can be called with no arguments, causing both **a** and **b** to default to 0. That is, the following invocations of **f( )** are all valid:

```
f(); // a and b default to 0
f(10); // a is 10, b defaults to 0
f(10, 99) // a is 10, b is 99
```

In this example, it should be clear that there is no way to default **a** and specify **b**.

When you create a function that has one or more default arguments, those arguments must be specified only once: either in the function's prototype or in its definition if the definition precedes the function's first use. The defaults cannot be specified in both the prototype and the definition. This rule applies even if you simply duplicate the same defaults.

As you can probably guess, all default parameters must be to the right of any parameters that don't have defaults. Further, once you begin to define default parameters, you cannot specify any parameters that have no defaults.

One other point about default arguments: they must be constants or global variables. They cannot be local variables or other parameters.

EXAMPLES

1. Here is a program that illustrates the example described in the preceding discussion:

```
// A simple first example of default arguments.
#include <iostream>
using namespace std;

void f(int a=0, int b=0)
{
  cout << "a: " << a << ", b: " << b;
  cout << '\n';
}

int main()
{
  f();
  f(10);
  f(10, 99);
```

```
  return 0;
}
```

As you should expect, this program displays the
following output:

```
a: 0, b: 0
a: 10, b: 0
a: 10, b: 99
```

Remember that once the first default argument is specified, all
following parameters must have defaults as well. For example,
this slightly different version of **f( )** causes a compile-time error:

```
void f(int a=0, int b) // wrong! b must have default, too
{
  cout << "a: " << a << ", b: " << b;
  cout << '\n';
}
```

2. To understand how default arguments are related to function
   overloading, first consider the next program, which overloads
   the function called **rect_area( )**. This function returns the area
   of a rectangle.

```
// Compute area of a rectangle using overloaded functions.
#include <iostream>
using namespace std;

// Return area of a non-square rectangle.
double rect_area(double length, double width)
{
  return length * width;
}

// Return area of a square.
double rect_area(double length)
{
  return length * length;
}

int main()
{
  cout  << "10 x 5.8 rectangle has area: ";
  cout << rect_area(10.0, 5.8) << '\n';
```

```
    cout  << "10 x 10 square has area: ";
    cout << rect_area(10.0) << '\n';
    return 0;
}
```

In this program, **rect_area( )** is overloaded two ways. In the first way, both dimensions of a rectangle are passed to the function. This version is used when the rectangle is not a square. However, when the rectangle is a square, only one argument need be specified, and the second version of **rect_area( )** is called.

If you think about it, it is clear that in this situation there is really no need to have two different functions. Instead, the second parameter can be defaulted to some value that acts as a flag to **rect_area( )**. When this value is seen by the function, it uses the **length** parameter twice. Here is an example of this approach:

```
// Compute area of a rectangle using default arguments.
#include <iostream>
using namespace std;

// Return area of a rectangle.
double rect_area(double length, double width = 0)
{
  if(!width) width = length;
  return length * width;
}

int main()
{
  cout  << "10 x 5.8 rectangle has area: ";
  cout << rect_area(10.0, 5.8) << '\n';

  cout  << "10 x 10 square has area: ";
  cout << rect_area(10.0) << '\n';

  return 0;
}
```

Here 0 is the default value of **width**. This value was chosen because no rectangle will have a width of 0. (Actually, a rectangle with a width of 0 is a line.) Thus, if this default value is seen, **rect_area( )** automatically uses the value in **length** for the value of **width**.

As this example shows, default arguments often provide a simple alternative to function overloading. (Of course, there are many situations in which function overloading is still required.)

3. It is not only legal to give constructor functions default arguments, it is also common. As you saw earlier in this chapter, many times a constructor is overloaded simply to allow both initialized and uninitialized objects to be created. In many cases, you can avoid overloading a constructor by giving it one or more default arguments. For example, examine this program:

```
#include <iostream>
using namespace std;

class myclass {
  int x;
public:
  /* Use default argument instead of overloading
     myclass's constructor. */
  myclass(int n = 0) { x = n; }
  int getx() { return x; }
};

int main()
{
  myclass o1(10); // declare with initial value
  myclass o2; // declare without initializer

  cout << "o1: " << o1.getx() << '\n';
  cout << "o2: " << o2.getx() << '\n';

  return 0;
}
```

As this example shows, by giving **n** the default value of 0, it is possible to create objects that have explicit initial values and those for which the default value is sufficient.

4. Another good application for a default argument is found when a parameter is used to select an option. It is possible to give that parameter a default value that is used as a flag that tells the function to continue to use the previously selected option. For example, in the following program, the function **print( )**

displays a string on the screen. If its **how** parameter is set to **ignore**, the text is displayed as is. If **how** is **upper**, the text is displayed in uppercase. If **how** is **lower**, the text is displayed in lowercase. When **how** is not specified, it defaults to -1, which tells the function to reuse the last **how** value.

```cpp
#include <iostream>
#include <cctype>
using namespace std;

const int ignore = 0;
const int upper = 1;
const int lower = 2;

void print(char *s, int how = -1);

int main()
{
  print("Hello There\n", ignore);
  print("Hello There\n", upper);
  print("Hello There\n"); // continue in upper
  print("Hello there\n", lower);
  print("That's all\n");   // continue in lower

  return 0;
}

/* Print a string in the specified case. Use
   last case specified if none is given.
*/
void print(char *s, int how)
{
  static int oldcase = ignore;

  // reuse old case if none specified
  if(how<0) how = oldcase;
  while(*s) {
    switch(how) {
      case upper: cout << (char) toupper(*s);
        break;
      case lower: cout << (char) tolower(*s);
        break;
      default: cout << *s;
    }
    s++;
  }
```

```
    oldcase = how;
}
```

This function displays the following output:

```
Hello There
HELLO THERE
HELLO THERE
hello there
that's all
```

5. Earlier in this chapter you saw the general form of a copy constructor. This general form was shown with only one parameter. However, it is possible to create copy constructors that take additional arguments, as long as the additional arguments have default values. For example, the following is also an acceptable form of a copy constructor:

```
myclass(const myclass &obj, int x=0) {
    // body of constructor
}
```

As long as the first argument is a reference to the object being copied, and all other arguments default, the function qualifies as a copy constructor. This flexibility allows you to create copy constructors that have other uses.

6. Although default arguments are powerful and convenient, they can be misused. There is no question that, when used correctly, default arguments allow a function to perform its job in an efficient and easy-to-use manner. However, this is only the case when the default value given to a parameter makes sense. For example, if the argument is the value wanted nine times out ten, giving a function a default argument to this effect is obviously a good idea. However, in cases in which no one value is more likely to be used than another, or when there is no benefit to using a default argument as a flag value, it makes little sense to provide a default value. Actually, providing a default argument when one is not called for destructures your program and tends to mislead anyone else who has to use that function.

   As with function overloading, part of becoming an excellent C++ programmer is knowing when to use a default argument and when not to.

1. In the C++ standard library is the function **strtol( )**, which has this prototype:

   long strtol(const char *start, const **end, int base);

   The function converts the numeric string pointed to by start into a long integer. The number base of the numeric string is specified by base. Upon return, end points to the character in the string immediately following the end of the number. The long integer equivalent of the numeric string is returned. base must be in the range 2 to 38. However, most commonly, base 10 is used.

   Create a function called **mystrtol( )** that works the same as **strtol( )** except that base is given the default argument of 10. (Feel free to use **strtol( )** to actually perform the conversion. It requires the header **< cstdlib >**.) Demonstrate that your version works correctly.

2. What is wrong with the following function prototype?

   ```
   char *f(char *p, int x = 0, char *q);
   ```

3. Most C++ compilers supply nonstandard functions that allow cursor positioning and the like. If your compiler supplies such functions, create a function called **myclreol( )** that clears the line from the current cursor position to the end of the line. However, give this function a parameter that specifies the number of character positions to clear. If the parameter is not specified, automatically clear the entire line. Otherwise, clear only the number of character positions specified by the parameter.

4. What is wrong with the following prototype, which uses a default argument?

   ```
   int f(int count, int max = count);
   ```

5.5	***O****VERLOADING AND AMBIGUITY*

When you are overloading functions, it is possible to introduce ambiguity into your program. Overloading-caused ambiguity can be introduced through type conversions, reference parameters, and default arguments. Further, some types of ambiguity are caused by the overloaded functions themselves. Other types occur in the manner in which an overloaded function is called. Ambiguity must be removed before your program will compile without error.

EXAMPLES

1. One of the most common types of ambiguity is caused by C++'s automatic type conversion rules. As you know, when a function is called with an argument that is of a compatible (but not the same) type as the parameter to which it is being passed, the type of the argument is automatically converted to the target type. In fact, it is this sort of type conversion that allows a function such as **putchar( )** to be called with a character even though its argument is specified as an **int**. However, in some cases, this automatic type conversion will cause an ambiguous situation when a function is overloaded. To see how, examine this program:

```
// This program contains an ambiguity error.
#include <iostream>
using namespace std;

float f(float i)
{
  return i / 2.0;
}

double f(double i)
{
  return i / 3.0;
}

int main()
{
  float x = 10.09;
  double y = 10.09;
```

```
cout << f(x); // unambiguous - use f(float)
cout << f(y); // unambiguous - use f(double)

cout << f(10); // ambiguous, convert 10 to double or float??

return 0;
}
```

As the comments in **main( )** indicate, the compiler is able to select the correct version of **f( )** when it is called with either a **float** or a **double** variable. However, what happens when it is called with an integer? Does the compiler call **f(float)** or **f(double)**? (Both are valid conversions!) In either case, it is valid to promote an integer into either a **float** or a **double**. Thus, the ambiguous situation is created.

This example also points out that ambiguity can be introduced by the way an overloaded function is called. The fact is that there is no inherent ambiguity in the overloaded versions of **f( )** as long as each is called with an unambiguous argument.

2. Here is another example of function overloading that is not ambiguous in and of itself. However, when this function is called with the wrong type of argument, C++'s automatic conversion rules cause an ambiguous situation.

```
// This program is ambiguous.
#include <iostream>
using namespace std;

void f(unsigned char c)
{
  cout << c;
}

void f(char c)
{
  cout << c;
}

int main()
{
  f('c');
  f(86); // which f() is called???
```

```
    return 0;
}
```

Here, when **f( )** is called with the numeric constant 86, the compiler cannot know whether to call **f(unsigned char)** or **f(char)**. Either conversion is equally valid, thus leading to ambiguity.

3. One type of ambiguity is caused when you try to overload functions in which the only difference is the fact that one uses a reference parameter and the other uses the default call-by-value parameter. Given C++'s formal syntax, there is no way for the compiler to know which function to call. Remember, there is no syntactical difference between calling a function that takes a value parameter and calling a function that takes a reference parameter. For example:

```
// An ambiguous program.
#include <iostream>
using namespace std;

int f(int a, int b)
{
  return a+b;
}


// this is inherently ambiguous
int f(int a, int &b)
{
  return a-b;
}

int main()
{
  int x=1, y=2;

  cout << f(x, y); // which version of f() is called???

  return 0;
}
```

Here, **f(x, y)** is ambiguous because it could be calling either version of the function. In fact, the compiler will flag an error before this statement is even specified because the overloading of the two functions is inherently ambiguous and no reference to them could be resolved.

4. Another type of ambiguity is caused when you are overloading a function in which one or more overloaded functions use a default argument. Consider this program:

```cpp
// Ambiguity based on default arguments plus overloading.
#include <iostream>
using namespace std;

int f(int a)
{
  return a*a;
}

int f(int a, int b = 0)
{
  return a*b;
}

int main()
{
  cout << f(10, 2); // calls f(int, int)
  cout << f(10); // ambiguous - call f(int) or f(int, int)???

  return 0;
}
```

Here the call **f(10, 2)** is perfectly acceptable and unambiguous. However, the compiler has no way of knowing whether the call **f(10)** is calling the first version of **f( )** or the second version with **b** defaulting.

---

1. Try to compile each of the preceding ambiguous programs. Make a mental note of the types of error messages they generate. This will help you recognize ambiguity errors when they creep into your own programs.

5.6

*F*INDING THE ADDRESS OF AN OVERLOADED FUNCTION

To conclude this chapter, you will learn how to find the address of an overloaded function. Just as in C, you can assign the address of a function (that is, its entry point) to a pointer and access that function via that pointer. A function's address is obtained by putting its name on the right side of an assignment statement without any parentheses or arguments. For example, if **zap( )** is a function, assuming proper declarations, this is a valid way to assign **p** the address of **zap( )**:

```
p = zap;
```

   In C, any type of pointer can be used to point to a function because there is only one function that it can point to. However, in C++ the situation is a bit more complex because a function can be overloaded. Thus, there must be some mechanism that determines which function's address is obtained.

   The solution is both elegant and effective. When obtaining the address of an overloaded function, it is *the way the pointer is declared* that determines which overloaded function's address will be obtained. In essence, the pointer's declaration is matched against those of the overloaded functions. The function whose declaration matches is the one whose address is used.

EXAMPLE

1. Here is a program that contains two versions of a function called **space( )**. The first version outputs **count** number of spaces to the screen. The second version outputs **count** number of whatever type of character is passed to **ch**. In **main( )**, two function pointers are declared. The first one is specified as a pointer to a function having only one integer parameter. The second is declared as a pointer to a function taking two parameters.

```
/* Illustrate assigning function pointers to
   overloaded functions. */
#include <iostream>
using namespace std;
```

```
// Output count number of spaces.
void space(int count)
{
  for( ; count; count--) cout << ' ';
}

// Output count number of chs.
void space(int count, char ch)
{
  for( ; count; count--) cout << ch;
}

int main()
{
  /* Create a pointer to void function with
     one int parameter. */
  void (*fp1)(int);

  /* Create a pointer to void function with
     one int parameter and one character parameter. */
  void (*fp2)(int, char);

  fp1 = space; // gets address of space(int)

  fp2 = space; // gets address of space(int, char)

  fp1(22);   // output 22 spaces
  cout << "|\n";

  fp2(30, 'x'); // output 30 x's
  cout << "|\n";

  return 0;
}
```

As the comments illustrate, the compiler is able to determine which overloaded function to obtain the address of based upon how **fp1** and **fp2** are declared.

To review: When you assign the address of an overloaded function to a function pointer, it is the declaration of the pointer that determines which function's address is assigned. Further, the declaration of the function pointer must exactly match one and only one of the overloaded functions. If it does not, ambiguity will be introduced, causing a compile-time error.

EXERCISE

1. Following are two overloaded functions. Show how to obtain the address of each.

```
int dif(int a, int b)
{
  return a-b;
}

float dif(float a, float b)
{
  return a-b;
}
```

S KILLS CHECK

Mastery
Skills Check

At this point you should be able to perform the following exercises and answer the questions.

1. Overload the **date( )** constructor from Section 5.1, Example 3, so that it accepts a parameter of type **time_t**. (Remember, **time_t** is a type defined by the standard time and date functions found in your C++ compiler's library.)

2. What is wrong with the following fragment?

```
class samp {
  int a;
public:
  samp(int i) { a = i; }
  // ...
}:
```

```
// ...

int main()
{
  samp x, y(10);

  // ...
}
```

3. Give two reasons why you might want (or need) to overload a class's constructor.

4. What is the most common general form of a copy constructor?

5. What type of operations will cause the copy constructor to be invoked?

6. Briefly explain what the **overload** keyword does and why it is no longer needed.

7. Briefly describe a default argument.

8. Create a function called **reverse( )** that takes two parameters. The first parameter, called **str**, is a pointer to a string that will be reversed upon return from the function. The second parameter is called **count,** and it specifies how many characters of **str** to reverse. Give **count** a default value that, when present, tells **reverse( )** to reverse the entire string.

9. What is wrong with the following prototype?

```
char *wordwrap(char *str, int size=0, char ch);
```

10. Explain some ways that ambiguity can be introduced when you are overloading functions.

11. What is wrong with the following fragment?

```
void compute(double *num, int divisor=1);
void compute(double *num);
// ...
compute(&x);
```

12. When you are assigning the address of an overloaded function to a pointer, what is it that determines which version of the function is used?

**Cumulative
Skills Check**

This section checks how well you have integrated material in this chapter with that from the preceding chapters.

1. Create a function called **order( )** that takes two integer reference parameters. If the first argument is greater than the second argument, reverse the two arguments. Otherwise, take no action. That is, order the two arguments used to call **order( )** so that, upon return, the first argument will be less than the second. For example, given

```
int x=1, y=0;
order(x, y);
```

following the call, **x** will be 0 and **y** will be 1.

2. Why are the following two overloaded functions inherently ambiguous?

```
int f(int a);
int f(int &a);
```

3. Explain why using a default argument is related to function overloading.

4. Given the following partial class, add the necessary constructor functions so that both declarations within **main( )** are valid. (Hint: You need to overload **samp( )** twice.)

```
class samp {
  int a;
public:
  // add constructor functions
  int get_a() { return a; }
};

int main()
{
  samp ob(88); // init ob's a to 88
  samp obarray[10]; // noninitialized 10-element array

  // ...
}
```

5. Briefly explain why copy constructors are needed.

6

Introducing Operator Overloading

chapter objectives

6.1 The basics of operator overloading

6.2 Overloading binary operators

6.3 Overloading the relational and logical operators

6.4 Overloading a unary operator

6.5 Using friend operator functions

6.6 A closer look at the assignment operator

6.7 Overloading the **[ ]** subscript operator

T HIS chapter introduces another important C++ feature: operator overloading. This feature allows you to define the meaning of the C++ operators relative to classes that you define. By overloading operators, you can seamlessly add new data types to your program.

Review
Skills Check

Before proceeding, you should be able to correctly answer the following questions and do the exercises.

1. Show how to overload the constructor for the following class so that uninitialized objects can also be created. (When creating uninitialized objects, give **x** and **y** the value 0.)

```
class myclass {
  int x, y;
public:
  myclass(int i, int j) { x=i; y=j; }
  // ...
};
```

2. Using the class from Question 1, show how you can avoid overloading **myclass( )** by using default arguments.

3. What is wrong with the following declaration?

```
int f(int a=0, double balance);
```

4. What is wrong with these two overloaded functions?

```
void f(int a);
void f(int &a);
```

5. When is it appropriate to use default arguments? When is it probably a bad idea?

6. Given the following class definition, is it possible to dynamically allocate an array of these objects?

```
class test {
  char *p;
  int *q;
  int count;
public:
  test(char *x, int *y, int c) {
    p = x;
    q = y;
    count = c;
  }
  // ...
};
```

7. What is a copy constructor and under what circumstances is it called?

6.1   *THE BASICS OF OPERATOR OVERLOADING*

Operator overloading resembles function overloading. In fact, operator overloading is really just a type of function overloading. However, some additional rules apply. For example, an operator is always overloaded relative to a user-defined type, such as a class. Other differences will be discussed as needed.

When an operator is overloaded, that operator loses none of its original meaning. Instead, it gains additional meaning relative to the class for which it is defined.

To overload an operator, you create an *operator function.* Most often an operator function is a member or a friend of the class for which it is defined. However, there is a slight difference between a member operator function and a friend operator function. The first part of this chapter discusses the creation of member operator functions. Then friend operator functions are discussed.

The general form of a member operator function is shown here:

return-type class-name::operator#(arg-list)
{
  // operation to be performed
}

The return type of an operator function is often the class for which it is defined. (However, an operator function is free to return any type.) The operator being overloaded is substituted for the #. For example, if the + is being overloaded, the function name would be **operator +**. The contents of *arg-list* vary depending upon how the operator function is implemented and the type of operator being overloaded.

There are two important restrictions to remember when you are overloading an operator. First, the precedence of the operator cannot be changed. Second, the number of operands that an operator takes cannot be altered. For example, you cannot overload the / operator so that it takes only one operand.

Most C++ operators can be overloaded. The only operators that you cannot overload are shown here:

.   ::   .*   ?

Also, you cannot overload the preprocessor operators. (The **.*** operator is highly specialized and is beyond the scope of this book.)

Remember that C++ defines operators very broadly, including such things as the **[ ]** subscript operators, the **( )** function call operators, **new** and **delete**, and the **.** (dot) and **->** (arrow) operators. However, this chapter concentrates on overloading the most commonly used operators.

Except for the **=**, operator functions are inherited by any derived class. However, a derived class is free to overload any operator it chooses (including those overloaded by the base class) relative to itself.

You have been using two overloaded operators: **<<** and **>>**. These operators have been overloaded to perform console I/O. As mentioned, overloading these operators to perform I/O does not prevent them from performing their traditional jobs of left shift and right shift.

While it is permissible for you to have an operator function perform *any* activity—whether related to the traditional use of the operator or not—it is best to have an overloaded operator's actions stay within the spirit of the operator's traditional use. When you create overloaded operators that stray from this principle, you run the risk of substantially destructuring your program. For example, overloading the / so that the phrase "I like C++" is written to a disk file 300 times is a fundamentally confusing misuse of operator overloading!

The preceding paragraph notwithstanding, there will be times when you need to use an operator in a way not related to its traditional usage. The two best examples of this are the << and >> operators, which are overloaded for console I/O. However, even in these cases, the left and right arrows provide a visual "clue" to their meaning. Therefore, if you need to overload an operator in a nonstandard way, make the greatest effort possible to use an appropriate operator.

One final point: operator functions cannot have default arguments.

6.2 OVERLOADING BINARY OPERATORS

When a member operator function overloads a binary operator, the function will have only one parameter. This parameter will receive the object that is on the right side of the operator. The object on the left side is the object that generates the call to the operator function and is passed implicitly by **this**.

It is important to understand that operator functions can be written with many variations. The examples here and elsewhere in this chapter are not exhaustive, but they do illustrate several of the most common techniques.

EXAMPLES

1. The following program overloads the **+** operator relative to the **coord** class. This class is used to maintain X,Y coordinates.

```
// Overload the + relative to coord class.
#include <iostream>
using namespace std;

class coord {
  int x, y; // coordinate values
public:
  coord() { x=0; y=0; }
  coord(int i, int j) { x=i; y=j; }
  void get_xy(int &i, int &j) { i=x; j=y; }
  coord operator+(coord ob2);
};

// Overload + relative to coord class.
coord coord::operator+(coord ob2)
{
```

```
   coord temp;
   temp.x = x + ob2.x;
   temp.y = y + ob2.y;

   return temp;
}

int main()
{
   coord o1(10, 10), o2(5, 3), o3;
   int x, y;

   o3 = o1 + o2; // add two objects - this calls operator+()

   o3.get_xy(x, y);
   cout << "(o1+o2) X: " << x << ", Y: " << y << "\n";

   return 0;
}
```

This program displays the following:

```
(o1+o2) X: 15, Y: 13
```

Let's look closely at this program. The **operator + ( )** function
returns an object of type **coord** that has the sum of each
operand's X coordinates in **x** and the sum of the Y coordinates
in **y**. Notice that a temporary object called **temp** is used inside
operator + ( ) to hold the result, and it is this object that is
returned. Notice also that neither operand is modified. The
reason for **temp** is easy to understand. In this situation (as in
most), the **+** has been overloaded in a manner consistent with
its normal arithmetic use. Therefore, it was important that
neither operand be changed. For example, when you add $10 + 4$,
the result is 14, but neither the 10 nor the 4 is modified. Thus, a
temporary object is needed to hold the result.

The reason that the **operator + ( )** function returns an object
of type **coord** is that it allows the result of the addition
of **coord** objects to be used in larger expressions. For example,
the statement

```
o3 = o1 + o2;
```

is valid only because the result of **o1 + o2** is a **coord** object that can be assigned to **o3**. If a different type had been returned, this statement would have been invalid. Further, by returning a **coord** object, the addition operator allows a string of additions. For example, this is a valid statement:

```
o3 = o1 + o2 + o1 + o3;
```

Although there will be situations in which you want an operator function to return something other than an object for which it is defined, most of the time operator functions that you create will return an object of their class. (The major exception to this rule is when the relational and logical operators are overloaded. This situation is examined in Section 6.3, "Overloading the Relational and Logical Operators," later in this chapter.)

One final point about this example. Because a **coord** object is returned, the following statement is also perfectly valid:

```
(o1+o2).get_xy(x, y);
```

Here the temporary object returned by **operator + ( )** is used directly. Of course, after this statement has executed, the temporary object is destroyed.

2. The following version of the preceding program overloads the **–** and the **=** operators relative to the **coord** class.

```
// Overload the +, -, and = relative to coord class.
#include <iostream>
using namespace std;

class coord {
  int x, y; // coordinate values
public:
  coord() { x=0; y=0; }
  coord(int i, int j) { x=i; y=j; }
  void get_xy(int &i, int &j) { i=x; j=y; }
  coord operator+(coord ob2);
  coord operator-(coord ob2);
  coord operator=(coord ob2);
};

// Overload + relative to coord class.
```

```
coord coord::operator+(coord ob2)
{
  coord temp;

  temp.x = x + ob2.x;
  temp.y = y + ob2.y;

  return temp;
}

// Overload - relative to coord class.
coord coord::operator-(coord ob2)
{
  coord temp;

  temp.x = x - ob2.x;
  temp.y = y - ob2.y;

  return temp;
}

// Overload = relative to coord.
coord coord::operator=(coord ob2)
{
  x = ob2.x;
  y = ob2.y;

  return *this; // return the object that is assigned
}

int main()
{
  coord o1(10, 10), o2(5, 3), o3;
  int x, y;

  o3 = o1 + o2; // add two objects - this calls operator+()
  o3.get_xy(x, y);
  cout << "(o1+o2) X: " << x << ", Y: " << y << "\n";

  o3 = o1 - o2; // subtract two objects
  o3.get_xy(x, y);
  cout << "(o1-o2) X: " << x << ", Y: " << y << "\n";

  o3 = o1; // assign an object
```

```
        o3.get_xy(x, y);
        cout << "(o3=o1) X: " << x << ", Y: " << y << "\n";

        return 0;
}
```

The **operator–( )** function is implemented similarly to **operator+( )**. However, the above example illustrates a crucial point when you are overloading an operator in which the order of the operands is important. When the **operator+ ( )** function was created, it did not matter which order the operands were in. (That is, A + B is the same as B + A.) However, the subtraction operation is order dependent. Therefore, to correctly overload the subtraction operator, it is necessary to subtract the operand on the right from the operand on the left. Because it is the left operand that generates the call to **operator–( )**, the subtraction must be in this order:

```
x - ob2.x;
```

Remember *When a binary operator is overloaded, the left operand is passed implicitly to the function and the right operand is passed as an argument.*

Now look at the assignment operator function. The first thing you should notice is that the left operand (that is, the object being assigned a value) is modified by the operation. This is in keeping with the normal meaning of assignment. The second thing to notice is that the function returns ***this**. That is, the **operator=( )** function returns the object that is being assigned to. The reason for this is to allow a series of assignments to be made. As you should know, in C++, the following type of statement is syntactically correct (and, indeed, very common):

```
a = b = c = d = 0;
```

By returning ***this,** the overloaded assignment operator allows objects of type **coord** to be used in a similar fashion. For example, this is perfectly valid:

```
o3 = o2 = o1;
```

Keep in mind that there is no rule that requires an overloaded assignment function to return the object that receives the assignment. However, if you want the overloaded = to behave relative to its class the way it does for the built-in types, it must return *this.

3. It is possible to overload an operator relative to a class so that the operand on the right side is an object of a built-in type, such as an integer, instead of the class for which the operator function is a member. For example, here the + operator is overloaded to add an integer value to a **coord** object:

```cpp
// Overload + for ob + int as well as ob + ob.
#include <iostream>
using namespace std;

class coord {
  int x, y; // coordinate values
public:
  coord() { x=0; y=0; }
  coord(int i, int j) { x=i; y=j; }
  void get_xy(int &i, int &j) { i=x; j=y; }
  coord operator+(coord ob2); // ob + ob
  coord operator+(int i); // ob + int
};

// Overload + relative to coord class.
coord coord::operator+(coord ob2)
{
  coord temp;

  temp.x = x + ob2.x;
  temp.y = y + ob2.y;

  return temp;
}

// Overload + for ob + int
coord coord::operator+(int i)
{
  coord temp;

  temp.x = x + i;
  temp.y = y + i;
  return temp;
```

```
}

int main()
{
  coord o1(10, 10), o2(5, 3), o3;
  int x, y;

  o3 = o1 + o2; // add two objects - calls operator+(coord)
  o3.get_xy(x, y);
  cout << "(o1+o2) X: " << x << ", Y: " << y << "\n";

  o3 = o1 + 100; // add object + int - calls operator+(int)
  o3.get_xy(x, y);
  cout << "(o1+100) X: " << x << ", Y: " << y << "\n";

  return 0;
}
```

It is important to remember that when you are overloading a
member operator function so that an object can be used in an
operation involving a built-in type, the built-in type must be on
the right side of the operator. The reason for this is easy to
understand: It is the object on the left that generates the call to
the operator function. For instance, what happens when the
compiler sees the following statement?

```
o3 = 19 + o1;  // int + ob
```

There is no built-in operation defined to handle the addition of
an integer to an object. The overloaded **operator + (int i)**
function works only when the object is on the left. Therefore,
this statement generates a compile-time error. (Soon you will
see one way around this restriction.)

4. You can use a reference parameter in an operator function. For
   example, this is a perfectly acceptable way to overload the **+**
   operator relative to the **coord** class:

```
// Overload + relative to coord class using references.
coord coord::operator+(coord &ob2)
{
  coord temp;
```

```
temp.x = x + ob2.x;
temp.y = y + ob2.y;

return temp;
}
```

One reason for using a reference parameter in an operator function is efficiency. Passing objects as parameters to functions often incurs a large amount of overhead and consumes a significant number of CPU cycles. However, passing the address of an object is always quick and efficient. If the operator is going to be used often, using a reference parameter will generally improve performance significantly.

Another reason for using a reference parameter is to avoid the trouble caused when a copy of an operand is destroyed. As you know from previous chapters, when an argument is passed by value, a copy of that argument is made. If that object has a destructor function, when the function terminates, the copy's destructor is called. In some cases it is possible for the destructor to destroy something needed by the calling object. If this is the case, using a reference parameter instead of a value parameter is an easy (and efficient) way around the problem. Of course, you could also define a copy constructor that would prevent this problem in the general case.

EXERCISES

1. Relative to **coord**, overload the * and / operators. Demonstrate that they work.

2. Why would the following be an inappropriate use of an overloaded operator?

```
coord coord::operator%(coord ob)
{
  double i;

  cout << "Enter a number: ";
  cin >> i;
  cout << "root of " << i << " is ";
```

```
    cout << sqr(i);
}
```

3. On your own, experiment by changing the return types of the operator functions to something other than **coord**. See what types of errors result.

6.3 # *O*VERLOADING THE RELATIONAL AND LOGICAL OPERATORS

It is possible to overload the relational and logical operators. When you overload the relational and logical operators so that they behave in their traditional manner, you will not want the operator functions to return an object of the class for which they are defined. Instead, they will return an integer that indicates either true or false. This not only allows these operator functions to return a true/false value, it also allows the operators to be integrated into larger relational and logical expressions that involve other types of data.

Note

*If you are using a modern C++ compiler, you can also have an overloaded relational or logical operator function return a value of type **bool**, although there is no advantage to doing so. As explained in Chapter 1, the **bool** type defines only two values: **true** and **false**. These values are automatically converted into nonzero and 0 values. Integer nonzero and 0 values are automatically converted into **true** and **false**.*

EXAMPLE

1. In the following program, the **= =** and **&&** operators are overloaded:

```
// Overload the == and && relative to coord class.
#include <iostream>
using namespace std;

class coord {
  int x, y; // coordinate values
```

```cpp
public:
  coord() { x=0; y=0; }
  coord(int i, int j) { x=i; y=j; }
  void get_xy(int &i, int &j) { i=x; j=y; }
  int operator==(coord ob2);
  int operator&&(coord ob2);
};

// Overload the == operator for coord.
int coord::operator==(coord ob2)
{
  return x==ob2.x && y==ob2.y;
}

// Overload the && operator for coord.
int coord::operator&&(coord ob2)
{
  return (x && ob2.x) && (y && ob2.y);
}

int main()
{
  coord o1(10, 10), o2(5, 3), o3(10, 10), o4(0, 0);

  if(o1==o2) cout << "o1 same as o2\n";
  else cout << "o1 and o2 differ\n";

  if(o1==o3) cout << "o1 same as o3\n";
  else cout << "o1 and o3 differ\n";

  if(o1&&o2) cout << "o1 && o2 is true\n";
  else cout << "o1 && o2 is false\n";

  if(o1&&o4) cout << "o1 && o4 is true\n";
  else cout << "o1 && o4 is false\n";

  return 0;
}
```

1. Overload the < and > operators relative to the **coord** class.

6.4 *O*VERLOADING A UNARY OPERATOR

Overloading a unary operator is similar to overloading a binary operator except that there is only one operand to deal with. When you overload a unary operator using a member function, the function has no parameters. Since there is only one operand, it is this operand that generates the call to the operator function. There is no need for another parameter.

1. The following program overloads the increment operator (+ +) relative to the **coord** class:

```
// Overload ++ relative to coord class.
#include <iostream>
using namespace std;

class coord {
  int x, y; // coordinate values

public:
  coord() { x=0; y=0; }
  coord(int i, int j) { x=i; y=j; }
  void get_xy(int &i, int &j) { i=x; j=y; }
  coord operator++();
};

// Overload ++ for coord class.
coord coord::operator++()
{
  x++;
  y++;
```

```
   return *this;
}

int main()
{
  coord o1(10, 10);
  int x, y;

  ++o1; // increment an object
  o1.get_xy(x, y);
  cout << "(++o1) X: " << x << ", Y: " << y << "\n";

  return 0;
}
```

Since the increment operator is designed to increase its operand by 1, the overloaded **+ +** modifies the object it operates upon. The function also returns the object that it increments. This allows the increment operator to be used as part of a larger statement, such as this:

```
o2 = ++o1;
```

As with the binary operators, there is no rule that says you must overload a unary operator so that it reflects its normal meaning. However, most of the time this is what you will want to do.

2. In early versions of C++, when an increment or decrement operator was overloaded, there was no way to determine whether an overloaded **+ +** or **– –** preceded or followed its operand. That is, assuming the preceding program, these two statements would have been identical:

```
o1++;
++o1;
```

However, the modern specification for C++ has defined a way by which the compiler can distinguish between these two statements. To accomplish this, create two versions of the **operator + +( )** function. The first is defined as shown in the preceding example. The second is declared like this:

```
coord coord::operator++(int notused);
```

If the **+ +** precedes its operand, the **operator + +( )** function is called. However, if the **+ +** follows its operand, the **operator + +(int notused)** function is used. In this case, **notused** will always be passed the value 0. Therefore, if the difference between prefix and postfix increment or decrement is important to your class objects, you will need to implement both operator functions.

3. As you know, the minus sign is both a binary and a unary operator in C++. You might be wondering how you can overload it so that it retains both of these uses relative to a class that you create. The solution is actually quite easy: you simply overload it twice, once as a binary operator and once as a unary operator. This program shows how:

```cpp
// Overload the - relative to coord class.
#include <iostream>
using namespace std;

class coord {
  int x, y; // coordinate values
public:
  coord() { x=0; y=0; }
  coord(int i, int j) { x=i; y=j; }
  void get_xy(int &i, int &j) { i=x; j=y; }
  coord operator-(coord ob2); // binary minus
  coord operator-(); // unary minus
};

// Overload - relative to coord class.
coord coord::operator-(coord ob2)
{
  coord temp;

  temp.x = x - ob2.x;
  temp.y = y - ob2.y;

  return temp;
}

// Overload unary - for coord class.
coord coord::operator-()
```

```
{
  x = -x;
  y = -y;
  return *this;
}

int main()
{
  coord o1(10, 10), o2(5, 7);
  int x, y;

  o1 = o1 - o2; // subtraction
  o1.get_xy(x, y);
  cout << "(o1-o2) X: " << x << ", Y: " << y << "\n";

  o1 = -o1; // negation
  o1.get_xy(x, y);
  cout << "(-o1) X: " << x << ", Y: " << y << "\n";

  return 0;
}
```

As you can see, when the minus is overloaded as a binary operator, it takes one parameter. When it is overloaded as a unary operator, it takes no parameter. This difference in the number of parameters is what makes it possible for the minus to be overloaded for both operations. As the program indicates, when the minus sign is used as a binary operator, the **operator–(coord ob2)** function is called. When it is used as a unary minus, the **operator–( )** function is called.

EXERCISES

1. Overload the **– –** operator for the **coord** class. Create both its prefix and postfix forms.

2. Overload the **+** operator for the **coord** class so that it is both a binary operator (as shown earlier) and a unary operator. When it is used as a unary operator, have the **+** make any negative coordinate value positive.

*U*SING FRIEND OPERATOR FUNCTIONS

As mentioned at the start of this chapter, it is possible to overload an operator relative to a class by using a friend rather than a member function. As you know, a friend function does not have a **this** pointer. In the case of a binary operator, this means that a friend operator function is passed both operands explicitly. For unary operators, the single operand is passed. All other things being equal, there is no reason to use a friend rather than a member operator function, with one important exception, which is discussed in the examples.

Remember

You cannot use a friend to overload the assignment operator. The assignment operator can be overloaded only by a member operator function.

EXAMPLES

1. Here **operator + ( )** is overloaded for the **coord** class by using a friend function:

```
// Overload the + relative to coord class using a friend.
#include <iostream>
using namespace std;

class coord {
  int x, y; // coordinate values
public:
  coord() { x=0; y=0; }
  coord(int i, int j) { x=i; y=j; }
  void get_xy(int &i, int &j) { i=x; j=y; }
  friend coord operator+(coord ob1, coord ob2);
};

// Overload + using a friend.
coord operator+(coord ob1, coord ob2)
{
  coord temp;

  temp.x = ob1.x + ob2.x;
  temp.y = ob1.y + ob2.y;
```

```
    return temp;
}

int main()
{
    coord o1(10, 10), o2(5, 3), o3;
    int x, y;

    o3 = o1 + o2; // add two objects - this calls operator+()
    o3.get_xy(x, y);
    cout << "(o1+o2) X: " << x << ", Y: " << y << "\n";

    return 0;
}
```

Notice that the left operand is passed to the first parameter and the right operand is passed to the second parameter.

2. Overloading an operator by using a friend provides one very important feature that member functions do not. Using a friend operator function, you can allow objects to be used in operations involving built-in types in which the built-in type is on the left side of the operator. As you saw earlier in this chapter, it is possible to overload a binary member operator function such that the left operand is an object and the right operand is a built-in type. But it is not possible to use a member function to allow the built-in type to occur on the left side of the operator. For example, assuming an overloaded member operator function, the first statement shown here is legal; the second is not:

```
ob1 = ob2 + 10; // legal
ob1 = 10 + ob2; // illegal
```

While it is possible to organize such statements like the first, always having to make sure that the object is on the left side of the operand and the built-in type on the right can be a cumbersome restriction. The solution to this problem is to make the overloaded operator functions friends and define both possible situations.

As you know, a friend operator function is explicitly passed *both* operands. Thus, it is possible to define one overloaded friend function so that the left operand is an object and the right operand is the other type. Then you could overload the operator again with the left operand being the built-in type and the right operand being the object. The following program illustrates this method:

```cpp
// Use friend operator functions to add flexibility.
#include <iostream>
using namespace std;

class coord {
  int x, y; // coordinate values

public:
  coord() { x=0; y=0; }
  coord(int i, int j) { x=i; y=j; }
  void get_xy(int &i, int &j) { i=x; j=y; }
  friend coord operator+(coord ob1, int i);
  friend coord operator+(int i, coord ob1);
};

// Overload for ob + int.
coord operator+(coord ob1, int i)
{
  coord temp;

  temp.x = ob1.x + i;
  temp.y = ob1.y + i;

  return temp;
}

// Overload for int + ob.
coord operator+(int i, coord ob1)
{
  coord temp;

  temp.x = ob1.x + i;
  temp.y = ob1.y + i;

  return temp;
}

int main()
{
```

```
coord o1(10, 10);
int x, y;


o1 = o1 + 10; // object + integer
o1.get_xy(x, y);
cout << "(o1+10) X: " << x << ", Y: " << y << "\n";

o1 = 99 + o1; // integer + object
o1.get_xy(x, y);
cout << "(99+o1) X: " << x << ", Y: " << y << "\n";

return 0;
}
```

As a result of overloading friend operator functions for both
situations, both of these statements are now valid:

```
o1 = o1 + 10;
o1 = 99 + o1;
```

3. If you want to use a friend operator function to overload either
the **+ +** or **– –** unary operator, you must pass the operand to the
function as a reference parameter. This is because friend
functions do not have **this** pointers. Remember that the
increment and decrement operators imply that the operand will
be modified. However, if you overload these operators by using
a friend that uses a value parameter, any modifications that
occur to the parameter inside the friend operator function will
not affect the object that generated the call. And since no
pointer to the object is passed implicitly (that is, there is no **this**
pointer) when a friend is used, there is no way for the
increment or decrement to affect the operand.

However, if you pass the operand to the friend as a
reference parameter, changes that occur inside the friend
function affect the object that generates the call. For example,
here is a program that overloads the **+ +** operator by using a
friend function:

```
// Overload the ++ using a friend.
#include <iostream>
using namespace std;
```

```
class coord {
  int x, y; // coordinate values
public:
  coord() { x=0; y=0; }
  coord(int i, int j) { x=i; y=j; }
  void get_xy(int &i, int &j) { i=x; j=y; }
  friend coord operator++(coord &ob);
};

// Overload ++ using a friend.
coord operator++(coord &ob) // use reference parameter
{
  ob.x++;
  ob.y++;

  return ob; // return object generating the call
}

int main()
{
  coord o1(10, 10);
  int x, y;

  ++o1;  // o1 is passed by reference
  o1.get_xy(x, y);
  cout << "(++o1) X: " << x << ", Y: " << y << "\n";

  return 0;
}
```

If you are using a modern compiler, you can also distinguish
between the prefix and postfix forms of the increment or
decrement operators when using a friend operator function in
much the same way you did when using member functions. You
simply add an integer parameter when defining the postfix
version. For example, here are the prototypes for both the prefix
and postfix versions of the increment operator relative to the
coord class:

```
coord operator++(coord &ob); // prefix
coord operator++(coord &ob, int notused); // postfix
```

If the **+ +** precedes its operand, the **operator + +(coord &ob)** function is called. However, if the **+ +** follows its operand, the **operator + +(coord &ob, int notused)** function is used. In this case, **notused** will be passed the value 0.

EXERCISES

1. Overload the **−** and **/** operators for the **coord** class using friend functions.

2. Overload the **coord** class so it can use **coord** objects in operations in which an integer value can be multiplied by each coordinate. Allow the operations to use either order: *ob * int* or *int * ob*.

3. Explain why the solution to Exercise 2 requires the use of friend operator functions.

4. Using a friend, show how to overload the **− −** relative to the **coord** class. Define both the prefix and postfix forms.

6.6   *A CLOSER LOOK AT THE ASSIGNMENT OPERATOR*

As you have seen, it is possible to overload the assignment operator relative to a class. By default, when the assignment operator is applied to an object, a bitwise copy of the object on the right is put into the object on the left. If this is what you want, there is no reason to provide your own **operator =( )** function. However, there are cases in which a strict bitwise copy is not desirable. You saw some examples of this in Chapter 3, in cases in which an object allocates memory. In these types of situations, you will want to provide a special assignment operation.

EXAMPLE

1. Here is another version of the **strtype** class that you have seen in various forms in the preceding chapters. However, this version overloads the **=** operator so that the pointer **p** is not overwritten by an assignment operation.

```cpp
#include <iostream>
#include <cstring>
#include <cstdlib>
using namespace std;

class strtype {
  char *p;
  int len;
public:
  strtype(char *s);
  ~strtype() {
    cout << "Freeing " << (unsigned) p << '\n';
    delete [] p;
   }
  char *get() { return p; }
  strtype &operator=(strtype &ob);
};

strtype::strtype(char *s)
{
  int l;

  l = strlen(s)+1;

  p = new char [l];
  if(!p) {
    cout << "Allocation error\n";
    exit(1);
  }

  len = l;
  strcpy(p, s);
}
```

```
// Assign an object.
strtype &strtype::operator=(strtype &ob)
{
  // see if more memory is needed
  if(len < ob.len) { // need to allocate more memory
    delete [] p;
    p = new char [ob.len];
    if(!p) {
      cout << "Allocation error\n";
      exit(1);
    }
  }
  len = ob.len;
  strcpy(p, ob.p);
  return *this;
}

int main()
{
  strtype a("Hello"), b("There");

  cout << a.get() << '\n';
  cout << b.get() << '\n';

  a = b; // now p is not overwritten

  cout << a.get() << '\n';
  cout << b.get() << '\n';

  return 0;
}
```

As you can see, the overloaded assignment operator prevents **p** from being overwritten. It first checks to see if the object on the left has allocated enough memory to hold the string that is being assigned to it. If it hasn't, that memory is freed and another portion is allocated. Then the string is copied to that memory and the length is copied into **len**.

Notice two other important features about the **operator = ( )** function. First, it takes a reference parameter. This prevents a copy of the object on the right side of the assignment from being made. As you know from previous chapters, when a copy of an object is made when passed to a function, that copy is destroyed when the function terminates. In this case, destroying the copy would call the destructor function, which would free **p**. However, this is the same **p** still needed by the object used as an argument. Using a reference parameter prevents this problem.

The second important feature of the **operator = ( )** function is that it returns a reference, not an object. The reason for this is the same as the reason it uses a reference parameter. When a function returns an object, a temporary object is created that is destroyed after the return is complete. However, this means that the temporary object's destructor will be called, causing **p** to be freed, but **p** (and the memory it points to) is still needed by the object being assigned a value. Therefore, by returning a reference, you prevent a temporary object from being created.

As you learned in Chapter 5, creating a copy constructor is another way to prevent both of the problems described in the preceding two paragraphs. But the copy constructor might not be as efficient a solution as using a reference parameter and a reference return type. This is because using a reference prevents the overhead associated with copying an object in either circumstance. As you can see, there are often several ways to accomplish the same end in C++. Learning to choose between them is part of becoming an excellent C++ programmer.

EXERCISE

1. Given the following class declaration, fill in all the details that will create a dynamic array type. That is, allocate memory for the array, storing a pointer to this memory in **p**. Store the size of the array, in bytes, in **size**. Have **put( )** return a reference to the specified element, and have **get( )** return the value of a specified element. Don't allow the boundaries of the array to be overrun. Also, overload the assignment operator so that the allocated memory of each array is not accidentally destroyed when one array is assigned to another. (In the next section you will see a way to improve your solution to this exercise.)

```
class dynarray {
  int *p;
  int size;
public:
  dynarray(int s); // pass size of array in s
  int &put(int i); // return reference to element i
  int get(int i);  // return value of element i
  // create operator=() function
};
```

6.7 *O*VERLOADING THE [ ] SUBSCRIPT OPERATOR

The last operator that we will overload is the **[ ]** array subscripting operator. In C++, the **[ ]** is considered a binary operator for the purposes of overloading. The **[ ]** can be overloaded only by a member function. Therefore, the general form of a member **operator[ ]( )** function is as shown here:

type class-name::operator[ ](int *index*)
{
  // ...
}

Technically, the parameter does not have to be of type **int**, but **operator[ ]( )** functions are typically used to provide array subscripting and as such an integer value is generally used.

To understand how the **[ ]** operator works, assume that an object called **O** is indexed as shown here:

```
O[9]
```

This index will translate into the following call to the **operator[ ]( )** function:

```
O.operator[](9)
```

That is, the value of the expression within the subscripting operator is passed to the **operator[ ]( )** function in its explicit parameter. The **this** pointer will point to **O**, the object that generated the call.

EXAMPLES

1. In the following program, **arraytype** declares an array of five integers. Its constructor function initializes each member of the array. The overloaded **operator[ ]( )** function returns the value of the element specified by its parameter.

```
#include <iostream>
using namespace std;

const int SIZE = 5;

class arraytype {
  int a[SIZE];
public:
  arraytype() {
    int i;
    for(i=0; i<SIZE; i++) a[i] = i;
  }
  int operator[](int i) { return a[i]; }
};

int main()
{
  arraytype ob;
  int i;

  for(i=0; i<SIZE; i++)
    cout << ob[i] << " ";

  return 0;
}
```

This program displays the following output:

```
0 1 2 3 4
```

The initialization of the array **a** by the constructor in this and the following programs is for the sake of illustration only. It is not required.

2. It is possible to design the **operator[ ]( )** function in such a way that the **[ ]** can be used on both the left and right sides of an assignment statement. To do this, return a reference to the element being indexed. For example, this program makes this change and illustrates its use:

```cpp
#include <iostream>
using namespace std;

const int SIZE = 5;

class arraytype {
  int a[SIZE];
public:
  arraytype() {
    int i;
    for(i=0; i<SIZE; i++) a[i] = i;
  }
  int &operator[](int i) { return a[i]; }
};

int main()
{
  arraytype ob;
  int i;

  for(i=0; i<SIZE; i++)
    cout << ob[i] << " ";

  cout << "\n";

  // add 10 to each element in the array
  for(i=0; i<SIZE; i++)
    ob[i] = ob[i]+10;  // [] on left of =

  for(i=0; i<SIZE; i++)
    cout << ob[i] << " ";

  return 0;
}
```

This program displays the following output:

```
0 1 2 3 4
10 11 12 13 14
```

Because the **operator[ ]( )** function now returns a reference to the array element indexed by **i**, it can be used on the left side of an assignment to modify an element of the array. (Of course, it can still be used on the right side as well.) As you can see, this makes objects of **arraytype** act like normal arrays.

3. One advantage of being able to overload the **[ ]** operator is that it allows a better means of implementing safe array indexing. Earlier in this book you saw a simplified way to implement a safe array that relied upon functions such as **get( )** and **put( )** to access the elements of the array. Here you will see a better way to create a safe array that utilizes an overloaded **[ ]** operator. Recall that a safe array is an array that is encapsulated within a class that performs bounds checking. This approach prevents the array boundaries from being overrun. By overloading the **[ ]** operator for such an array, you allow it to be accessed just like a regular array.

   To create a safe array, simply add bounds checking to the **operator[ ]( )** function. The **operator[ ]( )** must also return a reference to the element being indexed. For example, this program adds a range check to the previous array program and proves that it works by generating a boundary error:

```
// A safe array example.
#include <iostream>
#include <cstdlib>
using namespace std;

const int SIZE = 5;

class arraytype {
  int a[SIZE];
public:
  arraytype() {
    int i;
    for(i=0; i<SIZE; i++) a[i] = i;
  }
  int &operator[](int i);
};

// Provide range checking for arraytype.
int &arraytype::operator[](int i)
{
```

```
      if(i<0 || i> SIZE-1) {
        cout << "\nIndex value of ";
        cout << i << " is out of bounds.\n";
        exit(1);
      }
      return a[i];
    }

int main()
{
    arraytype ob;
    int i;

    // this is OK
    for(i=0; i<SIZE; i++)
      cout << ob[i] << " ";

    /* this generates a run-time error because
       SIZE+100 is out of range */
    ob[SIZE+100] = 99; // error!

    return 0;
}
```

In this program, when the statement

```
ob[SIZE+100] = 99;
```

executes, the boundary error is intercepted by **operator[ ]( )** and the program is terminated before any damage can be done.

Because the overloading of the **[ ]** operator allows you to create safe arrays that look and act just like regular arrays, they can be seamlessly integrated into your programming environment. But be careful. A safe array adds overhead that might not be acceptable in all situations. In fact, the added overhead is why C++ does not perform boundary checking on arrays in the first place. However, in applications in which you want to be sure that a boundary error does not take place, a safe array will be worth the effort.

EXERCISES

1. Modify Example 1 in Section 6.6 so that **strtype** overloads the [ ] operator. Have this operator return the character at the specified index. Also, allow the [ ] to be used on the left side of the assignment statement. Demonstrate its use.

2. Modify your answer to Exercise 1 from Section 6.6 so that it uses [ ] to index the dynamic array. That is, replace the **get( )** and **put( )** functions with the [ ] operator.

S*KILLS CHECK*

At this point you should be able to perform the following exercises and answer the questions.

1. Overload the **> >** and **< <** shift operators relative to the **coord** class so that the following types of operations are allowed:

```
ob << integer
ob >> integer
```

Make sure your operators shift the **x** and **y** values by the amount specified.

2. Given the class

```
class three_d {
  int x, y, z;
public:
  three_d(int i, int j, int k)
  {
    x = i; y = j; z = k;
```

```
    }
    three_d() { x=0; y=0; z=0; }
    void get(int &i, int &j, int &k)
    {
        i = x; j = y; k = z;
    }
};
```

overload the +, −, ++, and − − operators for this class. (For the increment and decrement operators, overload only the prefix form.)

3. Rewrite your answer to Question 2 so that it uses reference parameters instead of value parameters to the operator functions. (Hint: You will need to use friend functions for the increment and decrement operators.)

4. How do friend operator functions differ from member operator functions?

5. Explain why you might need to overload the assignment operator.

6. Can **operator = ( )** be a friend function?

7. Overload the + for the **three_d** class in Question 2 so that it accepts the following types of operations:

```
ob + int;
int + ob;
```

8. Overload the = =, ! =, and || operators relative to the **three_d** class from Question 2.

9. Explain the main reason for overloading the [ ] operator.

Cumulative
Skills Check

This section checks how well you have integrated material in this chapter with that from the preceding chapters.

1. Create a **strtype** class that allows the following types of operators:

   ▼ string concatenation using the + operator

   ▼ string assignment using the = operator

   ▼ string comparisons using <, >, and ==

   Feel free to use fixed-length strings. This is a challenging assignment, but with some thought (and experimentation), you should be able to accomplish it.

7

Inheritance

Y OU were introduced to the concept of inheritance earlier in this book. Now it is time to explore it more thoroughly. Inheritance is one of the three principles of OOP and, as such, it is an important feature of C++. Inheritance does more than just support the concept of hierarchical classification; in Chapter 10 you will learn how inheritance provides support for polymorphism, another principal feature of OOP.

The topics covered in this chapter include base class access control and the **protected** access specifier, inheriting multiple base classes, passing arguments to base class constructors, and virtual base classes.

Before proceeding, you should be able to correctly answer the following questions and do the exercises.

1. When an operator is overloaded, does it lose any of its original functionality?

2. Must an operator be overloaded relative to a user-defined type, such as a class?

3. Can the precedence of an overloaded operator be changed? Can the number of operands be altered?

4. Given the following partially completed program, fill in the needed operator functions:

```cpp
#include <iostream>
using namespace std;

class array {
  int nums[10];
public:
  array();
  void set(int n[10]);
  void show();
  array operator+(array ob2);
  array operator-(array ob2);
  int operator==(array ob2);
```

```
};

array::array()
{
  int i;
  for(i=0; i<10; i++) nums[i] = 0;
}

void array::set(int *n)
{
  int i;

  for(i=0; i<10; i++) nums[i] = n[i];
}

void array::show()
{
  int i;

  for(i=0; i<10; i++)
    cout << nums[i] << ' ';

  cout << "\n";
}

// Fill in operator functions.

int main()
{
  array o1, o2, o3;

  int i[10] = {1, 2, 3, 4, 5, 6, 7, 8, 9, 10 };

  o1.set(i);
  o2.set(i);

  o3 = o1 + o2;
  o3.show();

  o3 = o1 - o3;
  o3.show();

  if(o1==o2) cout << "o1 equals o2\n";
  else cout << "o1 does not equal o2\n";
```

```
    if(o1==o3) cout << "o1 equals o3\n";
    else cout << "o1 does not equal o3\n";

    return 0;
}
```

Have the overloaded **+** add each element of each operand. Have the overloaded **−** subtract each element of the right operand from the left. Have the overloaded **= =** return true if each element of each operand is the same and return false otherwise.

5. Convert the solution to Exercise 4 so it overloads the operators by using friend functions.

6. Using the class and support functions from Exercise 4, overload the **+ +** operator by using a member function and overload the **− −** operator by using a friend. (Overload only the prefix forms of **+ +** and **− −**.)

7. Can the assignment operator be overloaded by using a friend function?

7.1 ▮▮▮ **B**ASE CLASS ACCESS CONTROL

When one class inherits another, it uses this general form:

class *derived-class-name* : *access base-class-name* {
  // ...
}

Here *access* is one of three keywords: **public**, **private**, or **protected**. A discussion of the **protected** access specifier is deferred until the next section of this chapter. The other two are discussed here.

The access specifier determines how elements of the base class are inherited by the derived class. When the access specifier for the inherited base class is **public**, all public members of the base become public members of the derived class. If the access specifier is **private**, all public members of the base class become private members of the derived class. In either case, any private members of the base remain private to it and are inaccessible by the derived class.

It is important to understand that if the access specifier is **private**, public members of the base become private members of the derived class, but these members are still accessible by member functions of the derived class.

Technically, *access* is optional. If the specifier is not present, it is **private** by default if the derived class is a **class**. If the derived class is a **struct**, **public** is the default in the absence of an explicit access specifier. Frankly, most programmers explicitly specify *access* for the sake of clarity.

EXAMPLES

1. Here is a short base class and a derived class that inherits it (as public):

```
#include <iostream>
using namespace std;

class base {
  int x;
public:
  void setx(int n) { x = n; }
  void showx() { cout << x << '\n'; }
};

// Inherit as public.
class derived : public base {
  int y;
public:
  void sety(int n) { y = n; }
  void showy() { cout << y << '\n'; }
};

int main()
{
  derived ob;

  ob.setx(10); // access member of base class
  ob.sety(20); // access member of derived class

  ob.showx(); // access member of base class
  ob.showy(); // access member of derived class

  return 0;
}
```

As this program illustrates, because **base** is inherited as public, the public members of **base–setx( )** and **showx( )–** become public members of **derived** and are, therefore, accessible by any other part of the program. Specifically, they are legally called within **main( )**.

2. It is important to understand that just because a derived class inherits a base as public, it does not mean that the derived class has access to the base's private members. For example, this addition to **derived** from the preceding example is incorrect:

```
class base {
  int x;
public:
  void setx(int n) { x = n; }
  void showx() { cout << x << '\n'; }
};

// Inherit as public - this has an error!
class derived : public base {
  int y;
public:
  void sety(int n) { y = n; }

  /* Cannot access private member of base class.
     x is a private member of base and not available
     within derived. */
  void show_sum() { cout << x+y << '\n'; } // Error!

  void showy() { cout << y << '\n'; }
};
```

In this example, the **derived** class attempts to access **x**, which is a private member of **base**. This is an error because the private parts of a base class remain private to it *no matter how it is inherited*.

3. Here is a variation of the program shown in Example 1; this time **derived** inherits **base** as private. This change causes the program to be in error, as indicated in the comments.

```
// This program contains an error.
#include <iostream>
using namespace std;
```

```
class base {
  int x;
public:
  void setx(int n) { x = n; }
  void showx() { cout << x << '\n'; }
};

// Inherit base as private.
class derived : private base {
  int y;
public:
  void sety(int n) { y = n; }
  void showy() { cout << y << '\n'; }
};

int main()
{
  derived ob;

  ob.setx(10); // ERROR - now private to derived class
  ob.sety(20); // access member of derived class - OK

  ob.showx(); // ERROR - now private to derived class
  ob.showy(); // access member of derived class - OK

  return 0;
}
```

As the comments in this (incorrect) program illustrate, both **showx( )** and **setx( )** become private to **derived** and are not accessible outside of it.

Keep in mind that **showx( )** and **setx( )** are still public within **base** no matter how they are inherited by some derived class. This means that an object of type **base** could access these functions anywhere. However, relative to objects of type **derived**, they become private. For example, given this fragment:

```
base base_ob;
```

```
base_ob.setx(1); // is legal because base_ob is of type base
```

the call to **setx( )** is legal because **setx( )** is public within **base**.

4. As stated, even though public members of a base class become private members of a derived class when inherited using the **private** specifier, they are still accessible *within* the derived class. For example, here is a "fixed" version of the preceding program:

```cpp
// This program is fixed.
#include <iostream>
using namespace std;

class base {
  int x;
public:
  void setx(int n) { x = n; }
  void showx() { cout << x << '\n'; }
};

// Inherit base as private.
class derived : private base {
  int y;
public:
  // setx is accessible from within derived
  void setxy(int n, int m) { setx(n); y = m; }
  // showx is accessible from within derived
  void showxy() { showx(); cout << y << '\n'; }
};

int main()
{
  derived ob;

  ob.setxy(10, 20);

  ob.showxy();

  return 0;
}
```

In this case, the functions **setx( )** and **showx( )** are accessed inside the derived class, which is perfectly legal because they are private members of that class.

EXERCISES

1. Examine this skeleton:

```
#include <iostream>
using namespace std;

class mybase {
  int a, b;
public:
  int c;
  void setab(int i, int j) { a = i; b = j; }
  void getab(int &i, int &j) { i = a; j = b; }
};

class derived1 : public mybase {
// ...
};

class derived2 : private mybase {
// ...
};

int main()
{
  derived1 o1;
  derived2 o2;
  int i, j;

  // ...
}
```

Within **main( ),** which of the following statements are legal?

```
A. o1.getab(i, j);
B. o2.getab(i, j);
C. o1.c = 10;
D. o2.c = 10;
```

2. What happens when a public member is inherited as public? What happens when it is inherited as private?

3. If you have not done so, try all the examples presented in this section. On your own, try various changes relative to the access specifiers and observe the results.

7.2 *U*SING PROTECTED MEMBERS

As you know from the preceding section, a derived class does not have access to the private members of the base class. This means that if the derived class needs access to some member of the base, that member must be public. However, there will be times when you want to keep a member of a base class private but still allow a derived class access to it. To accomplish this goal, C++ includes the **protected** access specifier.

The **protected** access specifier is equivalent to the **private** specifier with the sole exception that protected members of a base class are accessible to members of any class derived from that base. Outside the base or derived classes, protected members are not accessible.

The **protected** access specifier can occur anywhere in the class declaration, although typically it occurs after the (default) private members are declared and before the public members. The full general form of a class declaration is shown here:

```
class class-name {
   // private members
protected: // optional
   // protected members
public:
   // public members
};
```

When a protected member of a base class is inherited as public by the derived class, it becomes a protected member of the derived class. If the base is inherited as private, a protected member of the base becomes a private member of the derived class.

A base class can also be inherited as protected by a derived class. When this is the case, public and protected members of the base class become protected members of the derived class. (Of course, private members of the base class remain private to it and are not accessible by the derived class.)

The **protected** access specifier can also be used with structures.

EXAMPLES

1. This program illustrates how public, private, and protected members of a class can be accessed:

```cpp
#include <iostream>
using namespace std;

class samp {
  // private by default
  int a;
protected: // still private relative to samp
  int b;
public:
  int c;

  samp(int n, int m) { a = n; b = m; }
  int geta() { return a; }
  int getb() { return b; }
};

int main()
{
  samp ob(10, 20);

  // ob.b = 99;  Error! b is protected and thus private
  ob.c = 30; // OK, c is public

  cout << ob.geta() << ' ';
  cout << ob.getb() << ' ' << ob.c << '\n';

  return 0;
}
```

As you can see, the commented-out line is not permissible in **main( )** because **b** is protected and is thus still private to **samp**.

2. The following program illustrates what occurs when protected members are inherited as public:

```cpp
#include <iostream>
using namespace std;
```

```
class base {
protected:  // private to base
  int a, b; // but still accessible by derived
public:
  void setab(int n, int m) { a = n; b = m; }
};

class derived : public base {
  int c;
public:
  void setc(int n) { c = n; }

  // this function has access to a and b from base
  void showabc() {
    cout << a << ' ' << b << ' ' << c << '\n';
  }
};

int main()
{
  derived ob;

  /* a and b are not accessible here because they are
     private to both base and derived. */

  ob.setab(1, 2);
  ob.setc(3);

  ob.showabc();

  return 0;
}
```

Because **a** and **b** are protected in **base** and inherited as public by **derived**, they are available for use by member functions of **derived**. However, outside of these two classes, **a** and **b** are effectively private and unaccessible.

3. As mentioned earlier, when a base class is inherited as protected, public and protected members of the base class become protected members of the derived class. For example, here the preceding program is changed slightly, inheriting **base** as protected instead of public:

```
// This program will not compile.
#include <iostream>
using namespace std;

class base {
protected:  // private to base
  int a, b; // but still accessible by derived
public:
  void setab(int n, int m) { a = n; b = m; }
};

class derived : protected base { // inherit as protected
  int c;
public:
  void setc(int n) { c = n; }

  // this function has access to a and b from base
  void showabc() {
    cout << a << ' ' << b << ' ' << c << '\n';
  }
};

int main()
{
  derived ob;

  // ERROR: setab() is now a protected member of base.
  ob.setab(1, 2); // setab() is not accessible here.

  ob.setc(3);

  ob.showabc();

  return 0;
}
```

As the comments now describe, because **base** is inherited as protected, its public and protected elements become protected members of **derived** and are therefore inaccessible within **main( )**.

1. What happens when a protected member is inherited as public? What happens when it is inherited as private? What happens when it is inherited as protected?

2. Explain why the protected category is needed.

3. In Exercise 1 from Section 7.1, if the **a** and **b** inside **myclass** were made into protected instead of private (by default) members, would any of your answers to that exercise change? If so, how?

7.3 CONSTRUCTORS, DESTRUCTORS, AND INHERITANCE

It is possible for the base class, the derived class, or both to have constructor and/or destructor functions. Several issues that relate to these situations are examined in this section.

When a base class and a derived class both have constructor and destructor functions, the constructor functions are executed in order of derivation. The destructor functions are executed in reverse order. That is, the base class constructor is executed before the constructor in the derived class. The reverse is true for destructor functions: the derived class's destructor is executed before the base class's destructor.

If you think about it, it makes sense that constructor functions are executed in order of derivation. Because a base class has no knowledge of any derived class, any initialization it performs is separate from and possibly prerequisite to any initialization performed by the derived class. Therefore, it must be executed first.

On the other hand, a derived class's destructor must be executed before the destructor of the base class because the base class underlies the derived class. If the base class's destructor were executed first, it would imply the destruction of the derived class. Thus, the derived class's destructor must be called before the object goes out of existence.

So far, none of the preceding examples have passed arguments to either a derived or base class constructor. However, it is possible to do this. When only the derived class takes an initialization, arguments are passed to the derived class's constructor in the normal fashion. However, if you need to pass an argument to the constructor of the base class, a little more effort is needed. To accomplish this, a chain of argument passing is established. First, all necessary arguments to both the base class and the derived class are passed to the derived class's constructor. Using an expanded form of the derived class's constructor declaration, you then pass the appropriate arguments along to the base class. The syntax for passing along an argument from the derived class to the base class is shown here:

```
derived-constructor (arg-list) : base(arg-list) {
   // body of derived class constructor
}
```

Here *base* is the name of the base class. It is permissible for both the derived class and the base class to use the same argument. It is also possible for the derived class to ignore all arguments and just pass them along to the base.

EXAMPLES

1. Here is a very short program that illustrates when base class and derived class constructor and destructor functions are executed:

```cpp
#include <iostream>
using namespace std;

class base {
public:
  base() { cout << "Constructing base class\n"; }
  ~base() { cout << "Destructing base class\n"; }
};

class derived : public base {
public:
  derived() { cout << "Constructing derived class\n"; }
  ~derived() { cout << "Destructing derived class\n"; }
};

int main()
{
```

```
    derived o;

    return 0;
}
```

This program displays the following output:

```
Constructing base class
Constructing derived class
Destructing derived class
Destructing base class
```

As you can see, the constructors are executed in order of derivation and the destructors are executed in reverse order.

2. This program shows how to pass an argument to a derived class's constructor:

```
#include <iostream>
using namespace std;

class base {
public:
  base() { cout << "Constructing base class\n"; }
  ~base() { cout << "Destructing base class\n"; }
};

class derived : public base {
  int j;
public:
  derived(int n) {
    cout << "Constructing derived class\n";
    j = n;
  }
  ~derived() { cout << "Destructing derived class\n"; }
  void showj() { cout << j << '\n'; }
};

int main()
{
  derived o(10);

  o.showj();

  return 0;
}
```

Notice that the argument is passed to the derived class's constructor in the normal fashion.

3. In the following example, both the derived class and the base class constructors take arguments. In this specific case, both use the same argument, and the derived class simply passes along the argument to the base.

```cpp
#include <iostream>
using namespace std;

class base {
  int i;
public:
  base(int n) {
    cout << "Constructing base class\n";
    i = n;
  }
  ~base() { cout << "Destructing base class\n"; }
  void showi() { cout << i << '\n'; }
};

class derived : public base {
  int j;
public:
  derived(int n) : base(n) { // pass arg to base class
    cout << "Constructing derived class\n";
    j = n;
  }
  ~derived() { cout << "Destructing derived class\n"; }
  void showj() { cout << j << '\n'; }
};

int main()
{
  derived o(10);

  o.showi();
  o.showj();

  return 0;
}
```

Pay special attention to the declaration of **derived**'s constructor. Notice how the parameter **n** (which receives the initialization argument) is both used by **derived( )** and passed to **base( )**.

4. In most cases, the constructor functions for the base and derived classes will *not* use the same argument. When this is the case and you need to pass one or more arguments to each, you must pass to the derived class's constructor *all* arguments needed by *both* the derived class and the base class. Then the derived class simply passes along to the base those arguments required by it. For example, this program shows how to pass an argument to the derived class's constructor and another one to the base class:

```cpp
#include <iostream>
using namespace std;

class base {
  int i;
public:
  base(int n) {
    cout << "Constructing base class\n";
    i = n;
  }
  ~base() { cout << "Destructing base class\n"; }
  void showi() { cout << i << '\n'; }
};

class derived : public base {
  int j;
public:
  derived(int n, int m) : base(m) { // pass arg to base class
    cout << "Constructing derived class\n";
    j = n;
  }
  ~derived() { cout << "Destructing derived class\n"; }
  void showj() { cout << j << '\n'; }
};

int main()
{
  derived o(10, 20);
```

```
    o.showi();
    o.showj();

    return 0;
}
```

5. It is not necessary for the derived class' constructor to actually use an argument in order to pass one to the base class. If the derived class does not need an argument, it ignores the argument and simply passes it along. For example, in this fragment, parameter **n** is not used by **derived( )**. Instead, it is simply passed to **base( )**:

```
class base {
  int i;
public:
  base(int n) {
    cout << "Constructing base class\n";
    i = n;
  }
  ~base() { cout << "Destructing base class\n"; }
  void showi() { cout << i << '\n'; }
};

class derived : public base {
  int j;
public:
  derived(int n) : base(n) { // pass arg to base class
    cout << "Constructing derived class\n";
    j = 0; // n not used here
  }
  ~derived() { cout << "Destructing derived class\n"; }
  void showj() { cout << j << '\n'; }
};
```

EXERCISES

1. Given the following skeleton, fill in the constructor function for **myderived**. Have it pass along a pointer to an initialization string to **mybase**. Also, have **myderived( )** initialize **len** to the length of the string.

```
#include <iostream>
#include <cstring>
using namespace std;

class mybase {
  char str[80];
public:
  mybase(char *s) { strcpy(str, s); }
  char *get() { return str; }
};

class myderived : public mybase {
  int len;
public:
  // add myderived() here
  int getlen() { return len; }
  void show() { cout << get() << '\n'; }
};

int main()
{
  myderived ob("hello");

  ob.show();
  cout << ob.getlen() << '\n';

  return 0;
}
```

2. Using the following skeleton, create appropriate **car( )** and **truck( )** constructor functions. Have each pass along appropriate arguments to **vehicle**. In addition, have **car( )** initialize **passengers** as specified when an object is created. Have **truck( )** initialize **loadlimit** as specified when an object is created.

```
#include <iostream>
using namespace std;

// A base class for various types of vehicles.
class vehicle {
  int num_wheels;
  int range;
public:
  vehicle(int w, int r)
```

```
    {
      num_wheels = w; range = r;
    }
    void showv()
    {
      cout << "Wheels: " << num_wheels << '\n';
      cout << "Range: " << range << '\n';
    }
};

class car : public vehicle {
  int passengers;
public:
  // insert car() constructor here
  void show()
  {
    showv();
    cout << "Passengers: " << passengers << '\n';
  }
};

class truck : public vehicle {
  int loadlimit;
public:
  // insert truck() constructor here
  void show()
  {
    showv();
    cout << "loadlimit " << loadlimit << '\n';
  }
};

int main()
{
  car c(5, 4, 500);
  truck t(30000, 12, 1200);

  cout << "Car: \n";
  c.show();
  cout << "\nTruck:\n";
  t.show();

  return 0;
}
```

Have **car( )** and **truck( )** declare objects like this:

```
car ob(passengers, wheels, range);
truck ob(loadlimit, wheels, range);
```

MULTIPLE INHERITANCE

There are two ways that a derived class can inherit more than one base class. First, a derived class can be used as a base class for another derived class, creating a multilevel class hierarchy. In this case, the original base class is said to be an *indirect* base class of the second derived class. (Keep in mind that any class—no matter how it is created—can be used as a base class.) Second, a derived class can directly inherit more than one base class. In this situation, two or more base classes are combined to help create the derived class. There are several issues that arise when multiple base classes are involved, and these issues are examined in this section.

When a base class is used to derive a class that is used as a base class for another derived class, the constructor functions of all three classes are called in order of derivation. (This is a generalization of the principle you learned earlier in this chapter.) Also, destructor functions are called in reverse order. Thus, if class *B1* is inherited by *D1*, and *D1* is inherited by *D2*, *B1*'s constructor is called first, followed by *D1*'s, followed by *D2* 's. The destructors are called in reverse order.

When a derived class directly inherits multiple base classes, it uses this expanded declaration:

```
class derived-class-name : access base1, access base2, . . . , access baseN
{
   // ... body of class
}
```

Here *base1* through *baseN* are the base class names and *access* is the access specifier, which can be different for each base class. When multiple base classes are inherited, constructors are executed in the order, left to right, that the base classes are specified. Destructors are executed in the opposite order.

When a class inherits multiple base classes that have constructors that require arguments, the derived class passes the necessary arguments to them by using this expanded form of the derived class' constructor function:

derived-constructor(arg-list) : base1(arg-list), base2(arg-list), . . . ,
   baseN(arg-list)
{
   // body of derived class constructor
}

Here *base1* through *baseN* are the names of the base classes.

When a derived class inherits a hierarchy of classes, each derived class in the chain must pass back to its preceding base any arguments it needs.

EXAMPLES

1. Here is an example of a derived class that inherits a class derived from another class. Notice how arguments are passed along the chain from **D2** to **B1**.

```cpp
// Multiple Inheritance
#include <iostream>
using namespace std;

class B1 {
  int a;
public:
  B1(int x) { a = x; }
  int geta() { return a; }
};

// Inherit direct base class.
class D1 : public B1 {
  int b;
public:
  D1(int x, int y) : B1(y) // pass y to B1
  {
    b = x;
  }
  int getb() { return b; }
};
```

```
// Inherit a derived class and an indirect base.
class D2 : public D1 {
  int c;
public:
  D2(int x, int y, int z) : D1(y, z) // pass args to D1
  {
    c = x;
  }

  /* Because bases inherited as public, D2 has access
     to public elements of both B1 and D1. */
  void show() {
    cout << geta() << ' ' << getb() << ' ';
    cout << c << '\n';
  }
};

int main()
{
  D2 ob(1, 2, 3);

  ob.show();
  // geta() and getb() are still public here
  cout << ob.geta() << ' ' << ob.getb() << '\n';

  return 0;
}
```

The call to **ob.show( )** displays **3 2 1**. In this example, **B1** is an indirect base class of **D2**. Notice that **D2** has access to the public members of both **D1** and **B1**. As you should remember, when public members of a base class are inherited as public, they become public members of the derived class. Therefore, when **D1** inherits **B1**, **geta( )** becomes a public member of **D1**, which becomes a public member of **D2**.

As the program illustrates, each class in a class hierarchy must pass all arguments required by each preceding base class. Failure to do so will generate a compile-time error.

The class hierarchy created in this program is illustrated here:

B1

D1

D2

Before we move on, a short discussion about how to draw C++-style inheritance graphs is in order. In the preceding graph, notice that the arrows point up instead of down. Traditionally, C++ programmers usually draw inheritance charts as directed graphs in which the arrow points from the derived class to the base class. While newcomers sometimes find this approach counter-intuitive, it is nevertheless the way inheritance charts are usually depicted in C++.

2. Here is a reworked version of the preceding program, in which a derived class directly inherits two base classes:

```
#include <iostream>
using namespace std;

// Create first base class.
class B1 {
  int a;
public:
  B1(int x) { a = x; }
  int geta() { return a; }
};

// Create second base class.
class B2 {
  int b;
public:
  B2(int x)
  {
    b = x;
  }
```

```
  int getb() { return b; }
};

// Directly inherit two base classes.
class D : public B1, public B2 {
  int c;
public:
  // here z and y are passed directly to B1 and B2
  D(int x, int y, int z) : B1(z), B2(y)
  {
    c = x;
  }

  /* Because bases inherited as public, D has access
     to public elements of both B1 and B2. */
  void show() {
    cout << geta() << ' ' << getb() << ' ';
    cout << c << '\n';
  }
};

int main()
{
  D ob(1, 2, 3);

  ob.show();

  return 0;
}
```

In this version, the arguments to **B1** and **B2** are passed individually to these classes by **D**. This program creates a class that looks like this:

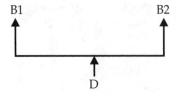

3. The following program illustrates the order in which constructor and destructor functions are called when a derived class directly inherits multiple base classes:

```
#include <iostream>
using namespace std;

class B1 {
public:
  B1() { cout << "Constructing B1\n"; }
  ~B1() { cout << "Destructing B1\n"; }
};

class B2 {
  int b;
public:
  B2() { cout << "Constructing B2\n"; }
  ~B2() { cout << "Destructing B2\n"; }
};

// Inherit two base classes.
class D : public B1, public B2 {
public:
  D() { cout << "Constructing D\n"; }
  ~D() { cout << "Destructing D\n"; }
};

int main()
{
  D ob;

  return 0;
}
```

This program displays the following:

```
Constructing B1
Constructing B2
Constructing D
Destructing D
Destructing B2
Destructing B1
```

As you have learned, when multiple direct base classes are inherited, constructors are called in order, left to right, as specified in the inheritance list. Destructors are called in reverse order.

1. What does the following program display? (Try to determine this without actually running the program.)

```cpp
#include <iostream>
using namespace std;

class A {
public:
  A() { cout << "Constructing A\n"; }
  ~A() { cout << "Destructing A\n"; }
};

class B {
public:
  B() { cout << "Constructing B\n"; }
  ~B() { cout << "Destructing B\n"; }
};

class C : public A, public B {
public:
  C() { cout << "Constructing C\n"; }
  ~C() { cout << "Destructing C\n"; }
};

int main()
{
  C ob;

  return 0;
}
```

2. Using the following class hierarchy, create **C**'s constructor so that it initializes **k** and passes on arguments to **A( )** and **B( )**.

```cpp
#include <iostream>
using namespace std;

class A {
  int i;
public:
  A(int a) { i = a; }
};
```

```
class B {
  int j;
public:
  B(int a) { j = a; }
};

class C : public A, public B {
  int k;
public:
  /* Create C() so that it initializes k
     and passes arguments to both A() and B() */
};
```

7.5 **VIRTUAL BASE CLASSES**

A potential problem exists when multiple base classes are directly inherited by a derived class. To understand what this problem is, consider the following class hierarchy:

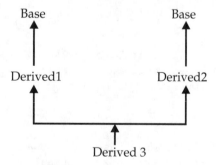

Here the base class *Base* is inherited by both *Derived1* and *Derived2*. *Derived3* directly inherits both *Derived1* and *Derived2*. However, this implies that *Base* is actually inherited twice by *Derived3*—first it is inherited through *Derived1*, and then again through *Derived2*. This causes ambiguity when a member of *Base* is used by *Derived3*. Since two copies of *Base* are included in *Derived3*, is a reference to a member of *Base* referring to the *Base* inherited indirectly through *Derived1* or to the *Base* inherited indirectly through *Derived2*? To resolve this ambiguity, C++ includes a mechanism by which only one copy of *Base* will be included in *Derived3*. This feature is called a *virtual base class*.

In situations like the one just described, in which a derived class indirectly inherits the same base class more than once, it is possible to prevent two copies of the base from being present in the derived object by having that base class inherited as virtual by any derived classes. Doing this prevents two (or more) copies of the base from being present in any subsequent derived class that inherits the base class indirectly. The **virtual** keyword precedes the base class access specifier when it is inherited by a derived class.

EXAMPLES

1. Here is an example that uses a virtual base class to prevent two copies of **base** from being present in **derived3**.

```
// This program uses a virtual base class.
#include <iostream>
using namespace std;

class base {
public:
  int i;
};

// Inherit base as virtual.
class derived1 : virtual public base {
public:
  int j;
};

// Inherit base as virtual here, too.
class derived2 : virtual public base {
public:
  int k;
};

/* Here, derived3 inherits both derived1 and derived2.
   However, only one copy of base is present.
*/
class derived3 : public derived1, public derived2 {
public:
  int product() { return i * j * k; }
```

```
};

int main()
{
  derived3 ob;

  ob.i = 10; // unambiguous because only one copy present
  ob.j = 3;
  ob.k = 5;

  cout << "Product is " << ob.product() << '\n';

  return 0;
}
```

If **derived1** and **derived2** had not inherited **base** as virtual, the statement

```
ob.i = 10;
```

would have been ambiguous and a compile-time error would have resulted. (See Exercise 1, below.)

2. It is important to understand that when a base class is inherited as virtual by a derived class, that base class still exists within that derived class. For example, assuming the preceding program, this fragment is perfectly valid:

```
derived1 ob;
ob.i = 100;
```

The only difference between a normal base class and a virtual one occurs when an object inherits the base more than once. If virtual base classes are used, only one base class is present in the object. Otherwise, multiple copies will be found.

EXERCISES

1. Using the program in Example 1, remove the **virtual** keyword and try to compile the program. See what types of errors result.

2. Explain why a virtual base class might be necessary.

Mastery
Skills Check

SKILLS CHECK

At this point you should be able to perform the following exercises and answer the questions.

1. Create a generic base class called **building** that stores the number of floors a building has, the number of rooms, and its total square footage. Create a derived class called **house** that inherits **building** and also stores the number of bedrooms and the number of bathrooms. Next, create a derived class called **office** that inherits **building** and also stores the number of fire extinguishers and the number of telephones. Note: Your solution may differ from the answer given in the back of this book. However, if it is functionally the same, count it as correct.

2. When a base class is inherited as public by the derived class, what happens to its public members? What happens to its private members? If the base is inherited as private by the derived class, what happens to its public and private members?

3. Explain what **protected** means. (Be sure to explain what it means both when referring to members of a class and when it is used as an inheritance access specifier.)

4. When one class inherits another, when are the classes' constructors called? When are their destructors called?

5. Given this skeleton, fill in the details as indicated in the comments:

```cpp
#include <iostream>
using namespace std;

class planet {
protected:
  double distance; // miles from the sun
  int revolve;   // in days
public:
```

```
  planet(double d, int r) { distance = d; revolve = r; }
};

class earth : public planet {
  double circumference; // circumference of orbit
public:
  /* Create earth(double d, int r). Have it pass the
     distance and days of revolution back to planet.
     Have it compute the circumference of the orbit.
     (Hint: circumference = 2r*3.1416.)
  */
  /* Create a function called show() that displays the
     information. */
};

int main()
{
  earth ob(93000000, 365);

  ob.show();

  return 0;
}
```

6. Fix the following program:

```
/* A variation on the vehicle hierarchy. But
   this program contains an error. Fix it. Hint:
   try compiling it as is and observe the error
   messages.
*/
#include <iostream>
using namespace std;

// A base class for various types of vehicles.
class vehicle {
  int num_wheels;
  int range;
public:
  vehicle(int w, int r)
  {
    num_wheels = w; range = r;
  }
  void showv()
  {
```

```
    cout << "Wheels: " << num_wheels << '\n';
    cout << "Range: " << range << '\n';
  }
};

enum motor {gas, electric, diesel};

class motorized : public vehicle {
  enum motor mtr;
public:
  motorized(enum motor m, int w, int r) : vehicle(w, r)
  {
    mtr = m;
  }
  void showm() {
    cout << "Motor: ";
    switch(mtr) {
      case gas : cout << "Gas\n";
        break;
      case electric : cout << "Electric\n";
        break;
      case diesel : cout << "Diesel\n";
        break;
    }
  }
};

class road_use : public vehicle {
  int passengers;
public:
  road_use(int p, int w, int r) : vehicle(w, r)
  {
    passengers = p;
  }
  void showr()
  {
    cout << "Passengers: " << passengers << '\n';
  }
};

enum steering { power, rack_pinion, manual };

class car : public motorized, public road_use {
  enum steering strng;
public:
```

```
    car(enum steering s, enum motor m, int w, int r, int p) :
      road_use(p, w, r), motorized(m, w, r), vehicle(w, r)
    {
      strng = s;
    }
    void show() {
      showv(); showr(); showm();
      cout << "Steering: ";
      switch(strng) {
        case power : cout << "Power\n";
          break;
        case rack_pinion : cout << "Rack and Pinion\n";
          break;
        case manual : cout << "Manual\n";
          break;
      }
    }
};

int main()
{
  car c(power, gas, 4, 500, 5);

  c.show();

  return 0;
}
```

This section checks how well you have integrated material in this
chapter with that from the preceding chapters.

1. In Exercise 6 from the preceding Mastery Skills Check section,
   you might have seen a warning message (or perhaps an error
   message) concerning the use of the **switch** statement within **car**
   and **motorized**. Why?

2. As you know from the preceding chapter, most operators
   overloaded in a base class are available for use in a derived

class. Which one or ones are not? Can you offer a reason why this is the case?

3. Following is a reworked version of the **coord** class from the previous chapter. This time it is used as a base for another class called **quad**, which also maintains the quadrant the specific point is in. On your own, run this program and try to understand its output.

```
/* Overload the +, -, and = relative to coord class. Then
   use coord as a base for quad. */
#include <iostream>
using namespace std;

class coord {
public:
  int x, y; // coordinate values
  coord() { x=0; y=0; }
  coord(int i, int j) { x=i; y=j; }
  void get_xy(int &i, int &j) { i=x; j=y; }
  coord operator+(coord ob2);
  coord operator-(coord ob2);
  coord operator=(coord ob2);
};

// Overload + relative to coord class.
coord coord::operator+(coord ob2)
{
  coord temp;

  cout << "Using coord operator+()\n";

  temp.x = x + ob2.x;
  temp.y = y + ob2.y;

  return temp;
}

// Overload - relative to coord class.
coord coord::operator-(coord ob2)
{
  coord temp;

  cout << "Using coord operator-()\n";
```

```
    temp.x = x - ob2.x;
    temp.y = y - ob2.y;

    return temp;
}

// Overload = relative to coord.
coord coord::operator=(coord ob2)
{
    cout << "Using coord operator=()\n";

    x = ob2.x;
    y = ob2.y;

    return *this; // return the object that is assigned to
}

class quad : public coord {
    int quadrant;
public:
    quad() { x = 0; y = 0; quadrant = 0; }
    quad(int x, int y) : coord(x, y)
    {
        if(x>=0 && y>=0) quadrant = 1;
        else if(x<0 && y>=0) quadrant = 2;
        else if(x<0 && y<0) quadrant = 3;
        else quadrant = 4;
    }
    void showq()
    {
        cout << "Point in Quadrant: " << quadrant << '\n';
    }
    quad operator=(coord ob2);
};

quad quad::operator=(coord ob2)
{
    cout << "Using quad operator=()\n";

    x = ob2.x;
    y = ob2.y;
    if(x>=0 && y>=0) quadrant = 1;
    else if(x<0 && y>=0) quadrant = 2;
    else if(x<0 && y<0) quadrant = 3;
    else quadrant = 4;
```

```
      return *this;
    }

    int main()
    {
      quad o1(10, 10), o2(15, 3), o3;
      int x, y;

      o3 = o1 + o2; // add two objects - this calls operator+()
      o3.get_xy(x, y);
      o3.showq();
      cout << "(o1+o2) X: " << x << ", Y: " << y << "\n";

      o3 = o1 - o2; // subtract two objects
      o3.get_xy(x, y);
      o3.showq();
      cout << "(o1-o2) X: " << x << ", Y: " << y << "\n";

      o3 = o1; // assign an object
      o3.get_xy(x, y);
      o3.showq();
      cout << "(o3=o1) X: " << x << ", Y: " << y << "\n";

      return 0;
    }
```

4. Again on your own, convert the program shown in Exercise 3 so that it uses friend operator functions.

8

Introducing the C++ I/O System

chapter objectives

8.1 Some C++ I/O basics

8.2 Formatted I/O

8.3 Using **width( )**, **precision( )**, and **fill( )**

8.4 Using I/O manipulators

8.5 Creating your own inserters

8.6 Creating extractors

ALTHOUGH you have been using C++-style I/O since the first chapter of this book, it is time to explore it more fully. Like its predecessor, C, the C++ language includes a rich I/O system that is both flexible and powerful. It is important to understand that C++ still supports the entire C I/O system. However, C++ supplies a complete set of object-oriented I/O routines. The major advantage of the C++ I/O system is that it can be overloaded relative to classes that you create. Put differently, the C++ I/O system allows you to seamlessly integrate new types that you create.

Like the C I/O system, the C++ object-oriented I/O system makes little distinction between console and file I/O. File and console I/O are really just different perspectives on the same mechanism. The examples in this chapter use console I/O, but the information presented is applicable to file I/O as well. (File I/O is examined in detail in Chapter 9.)

At the time of this writing, there are two versions of the I/O library in use: the older one that is based on the original specifications for C++ and the newer one defined by Standard C++. For the most part the two libraries appear the same to the programmer. This is because the new I/O library is, in essence, simply an updated and improved version of the old one. In fact, the vast majority of the differences between the two occur beneath the surface, in the way that the libraries are implemented—not in the way that they are used. From the programmer's perspective, the main difference is that the new I/O library contains a few additional features and defines some new data types. Thus, the new I/O library is essentially a superset of the old one. Nearly all programs originally written for the old library will compile without substantive changes when the new library is used. Since the old-style I/O library is now obsolete, this book describes only the new I/O library as defined by Standard C++. But most of the information is applicable to the old I/O library as well.

This chapter covers several aspects of C++'s I/O system, including formatted I/O, I/O manipulators, and creating your own I/O inserters and extractors. As you will see, the C++ I/O system shares many features with the C I/O system.

Before proceeding, you should be able to correctly answer the
following questions and do the exercises.

1. Create a class hierarchy that stores information about airships.
   Start with a general base class called **airship** that stores the
   number of passengers and the amount of cargo (in pounds) that
   can be carried. Then create two derived classes called **airplane**
   and **balloon** from **airship**. Have **airplane** store the type of
   engine used (propeller or jet) and range, in miles. Have **balloon**
   store information about the type of gas used to lift the balloon
   (hydrogen or helium) and its maximum altitude (in feet). Create
   a short program that demonstrates this class hierarchy. (Your
   solution will, no doubt, differ from the answer shown in the
   back of this book. If it is functionally similar, count it as correct.)

2. What is **protected** used for?

3. Given the following class hierarchy, in what order are the
   constructor functions called? In what order are the destructor
   functions called?

```cpp
#include <iostream>
using namespace std;

class A {
public:
  A() { cout << "Constructing A\n"; }
  ~A() { cout << "Destructing A\n"; }
};

class B : public A {
public:
  B() { cout << "Constructing B\n"; }
  ~B() { cout << "Destructing B\n"; }
};
```

```
class C : public B {
public:
  C() { cout << "Constructing C\n"; }
  ~C() { cout << "Destructing C\n"; }
};

int main()
{
  C ob;

  return 0;
}
```

4. Given the following fragment, in what order are the constructor functions called?

```
class myclass : public A, public B, public C { ...
```

5. Fill in the missing constructor functions in this program:

```
#include <iostream>
using namespace std;

class base {
  int i, j;
public:
  // need constructor
  void showij() { cout << i << ' ' << j << '\n'; }
};

class derived : public base {
  int k;
public:
  // need constructor
  void show() { cout << k << ' '; showij(); }
};

int main()
{
  derived ob(1, 2, 3);

  ob.show();
```

```
    return 0;
}
```

6. In general, when you define a class hierarchy, you begin with
the most _____ class and move to the most
_____ class. (Fill in the missing words.)

SOME C++ I/O BASICS

Before we begin our examination of C++ I/O, a few general comments
are in order. The C++ I/O system, like the C I/O system, operates
through *streams.* Because of your C programming experience, you
should already know what a stream is, but here is a summary. A
stream is a logical device that either produces or consumes
information. A stream is linked to a physical device by the C++ I/O
system. All streams behave in the same manner, even if the actual
physical devices they are linked to differ. Because all streams act the
same, the I/O system presents the programmer with a consistent
interface, even though it operates on devices with differing
capabilities. For example, the same function that you use to write to
the screen can be used to write to a disk file or to the printer.

As you know, when a C program begins execution, three predefined
streams are automatically opened: **stdin**, **stdout**, and **stderr**. A similar
thing happens when a C++ program starts running. When a C++
program begins, these four streams are automatically opened:

Stream	Meaning	Default Device
cin	Standard input	Keyboard
cout	Standard output	Screen
cerr	Standard error	Screen
clog	Buffered version of **cerr**	Screen

As you have probably guessed, the streams **cin**, **cout**, and **cerr**
correspond to C's **stdin**, **stdout**, and **stderr**. You have already been
using **cin** and **cout**. The stream **clog** is simply a buffered version of
cerr. Standard C++ also opens wide (16-bit) character versions of
these streams called **wcin**, **wcout**, **wcerr**, and **wclog**, but we won't be

using them in this book. The wide character streams exist to support languages, such as Chinese, that require large character sets.

By default, the standard streams are used to communicate with the console. However, in environments that support I/O redirection, these streams can be redirected to other devices.

As you learned in Chapter 1, C++ provides support for its I/O system in the header file **< iostream >**. In this file, a rather complicated set of class hierarchies is defined that supports I/O operations. The I/O classes begin with a system of *template classes*. Template classes, also called generic classes, will be discussed more fully in Chapter 11; briefly, a template class defines the form of a class without fully specifying the data upon which it will operate. Once a template class has been defined, specific instances of it can be created. As it relates to the I/O library, Standard C++ creates two specific versions of the I/O template classes: one for 8-bit characters and another for wide characters. This book will discuss only the 8-bit character classes, since they are by far the most frequently used.

The C++ I/O system is built upon two related, but different, template class hierarchies. The first is derived from the low-level I/O class called **basic_streambuf**. This class supplies the basic, low-level input and output operations and provides the underlying support for the entire C++ I/O system. Unless you are doing advanced I/O programming, you will not need to use **basic_streambuf** directly. The class hierarchy that you will most commonly be working with is derived from **basic_ios**. This is a high-level I/O class that provides formatting, error-checking, and status information related to stream I/O. **basic_ios** is used as a base for several derived classes, including **basic_istream**, **basic_ostream**, and **basic_iostream**. These classes are used to create streams capable of input, output, and input/output, respectively.

As explained earlier, the I/O library creates two specific versions of the class hierarchies just described: one for 8-bit characters and one for wide characters. The following table shows the mapping of the template class names to their 8-bit character-based versions (including some that will be used in Chapter 9):

Template Class	8-Bit Character-Based Class
basic_streambuf	streambuf
basic_ios	ios

Template Class	8-Bit Character-Based Class
basic_istream	istream
basic_ostream	ostream
basic_iostream	iostream
basic_fstream	fstream
basic_ifstream	ifstream
basic_ofstream	ofstream

The character-based names will be used throughout the remainder of this book, since they are the names that you will use in your programs. They are also the same names that were used by the old I/O library. This is why the old and the new I/O libraries are compatible at the source code level.

One last point: The **ios** class contains many member functions and variables that control or monitor the fundamental operation of a stream. It will be referred to frequently. Just remember that if you include **< iostream >** in your program, you will have access to this important class.

8.2 *F*ORMATTED I/O

Until now, all examples in this book displayed information to the screen using C++'s default formats. However, it is possible to output information in a wide variety of forms. In fact, you can format data using C++'s I/O system in much the same way that you do using C's **printf( )** function. Also, you can alter certain aspects of the way information is input.

Each stream has associated with it a set of format flags that control the way information is formatted. The **ios** class declares a bitmask enumeration called **fmtflags**, in which the following values are defined:

adjustfield	floatfield	right	skipws
basefield	hex	scientific	unitbuf
boolalpha	internal	showbase	uppercase
dec	left	showpoint	
fixed	oct	showpos	

These values are used to set or clear the format flags and are defined within **ios**. If you are using an older, nonstandard compiler, it may not define the **fmtflags** enumeration type. In this case, the format flags will be encoded into a long integer.

When the **skipws** flag is set, leading whitespace characters (spaces, tabs, and newlines) are discarded when input is being performed on a stream. When **skipws** is cleared, whitespace characters are not discarded.

When the **left** flag is set, output is left justified. When **right** is set, output is right justified. When the **internal** flag is set, a numeric value is padded to fill a field by inserting spaces between any sign or base character. If none of these flags is set, output is right justified by default.

By default, numeric values are output in decimal. However, it is possible to change the number base. Setting the **oct** flag causes output to be displayed in octal. Setting the **hex** flag causes output to be displayed in hexadecimal. To return output to decimal, set the **dec** flag.

Setting **showbase** causes the base of numeric values to be shown. For example, if the conversion base is hexadecimal, the value 1F will be displayed as 0x1F.

By default, when scientific notation is displayed, the e is lowercase. Also, when a hexadecimal value is displayed, the x is lowercase. When **uppercase** is set, these characters are displayed uppercase.

Setting **showpos** causes a leading plus sign to be displayed before positive values.

Setting **showpoint** causes a decimal point and trailing zeros to be displayed for all floating-point output—whether needed or not.

If the **scientific** flag is set, floating-point numeric values are displayed using scientific notation. When **fixed** is set, floating-point values are displayed using normal notation. When neither flag is set, the compiler chooses an appropriate method.

When **unitbuf** is set, the buffer is flushed after each insertion operation.

When **boolalpha** is set, Booleans can be input or output using the keywords **true** and **false**.

Since it is common to refer to the **oct**, **dec**, and **hex** fields, they can be collectively referred to as **basefield**. Similarly, the **left**, **right**, and **internal** fields can be referred to as **adjustfield**. Finally, the **scientific** and **fixed** fields can be referenced as **floatfield**.

To set a format flag, use the **setf( )** function. This function is a member of **ios**. Its most common form is shown here:

fmtflags setf(fmtflags *flags*);

This function returns the previous settings of the format flags and turns on those flags specified by *flags*. (All other flags are unaffected.) For example, to turn on the **showpos** flag, you can use this statement:

stream.setf(ios::showpos);

Here *stream* is the stream you wish to affect. Notice the use of the scope resolution operator. Remember, **showpos** is an enumerated constant within the **ios** class. Therefore, it is necessary to tell the compiler this fact by preceding **showpos** with the class name and the scope resolution operator. If you don't, the constant **showpos** will simply not be recognized.

It is important to understand that **setf( )** is a member function of the **ios** class and affects streams created by that class. Therefore, any call to **setf( )** is done relative to a specific stream. There is no concept of calling **setf( )** by itself. Put differently, there is no concept in C++ of global format status. Each stream maintains its own format status information individually.

It is possible to set more than one flag in a single call to **setf( )**, rather than making multiple calls. To do this, OR together the values of the flags you want to set. For example, this call sets the **showbase** and **hex** flags for **cout**:

```
cout.setf(ios::showbase | ios::hex);
```

*Because the format flags are defined within the **ios** class, you must access their values by using **ios** and the scope resolution operator. For example, **showbase** by itself will not be recognized; you must specify **ios::showbase**.*

The complement of **setf( )** is **unsetf( )**. This member function of **ios** clears one or more format flags. Its most common prototype form is shown here:

void unsetf(fmtflags *flags*);

The flags specified by *flags* are cleared. (All other flags are unaffected.)

There will be times when you want to know, but not alter, the current format settings. Since both **setf( )** and **unsetf( )** alter the setting of one or more flags, **ios** also includes the member function **flags( )**, which simply returns the current setting of each format flag. Its prototype is shown here:

fmtflags flags( );

The **flags( )** function has a second form that allows you to set *all* format flags associated with a stream to those specified in the argument to **flags( )**. The prototype for this version of **flags( )** is shown here:

fmtflags flags(fmtflags *f*) ;

When you use this version, the bit pattern found in *f* is copied to the variable used to hold the format flags associated with the stream, thus overwriting all previous flag settings. The function returns the previous settings.

EXAMPLES

1. Here is an example that shows how to set several of the format flags:

```cpp
#include <iostream>
using namespace std;

int main()
{
  // display using default settings
  cout << 123.23 << " hello " << 100 << '\n';
  cout << 10 << ' ' << -10 << '\n';
  cout << 100.0 << "\n\n";

  // now, change formats
  cout.unsetf(ios::dec); // not required by all compilers
  cout.setf(ios::hex | ios::scientific);
  cout << 123.23 << " hello " << 100 << '\n';

  cout.setf(ios::showpos);
  cout << 10 << ' ' << -10 << '\n';
```

```
    cout. setf(ios::showpoint | ios::fixed);
    cout << 100.0;

    return 0;
}
```

This program displays the following output:

```
123.23 hello 100
10 -10
100

1.232300e+02 hello 64
a fffffff6
+100.000000
```

Notice that the **showpos** flag affects only decimal output. It does not affect the value 10 when output in hexadecimal. Also notice the **unsetf( )** call that turns off the **dec** flag (which is on by default). This call is not needed by all compilers. But for some compilers, the **dec** flag overrides the other flags, so it is necessary to turn it off when turning on either **hex** or **oct**. In general, for maximum portability, it is better to set only the number base that you want to use and clear the others.

2. The following program illustrates the effect of the **uppercase** flag. It first sets the **uppercase**, **showbase**, and **hex** flags. It then outputs 88 in hexadecimal. In this case, the X used in the hexadecimal notation is uppercase. Next, it clears the **uppercase** flag by using **unsetf( )** and again outputs 88 in hexadecimal. This time, the x is lowercase.

```
#include <iostream>
using namespace std;

int main()
{
  cout.unsetf(ios::dec);
  cout.setf(ios::uppercase | ios::showbase | ios::hex);

  cout << 88 << '\n';

  cout.unsetf(ios::uppercase);

  cout << 88 << '\n';
```

```
          return 0;
      }
```

3. The following program uses **flags( )** to display the settings of the format flags relative to **cout**. Pay special attention to the **showflags( )** function. You might find it useful in programs you write.

```cpp
#include <iostream>
using namespace std;

void showflags();

int main()
{
  // show default condition of format flags
  showflags();

  cout.setf(ios::oct | ios::showbase | ios::fixed);

  showflags();

  return 0;
}

// This function displays the status of the format flags.
void showflags()
{
  ios::fmtflags f;

  f = cout.flags();  // get flag settings

  if(f & ios::skipws) cout << "skipws on\n";
  else cout << "skipws off\n";

  if(f & ios::left) cout << "left on\n";
  else cout << "left off\n";

  if(f & ios::right) cout << "right on\n";
  else cout << "right off\n";

  if(f & ios::internal) cout << "internal on\n";
  else cout << "internal off\n";
```

```
      if(f & ios::dec) cout << "dec on\n";
      else cout << "dec off\n";

      if(f & ios::oct) cout << "oct on\n";
      else cout << "oct off\n";

      if(f & ios::hex) cout << "hex on\n";
      else cout << "hex off\n";

      if(f & ios::showbase) cout << "showbase on\n";
      else cout << "showbase off\n";

      if(f & ios::showpoint) cout << "showpoint on\n";
      else cout << "showpoint off\n";

      if(f & ios::showpos) cout << "showpos on\n";
      else cout << "showpos off\n";

      if(f & ios::uppercase) cout << "uppercase on\n";
      else cout << "uppercase off\n";

      if(f & ios::scientific) cout << "scientific on\n";
      else cout << "scientific off\n";

      if(f & ios::fixed) cout << "fixed on\n";
      else cout << "fixed off\n";

      if(f & ios::unitbuf) cout << "unitbuf on\n";
      else cout << "unitbuf off\n";

      if(f & ios::boolalpha) cout << "boolalpha on\n";
      else cout << "boolalpha off\n";

      cout << "\n";
}
```

Inside **showflags( )**, the local variable **f** is declared to be of type
fmtflags. If your compiler does not define **fmtflags**, declare
this variable as **long** instead. The output from the program is
shown here:

```
skipws on
left off
right off
internal off
```

```
dec on
oct off
hex off
showbase off
showpoint off
showpos off
uppercase off
scientific off
fixed off
unitbuf off
boolalpha off

skipws on
left off
right off
internal off
dec on
oct on
hex off
showbase on
showpoint off
showpos off
uppercase off
scientific off
fixed on
unitbuf off
boolalpha off
```

4. The next program illustrates the second version of **flags( )**. It first constructs a flag mask that turns on **showpos**, **showbase**, **oct**, and **right**. It then uses **flags( )** to set the flag variable associated with **cout** to these settings. The function **showflags( )** verifies that the flags are set as indicated. (This is the same function used in the previous program.)

```
#include <iostream>
using namespace std;

void showflags() ;

int main()
{
  // show default condition of format flags
  showflags();
```

```
// showpos, showbase, oct, right are on, others off
ios::fmtflags f = ios::showpos | ios::showbase |
                  ios::oct | ios::right;

cout.flags(f);  // set flags

showflags();

return 0;
}
```

EXERCISES

1. Write a program that sets **cout**'s flags so that integers display a + sign when positive values are displayed. Demonstrate that you have set the format flags correctly.

2. Write a program that sets **cout**'s flags so that the decimal point is always shown when floating-point values are displayed. Also, display all floating-point values in scientific notation with an uppercase E.

3. Write a program that saves the current state of the format flags, sets **showbase** and **hex**, and displays the value 100. Then reset the flags to their previous values.

8.3   USING width( ), precision( ), AND fill( )

In addition to the formatting flags, there are three member functions defined by **ios** that set these format parameters: the field width, the precision, and the fill character. These are **width( )**, **precision( )**, and **fill( )**, respectively.

By default, when a value is output, it occupies only as much space as the number of characters it takes to display it. However, you can specify a minimum field width by using the **width( )** function. Its prototype is shown here:

```
streamsize width(streamsize w);
```

Here w becomes the field width, and the previous field width is returned. The **streamsize** type is defined by **< iostream >** as some form of integer. In some implementations, each time an output operation is performed, the field width returns to its default setting, so it might be necessary to set the minimum field width before each output statement.

After you set a minimum field width, when a value uses less than the specified width, the field is padded with the current fill character (the space, by default) so that the field width is reached. However, keep in mind that if the size of the output value exceeds the minimum field width, the field will be overrun. No values are truncated.

By default, six digits of precision are used. You can set this number by using the **precision( )** function. Its prototype is shown here:

```
streamsize precision(streamsize p);
```

Here the precision is set to p and the old value is returned.

By default, when a field needs to be filled, it is filled with spaces. You can specify the fill character by using the **fill( )** function. Its prototype is shown here:

```
char fill(char ch);
```

After a call to **fill( )**, ch becomes the new fill character, and the old one is returned.

EXAMPLES

1. Here is a program that illustrates the format functions:

```cpp
#include <iostream>
using namespace std;

int main()
{
  cout.width(10);             // set minimum field width
```

```
cout << "hello" << '\n'; // right-justify by default
cout.fill('%');          // set fill character
cout.width(10);          // set width
cout << "hello" << '\n'; // right-justify by default
cout.setf(ios::left);    // left-justify
cout.width(10);          // set width
cout << "hello" << '\n'; // output left justified

cout.width(10);          // set width
cout.precision(10);      // set 10 digits of precision
cout << 123.234567 << '\n';
cout.width(10);          // set width
cout.precision(6);       // set 6 digits of precision
cout << 123.234567 << '\n';

return 0;
}
```

This program displays the following output:

```
     hello
%%%%%hello
hello%%%%%
123.234567
123.235%%%
```

Notice that the field width is set before each output statement.

2. The following program shows how to use the C++ I/O format functions to create an aligned table of numbers:

```
// Create a table of square roots and squares.
#include <iostream>
#include <cmath>
using namespace std;

int main()
{
  double x;

  cout.precision(4);
  cout << "        x    sqrt(x)      x^2\n\n";

  for(x = 2.0; x <= 20.0; x++) {
    cout.width(7);
    cout << x << "  ";
```

```
    cout.width(7);
    cout << sqrt(x) << "   ";
    cout.width(7);
    cout << x*x << '\n';
  }

  return 0;
}
```

This program creates the following table:

```
    x      sqrt(x)    x^2

    2      1.414        4
    3      1.732        9
    4          2       16
    5      2.236       25
    6      2.449       36
    7      2.646       49
    8      2.828       64
    9          3       81
   10      3.162      100
   11      3.317      121
   12      3.464      144
   13      3.606      169
   14      3.742      196
   15      3.873      225
   16          4      256
   17      4.123      289
   18      4.243      324
   19      4.359      361
   20      4.472      400
```

EXERCISES

1. Create a program that prints the natural log and base 10 log of the numbers from 2 to 100. Format the table so the numbers are right justified within a field width of 10, using a precision of five decimal places.

2. Create a function called **center( )** that has this prototype:

void center(char *s);

Have this function center the specified string on the screen. To accomplish this, use the **width( )** function. Assume that the screen is 80 characters wide. (For simplicity, you may assume that no string exceeds 80 characters.) Write a program that demonstrates that your function works.

3. On your own, experiment with the format flags and the format functions. Once you become familiar with the C++ I/O system, you will have no trouble using it to format output any way you like.

8.4 USING I/O MANIPULATORS

There is a second way that you can format information using C++'s I/O system. This method uses special functions called *I/O manipulators.* As you will see, I/O manipulators are, in some situations, easier to use than the **ios** format flags and functions.

I/O manipulators are special I/O format functions that can occur *within* an I/O statement, instead of separate from it the way the **ios** member functions must. The standard manipulators are shown in Table 8-1. As you can see, many of the I/O manipulators parallel member functions of the **ios** class. Many of the manipulators shown in Table 8-1 were added recently to Standard C++ and will be supported only by modern compilers.

To access manipulators that take parameters, such as **setw( )**, you must include **< iomanip >** in your program. This is not necessary when you are using a manipulator that does not require an argument.

As stated above, the manipulators can occur in the chain of I/O operations. For example:

```
cout << oct << 100 << hex << 100;
cout << setw(10) << 100;
```

The first statement tells **cout** to display integers in octal and then outputs 100 in octal. It then tells the stream to display integers in hexadecimal and then outputs 100 in hexadecimal format. The second

Manipulator	Purpose	Input/Output
boolalpha	Turns on **boolalpha** flag	Input/Output
dec	Turns on **dec** flag	Input/Output
endl	Outputs a newline character and flushes the stream	Output
ends	Outputs a null	Output
fixed	Turns on **fixed** flag	Output
flush	Flushes a stream	Output
hex	Turns on **hex** flag	Input/Output
internal	Turns on **internal** flag	Output
left	Turns on **left** flag	Output
noboolalpha	Turns off **boolalpha** flag	Input/Output
noshowbase	Turns off **showbase** flag	Output
noshowpoint	Turns off **showpoint** flag	Output
noshowpos	Turns off **showpos** flag	Output
noskipws	Turns off **skipws** flag	Input
nounitbuf	Turns off **unitbuf** flag	Output
nouppercase	Turns off **uppercase** flag	Output
oct	Turns on **oct** flag	Input/Output
resetiosflags(fmtflags _f_)	Turns off the flags specified in _f_	Input/Output
right	Turns on **right** flag	Output
scientific	Turns on **scientific** flag	Output
setbase(int _base_)	Sets the number base to _base_	Input/Output
setfill(int _ch_)	Sets the fill character to _ch_	Output
setiosflags(fmtflags _f_)	Turns on the flags specified in _f_	Input/Output
setprecision(int _p_)	Sets the number of digits of precision	Output
setw(int _w_)	Sets the field width to _w_	Output
showbase	Turns on **showbase** flag	Output
showpoint	Turns on **showpoint** flag	Output
showpos	Turns on **showpos** flag	Output
skipws	Turns on **skipws** flag	Input
unitbuf	Turns on **unitbuf** flag	Output
uppercase	Turns on **uppercase** flag	Output
ws	Skips leading white space	Input

TABLE 8-1 _The Standard C++ I/O Manipulators_ ▼

statement sets the field width to 10 and then displays 100 in hexadecimal format again. Notice that when a manipulator does not take an argument, such as **oct** in the example, it is not followed by parentheses. This is because it is the address of the manipulator that is passed to the overloaded < < operator.

Keep in mind that an I/O manipulator affects only the stream of which the I/O expression is a part. I/O manipulators do *not* affect all streams currently opened for use.

As the preceding example suggests, the main advantages of using manipulators over the **ios** member functions is that they are often easier to use and allow more compact code to be written.

If you wish to set specific format flags manually by using a manipulator, use **setiosflags( )**. This manipulator performs the same function as the member function **setf( )**. To turn off flags, use the **resetiosflags( )** manipulator. This manipulator is equivalent to **unsetf( )**.

EXAMPLES

1. This program demonstrates several of the I/O manipulators:

```
#include <iostream>
#include <iomanip>
using namespace std;

int main()
{
  cout << hex << 100 << endl;
  cout << oct << 10 << endl;

  cout << setfill('X') << setw(10);
  cout << 100 << " hi " << endl;

  return 0;
}
```

This program displays the following:

```
64
12
XXXXXXX144 hi
```

2. Here is another version of the program that displays a table of the squares and square roots of the numbers 2 through 20. This version uses I/O manipulators instead of member functions and format flags.

```cpp
/* This version uses I/O manipulators to display
   the table of squares and square roots. */
#include <iostream>
#include <iomanip>
#include <cmath>
using namespace std;

int main()
{
  double x;

  cout << setprecision(4);
  cout << "      x    sqrt(x)      x^2\n\n";

  for(x = 2.0; x <= 20.0; x++) {
    cout << setw(7) << x << "   ";
    cout << setw(7) << sqrt(x) << "   ";
    cout << setw(7) << x*x << '\n';
  }

  return 0;
}
```

3. One of the most interesting format flags added by the new I/O library is **boolalpha**. This flag can be set either directly or by using the new manipulators **boolalpha** or **noboolalpha**. What makes **boolalpha** so interesting is that setting it allows you to input and output Boolean values using the keywords **true** and **false**. Normally you must enter 1 for true and 0 for false. For example, consider the following program:

```cpp
// Demonstrate boolalpha format flag.
#include <iostream>
using namespace std;

int main()
{
  bool b;

  cout << "Before setting boolalpha flag: ";
```

```
    b = true;
    cout << b << " ";
    b = false;
    cout << b << endl;

    cout << "After setting boolalpha flag: ";
    b = true;
    cout << boolalpha << b << " ";
    b = false;
    cout << b << endl;

    cout << "Enter a Boolean value: ";
    cin >> boolalpha >> b; // you can enter true or false
    cout << "You entered " << b;

    return 0;
}
```

Here is a sample run:

```
Before setting boolalpha flag: 1 0
After setting boolalpha flag: true false
Enter a Boolean value: true
You entered true
```

As you can see, once the **boolalpha** flag has been set, Boolean values are input and output using the words **true** or **false**. Notice that you must set the **boolalpha** flags for **cin** and **cout** separately. As with all format flags, setting **boolalpha** for one stream does not imply that it is also set for another.

<hr>

EXERCISES

1. Redo Exercises 1 and 2 from Section 8.3, this time using I/O manipulators instead of member functions and format flags.

2. Show the I/O statement that outputs the value 100 in hexadecimal with the base indicator (the 0x) shown. Use the **setiosflags( )** manipulator to accomplish this.

3. Explain the effect of setting the **boolalpha** flag.

*C*REATING YOUR OWN INSERTERS

As stated earlier, one of the advantages of the C++ I/O system is that you can overload the I/O operators for classes that you create. By doing so, you can seamlessly incorporate your classes into your C++ programs. In this section you learn how to overload C++'s output operator < <.

In the language of C++, the output operation is called an *insertion* and the < < is called the *insertion operator*. When you overload the < < for output, you are creating an *inserter function,* or *inserter* for short. The rationale for these terms comes from the fact that an output operator *inserts* information into a stream.

All inserter functions have this general form:

```
ostream &operator <<(ostream &stream, class-name ob)
{
    // body of inserter
    return stream;
}
```

The first parameter is a reference to an object of type **ostream**. This means that *stream* must be an output stream. (Remember, **ostream** is derived from the **ios** class.) The second parameter receives the object that will be output. (This can also be a reference parameter, if that is more suitable to your application.) Notice that the inserter function returns a reference to *stream,* which is of type **ostream**. This is required if the overloaded < < is going to be used in a series of I/O expressions, such as

```
cout << ob1 << ob2 << ob3;
```

Within an inserter you can perform any type of procedure. What an inserter does is completely up to you. However, for the inserter to be consistent with good programming practices, you should limit its operations to outputting information to a stream.

Although you might find this surprising at first, an inserter *cannot* be a member of the class on which it is designed to operate. Here is why: When an operator function of any type is a member of a class, the left operand, which is passed implicitly through the **this** pointer, is the object that generates the call to the operator function. This implies that the left operand is an object of that class. Therefore, if an overloaded operator function is a member of a class, the left operand must be an object of that class. However, when you create an inserter, the left operand is a stream and the right operand is the object that you want to output. Therefore, an inserter cannot be a member function.

The fact that an inserter cannot be a member function might appear to be a serious flaw in C++ because it seems to imply that all data of a class that will be output using an inserter will need to be public, thus violating the key principle of encapsulation. However, this is not the case. Even though inserters cannot be members of the class upon which they are designed to operate, they can be friends of the class. In fact, in most programming situations you will encounter, an overloaded inserter will be a friend of the class for which it was created.

EXAMPLES

1. As a simple first example, this program contains an inserter for the **coord** class, developed in a previous chapter:

```cpp
// Use a friend inserter for objects of type coord.
#include <iostream>
using namespace std;

class coord {
  int x, y;
public:
  coord() { x = 0; y = 0; }
  coord(int i, int j) { x = i; y = j; }
  friend ostream &operator<<(ostream &stream, coord ob);
};

ostream &operator<<(ostream &stream, coord ob)
{
  stream << ob.x << ", " << ob.y << '\n';
  return stream;
}

int main()
{
  coord a(1, 1), b(10, 23);
```

```
  cout << a << b;

  return 0;
}
```

This program displays the following:

```
1, 1
10, 23
```

The inserter in this program illustrates one very important point about creating your own inserters: make them as general as possible. In this case, the I/O statement inside the inserter outputs the values of **x** and **y** to **stream**, which is whatever stream is passed to the function. As you will see in the following chapter, when written correctly the same inserter that outputs to the screen can be used to output to *any* stream. Sometimes beginners are tempted to write the **coord** inserter like this:

```
ostream &operator<<(ostream &stream, coord ob)
{
  cout << ob.x << ", " << ob.y << '\n';
  return stream;
}
```

In this case, the output statement is hard-coded to display information on the standard output device linked to **cout**. However, this prevents the inserter from being used by other streams. The point is that you should make your inserters as general as possible because there is no disadvantage to doing so.

2. For the sake of illustration, here is the preceding program revised so that the inserter is *not* a friend of the **coord** class. Because the inserter does not have access to the private parts of **coord**, the variables **x** and **y** have to be made public.

```
/* Create an inserter for objects of type coord, using
   a non-friend inserter. */

#include <iostream>
using namespace std;

class coord {
public:
  int x, y;  // must be public
```

```
   coord() { x = 0; y = 0; }
   coord(int i, int j) { x = i; y = j; }
};

// An inserter for the coord class.
ostream &operator<<(ostream &stream, coord ob)
{
  stream << ob.x << ", " << ob.y << '\n';
  return stream;
}

int main()
{
  coord a(1, 1), b(10, 23);
  cout << a << b;

  return 0;
}
```

3. An inserter is not limited to displaying only textual information.
   An inserter can perform any operation or conversion necessary
   to output information in a form needed by a particular device or
   situation. For example, it is perfectly valid to create an inserter
   that sends information to a plotter. In this case, the inserter will
   need to send appropriate plotter codes in addition to the
   information. To allow you to taste the flavor of this type of
   inserter, the following program creates a class called **triangle**,
   which stores the width and height of a right triangle. The
   inserter for this class displays the triangle on the screen.

```
// This program draws right triangles
#include <iostream>
using namespace std;

class triangle {
  int height, base;
public:
  triangle(int h, int b) { height = h; base = b; }
  friend ostream &operator<<(ostream &stream, triangle ob);
};

// Draw a triangle.
ostream &operator<<(ostream &stream, triangle ob)
{
```

```
    int i, j, h, k;

    i = j = ob.base-1;
    for(h=ob.height-1; h; h--) {
      for(k=i; k; k--)
        stream << ' ';
      stream << '*';

      if(j!=i) {
        for(k=j-i-1; k; k--)
          stream << ' ';
        stream << '*';
      }

      i--;
      stream << '\n';
    }
    for(k=0; k<ob.base; k++) stream << '*';
    stream << '\n';

    return stream;
}

int main()
{
  triangle t1(5, 5), t2(10, 10), t3(12, 12);

  cout << t1;
  cout << endl << t2 << endl << t3;

  return 0;
}
```

Notice that this program illustrates how a properly designed inserter can be fully integrated into a "normal" I/O expression. This program displays the following:

```
    *
   **
  *  *
 *    *
*****

        *
       **
      *  *
     *    *
    *     *
   *      *
  *       *
 *        *
*         *
**********

         *
        **
       *  *
      *    *
     *     *
    *      *
   *       *
  *        *
 *         *
*          *
***********
```

EXERCISES

1. Given the following **strtype** class and partial program, create an inserter that displays a string:

```cpp
#include <iostream>
#include <cstring>
#include <cstdlib>
using namespace std;

class strtype {
  char *p;
```

```
    int len;
public:
    strtype(char *ptr);
    ~strtype() {delete [] p;}
    friend ostream &operator<<(ostream &stream, strtype &ob);
};

strtype::strtype(char *ptr)
{
    len = strlen(ptr)+1;
    p = new char [len];
    if(!p) {
        cout << "Allocation error\n";
        exit(1);
    }
    strcpy(p, ptr);
}

// Create operator<< inserter function here.

int main()
{
    strtype s1("This is a test."), s2("I like C++.");

    cout << s1 << '\n' << s2;

    return 0;
}
```

2. Replace the **show( )** function in the following program with an
   inserter function:

```
#include <iostream>
using namespace std;

class planet {
protected:
    double distance; // miles from the sun
    int revolve;  // in days
public:
    planet(double d, int r) { distance = d; revolve = r; }
};

class earth : public planet {
    double circumference; // circumference of orbit
```

```
public:
  earth(double d, int r) : planet(d, r) {
    circumference = 2*distance*3.1416;
  }

  /* Rewrite this so that it displays the information using
     an inserter function. */
  void show() {
    cout << "Distance from sun: " << distance << '\n';
    cout << "Days in obit: " << revolve << '\n';
    cout << "Circumference of orbit: " << circumference << '\n';
  }
};

int main()
{
  earth ob(93000000, 365);

  cout << ob;

  return 0;
}
```

3. Explain why an inserter cannot be a member function.

8.6 CREATING EXTRACTORS

Just as you can overload the < < output operator, you can overload the
> > input operator. In C++, the > > is referred to as the *extraction
operator* and a function that overloads it is called an *extractor*. The
reason for this term is that the act of inputting information from a
stream removes (that is, extracts) data from it.

The general form of an extractor function is shown here:

istream &operator>>(istream &*stream*, *class-name* &*ob*)
{
   // *body of extractor*
   return *stream*;
}

Extractors return a reference to **istream**, which is an input stream. The first parameter must be a reference to an input stream. The second parameter is a reference to the object that is receiving input.

For the same reason that an inserter cannot be a member function, an extractor cannot be a member function. Although you can perform any operation within an extractor, it is best to limit its activity to inputting information.

EXAMPLES

1. This program adds an extractor to the **coord** class:

```cpp
// Add a friend extractor for objects of type coord.
#include <iostream>
using namespace std;

class coord {
  int x, y;
public:
  coord() { x = 0; y = 0; }
  coord(int i, int j) { x = i; y = j; }
  friend ostream &operator<<(ostream &stream, coord ob);
  friend istream &operator>>(istream &stream, coord &ob);
};

ostream &operator<<(ostream &stream, coord ob)
{
  stream << ob.x << ", " << ob.y << '\n';
  return stream;
}

istream &operator>>(istream &stream, coord &ob)
{
  cout << "Enter coordinates: ";
  stream >> ob.x >> ob.y;
  return stream;
}

int main()
{
  coord a(1, 1), b(10, 23);
```

```
  cout << a << b;

  cin >> a;
  cout << a;

  return 0;
}
```

Notice how the extractor also prompts the user for input. Although such prompting is not required (or even desired) for most situations, this function shows how a customized extractor can simplify coding when a prompting message is needed.

2. Here an inventory class is created that stores the name of an item, the number on hand, and its cost. The program includes both an inserter and an extractor for this class.

```
#include <iostream>
#include <cstring>
using namespace std;

class inventory {
  char item[40]; // name of item
  int onhand; // number on hand
  double cost;  // cost of item
public:
  inventory(char *i, int o, double c)
  {
    strcpy(item, i);
    onhand = o;
    cost = c;
  }
  friend ostream &operator<<(ostream &stream, inventory ob);
  friend istream &operator>>(istream &stream, inventory &ob);
};

ostream &operator<<(ostream &stream, inventory ob)
{
  stream << ob.item << ": " << ob.onhand;
  stream << " on hand at $" << ob.cost << '\n';

  return stream;
}

istream &operator>>(istream &stream, inventory &ob)
```

```
{
  cout << "Enter item name: ";
  stream >> ob.item;
  cout << "Enter number on hand: ";
  stream >> ob.onhand;
  cout << "Enter cost: ";
  stream >> ob.cost;

  return stream;
}

int main()
{
  inventory ob("hammer", 4, 12.55);

  cout << ob;

  cin >> ob;

  cout << ob;

  return 0;
}
```

EXERCISES

1. Add an extractor to the **strtype** class from Exercise 1 in the preceding section.

2. Create a class that stores an integer value and its lowest factor. Create both an inserter and an extractor for this class.

SKILLS CHECK

Mastery
Skills Check

At this point you should be able to perform the following exercises and answer the questions.

1. Write a program that displays the number 100 in decimal, hexadecimal, and octal. (Use the **ios** format flags.)

2. Write a program that displays the value 1000.5364 in a 20-character field, left justified, with two decimal places, using * as a fill character. (Use the **ios** format flags.)

3. Rewrite your answers to Exercises 1 and 2 so that they use I/O manipulators.

4. Show how to save the format flags for **cout** and how to restore them. Use either member functions or manipulators.

5. Create an inserter and an extractor for this class:

```
class pwr {
  int base;
  int exponent;
  double result; // base to the exponent power
public:
  pwr(int b, int e);
};

pwr::pwr(int b, int e)
{
  base = b;
  exponent = e;

  result = 1;
  for( ; e; e--) result = result * base;
}
```

6. Create a class called **box** that stores the dimensions of a square. Create an inserter that displays a square box on the screen. (Use any method you like to display the box.)

This section checks how well you have integrated material in this chapter with that from the preceding chapters.

1. Using the **stack** class shown here, create an inserter that displays the contents of the stack. Demonstrate that your inserter works.

```cpp
#include <iostream>
using namespace std;

#define SIZE 10

// Declare a stack class for characters
class stack {
  char stck[SIZE]; // holds the stack
  int tos; // index of top-of-stack
public:
  stack();
  void push(char ch); // push character on stack
  char pop(); // pop character from stack
};

// Initialize the stack
stack::stack()
{
  tos = 0;
}

// Push a character.
void stack::push(char ch)
{
  if(tos==SIZE) {
    cout << "Stack is full\n";
    return;
  }
  stck[tos] = ch;
  tos++;
}
```

```
// Pop a character.
char stack::pop()
{
  if(tos==0) {
    cout << "Stack is empty\n";
    return 0; // return null on empty stack
  }
  tos--;
  return stck[tos];
}
```

2. Write a program that contains a class called **watch**. Using the standard time functions, have this class's constructor read the system time and store it. Create an inserter that displays the time.

3. Using the following class, which converts feet to inches, create an extractor that prompts the user for feet. Also, create an inserter that displays the number of feet and inches. Include a program that demonstrates that your inserter and extractor work.

```
class ft_to_inches {
  double feet;
  double inches;
public:
  void set(double f) {
    feet = f;
    inches = f * 12;
  }
};
```

9

Advanced C++ I/O

THIS chapter continues the examination of the C++ I/O system. In it you will learn to create your own I/O manipulators and work with files. Keep in mind that the C++ I/O system is both rich and flexible and contains many features. While it is beyond the scope of this book to include all of those features, the most important ones are discussed here. A complete description of the C++ I/O system can be found in my book *C++: The Complete Reference* (Berkeley: Osborne/McGraw-Hill).

The C++ I/O system described in this chapter reflects the one defined by Standard C++ and is compatible with all major C++ compilers. If you have an older or nonconforming compiler, its I/O system will not have all the capabilities described here.

Review
Skills Check

Before proceeding, you should be able to correctly answer the following questions and do the exercises.

1. Write a program that displays the sentence "C++ is fun" in a 40-character-wide field using a colon (:) as the fill character.

2. Write a program that displays the outcome of 10/3 to three decimal places. Use **ios** member functions to do this.

3. Redo the preceding program using I/O manipulators.

4. What is an inserter? What is an extractor?

5. Given the following class, create an inserter and an extractor for it.

```
class date {
  char d[9]; // store date as string: mm/dd/yy
public:
  // add inserter and extractor
};
```

6. What header must be included if your program is to use I/O manipulators that take parameters?

7. What predefined streams are created when a C++ program begins execution?

CREATING YOUR OWN MANIPULATORS

In addition to overloading the insertion and extraction operators, you can further customize C++'s I/O system by creating your own manipulator functions. Custom manipulators are important for two main reasons. First, a manipulator can consolidate a sequence of several separate I/O operations. For example, it is not uncommon to have situations in which the same sequence of I/O operations occurs frequently within a program. In these cases you can use a custom manipulator to perform these actions, thus simplifying your source code and preventing accidental errors. Second, a custom manipulator can be important when you need to perform I/O operations on a nonstandard device. For example, you could use a manipulator to send control codes to a special type of printer or an optical recognition system.

Custom manipulators are a feature of C++ that supports OOP, but they can also benefit programs that aren't object oriented. As you will see, custom manipulators can help make any I/O-intensive program clearer and more efficient.

As you know, there are two basic types of manipulators: those that operate on input streams and those that operate on output streams. In addition to these two broad categories, there is a secondary division: those manipulators that take an argument and those that don't. There are some significant differences between the way a parameterless manipulator and a parameterized manipulator are created. Further, creating parameterized manipulators is substantially more difficult than creating parameterless ones and is beyond the scope of this book. However, writing your own parameterless manipulators is quite easy and is examined here.

All parameterless manipulator output functions have this skeleton:

```
ostream &manip-name(ostream &stream)
{
  // your code here
  return stream;
}
```

Here *manip-name* is the name of the manipulator and *stream* is a reference to the invoking stream. A reference to the stream is returned. This is necessary if a manipulator is used as part of a larger I/O expression. It is important to understand that even though the manipulator has as its single argument a reference to the stream upon which it is operating, no argument is used when the manipulator is called in an output operation.

All parameterless input manipulator functions have this skeleton:

```
istream &manip-name(istream &stream)
{
   // your code here
   return stream;
}
```

An input manipulator receives a reference to the stream on which it was invoked. This stream must be returned by the manipulator.

Remember

It is crucial that your manipulators return a reference to the invoking stream. If this is not done, your manipulators cannot be used in a sequence of input or output operations.

EXAMPLES

1. As a simple first example, the following program creates a manipulator called **setup( )** that sets the field width to 10, the precision to 4, and the fill character to *.

```
#include <iostream>
using namespace std;

ostream &setup(ostream &stream)
{
  stream.width(10);
  stream.precision(4);
  stream.fill('*');

  return stream;
}

int main()
```

```
{
  cout << setup << 123.123456;

  return 0;
}
```

As you can see, **setup** is used as part of an I/O expression in the same way that any of the built-in manipulators would be used.

2. Custom manipulators need not be complex to be useful. For example, the simple manipulators **atn( )** and **note( )**, shown here, provide a shorter way to output frequently used words or phrases.

```
#include <iostream>
using namespace std;

// Attention:
ostream &atn(ostream &stream)
{
  stream << "Attention: ";
  return stream;
}

// Please note:
ostream &note(ostream &stream)
{
  stream << "Please Note: ";
  return stream;
}

int main()
{
  cout << atn << "High voltage circuit\n";
  cout << note << "Turn off all lights\n";

  return 0;
}
```

Even though they are simple, if used frequently, these manipulators save you from some tedious typing.

3. This program creates the **getpass( )** input manipulator, which rings the bell and then prompts for a password:

```
#include <iostream>
#include <cstring>
using namespace std;

// A simple input manipulator
istream &getpass(istream &stream)
{
  cout << '\a';  // sound bell
  cout << "Enter password: ";

  return stream;
}

int main()
{
  char pw[80];

  do {
    cin >> getpass >> pw;
  } while (strcmp(pw, "password"));

  cout << "Logon complete\n";

  return 0;
}
```

EXERCISES

1. Create an output manipulator that displays the current system time and date. Call this manipulator **td( )**.

2. Create an output manipulator called **sethex( )** that sets output to hexadecimal and turns on the **uppercase** and **showbase** flags. Also, create an output manipulator called **reset( )** that undoes the changes made by **sethex( )**.

3. Create an input manipulator called **skipchar( )** that reads and ignores the next ten characters from the input stream.

9.2 *F*ILE I/O BASICS

It is now time to turn our attention to file I/O. As mentioned in the preceding chapter, file I/O and console I/O are closely related. In fact, the same class hierarchy that supports console I/O also supports file I/O. Thus, most of what you have already learned about I/O applies to files as well. Of course, file handling makes use of several new features.

To perform file I/O, you must include the header **< fstream >** in your program. It defines several classes, including **ifstream**, **ofstream**, and **fstream**. These classes are derived from **istream** and **ostream**. Remember, **istream** and **ostream** are derived from **ios**, so **ifstream**, **ofstream**, and **fstream** also have access to all operations defined by **ios** (discussed in the preceding chapter).

In C++, a file is opened by linking it to a stream. There are three types of streams: input, output, and input/output. Before you can open a file, you must first obtain a stream. To create an input stream, declare an object of type **ifstream**. To create an output stream, declare an object of type **ofstream**. Streams that will be performing both input and output operations must be declared as objects of type **fstream**. For example, this fragment creates one input stream, one output stream, and one stream capable of both input and output:

```
ifstream in;   // input
ofstream out;  // output
fstream io;    // input and output
```

Once you have created a stream, one way to associate it with a file is by using the function **open( )**. This function is a member of each of the three file stream classes. The prototype for each is shown here:

void ifstream::open(const char *filename,
                    openmode mode = ios::in);

void ofstream::open(const char *filename,
                    openmode mode = ios::out | ios::trunc);

void fstream::open(const char *filename,
                    openmode mode = ios::in | ios::out);

Here *filename* is the name of the file, which can include a path specifier. The value of *mode* determines how the file is opened. It must be a value of type **openmode**, which is an enumeration defined by **ios** that contains the following values:

ios::app
ios::ate
ios::binary
ios::in
ios::out
ios::trunc

You can combine two or more of these values by ORing them together. Let's see what each of these values means.

Including **ios::app** causes all output to that file to be appended to the end. This value can be used only with files capable of output. Including **ios::ate** causes a seek to the end of the file to occur when the file is opened. Although **ios::ate** causes a seek to end-of-file, I/O operations can still occur anywhere within the file.

The **ios::in** value specifies that the file is capable of input. The **ios::out** value specifies that the file is capable of output.

The **ios::binary** value causes a file to be opened in binary mode. By default, all files are opened in text mode. In text mode, various character translations might take place, such as carriage return/linefeed sequences being converted into newlines. However, when a file is opened in binary mode, no such character translations will occur. Keep in mind that any file, whether it contains formatted text or raw data, can be opened in either binary or text mode. The only difference is whether character translations take place.

The **ios::trunc** value causes the contents of a preexisting file by the same name to be destroyed and the file to be truncated to zero length. When you create an output stream using **ofstream**, any preexisting file with the same name is automatically truncated.

The following fragment opens an output file called **test**:

```
ofstream mystream;
mystream.open("test");
```

Since the _mode_ parameter to **open( )** defaults to a value appropriate to the type of stream being opened, there is no need to specify its value in the preceding example.

If **open( )** fails, the stream will evaluate to false when used in a Boolean expression. You can make use of this fact to confirm that the open operation succeeded by using a statement like this:

```
if(!mystream) {
  cout << "Cannot open file.\n";
  // handle error
}
```

In general, you should always check the result of a call to **open( )** before attempting to access the file.

You can also check to see if you have successfully opened a file by using the **is_open( )** function, which is a member of **fstream**, **ifstream**, and **ofstream**. It has this prototype.

bool is_open( );

It returns true if the stream is linked to an open file and false otherwise. For example, the following checks if **mystream** is currently open:

```
if(!mystream.is_open()) {
  cout << "File is not open.\n";
  // ...
```

Although it is entirely proper to open a file by using the **open( )** function, most of the time you will not do so because the **ifstream**, **ofstream**, and **fstream** classes have constructor functions that automatically open the file. The constructor functions have the same parameters and defaults as the **open( )** function. Therefore, the most common way you will see a file opened is shown in this example:

```
ifstream  mystream("myfile"); // open file for input
```

As stated, if for some reason the file cannot be opened, the stream variable will evaluate as false when used in a conditional statement. Therefore, whether you use a constructor function to open the file or an explicit call to **open( )**, you will want to confirm that the file has actually been opened by testing the value of the stream.

To close a file, use the member function **close( )**. For example, to close the file linked to a stream called **mystream**, use this statement:

```
mystream.close();
```

The **close( )** function takes no parameters and returns no value.

You can detect when the end of an input file has been reached by using the **eof( )** member function of **ios**. It has this prototype:

bool eof();

It returns true when the end of the file has been encountered and false otherwise.

Once a file has been opened, it is very easy to read textual data from it or write formatted, textual data to it. Simply use the << and >> operators the same way you do when performing console I/O, except that instead of using **cin** and **cout**, substitute a stream that is linked to a file. In a way, reading and writing files by using >> and << is like using C's **fprintf( )** and **fscanf( )** functions. All information is stored in the file in the same format it would be in if displayed on the screen. Therefore, a file produced by using << is a formatted text file, and any file read by >> must be a formatted text file. Typically, files that contain formatted text that you operate on using the >> and << operators should be opened for text rather than binary mode. Binary mode is best used on unformatted files, which are described later in this chapter.

EXAMPLES

1. Here is a program that creates an output file, writes information to it, closes the file and opens it again as an input file, and reads in the information:

```cpp
#include <iostream>
#include <fstream>
using namespace std;

int main()
{
  ofstream fout("test");  // create output file

  if(!fout) {
    cout << "Cannot open output file.\n";
    return 1;
  }

  fout << "Hello!\n";
  fout << 100 << ' ' << hex << 100 << endl;

  fout.close();
```

```
ifstream fin("test"); // open input file

if(!fin) {
  cout << "Cannot open input file.\n";
  return 1;
}

char str[80];
int i;

fin >> str >> i;
cout << str << ' ' << i << endl;

fin.close();

return 0;
}
```

After you run this program, examine the contents of **test**. It will contain the following:

```
Hello!
100 64
```

As stated earlier, when the **< <** and **> >** operators are used to perform file I/O, information is formatted exactly as it would appear on the screen.

2. Following is another example of disk I/O. This program reads strings entered at the keyboard and writes them to disk. The program stops when the user enters a **$** as the first character in a string. To use the program, specify the name of the output file on the command line.

```
#include <iostream>
#include <fstream>
using namespace std;

int main(int argc, char *argv[])
{
  if(argc!=2) {
    cout << "Usage: WRITE <filename>\n";
    return 1;
  }
```

```
ofstream out(argv[1]); // output file

if(!out) {
  cout << "Cannot open output file.\n";
  return 1;
}

char str[80];
cout << "Write strings to disk, '$' to stop\n";

do {
  cout << ": ";
  cin >> str;
  out << str << endl;
} while (*str != '$');

out.close();
return 0;
}
```

3. Following is a program that copies a text file and, in the process, converts all spaces into | symbols. Notice how **eof( )** is used to check for the end of the input file. Notice also how the input stream **fin** has its **skipws** flag turned off. This prevents leading spaces from being skipped.

```
// Convert spaces to |s.
#include <iostream>
#include <fstream>
using namespace std;

int main(int argc, char *argv[])
{
  if(argc!=3) {
    cout << "Usage: CONVERT <input> <output>\n";
    return 1;
  }

  ifstream fin(argv[1]); // open input file
  ofstream fout(argv[2]);  // create output file

  if(!fout) {
    cout << "Cannot open output file.\n";
    return 1;
  }
```

```
if(!fin) {
  cout << "Cannot open input file.\n";
  return 1;
}

char ch;

fin.unsetf(ios::skipws);  // do not skip spaces
while(!fin.eof()) {
  fin >> ch;
  if(ch==' ') ch = '|';
  if(!fin.eof()) fout << ch;
}

fin.close();
fout.close();

return 0;
}
```

4. There are a few differences between C++'s original I/O library and the modern Standard C++ library that you should be aware of, especially if you are converting older code. First, in the original I/O library, **open( )** allowed a third parameter, which specified the file's protection mode. This parameter defaulted to a normal file. The modern I/O library does not support this parameter.

Second, when you are using the old library to open a stream for input and output using **fstream**, you must explicitly specify both the **ios::in** and the **ios::out** *mode* values. No default value for *mode* is supplied. This applies to both the **fstream** constructor and to its **open( )** function. For example, using the old I/O library you must use a call to **open( )** as shown here to open a file for input and output:

```
fstream mystream;
mystream.open("test", ios::in | ios::out);
```

In the modern I/O library, an object of type **fstream** automatically opens files for input and output when the *mode* parameter is not supplied.

Finally, in the old I/O system, the *mode* parameter could also include either **ios::nocreate**, which causes the **open( )**

function to fail if the file does not already exist, or
ios::noreplace, which causes the **open( )** function to fail if the
file does already exist. These values are not supported by
Standard C++.

EXERCISES

---

1. Write a program that will copy a text file. Have this program
   count the number of characters copied and display this result.
   Why does the number displayed differ from that shown when
   you list the output file in the directory?

2. Write a program that writes the following table of information to
   a file called **phone**:

   Isaac Newton, 415 555-3423
   Robert Goddard, 213 555-2312
   Enrico Fermi, 202 555-1111

3. Write a program that counts the number of words in a file. For
   simplicity, assume that anything surrounded by whitespace
   is a word.

4. What does **is_open( )** do?

9.3 UNFORMATTED, BINARY I/O

Although formatted text files such as those produced by the preceding
examples are useful in a variety of situations, they do not have the
flexibility of unformatted, binary files. Unformatted files contain the
same binary representation of the data as that used internally by your
program rather than the human-readable text that data is translated
into by the < < and > > operators. Thus, unformatted I/O is also
referred to as "raw" I/O. C++ supports a wide range of unformatted
file I/O functions. The unformatted functions give you detailed
control over how files are written and read.

The lowest-level unformatted I/O functions are **get( )** and **put( )**. You can read a byte by using **get( )** and write a byte by using **put( )**. These functions are members of all input and output stream classes, respectively. The **get( )** function has many forms, but the most commonly used version is shown here, along with **put( )**:

```
istream &get(char &ch);
ostream &put(char ch);
```

The **get( )** function reads a single character from the associated stream and puts that value in *ch*. It returns a reference to the stream. If a read is attempted at end-of-file, on return the invoking stream will evaluate to false when used in an expression. The **put( )** function writes *ch* to the stream and returns a reference to the stream.

To read and write blocks of data, use the **read( )** and **write( )** functions, which are also members of the input and output stream classes, respectively. Their prototypes are shown here:

```
istream &read(char *buf, streamsize num);
ostream &write(const char *buf, streamsize num);
```

The **read( )** function reads *num* bytes from the invoking stream and puts them in the buffer pointed to by *buf*. The **write( )** function writes *num* bytes to the associated stream from the buffer pointed to by *buf*. The **streamsize** type is some form of integer. An object of type **streamsize** is capable of holding the largest number of bytes that will be transferred in any one I/O operation.

If the end of the file is reached before *num* characters have been read, **read( )** simply stops, and the buffer contains as many characters as were available. You can find out how many characters have been read by using the member function **gcount( )**, which has this prototype:

```
streamsize gcount();
```

It returns the number of characters read by the last unformatted input operation.

When you are using the unformatted file functions, most often you will open a file for binary rather than text operations. The reason for this is easy to understand: specifying **ios::binary** prevents any character translations from occurring. This is important when the binary representations of data such as integers, **float**s, and pointers are stored in the file. However, it is perfectly acceptable to use the unformatted functions on a file opened in text mode—as long as that file actually contains only text. But remember, some character translations may occur.

EXAMPLES

1. The next program will display the contents of any file on the screen. It uses the **get( )** function.

```cpp
#include <iostream>
#include <fstream>
using namespace std;

int main(int argc, char *argv[])
{
  char ch;

  if(argc!=2) {
    cout << "Usage: PR <filename>\n";
    return 1;
  }

  ifstream in(argv[1], ios::in | ios::binary);
  if(!in) {
    cout << "Cannot open file.\n";
    return 1;
  }

  while(!in.eof()) {
    in.get(ch);
    cout << ch;
  }

  in.close();

  return 0;
}
```

2. This program uses **put( )** to write characters to a file until the user enters a dollar sign:

```cpp
#include <iostream>
#include <fstream>
```

```
using namespace std;

int main(int argc, char *argv[])
{
  char ch;

  if(argc!=2) {
    cout << "Usage: WRITE <filename>\n";
    return 1;
  }

  ofstream out(argv[1], ios::out | ios::binary);

  if(!out) {
    cout << "Cannot open file.\n";
    return 1;
  }

  cout << "Enter a $ to stop\n";
  do {
    cout << ": ";
    cin.get(ch);
    out.put(ch);
  } while (ch!='$');

  out.close();

  return 0;
}
```

Notice that the program uses **get( )** to read characters from **cin**. This prevents leading spaces from being discarded.

3. Here is a program that uses **write( )** to write a **double** and a string to a file called **test**:

```
#include <iostream>
#include <fstream>
#include <cstring>
using namespace std;

int main()
{
  ofstream out("test", ios::out | ios::binary);

  if(!out) {
```

```
       cout << "Cannot open output file.\n";
       return 1;
    }

    double num = 100.45;
    char str[] = "This is a test";

    out.write((char *) &num, sizeof(double));
    out.write(str, strlen(str));

    out.close();

    return 0;
}
```

*The type cast to **(char *)** inside the call to **write( )** is necessary when outputting a buffer that is not defined as a character array. Because of C++'s strong type checking, a pointer of one type will not automatically be converted into a pointer of another type.*

4. This program uses **read( )** to read the file created by the program in Example 3:

```
#include <iostream>
#include <fstream>
using namespace std;

int main()
{
    ifstream in("test", ios::in | ios::binary);

    if(!in) {
       cout << "Cannot open input file.\n";
       return 1;
    }

    double num;
    char str[80];

    in.read((char *) &num, sizeof(double));
    in.read(str, 14);
    str[14] = '\0'; // null terminate str
```

```
  cout << num << ' ' << str;

  in.close();

  return 0;
}
```

As is the case with the program in the preceding example, the type cast inside **read( )** is necessary because C++ will not automatically convert a pointer of one type to another.

5. The following program first writes an array of **double** values to a file and then reads them back. It also reports the number of characters read.

```
// Demonstrate gcount().
#include <iostream>
#include <fstream>
using namespace std;

int main()
{
  ofstream out("test", ios::out | ios::binary);

  if(!out) {
    cout << "Cannot open output file.\n";
    return 1;
  }

  double nums[4] = {1.1, 2.2, 3.3, 4.4 };

  out.write((char *) nums, sizeof(nums));
  out.close();

  ifstream in("test", ios::in | ios::binary);

  if(!in) {
    cout << "Cannot open input file.\n";
    return 1;
  }

  in.read((char *) &nums, sizeof(nums));

  int i;
  for(i=0; i<4; i++)
```

```
       cout << nums[i] << ' ';

    cout << '\n';

    cout << in.gcount() << " characters read\n";
    in.close();

    return 0;
}
```

1. Rewrite your answers to Exercises 1 and 3 in the preceding section (Section 9.2) so that they use **get( )**, **put( )**, **read( )**, and/or **write( )**. (Use whichever of these functions you deem most appropriate.)

2. Given the following class, write a program that outputs the contents of the class to a file. Create an inserter function for this purpose.

```
class account {
  int custnum;
  char name[80];
  double balance;
public:
  account(int c, char *n, double b)
  {
    custnum = c;
    strcpy(name, n);
    balance = b;
  }
  // create inserter here
};
```

9.4 $\boldsymbol{M}$ORE UNFORMATTED I/O FUNCTIONS

In addition to the form shown earlier, there are several different ways in which the **get( )** function is overloaded. The prototypes for the three most commonly used overloaded forms are shown here:

```
istream &get(char *buf, streamsize num);
istream &get(char *buf, streamsize num, char delim);
int get( );
```

The first form reads characters into the array pointed to by *buf* until either *num*-1 characters have been read, a newline is found, or the end of the file has been encountered. The array pointed to by *buf* will be null terminated by **get( )**. If the newline character is encountered in the input stream, it is *not* extracted. Instead, it remains in the stream until the next input operation.

The second form reads characters into the array pointed to by *buf* until either *num*-1 characters have been read, the character specified by *delim* has been found, or the end of the file has been encountered. The array pointed to by *buf* will be null terminated by **get( )**. If the delimiter character is encountered in the input stream, it is *not* extracted. Instead, it remains in the stream until the next input operation.

The third overloaded form of **get( )** returns the next character from the stream. It returns EOF if the end of the file is encountered. This form of **get( )** is similar to C's **getc( )** function.

Another function that performs input is **getline( )**. It is a member of each input stream class. Its prototypes are shown here:

```
istream &getline(char *buf, streamsize num);
istream &getline(char *buf, streamsize num, char delim);
```

The first form reads characters into the array pointed to by *buf* until either *num*-1 characters have been read, a newline character has been found, or the end of the file has been encountered. The array pointed to by *buf* will be null terminated by **getline( )**. If the newline character is encountered in the input stream, it is extracted, but it is not put into *buf.*

The second form reads characters into the array pointed to by *buf* until either *num*-1 characters have been read, the character specified by *delim* has been found, or the end of the file has been encountered. The array pointed to by *buf* will be null terminated by **getline( )**. If the delimiter character is encountered in the input stream, it is extracted, but it is not put into *buf.*

As you can see, the two versions of **getline( )** are virtually identical to the **get(***buf, num***)** and **get(***buf, num, delim***)** versions of **get( )**. Both read characters from input and put them into the array pointed to by *buf* until either *num*-1 characters have been read or until the delimiter character or the end of the file is encountered. The difference between **get( )** and **getline( )** is that **getline( )** reads and removes the delimiter from the input stream; **get( )** does not.

You can obtain the next character in the input stream without removing it from that stream by using **peek( )**. This function is a member of the input stream classes and has this prototype:

```
int peek();
```

It returns the next character in the stream; it returns EOF if the end of the file is encountered.

You can return the last character read from a stream to that stream by using **putback( )**, which is a member of the input stream classes. Its prototype is shown here:

```
istream &putback(char c);
```

where *c* is the last character read.

When output is performed, data is not immediately written to the physical device linked to the stream. Instead, information is stored in an internal buffer until the buffer is full. Only then are the contents of that buffer written to disk. However, you can force the information to be physically written to disk before the buffer is full by calling **flush( )**. **flush( )** is a member of the output stream classes and has this prototype:

```
ostream &flush();
```

Calls to **flush( )** might be warranted when a program is going to be used in adverse environments (in situations where power outages occur frequently, for example).

EXAMPLES

1. As you know, when you use **> >** to read a string, it stops reading when the first whitespace character is encountered. This makes it useless for reading a string containing spaces. However, you can overcome this problem by using **getline( )**, as this program illustrates:

```
// Use getline() to read a string that contains spaces.
#include <iostream>
#include <fstream>
using namespace std;

int main()
{
  char str[80];

  cout << "Enter your name: ";
  cin.getline(str, 79);

  cout << str << '\n';

  return 0;
}
```

In this program, the delimiter used by **getline( )** is the newline. This makes **getline( )** act much like the standard **gets( )** function.

2. In real programming situations, the functions **peek( )** and **putback( )** are especially useful because they let you more easily handle situations in which you do not know what type of information is being input at any point in time. The following program gives the flavor of this. It reads either strings or integers from a file. The strings and integers can occur in any order.

```
// Demonstrate peek().
#include <iostream>
#include <fstream>
#include <cctype>
using namespace std;

int main()
{
  char ch;
  ofstream out("test", ios::out | ios::binary);

  if(!out) {
    cout << "Cannot open output file.\n";
    return 1;
  }

  char str[80], *p;

  out << 123 << "this is a test" << 23;
  out << "Hello there!" << 99 << "sdf" << endl;
  out.close();

  ifstream in("test", ios::in | ios::binary);

  if(!in) {
    cout << "Cannot open input file.\n";
    return 1;
  }

  do {
    p = str;
    ch = in.peek(); // see what type of char is next
    if(isdigit(ch)) {
      while(isdigit(*p=in.get())) p++; // read integer
      in.putback(*p); // return char to stream
      *p = '\0'; // null-terminate the string
      cout << "Integer: " << atoi(str);
    }
    else if(isalpha(ch)) { // read a string
      while(isalpha(*p=in.get())) p++;
      in.putback(*p); // return char to stream
      *p = '\0'; // null-terminate the string
      cout << "String: " << str;
    }
    else in.get(); // ignore
```

```
    cout << '\n';
} while(!in.eof());

in.close();
return 0;
}
```

1. Rewrite the program in Example 1 so it uses **get( )** instead of **getline( )**. Does the program function differently?

2. Write a program that reads a text file one line at a time and displays each line on the screen. Use **getline( )**.

3. On your own, think about why there may be cases in which a call to **flush( )** is appropriate.

9.5 *R*ANDOM ACCESS

In C++'s I/O system, you perform random access by using the **seekg( )** and **seekp( )** functions, which are members of the input and output stream classes, respectively. Their most common forms are shown here:

```
istream &seekg(off_type offset, seekdir origin);
ostream &seekp(off_type offset, seekdir origin);
```

Here **off_type** is an integer type defined by **ios** that is capable of containing the largest valid value that *offset* can have. **seekdir** is an enumeration defined by **ios** that has these values:

Value	Meaning
ios::beg	Seek from beginning
ios::cur	Seek from current location
ios::end	Seek from end

The C++ I/O system manages two pointers associated with a file. One is the *get pointer*, which specifies where in the file the next input operation will occur. The other is the *put pointer*, which specifies where in the file the next output operation will occur. Each time an input or output operation takes place, the appropriate pointer is automatically sequentially advanced. However, by using the **seekg( )** and **seekp( )** functions, it is possible to access the file in a nonsequential fashion.

The **seekg( )** function moves the associated file's current get pointer *offset* number of bytes from the specified *origin*. The **seekp( )** function moves the associated file's current put pointer *offset* number of bytes from the specified *origin*.

In general, files that will be accessed via **seekg( )** and **seekp( )** should be opened for binary file operations. This prevents character translations from occuring which may affect the apparent position of an item within a file.

You can determine the current position of each file pointer by using these member functions:

```
pos_type tellg( );
pos_type tellp( );
```

Here **pos_type** is an integer type defined by **ios** that is capable of holding the largest value that defines a file position.

There are overloaded versions of **seekg( )** and **seekp( )** that move the file pointers to the location specified by the return values of **tellg( )** and **tellp( )**. Their prototypes are shown here.

```
istream &seekg(pos_type position);
ostream &seekp(pos_type position);
```

EXAMPLES

1. The following program demonstrates the **seekp( )** function. It allows you to change a specific character in a file. Specify a file name on the command line, followed by the number of the byte in the file you want to change, followed by the new character. Notice that the file is opened for read/write operations.

```
#include <iostream>
#include <fstream>
```

```
#include <cstdlib>
using namespace std;

int main(int argc, char *argv[])
{
  if(argc!=4) {
    cout << "Usage: CHANGE <filename> <byte> <char>\n";
    return 1;
  }

  fstream out(argv[1], ios::in | ios::out | ios::binary);

  if(!out) {
    cout << "Cannot open file.\n";
    return 1;
  }

  out.seekp(atoi(argv[2]), ios::beg);

  out.put(*argv[3]);
  out.close();

  return 0;
}
```

2. The next program uses **seekg( )** to position the get pointer into the middle of a file and then displays the contents of that file from that point. The name of the file and the location to begin reading from are specified on the command line.

```
// Demonstrate seekg().
#include <iostream>
#include <fstream>
#include <cstdlib>
using namespace std;

int main(int argc, char *argv[])
{
  char ch;

  if(argc!=3) {
    cout << "Usage: LOCATE <filename> <loc>\n";
    return 1;
  }
```

```
ifstream in(argv[1], ios::in | ios::binary);

if(!in) {
  cout << "Cannot open input file.\n";
  return 1;
}

in.seekg(atoi(argv[2]), ios::beg);

while(!in.eof()) {
  in.get(ch);
  cout << ch;
}

in.close();

return 0;
}
```

EXERCISES

1. Write a program that displays a text file backwards. Hint: Think about this before creating your program. The solution is easier than you might imagine.

2. Write a program that swaps each character pair in a text file. For example, if the file contains "1234", then after the program is run, the file will contain "2143". (For simplicity, you may assume that the file contains an even number of characters.)

9.6 *C*HECKING THE I/O STATUS

The C++ I/O system maintains status information about the outcome of each I/O operation. The current status of an I/O stream is described in an object of type **iostate**, which is an enumeration defined by **ios** that includes these members:

Name	Meaning
goodbit	No errors occurred.
eofbit	End-of-file has been encountered.
failbit	A nonfatal I/O error has occurred.
badbit	A fatal I/O error has occurred.

For older compilers, the I/O status flags are held in an **int** rather than an object of type **iostate**.

There are two ways in which you can obtain I/O status information. First, you can call the **rdstate( )** function, which is a member of **ios**. It has this prototype:

    iostate rdstate( );

It returns the current status of the error flags. As you can probably guess from looking at the preceding list of flags, **rdstate( )** returns **goodbit** when no error has occurred. Otherwise, an error flag is returned.

The other way you can determine whether an error has occurred is by using one or more of these **ios** member functions.

    bool bad( );
    bool eof( );
    bool fail( );
    bool good( );

The **eof( )** function was discussed earlier. The **bad( )** function returns true if **badbit** is set. The **fail( )** function returns true if **failbit** is set. The **good( )** function returns true if there are no errors. Otherwise they return false.

Once an error has occurred, it might need to be cleared before your program continues. To do this, use the **ios** member function **clear( )**, whose prototype is shown here:

    void clear(iostate *flags* = ios::goodbit);

If *flags* is **goodbit** (as it is by default), all error flags are cleared. Otherwise, set *flags* to the settings you desire.

1. The following program illustrates **rdstate( )**. It displays the contents of a text file. If an error occurs, the function reports it by using **checkstatus( )**.

```cpp
#include <iostream>
#include <fstream>
using namespace std;

void checkstatus(ifstream &in);

int main(int argc, char *argv[])
{
  if(argc!=2) {
    cout << "Usage: DISPLAY <filename>\n";
    return 1;
  }

  ifstream in(argv[1]);

  if(!in) {
    cout << "Cannot open input file.\n";
    return 1;
  }

  char c;
  while(in.get(c)) {
    cout << c;
    checkstatus(in);
  }

  checkstatus(in);  // check final status
  in.close();

  return 0;
}

void checkstatus(ifstream &in)
{
  ios::iostate i;

  i = in.rdstate();

  if(i & ios::eofbit)
    cout << "EOF encountered\n";
```

```
   else if(i & ios::failbit)
     cout << "Non-Fatal I/O error\n";
   else if(i & ios::badbit)
     cout << "Fatal I/O error\n";
}
```

The preceding program will always report at least one "error."
After the **while** loop ends, the final call to **checkstatus( )**
reports, as expected, that an EOF has been encountered.

2. This program displays a text file. It uses **good( )** to detect a file error:

```
#include <iostream>
#include <fstream>
using namespace std;

int main(int argc, char *argv[])
{
  char ch;

  if(argc!=2) {
    cout << "PR: <filename>\n";
    return 1;
  }

  ifstream in(argv[1]);

  if(!in) {
    cout << "Cannot open input file.\n";
    return 1;
  }

  while(!in.eof()) {
    in.get(ch);
    // check for error
    if(!in.good() && !in.eof()) {
      cout << "I/O Error...terminating\n";
      return 1;
    }
    cout << ch;
  }

  in.close();

  return 0;
}
```

1. Add error checking to your answers to the exercises from the preceding section.

9.7   *C*USTOMIZED I/O AND FILES

In the preceding chapter, you learned how to overload the insertion and extraction operators relative to your own classes. In that chapter, only console I/O was performed. However, because all C++ streams are the same, the same overloaded inserter function, for example, can be used to output to the screen or to a file with no changes whatsoever. This is one of the most important and useful features of C++'s approach to I/O.

As stated in the previous chapter, overloaded inserters and extractors, as well as I/O manipulators, can be used with any stream as long as they are written in a general manner. If you "hard-code" a specific stream into an I/O function, its use is, of course, limited to only that stream. This is why you were urged to generalize your I/O functions whenever possible.

1. In the following program, the **coord** class overloads the < < and > > operators. Notice that you can use the operator functions to write both to the screen and to a file.

```
#include <iostream>
#include <fstream>
using namespace std;

class coord {
  int x, y;
public:
  coord(int i, int j) { x = i; y = j; }
  friend ostream &operator<<(ostream &stream, coord ob);
  friend istream &operator>>(istream &stream, coord &ob);
};
```

```cpp
ostream &operator<<(ostream &stream, coord ob)
{
  stream << ob.x << ' ' << ob.y << '\n';

  return stream;
}

istream &operator>>(istream &stream, coord &ob)
{
  stream >> ob.x >> ob.y;

  return stream;
}

int main()
{
  coord o1(1, 2), o2(3, 4);
  ofstream out("test");

  if(!out) {
    cout << "Cannot open output file.\n";
    return 1;
  }

  out << o1 << o2;

  out.close();

  ifstream in("test");

  if(!in) {
    cout << "Cannot open input file.\n";
    return 1;
  }

  coord o3(0, 0), o4(0, 0);
  in >> o3 >> o4;

  cout << o3 << o4;

  in.close();

  return 0;
}
```

2. All of the I/O manipulators can be used with files. For example, in this reworked version of a program presented earlier in this chapter, the same manipulator that writes to the screen will also write to a file:

```cpp
#include <iostream>
#include <fstream>
#include <iomanip>
using namespace std;

// Attention:
ostream &atn(ostream &stream)
{
  stream << "Attention: ";
  return stream;
}

// Please note:
ostream &note(ostream &stream)
{
  stream << "Please Note: ";
  return stream;
}

int main()
{
  ofstream out("test");

  if(!out) {
    cout << "Cannot open output file.\n";
    return 1;
  }

  // write to screen
  cout << atn << "High voltage circuit\n";
  cout << note << "Turn off all lights\n";

  // write to file
  out << atn << "High voltage circuit\n";
  out << note << "Turn off all lights\n";

  out.close();

  return 0;
}
```

EXERCISE

1. On your own, experiment with the programs from the preceding chapter, trying each on a disk file.

SKILLS CHECK

**Mastery
Skills Check**

At this point you should be able to perform the following exercises and answer the questions.

1. Create an output manipulator that outputs three tabs and then sets the field width to 20. Demonstrate that your manipulator works.

2. Create an input manipulator that reads and discards all nonalphabetical characters. When the first alphabetical character is read, have the manipulator return it to the input stream and return. Call this manipulator **findalpha**.

3. Write a program that copies a text file. In the process, reverse the case of all letters.

4. Write a program that reads a text file and then reports the number of times each letter in the alphabet occurs in the file.

5. If you have not done so, add complete error checking to your solutions to Exercises 3 and 4 above.

6. What function positions the get pointer? What function positions the put pointer?

Cumulative Skills Check

This section checks how well you have integrated material in this chapter with that from the preceding chapters.

1. Following is a reworked version of the **inventory** class presented in the preceding chapter. Write a program that fills in the functions **store( )** and **retrieve( )**. Next, create a small inventory file on disk containing a few entries. Then, using random I/O, allow the user to display the information about any item by specifying its record number.

```cpp
#include <fstream>
#include <iostream>
#include <cstring>
using namespace std;

#define SIZE 40

class inventory {
  char item[SIZE]; // name of item
  int onhand; // number on hand
  double cost;   // cost of item
public:
  inventory(char *i, int o, double c)
  {
    strcpy(item, i);
    onhand = o;
    cost = c;
  }
  void store(fstream &stream);
  void retrieve(fstream &stream);
  friend ostream &operator<<(ostream &stream, inventory ob);
  friend istream &operator>>(istream &stream, inventory &ob);
};

ostream &operator<<(ostream &stream, inventory ob)
{
  stream << ob.item << ": " << ob.onhand;
  stream << " on hand at $" << ob.cost << '\n';
```

```
    return stream;
}

istream &operator>>(istream &stream, inventory &ob)
{
    cout << "Enter item name: ";
    stream >> ob.item;
    cout << "Enter number on hand: ";
    stream >> ob.onhand;
    cout << "Enter cost: ";
    stream >> ob.cost;

    return stream;
}
```

2. As a special challenge, on your own, create a **stack** class for characters that stores them in a disk file rather than in an array in memory.

10

Virtual Functions

chapter objectives

10.1 Pointers to derived classes

10.2 Introduction to virtual functions

10.3 More about virtual functions

10.4 Applying polymorphism

THIS chapter examines another important aspect of C++: the virtual function. What makes virtual functions important is that they are used to support run-time polymorphism. Polymorphism is supported by C++ in two ways. First, it is supported at compile time, through the use of overloaded operators and functions. Second, it is supported at run time, through the use of virtual functions. As you will learn, run-time polymorphism provides the greatest flexibility.

At the foundation of virtual functions and run-time polymorphism are pointers to derived classes. For this reason this chapter begins with a discussion of such pointers.

Review
Skills Check

Before proceeding, you should be able to correctly answer the following questions and do the exercises.

1. Create a manipulator that causes numbers to be displayed in scientific notation, using a capital E.

2. Write a program that copies a text file. During the copy process, convert all tabs into the correct number of spaces.

3. Write a program that searches a text file for a word specified on the command line. Have the program display how many times the specified word is found. For simplicity, assume that anything surrounded by whitespace is a word.

4. Show the statement that sets the put pointer to the 234th byte in a file linked to a stream called **out**.

5. What functions report status information about the C++ I/O system?

6. Give one advantage of using the C++ I/O functions instead of the C-like I/O system.

10.1 *P*OINTERS TO DERIVED CLASSES

Although Chapter 4 discussed C++ pointers at some length, one special aspect was deferred until now because it relates specifically to virtual functions. The feature is this: A pointer declared as a pointer to a base class can also be used to point to any class derived from that base. For example, assume two classes called **base** and **derived**, where **derived** inherits **base**. Given this situation, the following statements are correct:

```
base *p; // base class pointer

base base_ob; // object of type base
derived derived_ob; // object of type derived

// p can, of course, point to base objects
p = &base_ob; // p points to base object

// p can also point to derived objects without error
p = &derived_ob; // p points to derived object
```

As the comments suggest, a base pointer can point to an object of any class derived from that base without generating a type mismatch error.

Although you can use a base pointer to point to a derived object, you can access only those members of the derived object that were inherited from the base. This is because the base pointer has knowledge only of the base class. It knows nothing about the members added by the derived class.

While it is permissible for a base pointer to point to a derived object, the reverse is not true. A pointer of the derived type cannot be used to access an object of the base class. (A type cast can be used to overcome this restriction, but its use is not recommended practice.)

One final point: Remember that pointer arithmetic is relative to the data type the pointer is declared as pointing to. Thus, if you point a base pointer to a derived object and then increment that pointer, it will not be pointing to the next derived object. It will be pointing to (what it thinks is) the next base object. Be careful about this.

1. Here is a short program that illustrates how a base class pointer can be used to access a derived class:

```cpp
// Demonstrate pointer to derived class.
#include <iostream>
using namespace std;

class base {
  int x;
public:
  void setx(int i) { x = i; }
  int getx() { return x; }
};

class derived : public base {
  int y;
public:
  void sety(int i) { y = i; }
  int gety() { return y; }
};

int main()
{
  base *p; // pointer to base type
  base b_ob; // object of base
  derived d_ob; // object of derived

  // use p to access base object
  p = &b_ob;
  p->setx(10); // access base object
  cout << "Base object x: " << p->getx() << '\n';

  // use p to access derived object
  p = &d_ob; // point to derived object
  p->setx(99); // access derived object

  // can't use p to set y, so do it directly
  d_ob.sety(88);
  cout << "Derived object x: " << p->getx() << '\n';
  cout << "Derived object y: " << d_ob.gety() << '\n';

  return 0;
}
```

Aside from illustrating pointers to derived classes, there is no value in using a base class pointer in the way shown in this example. However, in the next section you will see why base class pointers to derived objects are so important.

EXERCISE

1. On your own, try the preceding example and experiment with it. For example, try declaring a derived pointer and having it access an object of the base class.

10.2 *INTRODUCTION TO VIRTUAL FUNCTIONS*

A *virtual function* is a member function that is declared within a base class and redefined by a derived class. To create a virtual function, precede the function's declaration with the keyword **virtual**. When a class containing a virtual function is inherited, the derived class redefines the virtual function relative to the derived class. In essence, virtual functions implement the "one interface, multiple methods" philosophy that underlies polymorphism. The virtual function within the base class defines the *form* of the *interface* to that function. Each redefinition of the virtual function by a derived class implements its operation as it relates specifically to the derived class. That is, the redefinition creates a *specific method*. When a virtual function is redefined by a derived class, the keyword **virtual** is not needed.

A virtual function can be called just like any other member function. However, what makes a virtual function interesting—and capable of supporting run-time polymorphism—is what happens when a virtual function is called through a pointer. From the preceding section you know that a base class pointer can be used to point to a derived class object. When a base pointer points to a derived object that contains a virtual function and that virtual function is called through that pointer, C++ determines which version of that function will be executed based upon the *type of object being pointed to* by the pointer. And, this determination is made at *run time*. Put differently, it is the type of the object pointed to at the time when the call occurs that determines which version of the virtual function will be executed. Therefore, if two or more different classes are derived from a base class that contains a virtual function, then when different objects are pointed to by a base pointer, different versions of the virtual function are executed. This process is the way that run-time polymorphism is achieved. In fact, a class that contains a virtual function is referred to as a *polymorphic class*.

EXAMPLES

1. Here is a short example that uses a virtual function:

```cpp
// A simple example using a virtual function.
#include <iostream>
using namespace std;

class base {
public:
  int i;
  base(int x) { i = x; }
  virtual void func()
  {
    cout << "Using base version of func(): ";
    cout << i << '\n';
  }
};

class derived1 : public base {
public:
  derived1(int x) : base(x) {}
  void func()
  {
    cout << "Using derived1's version of func(): ";
    cout << i*i << '\n';
  }
};

class derived2 : public base {
public:
  derived2(int x) : base(x) {}
```

```
    void func()
    {
      cout << "Using derived2's version of func(): ";
      cout << i+i << '\n';
    }
};

int main()
{
  base *p;
  base ob(10);
  derived1 d_ob1(10);
  derived2 d_ob2(10);

  p = &ob;
  p->func(); // use base's func()

  p = &d_ob1;
  p->func(); // use derived1's func()

  p = &d_ob2;
  p->func(); // use derived2's func()

  return 0;
}
```

This program displays the following output:

```
Using base version of func(): 10
Using derived1's version of func(): 100
Using derived2's version of func(): 20
```

The redefinition of a virtual function inside a derived class might, at first, seem somewhat similar to function overloading. However, the two processes are distinctly different. First, an overloaded function must differ in type and/or number of parameters, while a redefined virtual function must have precisely the same type and number of parameters and the same return type. (In fact, if you change either the number or type of parameters when redefining a virtual function, it simply becomes an overloaded function and its virtual nature is lost.) Further, virtual functions must be class members. This is not the case for overloaded functions. Also, while destructor functions can be virtual, constructors cannot. Because of the differences between overloaded functions and redefined virtual functions, the term *overriding* is used to describe virtual function redefinition.

As you can see, the example program creates three classes. The **base** class defines the virtual function **func( )**. This class is then inherited by both **derived1** and **derived2**. Each of these classes overrides **func( )** with its individual implementation. Inside **main( )**, the base class pointer **p** is declared along with objects of type **base**, **derived1**, and **derived2**. First, **p** is assigned the address of **ob** (an object of type **base**). When **func( )** is called by using **p**, it is the version in **base** that is used. Next, **p** is assigned the address of **d_ob1** and **func( )** is called again. Because it is the type of the object pointed to that determines which virtual function will be called, this time it is the overridden version in **derived1** that is executed. Finally, **p** is assigned the address of **d_ob2** and **func( )** is called again. This time, it is the version of **func( )** defined inside **derived2** that is executed.

The key points to understand from the preceding example are that the type of the object being pointed to determines which version of an overridden virtual function will be executed when accessed via a base class pointer, and that this decision is made at run time.

2. Virtual functions are hierarchical in order of inheritance. Further, when a derived class does *not* override a virtual function, the function defined within its base class is used. For example, here is a slightly different version of the preceding program:

```
// Virtual functions are hierarchical.
#include <iostream>
using namespace std;

class base {
public:
  int i;
  base(int x) { i = x; }
  virtual void func()
  {
    cout << "Using base version of func(): ";
    cout << i << '\n';
  }
}
```

```
};

class derived1 : public base {
public:
  derived1(int x) : base(x) {}
  void func()
  {
    cout << "Using derived1's version of func(): ";
    cout << i*i << '\n';
  }
};

class derived2 : public base {
public:
  derived2(int x) : base(x) {}
  // derived2 does not override func()
};

int main()
{
  base *p;
  base ob(10);
  derived1 d_ob1(10);
  derived2 d_ob2(10);
  p = &ob;
  p->func(); // use base's func()

  p = &d_ob1;
  p->func(); // use derived1's func()
  p = &d_ob2;
  p->func(); // use base's func()

  return 0;
}
```

This program displays the following output:

```
Using base version of func(): 10
Using derived1's version of func(): 100
Using base version of func(): 10
```

In this version, **derived2** does not override **func( )**. When **p** is assigned **d_ob2** and **func( )** is called, **base**'s version is used because it is next up in the class hierarchy. In general, when a derived class does not override a virtual function, the base class' version is used.

3. The next example shows how a virtual function can respond to random events that occur at run time. This program selects between **d_ob1** and **d_ob2** based upon the value returned by the standard random number generator **rand( )**. Keep in mind that the version of **func( )** executed is resolved at run time. (Indeed, it is impossible to resolve the calls to **func( )** at compile time.)

```cpp
/* This example illustrates how a virtual function
   can be used to respond to random events occurring
   at run time.
*/
#include <iostream>
#include <cstdlib>
using namespace std;

class base {
public:
  int i;
  base(int x) { i = x; }
  virtual void func()
  {
    cout << "Using base version of func(): ";
    cout << i << '\n';
  }
};

class derived1 : public base {
public:
  derived1(int x) : base(x) {}
  void func()
  {
    cout << "Using derived1's version of func(): ";
    cout << i*i << '\n';
  }
};

class derived2 : public base {
public:
  derived2(int x) : base(x) {}
  void func()
  {
```

```
      cout << "Using derived2's version of func(): ";
      cout << i+i << '\n';
  }
};

int main()
{
  base *p;
  derived1 d_ob1(10);
  derived2 d_ob2(10);
  int i, j;

  for(i=0; i<10; i++) {
    j = rand();
    if((j%2)) p = &d_ob1; // if odd use d_ob1
    else p = &d_ob2; // if even use d_ob2
    p->func(); // call appropriate function
  }

  return 0;
}
```

4. Here is a more practical example of how a virtual function can be used. This program creates a generic base class called **area** that holds two dimensions of a figure. It also declares a virtual function called **getarea( )** that, when overridden by derived classes, returns the area of the type of figure defined by the derived class. In this case, the declaration of **getarea( )** inside the base class determines the nature of the interface. The actual implementation is left to the classes that inherit it. In this example, the area of a triangle and a rectangle are computed.

```
// Use virtual function to define interface.
#include <iostream>
using namespace std;

class area {
  double dim1, dim2; // dimensions of figure
public:
  void setarea(double d1, double d2)
  {
    dim1 = d1;
    dim2 = d2;
  }
```

```
  void getdim(double &d1, double &d2)
  {
    d1 = dim1;
    d2 = dim2;
  }
  virtual double getarea()
  {
    cout << "You must override this function\n";
    return 0.0;
  }
};

class rectangle : public area {
public:
  double getarea()
  {
    double d1, d2;
    getdim(d1, d2);
    return d1 * d2;
  }
};

class triangle : public area {
public:
  double getarea()
  {
    double d1, d2;

    getdim(d1, d2);
    return 0.5 * d1 * d2;
  }
};

int main()
{
  area *p;
  rectangle r;
  triangle t;

  r.setarea(3.3, 4.5);
  t.setarea(4.0, 5.0);

  p = &r;
  cout << "Rectangle has area: " << p->getarea() << '\n';
```

```
  p = &t;
  cout << "Triangle has area: " << p->getarea() << '\n';

  return 0;
}
```

Notice that the definition of **getarea( )** inside **area** is just a placeholder and performs no real function. Because **area** is not linked to any specific type of figure, there is no meaningful definition that can be given to **getarea( )** inside **area**. In fact, **getarea( )** must be overridden by a derived class in order to be useful. In the next section, you will see a way to enforce this.

EXERCISES

---

1. Write a program that creates a base class called **num**. Have this class hold an integer value and contain a virtual function called **shownum( )**. Create two derived classes called **outhex** and **outoct** that inherit **num**. Have the derived classes override **shownum( )** so that it displays the value in hexadecimal and octal, respectively.

2. Write a program that creates a base class called **dist** that stores the distance between two points in a **double** variable. In **dist**, create a virtual function called **trav_time( )** that outputs the time it takes to travel that distance, assuming that the distance is in miles and the speed is 60 miles per hour. In a derived class called **metric**, override **trav_time( )** so that it outputs the travel time assuming that the distance is in kilometers and the speed is 100 kilometers per hour.

10.3 ***M*ORE ABOUT VIRTUAL FUNCTIONS**

As Example 4 from the preceding section illustrates, sometimes when a virtual function is declared in the base class there is no meaningful operation for it to perform. This situation is common because often a base class does not define a complete class by itself. Instead, it simply supplies a core set of member functions and variables to which the derived class supplies the remainder. When there is no meaningful action for a base class virtual function to perform, the implication is that any derived class *must* override this function. To ensure that this will occur, C++ supports *pure virtual functions.*

A pure virtual function has no definition relative to the base class. Only the function's prototype is included. To make a pure virtual function, use this general form:

virtual *type func-name(parameter-list*) = 0;

The key part of this declaration is the setting of the function equal to 0. This tells the compiler that no body exists for this function relative to the base class. When a virtual function is made pure, it forces any derived class to override it. If a derived class does not, a compile-time error results. Thus, making a virtual function pure is a way to guarantee that a derived class will provide its own redefinition.

When a class contains at least one pure virtual function, it is referred to as an *abstract class.* Since an abstract class contains at least one function for which no body exists, it is, technically, an incomplete type, and no objects of that class can be created. Thus, abstract classes exist only to be inherited. They are neither intended nor able to stand alone. It is important to understand, however, that you can still create a pointer to an abstract class, since it is through the use of base class pointers that run-time polymorphism is achieved. (It is also permissible to have a reference to an abstract class.)

When a virtual function is inherited, so is its virtual nature. This means that when a derived class inherits a virtual function from a base class and then the derived class is used as a base for yet another derived class, the virtual function can be overridden by the final derived class (as well as the first derived class). For example, if base class B contains a virtual function called **f( )**, and D1 inherits B and D2 inherits D1, both D1 and D2 can override **f( )** relative to their respective classes.

EXAMPLES

1. Here is an improved version of the program shown in Example 4 in the preceding section. In this version, the function **getarea( )** is declared as pure in the base class **area**.

```cpp
// Create an abstract class.
#include <iostream>
using namespace std;

class area {
  double dim1, dim2; // dimensions of figure
public:
  void setarea(double d1, double d2)
  {
    dim1 = d1;
    dim2 = d2;
  }
  void getdim(double &d1, double &d2)
  {
    d1 = dim1;
    d2 = dim2;
  }
  virtual double getarea() = 0; // pure virtual function
};

class rectangle : public area {
public:
  double getarea()
  {
    double d1, d2;

    getdim(d1, d2);
    return d1 * d2;
  }
};

class triangle : public area {
```

```
public:
  double getarea()
  {
    double d1, d2;

    getdim(d1, d2);
    return 0.5 * d1 * d2;
  }
};

int main()
{
  area *p;
  rectangle r;
  triangle t;

  r.setarea(3.3, 4.5);
  t.setarea(4.0, 5.0);

  p = &r;
  cout << "Rectangle has area: " << p->getarea() << '\n';

  p = &t;
  cout << "Triangle has area: " << p->getarea() << '\n';

  return 0;
}
```

Now that **getarea( )** is pure, it ensures that each derived class will override it.

2. The following program illustrates how a function's virtual nature is preserved when it is inherited:

```
// Virtual functions retain their virtual nature when inherited.
#include <iostream>
using namespace std;

class base {
public:
  virtual void func()
  {
    cout << "Using base version of func()\n";
  }
};
```

```
class derived1 : public base {
public:
  void func()
  {
    cout << "Using derived1's version of func()\n";
  }
};

// Derived2 inherits derived1.
class derived2 : public derived1 {
public:
  void func()
  {
    cout << "Using derived2's version of func()\n";
  }
};

int main()
{
  base *p;
  base ob;
  derived1 d_ob1;
  derived2 d_ob2;

  p = &ob;
  p->func(); // use base's func()

  p = &d_ob1;
  p->func(); // use derived1's func()

  p = &d_ob2;
  p->func(); // use derived2's func()

  return 0;
}
```

In this program, the virtual function **func( )** is first inherited by **derived1**, which overrides it relative to itself. Next, **derived2** inherits **derived1**. In **derived2**, **func( )** is again overridden.

Because virtual functions are hierarchical, if **derived2** did not override **func( )**, when **d_ob2** was accessed, **derived1**'s **func( )** would have been used. If neither **derived1** nor **derived2** had overridden **func( )**, all references to it would have been routed to the one defined in **base**.

EXERCISES

1. On your own, experiment with the two example programs. Specifically, try creating an object by using **area** from Example 1 and observe the error message. In Example 2, try removing the redefinition of **func( )** within **derived2**. Confirm that, indeed, the version inside **derived1** is used.

2. Why can't an object be created by using an abstract class?

3. In Example 2, what happens if you remove only the redefinition of **func( )** inside **derived1**? Does the program still compile and run? If so, why?

10.4 $\boldsymbol{A}$PPLYING POLYMORPHISM

Now that you know how to use a virtual function to achieve run-time polymorphism, it is time to consider how and why to use it. As has been stated many times in this book, polymorphism is the process by which a common interface is applied to two or more similar (but technically different) situations, thus implementing the "one interface, multiple methods" philosophy. Polymorphism is important because it can greatly simplify complex systems. A single, well-defined interface is used to access a number of different but related actions, and artificial complexity is removed. In essence, polymorphism allows the logical relationship of similar actions to become apparent; thus, the program is easier to understand and maintain. When related actions are accessed through a common interface, you have less to remember.

There are two terms that are often linked to OOP in general and to C++ specifically. They are _early binding_ and _late binding_. It is important that you know what they mean. Early binding essentially refers to those events that can be known at compile time. Specifically, it refers to those function calls that can be resolved during compilation. Early bound entities include "normal" functions, overloaded functions, and nonvirtual member and friend functions. When these types of functions are compiled, all address information necessary to call them is known at compile time. The main advantage of early binding (and the reason that it is so widely used) is that it is very efficient. Calls to functions bound at compile time are the fastest types of function calls. The main disadvantage is lack of flexibility.

Late binding refers to events that must occur at run time. A late bound function call is one in which the address of the function to be called is not known until the program runs. In C++, a virtual function is a late bound object. When a virtual function is accessed via a base class pointer, the program must determine at run time what type of object is being pointed to and then select which version of the overridden function to execute. The main advantage of late binding is flexibility at run time. Your program is free to respond to random events without having to contain large amounts of "contingency code." Its primary disadvantage is that there is more overhead associated with a function call. This generally makes such calls slower than those that occur with early binding.

Because of the potential efficiency trade-offs, you must decide when it is appropriate to use early binding and when to use late binding.

EXAMPLES

1. Here is a program that illustrates "one interface, multiple methods." It defines an abstract list class for integer values. The interface to the list is defined by the pure virtual functions **store( )** and **retrieve( )**. To store a value, call the **store( )** function. To retrieve a value from the list, call **retrieve( )**. The base class **list** does not define any default methods for these actions. Instead, each derived class defines exactly what type of list will be maintained. In the program, two types of lists are implemented: a queue and a stack. Although the two lists operate completely differently, each is accessed using the same interface. You should study this program carefully.

```cpp
// Demonstrate virtual functions.
#include <iostream>
#include <cstdlib>
#include <cctype>
using namespace std;

class list {
public:
  list *head; // pointer to start of list
  list *tail; // pointer to end of list
```

```
  list *next; // pointer to next item
  int num; // value to be stored

  list() { head = tail = next = NULL; }
  virtual void store(int i) = 0;
  virtual int retrieve() = 0;
};

// Create a queue-type list.
class queue : public list {
public:
  void store(int i);
  int retrieve();
};

void queue::store(int i)
{
  list *item;

  item = new queue;
  if(!item) {
    cout << "Allocation error.\n";
    exit(1);
  }
  item->num = i;

  // put on end of list
  if(tail) tail->next = item;
  tail = item;
  item->next = NULL;
  if(!head) head = tail;
}

int queue::retrieve()
{
  int i;
  list *p;

  if(!head) {
    cout << "List empty.\n";
    return 0;
  }

  // remove from start of list
  i = head->num;
```

```cpp
  p = head;
  head = head->next;
  delete p;

  return i;
}

// Create a stack-type list.
class stack : public list {
public:
  void store(int i);
  int retrieve();
};

void stack::store(int i)
{
  list *item;

  item = new stack;
  if(!item) {
    cout << "Allocation error.\n";
    exit(1);
  }
  item->num = i;

  // put on front of list for stack-like operation
  if(head) item->next = head;
  head = item;
  if(!tail) tail = head;
}

int stack::retrieve()
{
  int i;
  list *p;

  if(!head) {
    cout << "List empty.\n";
    return 0;
  }

  // remove from start of list
  i = head->num;
  p = head;
  head = head->next;
```

```
      delete p;

      return i;
}

int main()
{
   list *p;

   // demonstrate queue
   queue q_ob;
   p = &q_ob; // point to queue

   p->store(1);
   p->store(2);
   p->store(3);

   cout << "Queue: ";
   cout << p->retrieve();
   cout << p->retrieve();
   cout << p->retrieve();

   cout << '\n';

   // demonstrate stack
   stack s_ob;
   p = &s_ob; // point to stack

   p->store(1);
   p->store(2);
   p->store(3);

   cout << "Stack: ";
   cout << p->retrieve();
   cout << p->retrieve();
   cout << p->retrieve();

   cout << '\n';

   return 0;
}
```

2. The **main( )** function in the list program just shown simply illustrates that the list classes do, indeed, work. However, to

begin to see why run-time polymorphism is so powerful, try
using this **main( )** instead:

```
int main()
{
  list *p;
  stack s_ob;
  queue q_ob;
  char ch;
  int i;

  for(i=0; i<10; i++) {
    cout << "Stack or Queue? (S/Q): ";
    cin >> ch;
    ch = tolower(ch);
    if(ch=='q') p = &q_ob;
    else p = &s_ob;
    p->store(i);
  }

  cout << "Enter T to terminate\n";
  for(;;) {
    cout << "Remove from Stack or Queue? (S/Q): ";
    cin >> ch;
    ch = tolower(ch);
    if(ch=='t') break;
    if(ch=='q') p = &q_ob;
    else p = &s_ob;
    cout << p->retrieve() << '\n';
  }

  cout << '\n';

  return 0;
}
```

This **main( )** illustrates how random events that occur at
run time can be easily handled by using virtual functions and
run-time polymorphism. The program executes a **for** loop
running from 0 to 9. Each iteration through the loop, you are
asked to choose into which type of list—the stack or the
queue—you want to put a value. According to your answer, the
base pointer **p** is set to point to the correct object and the
current value of **i** is stored. Once the loop is finished, another

loop begins that prompts you to indicate from which list to remove a value. Once again, it is your response that determines which list is selected.

While this example is trivial, you should be able to see how run-time polymorphism can simplify a program that must respond to random events. For instance, the Windows operating system interfaces to a program by sending it messages. As far as the program is concerned, these messages are generated at random, and your program must respond to each one as it is received. One way to respond to these messages is through the use of virtual functions.

EXERCISES

1. Add another type of list to the program in Example 1. Have this version maintain a sorted list (in ascending order). Call this list **sorted**.

2. On your own, think about ways in which you can apply run-time polymorphism to simplify the solutions to certain types of problems.

SKILLS CHECK

Mastery
Skills Check

At this point you should be able to perform the following exercises and answer the questions.

1. What is a virtual function?

2. What types of functions cannot be made virtual?

3. How does a virtual function help achieve run-time polymorphism? Be specific.

4. What is a pure virtual function?

5. What is an abstract class? What is a polymorphic class?

6. Is the following fragment correct? If not, why not?

```
class base {
public:
  virtual int f(int a) = 0;
  // ...
};

class derived : public base {
public:
  int f(int a, int b) { return a*b; }
  // ...
};
```

7. Is the virtual quality inherited?

8. On your own, experiment with virtual functions at this time. This is an important concept and you should master the technique.

**Cumulative
Skills Check**

This section checks how well you have integrated material in this chapter with that from the preceding chapters.

1. Enhance the list example from Section 10.4, Example 1, so that it overloads the **+** and **--** operators. Have the **+** store an element and the **--** retrieve an element.

2. How do virtual functions differ from overloaded functions?

3. On your own, reexamine some of the function overloading examples presented earlier in this book. Determine which can be converted to virtual functions. Also, think about ways in which a virtual function can solve some of your own programming problems.

11

Templates and Exception Handling

chapter objectives

11.1 Generic functions

11.2 Generic classes

11.3 Exception handling

11.4 More about exception handling

11.5 Handling exceptions thrown by **new**

THIS chapter discusses two of C++'s most important high-level features: *templates* and *exception handling*. While neither was part of the original specification for C++, both were added several years ago and are defined by Standard C++. They are supported by all modern C++ compilers. These two features help you achieve two of the most elusive goals in programming: the creation of reusable and resilient code.

Using templates, it is possible to create generic functions and classes. In a generic function or class, the type of data that is operated upon is specified as a parameter. This allows you to use one function or class with several different types of data without having to explicitly recode a specific version for each different data type. Thus, templates allow you to create reusable code. Both generic functions and generic classes are discussed here.

Exception handling is the subsystem of C++ that allows you to handle errors that occur at run time in a structured and controlled manner. With C++ exception handling, your program can automatically invoke an error handling routine when an error occurs. The principal advantage of exception handling is that it automates much of the error handling code that previously had to be coded "by hand" in any large program. The proper use of exception handling helps you to create resilient code.

Review
Skills Check

Before proceeding, you should be able to correctly answer the following questions and do the exercises.

1. What is a virtual function?

2. What is a pure virtual function? If a class declaration contains a pure virtual function, what is that class called, and what restrictions apply to its usage?

3. Run-time polymorphism is achieved through the use of _____ functions and _____ class pointers. (Fill in the missing words.)

4. If, in a class hierarchy, a derived class neglects to override a (non-pure) virtual function, what happens when an object of that derived class calls that function?

5. What is the main advantage of run-time polymorphism? What is its potential disadvantage?

11.1 *G*ENERIC FUNCTIONS

A generic function defines a general set of operations that will be applied to various types of data. A generic function has the type of data that it will operate upon passed to it as a parameter. Using this mechanism, the same general procedure can be applied to a wide range of data. As you know, many algorithms are logically the same no matter what type of data is being operated upon. For example, the Quicksort algorithm is the same whether it is applied to an array of integers or an array of **float**s. It is just that the type of the data being sorted is different. By creating a generic function, you can define, independent of any data, the nature of the algorithm. Once this is done, the compiler automatically generates the correct code for the type of data that is actually used when you execute the function. In essence, when you create a generic function you are creating a function that can automatically overload itself.

A generic function is created using the keyword **template**. The normal meaning of the word *template* accurately reflects the keyword's use in C++. It is used to create a template (or framework) that describes what a function will do, leaving it to the compiler to fill in the details as needed. The general form of a template function definition is shown here:

```
template <class Ttype> ret-type func-name( parameter list )
{
  // body of function
}
```

Here *Ttype* is a placeholder name for a data type used by the function. This name can be used within the function definition. However, it is only a placeholder; the compiler will automatically replace this placeholder with an actual data type when it creates a specific version of the function.

Although the use of the keyword **class** to specify a generic type in a template declaration is traditional, you can also use the keyword **typename**.

EXAMPLES

1. The following program creates a generic function that swaps the values of the two variables it is called with. Because the general process of exchanging two values is independent of the type of the variables, this process is a good choice to be made into a generic function.

```cpp
// Function template example.
#include <iostream>
using namespace std;

// This is a function template.
template <class X> void swapargs(X &a, X &b)
{
  X temp;

  temp = a;
  a = b;
  b = temp;
}

int main()
{
  int i=10, j=20;
  float x=10.1, y=23.3;

  cout << "Original i, j: " << i << ' ' << j << endl;
  cout << "Original x, y: " << x << ' ' << y << endl;

  swapargs(i, j); // swap integers
  swapargs(x, y); // swap floats

  cout << "Swapped i, j: " << i << ' ' << j << endl;
  cout << "Swapped x, y: " << x << ' ' << y << endl;

  return 0;
}
```

The keyword **template** is used to define a generic function. The line

```
template <class X> void swapargs(X &a, X &b)
```

tells the compiler two things: that a template is being created and that a generic definition is beginning. Here **X** is a generic type that is used as a placeholder. After the **template** portion, the function **swapargs( )** is declared, using **X** as the data type of the values that will be swapped. In **main( )**, the **swapargs( )** function is called using two different types of data: integers and **float**s. Because **swapargs( )** is a generic function, the compiler automatically creates two versions of **swapargs( )**—one that will exchange integer values and one that will exchange floating-point values. You should compile and try this program now.

Here are some other terms that are sometimes used when templates are discussed. and that you might encounter in other C++ literature. First, a generic function (that is, a function definition preceded by a **template** statement) is also called a *template function*. When the compiler creates a specific version of this function, it is said to have created a *generated function*. The act of generating a function is referred to as *instantiating* it. Put differently, a generated function is a specific instance of a template function.

2. The **template** portion of a generic function definition does not have to be on the same line as the function's name. For example, the following is also a common way to format the **swapargs( )** function:

```
template <class X>
void swapargs(X &a, X &b)
{
  X temp;

  temp = a;
  a = b;
  b = temp;
}
```

If you use this form, it is important to understand that no other statements can occur between the **template** statement and the start of the generic function definition. For example, the following fragment will not compile:

```
// This will not compile.
template <class X>
int i; // this is an error
void swapargs(X &a, X &b)
{
  X temp;

  temp = a;
  a = b;
  b = temp;
}
```

As the comments imply, the **template** specification must directly precede the rest of the function definition.

3. As mentioned, instead of using the keyword **class**, you can use the keyword **typename** to specify a generic type in a template definition. For example, here is another way to declare the **swapargs( )** function.

```
// Use typename.
template <typename X> void swapargs(X &a, X &b)
{
  X temp;

  temp = a;
  a = b;
  b = temp;
}
```

The **typename** keyword can also be used to specify an unknown type within a template, but this use is beyond the scope of this book.

4. You can define more than one generic data type with the **template** statement, using a comma-separated list. For example, this program creates a generic function that has two generic types:

```
#include <iostream>
using namespace std;

template <class type1, class type2>
```

```
void myfunc(type1 x, type2 y)
{
  cout << x << ' ' << y << endl;
}

int main()
{
  myfunc(10, "hi");

  myfunc(0.23, 10L);

  return 0;
}
```

In this example, the placeholder types **type1** and **type2** are replaced by the compiler with the data types **int** and **char *** and **double** and **long**, respectively, when the compiler generates the specific instances of **myfunc( )**.

Remember
When you create a generic function, you are, in essence, allowing the compiler to generate as many different versions of that function as necessary to handle the various ways that your program calls that function.

5. Generic functions are similar to overloaded functions except that they are more restrictive. When functions are overloaded, you can have different actions performed within the body of each function. But a generic function must perform the same general action for all versions. For example, the following overloaded functions *cannot* be replaced by a generic function because they do not do the same thing:

```
void outdata(int i)
{
  cout << i;
}

void outdata(double d)
{
  cout << setprecision(10) << setfill('#');
  cout << d;
```

```
cout << setprecision(6) << setfill(' ');
}
```

6. Even though a template function overloads itself as needed, you can explicitly overload one, too. If you overload a generic function, that overloaded function overrides (or "hides") the generic function relative to that specific version. For example, consider this version of Example 1:

```
// Overriding a template function.
#include <iostream>
using namespace std;

template <class X> void swapargs(X &a, X &b)
{
  X temp;

  temp = a;
  a = b;
  b = temp;
}

// This overrides the generic version of swapargs().
void swapargs(int a, int b)
{
  cout << "this is inside swapargs(int,int)\n";
}

int main()
{
  int i=10, j=20;
  float x=10.1, y=23.3;


  cout << "Original i, j: " << i << ' ' << j << endl;
  cout << "Original x, y: " << x << ' ' << y << endl;

  swapargs(i, j); // calls overloaded swapargs()
  swapargs(x, y); // swap floats

  cout << "Swapped i, j: " << i << ' ' << j << endl;
  cout << "Swapped x, y: " << x << ' ' << y << endl;
```

```
    return 0;
}
```

As the comments indicate, when **swapargs(i, j)** is called, it invokes the explicitly overloaded version of **swapargs( )** defined in the program. Thus, the compiler does not generate this version of the generic **swapargs( )** function because the generic function is overridden by the explicit overloading.

Manual overloading of a template, as shown in this example, allows you to tailor a version of a generic function to accommodate a special situation. However, in general, if you need to have different versions of a function for different data types, you should use overloaded functions rather than templates.

EXERCISES

1. If you have not done so, try each of the preceding examples.

2. Write a generic function, called **min( )**, that returns the lesser of its two arguments. For example, **min(3, 4)** will return 3 and **min('c', 'a')** will return a. Demonstrate your function in a program.

3. A good candidate for a template function is called **find( )**. This function searches an array for an object. It returns either the index of the matching object (if one is found) or -1 if no match is found. Here is the prototype for a specific version of **find( )**. Convert **find( )** into a generic function and demonstrate your solution within a program. (The **size** parameter specifies the number of elements in the array.)

```
int find(int object, int *list, int size)
{
  // ...
}
```

4. In your own words, explain why generic functions are valuable and may help simplify the source code to programs that you create.

*G*ENERIC CLASSES

In addition to defining generic functions, you can also define generic classes. When you do this, you create a class that defines all algorithms used by that class, but the actual type of the data being manipulated will be specified as a parameter when objects of that class are created.

Generic classes are useful when a class contains generalizable logic. For example, the same algorithm that maintains a queue of integers will also work for a queue of characters. Also, the same mechanism that maintains a linked list of mailing addresses will also maintain a linked list of auto part information. By using a generic class, you can create a class that will maintain a queue, a linked list, and so on for any type of data. The compiler will automatically generate the correct type of object based upon the type you specify when the object is created.

The general form of a generic class declaration is shown here:

```
template <class Ttype> class class-name {
    .
    .
    .
}
```

Here *Ttype* is the placeholder type name that will be specified when a class is instantiated. If necessary, you can define more than one generic data type by using a comma-separated list.

Once you have created a generic class, you create a specific instance of that class by using the following general form:

```
class-name <type> ob;
```

Here *type* is the type name of the data that the class will be operating upon.

Member functions of a generic class are, themselves, automatically generic. They need not be explicitly specified as such using **template**.

As you will see in Chapter 14, C++ provides a library that is built upon template classes. This library is usually referred to as the Standard Template Library, or STL for short. It provides generic versions of the most commonly used algorithms and data structures. If you want to use the STL effectively, you'll need a solid understanding of template classes and their syntax.

EXAMPLES

1. This program creates a very simple generic singly linked list class. It then demonstrates the class by creating a linked list that stores characters.

```cpp
// A simple generic linked list.
#include <iostream>
using namespace std;

template <class data_t> class list {
  data_t data;
  list *next;
public:
  list(data_t d);
  void add(list *node) {node->next = this; next = 0; }
  list *getnext() { return next; }
  data_t getdata() { return data; }
};

template <class data_t> list<data_t>::list(data_t d)
{
  data = d;
  next = 0;
}

int main()
{
  list<char> start('a');
  list<char> *p, *last;
  int i;

  // build a list
  last = &start;
  for(i=1; i<26; i++) {
    p = new list<char> ('a' + i);
    p->add(last);
    last = p;
  }

  // follow the list
  p = &start;
  while(p) {
    cout << p->getdata();
    p = p->getnext();
```

```
    }

    return 0;
}
```

As you can see, the declaration of a generic class is similar to that of a generic function. The actual type of data stored by the list is generic in the class declaration. It is not until an object of the list is declared that the actual data type is determined. In this example, objects and pointers are created inside **main( )** that specify that the data type of the list will be **char**. Pay special attention to this declaration:

```
list<char> start('a');
```

Notice how the desired data type is passed inside the angle brackets.

You should enter and execute this program. It builds a linked list that contains the characters of the alphabet and then displays them. However, by simply changing the type of data specified when **list** objects are created, you can change the type of data stored by the list. For example, you could create another object that stores integers by using this declaration:

```
list<int> int_start(1);
```

You can also use **list** to store data types that you create. For example, if you want to store address information, use this structure:

```
struct addr {
  char name[40];
  char street[40];
  char city[30];
  char state[3];
  char zip[12];
}
```

Then, to use **list** to generate objects that will store objects of type **addr**, use a declaration like this (assuming that **structvar** contains a valid **addr** structure):

```
list<addr> obj(structvar);
```

2. Here is another example of a generic class. It is a reworking of
the **stack** class first introduced in Chapter 1. However, in this
case, **stack** has been made into a template class. Thus, it can be
used to store any type of object. In the example shown here, a
character stack and a floating-point stack are created:

```cpp
// This function demonstrates a generic stack.
#include <iostream>
using namespace std;

#define SIZE 10

// Create a generic stack class
template <class StackType> class stack {
  StackType stck[SIZE]; // holds the stack
  int tos; // index of top of stack

public:
  void init() { tos = 0; } // initialize stack
  void push(StackType ch); // push object on stack
  StackType pop(); // pop object from stack
};

// Push an object.
template <class StackType>
void stack<StackType>:: push(StackType ob)
{
  if(tos==SIZE) {
    cout << "Stack is full.\n";
    return;
  }
  stck[tos] = ob;
  tos++;
}

// Pop an object.
template <class StackType>
StackType stack<StackType>::pop()
{
  if(tos==0) {
    cout << "Stack is empty.\n";
    return 0; // return null on empty stack
```

```
  }
  tos--;
  return stck[tos];
}

int main()
{
  // Demonstrate character stacks.
  stack<char> s1, s2;  // create two stacks
  int i;

  // initialize the stacks
  s1.init();
  s2.init();

  s1.push('a');
  s2.push('x');
  s1.push('b');
  s2.push('y');
  s1.push('c');
  s2.push('z');

  for(i=0; i<3; i++) cout << "Pop s1: " << s1.pop() << "\n";
  for(i=0; i<3; i++) cout << "Pop s2: " << s2.pop() << "\n";

  // demonstrate double stacks
  stack<double> ds1, ds2;  // create two stacks

  // initialize the stacks
  ds1.init();
  ds2.init();

  ds1.push(1.1);
  ds2.push(2.2);
  ds1.push(3.3);
  ds2.push(4.4);
  ds1.push(5.5);
  ds2.push(6.6);

  for(i=0; i<3; i++) cout << "Pop ds1: " << ds1.pop() << "\n";
  for(i=0; i<3; i++) cout << "Pop ds2: " << ds2.pop() << "\n";

  return 0;
}
```

As the **stack** class (and the preceding **list** class) illustrates, generic functions and classes provide a powerful tool that you can use to maximize your programming time because they allow you to define the general form of an algorithm that can be used with any type of data. You are saved from the tedium of creating separate implementations for each data type that you want the algorithm to work with.

3. A template class can have more than one generic data type. Simply declare all the data types required by the class in a comma-separated list within the **template** specification. For example, the following short example creates a class that uses two generic data types:

```cpp
/* This example uses two generic data types in a
   class definition.
*/
#include <iostream>
using namespace std;

template <class Type1, class Type2> class myclass
{
  Type1 i;
  Type2 j;
public:
  myclass(Type1 a, Type2 b) { i = a; j = b; }
  void show() { cout << i << ' ' << j << '\n'; }
};

int main()
{
  myclass<int, double> ob1(10, 0.23);
  myclass<char, char *> ob2('X', "This is a test");

  ob1.show(); // show int, double
  ob2.show(); // show char, char *

  return 0;
}
```

This program produces the following output:

```
10 0.23
X This is a test
```

The program declares two types of objects. **ob1** uses integer and **double** data. **ob2** uses a character and a character pointer. For both cases, the compiler automatically generates the appropriate data and functions to accommodate the way the objects are created.

EXERCISES

1. If you have not yet done so, compile and run the two generic class examples. Try declaring lists and/or stacks of different data types.

2. Create and demonstrate a generic queue class.

3. Create a generic class, called **input**, that does the following when its constructor is called:

   ▼ prompts the user for input,

   ▼ inputs the data entered by the user, and

   ▼ reprompts if the data is not within a predetermined range.

   Objects of type **input** should be declared like this:

   input ob("*prompt message*", *min-value, max-value*)

   Here *prompt message* is the message that prompts for input. The minimum and maximum acceptable values are specified by *min-value* and *max-value*, respectively. (Note: the type of data entered by the user will be the same as the type of *min-value* and *max-value*.)

11.3 *E*XCEPTION HANDLING

C++ provides a built-in error handling mechanism that is called *exception handling*. Using exception handling, you can more easily manage and respond to run-time errors. C++ exception handling is built upon three keywords: **try**, **catch**, and **throw**. In the most general terms, program statements that you want to monitor for exceptions are contained in a **try** block. If an exception (i.e., an error) occurs within the **try** block, it is thrown (using **throw**). The exception is caught, using **catch**, and processed. The following elaborates upon this general description.

As stated, any statement that throws an exception must have been executed from within a **try** block. (A function called from within a **try** block can also throw an exception.) Any exception must be caught by a **catch** statement that immediately follows the **try** statement that throws the exception. The general form of **try** and **catch** are shown here:

```
try {
    // try block
}
catch (type1 arg) {
    // catch block
}
catch (type2 arg) {
    // catch block
}
catch (type3 arg) {
    // catch block
}

    .

    .

    .

catch (typeN arg) {
    // catch block
}
```

The **try** block must contain the portion of your program that you want to monitor for errors. This can be as specific as monitoring a few statements within one function or as all-encompassing as enclosing the **main( )** function code within a **try** block (which effectively causes the entire program to be monitored).

When an exception is thrown, it is caught by its corresponding **catch** statement, which processes the exception. There can be more than one **catch** statement associated with a **try**. The **catch** statement that is used is determined by the type of the exception. That is, if the data type specified by a **catch** matches that of the exception, that

catch statement is executed (and all others are bypassed). When an exception is caught, *arg* will receive its value. If you don't need access to the exception itself, specify only *type* in the **catch** clause—*arg* is optional. Any type of data can be caught, including classes that you create. In fact, class types are frequently used as exceptions.

The general form of the **throw** statement is shown here:

throw *exception*;

throw must be executed either from within the **try** block proper or from any function that the code within the block calls (directly or indirectly). *exception* is the value thrown.

If you throw an exception for which there is no applicable **catch** statement, an abnormal program termination might occur. If your compiler complies with Standard C++, throwing an unhandled exception causes the standard library function **terminate( )** to be invoked. By default, **terminate( )** calls **abort( )** to stop your program, but you can specify your own termination handler, if you like. You will need to refer to your compiler's library reference for details.

EXAMPLES

1. Here is a simple example that shows the way C++ exception handling operates:

```
// A simple exception handling example.
#include <iostream>
using namespace std;

int main()
{
  cout << "start\n";

  try { // start a try block
    cout << "Inside try block\n";
    throw 10; // throw an error
    cout << "This will not execute";
  }
  catch (int i) { // catch an error
    cout << "Caught One! Number is: ";
    cout << i << "\n";
  }
```

```
    cout << "end";

    return 0;
}
```

This program displays the following output:

```
start
Inside try block
Caught One! Number is: 10
end
```

Look carefully at this program. As you can see, there is a **try** block containing three statements and a **catch(int i)** statement that processes an integer exception. Within the **try** block, only two of the three statements will execute: the first **cout** statement and the **throw**. Once an exception has been thrown, control passes to the **catch** expression and the **try** block is terminated. That is, **catch** is *not* called. Rather, program execution is transferred to it. (The stack is automatically reset as needed to accomplish this.) Thus, the **cout** statement following the **throw** will never execute.

After the **catch** statement executes, program control continues with the statements following the **catch**. Often, however, a **catch** block will end with a call to **exit( )**, **abort( )**, or some other function that causes program termination because exception handling is frequently used to handle catastrophic errors.

2. As mentioned, the type of the exception must match the type specified in a **catch** statement. For example, in the preceding example, if you change the type in the **catch** statement to **double**, the exception will not be caught and abnormal termination will occur. This change is shown here:

```
// This example will not work.
#include <iostream>
using namespace std;

int main()
{
  cout << "start\n";

  try { // start a try block
```

```
    cout << "Inside try block\n";
    throw 10; // throw an error
    cout << "This will not execute";
  }
  catch (double i) { // Won't work for an int exception
    cout << "Caught One! Number is: ";
    cout << i << "\n";
  }

  cout << "end";

  return 0;
}
```

This program produces the following output because the integer exception will not be caught by a **double catch** statement.

```
start
Inside try block
Abnormal program termination
```

3. An exception can be thrown from a statement that is outside the **try** block as long as the statement is within a function that is called from within the **try** block. For example, this is a valid program:

```
/* Throwing an exception from a function outside
   the try block.
*/
#include <iostream>
using namespace std;

void Xtest(int test)
{
  cout << "Inside Xtest, test is: " << test << "\n";
  if(test) throw test;
}

int main()
{
  cout << "start\n";

  try { // start a try block
    cout << "Inside try block\n";
```

```
    Xtest(0);
    Xtest(1);
    Xtest(2);
  }
  catch (int i) { // catch an error
    cout << "Caught One! Number is: ";
    cout << i << "\n";
  }

  cout << "end";

  return 0;
}
```

This program produces the following output:

```
start
Inside try block
Inside Xtest, test is: 0
Inside Xtest, test is: 1
Caught One! Number is: 1
end
```

4. A **try** block can be localized to a function. When this is the
   case, each time the function is entered, the exception
   handling relative to that function is reset. For example,
   examine this program:

```
#include <iostream>
using namespace std;

// A try/catch can be inside a function other than main().
void Xhandler(int test)
{
  try{
    if(test) throw test;
  }
  catch(int i) {
    cout << "Caught One!  Ex. #: " << i << '\n';
  }
}

int main()
{
  cout << "start\n";
```

```
    Xhandler(1);
    Xhandler(2);
    Xhandler(0);
    Xhandler(3);

    cout << "end";

    return 0;
}
```

This program displays this output:

```
start
Caught One!  Ex. #: 1
Caught One!  Ex. #: 2
Caught One!  Ex. #: 3
end
```

As you can see, three exceptions are thrown. After each exception, the function returns. When the function is called again, the exception handling is reset.

5. As stated earlier, you can have more than one **catch** associated with a **try**. In fact, it is common to do so. However, each **catch** must catch a different type of exception. For example, the following program catches both integers and strings:

```
#include <iostream>
using namespace std;

// Different types of exceptions can be caught.
void Xhandler(int test)
{
  try{
    if(test) throw test;
    else throw "Value is zero";
  }
  catch(int i) {
    cout << "Caught One!  Ex. #: " << i << '\n';
  }
  catch(char *str) {
    cout << "Caught a string: ";
    cout << str << '\n';
```

```
    }
}

int main()
{
  cout << "start\n";

  Xhandler(1);
  Xhandler(2);
  Xhandler(0);
  Xhandler(3);

  cout << "end";

  return 0;
}
```

This program produces the following output:

```
start
Caught One!   Ex. #: 1
Caught One!   Ex. #: 2
Caught a string: Value is zero
Caught One!   Ex. #: 3
end
```

As you can see, each **catch** statement responds only to its own type.

In general, **catch** expressions are checked in the order in which they occur in a program. Only a matching statement is executed. All other **catch** blocks are ignored.

EXERCISES

1. By far, the best way to understand how C++ exception handling works is to play with it. Enter, compile, and run the preceding example programs. Then experiment with them, altering pieces of them and observing the results.

2. What is wrong with this fragment?

```
int main()
{
    throw 12.23;
```

3. What is wrong with this fragment?

```
try {
  // ...
  throw 'a';
  // ...
}
catch(char *) {
 // ...
}
```

4. What will happen if an exception is thrown for which there is no corresponding **catch** statement?

11.4 *M*ORE ABOUT EXCEPTION HANDLING

There are several additional features and nuances to C++ exception handling that can make it easier and more convenient to use.

In some circumstances you will want an exception handler to catch all exceptions instead of just a certain type. This is easy to accomplish. Simply use this form of **catch**:

```
catch(...) {
  // process all exceptions
}
```

Here the ellipsis matches any type of data.

You can restrict the type of exceptions that a function can throw back to its caller. Put differently, you can control what type of exceptions a function can throw outside of itself. In fact, you can also prevent a function from throwing any exceptions whatsoever. To apply these restrictions, you must add a **throw** clause to the function definition. The general form of this is shown here:

```
ret-type func-name(arg-list) throw(type-list)
{
  // ...
}
```

Here only those data types contained in the comma-separated *type-list* may be thrown by the function. Throwing any other type of expression will cause abnormal program termination. If you don't want a function to be able to throw *any* exceptions, use an empty list.

If your compiler complies with Standard C++, when a function attempts to throw a disallowed exception the standard library function **unexpected( )** is called. By default, this causes the **terminate( )** function to be called, which causes abnormal program termination. However, you can specify your own termination handler, if you like. You will need to refer to your compiler's documentation for directions on how this can be accomplished.

If you wish to rethrow an expression from within an exception handler, you can do so by simply calling **throw**, by itself, with no exception. This causes the current exception to be passed on to an outer **try/catch** sequence.

EXAMPLES

1. The following program illustrates **catch(...)**:

```
// This example catches all exceptions.
#include <iostream>
using namespace std;

void Xhandler(int test)
{
  try{
    if(test==0) throw test; // throw int
    if(test==1) throw 'a'; // throw char
    if(test==2) throw 123.23; // throw double
  }
  catch(...) { // catch all exceptions
    cout << "Caught One!\n";
  }
}
```

```
int main()
{
  cout << "start\n";

  Xhandler(0);
  Xhandler(1);
  Xhandler(2);

  cout << "end";

  return 0;
}
```

This program displays the following output:

```
start
Caught One!
Caught One!
Caught One!
end
```

As you can see, all three **throw**s were caught using the one **catch** statement.

2. One very good use for **catch(...)** is as the last **catch** of a cluster of catches. In this capacity it provides a useful default or "catch all" statement. For example, this slightly different version of the preceding program explicitly catches integer exceptions but relies upon **catch(...)** to catch all others:

```
// This example uses catch(...) as a default.
#include <iostream>
using namespace std;

void Xhandler(int test)
{
  try{
    if(test==0) throw test; // throw int
    if(test==1) throw 'a'; // throw char
    if(test==2) throw 123.23; // throw double
  }
  catch(int i) { // catch an int exception
    cout << "Caught " << i << '\n';
  }
  catch(...) { // catch all other exceptions
    cout << "Caught One!\n";
```

```
    }
}

int main()
{
  cout << "start\n";

  Xhandler(0);
  Xhandler(1);
  Xhandler(2);

  cout << "end";

  return 0;
}
```

The output produced by this program is shown here:

```
start
Caught 0
Caught One!
Caught One!
end
```

As this example suggests, using **catch(...)** as a default
is a good way to catch all exceptions that you don't want to
handle explicitly. Also, by catching all exceptions, you
prevent an unhandled exception from causing an abnormal
program termination.

3. The following program shows how to restrict the types of
exceptions that can be thrown from a function:

```
// Restricting function throw types.
#include <iostream>
using namespace std;

// This function can only throw ints, chars, and doubles.
void Xhandler(int test) throw(int, char, double)
{
  if(test==0) throw test; // throw int
  if(test==1) throw 'a'; // throw char
  if(test==2) throw 123.23; // throw double
}

int main()
```

```
{
  cout << "start\n";

  try{
    Xhandler(0); // also, try passing 1 and 2 to Xhandler()
  }
  catch(int i) {
    cout << "Caught int\n";
  }
  catch(char c) {
    cout << "Caught char\n";
  }
  catch(double d) {
    cout << "Caught double\n";
  }

  cout << "end";

  return 0;
}
```

In this program, the function **Xhandler( )** can throw only integer, character, and **double** exceptions. If it attempts to throw any other type of exception, an abnormal program termination will occur. (That is, **unexpected( )** will be called.) To see an example of this, remove **int** from the list and retry the program.

It is important to understand that a function can only be restricted in what types of exceptions it throws back to the **try** block that called it. That is, a **try** block *within* a function can throw any type of exception so long as it is caught *within* that function. The restriction applies only when throwing an exception out of the function.

4. The following change to **Xhandler( )** prevents it from throwing any exceptions:

```
// This function can throw NO exceptions!
void Xhandler(int test) throw()
{
  /* The following statements no longer work.  Instead,
     they will cause an abnormal program termination. */
  if(test==0) throw test;
  if(test==1) throw 'a';
```

```
  if(test==2) throw 123.23;
}
```

5. As you have learned, you can rethrow an exception. The most likely reason for doing so is to allow multiple handlers access to the exception. For example, perhaps one exception handler manages one aspect of an exception and a second handler copes with another. An exception can only be rethrown from within a **catch** block (or from any function called from within that block). When you rethrow an exception, it will not be recaught by the same **catch** statement. It will propagate to an outer **catch** statement. The following program illustrates rethrowing an exception. It rethrows a **char** * exception.

```
// Example of rethrowing an exception.
#include <iostream>
using namespace std;

void Xhandler()
{
  try {
    throw "hello"; // throw a char *
  }
  catch(char *) { // catch a char *
    cout << "Caught char * inside Xhandler\n";
    throw ; // rethrow char * out of function
  }
}

int main()
{
  cout << "start\n";

  try{
    Xhandler();
  }
  catch(char *) {
    cout << "Caught char * inside main\n";
  }

  cout << "end";

  return 0;
}
```

This program displays the following output:

```
start
Caught char * inside Xhandler
Caught char * inside main
end
```

1. Before continuing, compile and run all of the examples in this section. Be sure you understand why each program produces the output that it does.

2. What is wrong with this fragment?

```
try {
  // ...
  throw 10;
}
catch(int *p) {
  // ...
}
```

3. Show one way to fix the preceding fragment.

4. What **catch** expression catches all types of exceptions?

5. Here is a skeleton for a function called **divide( )**.

```
double divide(double a, double b)
{
  // add error handling
  return a/b;
}
```

This function returns the result of dividing **a** by **b**. Add error checking to this function using C++ exception handling. Specifically, prevent a divide-by-zero error. Demonstrate your solution in a program.

*H*ANDLING EXCEPTIONS THROWN
BY new

In Chapter 4 you learned that the modern specification for the **new** operator states that it will throw an exception if an allocation request fails. Since in Chapter 4 exceptions had not yet been discussed, a description of how to handle that exception was deferred until later. Now the time has come to examine precisely what occurs when **new** fails.

Before we begin, it is necessary to state that the material in this section describes the behavior of **new** as specified by Standard C++. As you should recall from Chapter 4, the precise action that **new** takes on failure has been changed several times since C++ was invented. Specifically, when C++ was first invented, **new** returned null on failure. Later this was changed such that **new** caused an exception on failure. Also, the name of this exception has changed over time. Finally, it was decided that a **new** failure will generate an exception by default, but that a null pointer could be returned instead, as an option. Thus, **new** has been implemented differently, at different times, by compiler manufacturers. Although all compilers will eventually implement **new** in compliance with Standard C++, not all currently do. If the code examples shown here do not work with your compiler, check your compiler's documentation for details on how it implements **new**.

In Standard C++, when an allocation request cannot be honored, **new** throws a **bad_alloc** exception. If you don't catch this exception, your program will be terminated. Although this behavior is fine for short sample programs, in real applications you must catch this exception and process it in some rational manner. To have access to this exception, you must include the header < **new** > in your program.

Note

*Originally this exception was called **xalloc**, and at the time of this writing many compilers still use the older name. However, **bad_alloc** is the name specified by Standard C++, and it is the name that will be used in the future.*

In Standard C++ it is also possible to have **new** return null instead of throwing an exception when an allocation failure occurs. This form of **new** is most useful when you are compiling older code with a modern C++ compiler. It is also valuable when you are replacing calls to **malloc( )** with **new**. This form of **new** is shown here.

> *p_var* = new(nothrow) *type*;

Here *p_var* is a pointer variable of *type*. The **nothrow** form of **new** works like the original version of **new** from years ago. Since it returns null on failure, it can be "dropped into" older code and you won't have to add exception handling. However, for new code, exceptions provide a better alternative.

EXAMPLES

1. Here is an example of **new** that uses a **try/catch** block to monitor for an allocation failure.

```cpp
#include <iostream>
#include <new>
using namespace std;

int main()
{
  int *p;

   try {
    p = new int; // allocate memory for int
  } catch (bad_alloc xa) {
    cout << "Allocation failure.\n";
    return 1;
  }

  for(*p = 0; *p < 10; (*p)++)
    cout << *p << " ";

  delete p; // free the memory

  return 0;
}
```

Here if an allocation failure occurs, it is caught by the **catch** statement.

2. Since the previous program is unlikely to fail under any normal circumstance, the following program demonstrates **new**'s exception-throwing capability by forcing an allocation failure. It does this by allocating memory until it is exhausted.

```cpp
// Force an allocation failure.
#include <iostream>
#include <new>
using namespace std;

int main()
{
  double *p;

  // this will eventually run out of memory
  do {
    try {
      p = new double[100000];
    } catch (bad_alloc xa) {
      cout << "Allocation failure.\n";
      return 1;
    }
    cout << "Allocation OK.\n";
  } while(p);

  return 0;
}
```

3. The following program shows how to use the **new(nothrow)** alternative. It reworks the preceding program and forces an allocation failure.

```cpp
// Demonstrate the new(nothrow) alternative.
#include <iostream>
#include <new>
using namespace std;

int main()
{
  double *p;

  // this will eventually run out of memory
  do {
    p = new(nothrow) double[100000];
    if(p) cout << "Allocation OK.\n";
```

```
        else cout << "Allocation Error.\n";
    } while(p);

    return 0;
}
```

As this program demonstrates, when you use the **nothrow** approach, you must check the pointer returned by **new** after each allocation request.

---

1. Explain the difference between the behavior of **new** and **new(nothrow)** when an allocation failure occurs.

2. Given the following fragment, show two ways to convert it into modern C++-style code.

```
p = malloc(sizeof(int));

if(!p) {
    cout << "Allocation error.\n";
    exit(1);
}
```

S*KILLS CHECK*

Mastery
Skills Check

At this point you should be able to perform the following exercises and answer the questions.

1. Create a generic function that returns the mode of an array of values. (The _mode_ of a set is the value that occurs most often.)

2. Create a generic function that returns the summation of an array of values.

3. Create a generic bubble sort (or use any other sorting algorithm you like).

4. Rework the **stack** class so that it can store pairs of different-type objects on the stack. Demonstrate your solution.

5. Show the general forms of **try**, **catch**, and **throw**. In your own words, describe their operation.

6. Again, rework the **stack** class so that stack over- and underflows are handled as exceptions.

7. Check your compiler's documentation. See whether it supports the **terminate( )** and **unexpected( )** functions. Generally, these functions can be configured to call any function you choose. If this is the case with your compiler, try creating your own set of customized termination functions that handle otherwise unhandled exceptions.

8. Thought question: Give a reason why having **new** generate an exception is a better approach than having **new** return null on failure.

**Cumulative
Skills Check**

This section checks how well you have integrated material in this chapter with that from preceding chapters.

1. In Chapter 6, Section 6.7, Example 3, a safe array class was shown. On your own, convert it into a generic safe array.

2. In Chapter 1, overloaded versions of the **abs( )** function were created. As a better solution, create a generic **abs( )** function on your own that will return the absolute value of any numeric object.

12

Run-Time Type Identification and the Casting Operators

chapter objectives

12.1 Understanding Run-Time Type Identification (RTTI)

12.2 Using **dynamic_cast**

12.3 Using **const_cast**, **reinterpret_cast**, and **static_cast**

THIS chapter discusses two features that were recently added to the C++ language: run-time type identification (RTTI for short) and the new casting operators. RTTI allows you to identify the type of an object during the execution of your program. The casting operators give you safer, more controlled ways to cast. As you will see, one of the casting operators, **dynamic_cast**, relates directly to RTTI, so it makes sense to discuss these two subjects in the same chapter.

Review
Skills Check

Before proceeding, you should be able to correctly answer the following questions and do the exercises.

1. What is a generic function and what is its general form?

2. What is a generic class and what is its general form?

3. Write a generic function called **gexp( )** that returns the value of one of its arguments raised to the power of the other.

4. In Chapter 9, Section 9.7, Example 1, a **coord** class that holds integer coordinates was created and demonstrated in a program. Create a generic version of the **coord** class that can hold coordinates of any type. Demonstrate your solution in a program.

5. Briefly explain how **try**, **catch**, and **throw** work together to provide C++ exception handling.

6. Can **throw** be used if execution has not passed through a **try** block?

7. What purpose do **terminate( )** and **unexpected( )** serve?

8. What form of **catch** will handle all types of exceptions?

12.1   *U*NDERSTANDING RUN-TIME TYPE IDENTIFICATION (RTTI)

Run-time type information might be new to you because it is not found in non-polymorphic languages such as C. In non-polymorphic languages, there is no need for run-time type information because the type of each object is known at compile time (i.e., when the program is written). However, in polymorphic languages such as C++, there can be situations in which the type of an object is unknown at compile time because the precise nature of that object is not determined until the program is executed. As you know, C++ implements polymorphism through the use of class hierarchies, virtual functions, and base class pointers. In this approach, a base class pointer can be used to point to objects of the base class or to *any object derived from that base*. Thus, it is not always possible to know in advance what type of object will be pointed to by a base pointer at any given moment in time. This determination must be made at run time, using run-time type identification.

To obtain an object's type, use **typeid**. You must include the header **< typeinfo >** in order to use **typeid**. The most common form of **typeid** is shown here:

typeid(*object*)

Here *object* is the object whose type you will be obtaining. **typeid** returns a reference to an object of type **type_info** that describes the type of object defined by *object*. The **type_info** class defines the following public members:

```
bool operator==(const type_info &ob);
bool operator!=(const type_info &ob);
bool before(const type_info &ob);
const char *name( );
```

The overloaded **= =** and **! =** provide for the comparison of types. The **before( )** function returns true if the invoking object is before the object used as a parameter in collation order. (This function is mostly for internal use only. Its return value has nothing to do with inheritance or class hierarchies.) The **name( )** function returns a pointer to the name of the type.

While **typeid** will obtain the type of any object, its most important use is its application through a pointer of a polymorphic base class. In this case, it will automatically return the type of the actual object being pointed to, which can be a base class object or an object derived from that base. (Remember, a base class pointer can point to an object of the base class or of any class derived from that base.) Thus, using **typeid** you can determine at run time the type of the object that is being pointed to by a base class pointer. The same applies to references. When **typeid** is applied to a reference to an object of a polymorphic class, it will return the type of the object actually being referred to, which can be of a derived type. When **typeid** is applied to a non-polymorphic class, the base type of the pointer or reference is obtained.

There is a second form of **typeid,** one that takes a type name as its argument. This form is shown here:

typeid(*type-name*)

The main use of this form of **typeid** is to obtain a **type_info** object that describes the specified type so that it can be used in a type comparison statement.

Because **typeid** is commonly applied to a dereferenced pointer (i.e., one to which the * operator has been applied), a special exception has been created to handle the situation in which the pointer being dereferenced is null. In this case, **typeid** throws a **bad_typeid** exception.

Run-time type identification is not something that every program will use. However, when you are working with polymorphic types, it allows you to know what type of object is being operated upon in any given situation.

EXAMPLES

1. The following program demonstrates **typeid.** It first obtains type information about one of C++'s built-in types, **int**. It then displays the types of objects pointed to by **p**, which is a pointer of type **BaseClass**.

```
// An example that uses typeid.
#include <iostream>
#include <typeinfo>
```

```
using namespace std;

class BaseClass {
  virtual void f() {}; // make BaseClass polymorphic
  // ...
};

class Derived1: public BaseClass {
  // ...
};

class Derived2: public BaseClass {
  // ...
};

int main()
{
  int i;
  BaseClass *p, baseob;
  Derived1 ob1;
  Derived2 ob2;

  // First, display type name of a built-in type.
  cout << "Typeid of i is ";
  cout << typeid(i).name() << endl;

  // Demonstrate typeid with polymorphic types.
  p = &baseob;
  cout << "p is pointing to an object of type ";
  cout << typeid(*p).name() << endl;

  p = &ob1;
  cout << "p is pointing to an object of type ";
  cout << typeid(*p).name() << endl;

  p = &ob2;
  cout << "p is pointing to an object of type ";
  cout << typeid(*p).name() << endl;

  return 0;
}
```

The output produced by this program is shown here.

```
Typeid of i is int
p is pointing to an object of type class BaseClass
p is pointing to an object of type class Derived1
p is pointing to an object of type class Derived2
```

As explained, when **typeid** is applied to a base class pointer of a polymorphic type, the type of object pointed to will be determined at run time, as the output produced by the program shows. As an experiment, comment out the virtual function **f( )** in **BaseClass** and observe the results.

2. As explained, when **typeid** is applied to a reference to a polymorphic base class, the type returned is that of the actual object being referred to. The circumstance in which you will most often make use of this feature is when objects are passed to functions by reference. For example, in the following program, the function **WhatType( )** declares a reference parameter to objects of type **BaseClass**. This means that **WhatType( )** can be passed references to objects of type **BaseClass** or any class derived from **BaseClass**. When the **typeid** operator is applied to this parameter, it returns the actual type of the object being passed.

```
// Use a reference with typeid.
#include <iostream>
#include <typeinfo>
using namespace std;

class BaseClass {
  virtual void f() {}; // make BaseClass polymorphic
  // ...
};

class Derived1: public BaseClass {
  // ...
};

class Derived2: public BaseClass {
  // ...
};

// Demonstrate typeid with a reference parameter.
void WhatType(BaseClass &ob)
{
```

```
      cout << "ob is referencing an object of type ";
      cout << typeid(ob).name() << endl;
}


int main()
{
    int i;
    BaseClass baseob;
    Derived1 ob1;
    Derived2 ob2;

    WhatType(baseob);
    WhatType(ob1);
    WhatType(ob2);

    return 0;
}
```

The output produced by this program is shown here.

```
ob is referencing an object of type class BaseClass
ob is referencing an object of type class Derived1
ob is referencing an object of type class Derived2
```

3. Although obtaining the type name of an object is useful in some circumstances, often all you need to know is whether the type of one object matches that of another. Since the **type_info** object returned by **typeid** overloads the **= =** and **!=** operators, this too is easy to accomplish. The following program demonstrates the use of these operators.

```
// Demonstrate == and != relative to typeid.
#include <iostream>
#include <typeinfo>
using namespace std;

class X {
  virtual void f() {}
};

class Y {
  virtual void f() {}
};
```

```
int main()
{
  X x1, x2;
  Y y1;

  if(typeid(x1) == typeid(x2))
    cout << "x1 and x2 are same types\n";
  else
    cout << "x1 and x2 are different types\n";

  if(typeid(x1) != typeid(y1))
    cout << "x1 and y1 are different types\n";
  else
    cout << "x1 and y1 are same types\n";

  return 0;
}
```

The program displays the following output.

```
x1 and x2 are same types
x1 and y1 are different types
```

4. Although the preceding examples demonstrate the mechanics of using **typeid**, they don't show its full potential because the types in the preceding programs are knowable at compile time. In the following program, this is not the case. The program defines a simple class hierarchy that draws shapes on the screen. At the top of the hierarchy is the abstract class **Shape**. Four concrete subclasses are created: **Line**, **Square**, **Rectangle**, and **NullShape.** The function **generator( )** generates an object and returns a pointer to it. The actual object created is determined randomly based upon the outcome of the random number generator **rand( )**. (A function that produces objects is sometimes called an *object factory*.) Inside **main( )**, the shape of each object is displayed for all objects but **NullShape** objects, which have no shape. Since objects are generated randomly, there is no way to know in advance what type of object will be created next. Thus, the use of RTTI is required.

```
#include <iostream>
#include <cstdlib>
#include <typeinfo>
using namespace std;
```

```cpp
class Shape {
public:
  virtual void example() = 0;
};

class Rectangle: public Shape {
public:
  void example() {
    cout << "*****\n*   *\n*   *\n*****\n";
  }
};

class Triangle: public Shape {
public:
  void example() {
    cout << "*\n* *\n*   *\n*****\n";
  }
};

class Line: public Shape {
public:
  void example() {
    cout << "******\n";
  }
};

class NullShape: public Shape {
public:
  void example() {
  }
};

// A factory for objects derived from Shape.
Shape *generator()
{
  switch(rand() % 4) {
    case 0:
      return new Line;
    case 1:
      return new Rectangle;
    case 2:
      return new Triangle;
    case 3:
      return new NullShape;
  }
```

```
      return NULL;
}

int main()
{
  int i;
  Shape *p;

  for(i=0; i<10; i++) {
    p = generator(); // get next object

    cout << typeid(*p).name() << endl;

    // draw object only if it is not a NullShape
    if(typeid(*p) != typeid(NullShape))
      p->example();
  }

  return 0;
}
```

Sample output from the program is shown here.

```
class Rectangle
*****
*   *
*   *
*****
class NullShape
class Triangle
*
* *
*  *
*****
class Line
******
class Rectangle
*****
*   *
*   *
*****
class Line
******
```

```
class Triangle
*
* *
*  *
*****
class Triangle
*
* *
*  *
*****
class Triangle
*
* *
*  *
*****
class Line
******
```

5. The **typeid** operator can be applied to template classes. For example, consider the following program. It creates a hierarchy of template classes that store a value. The virtual function **get_val( )** returns a value that is defined by each class. For class **Num**, this is the value of the number itself. For **Square**, it is the square of the number, and for **Sqr_root**, it is the square root of the number. Objects derived from **Num** are generated by the **generator( )** function. The **typeid** operator is used to determine what type of object has been generated.

```cpp
// typeid can be used with templates.
#include <iostream>
#include <typeinfo>
#include <cmath>
#include <cstdlib>
using namespace std;

template <class T> class Num {
public:
  T x;
  Num(T i) { x = i; }
  virtual T get_val() { return x; };
};

template <class T>
class Square : public Num<T> {
```

```
public:
  Square(T i) : Num<T>(i) {}
  T get_val() { return x*x; }
};

template <class T>
class Sqr_root : public Num<T> {
public:
  Sqr_root(T i) : Num<T>(i) {}
  T get_val() { return sqrt((double) x); }
};

// A factory for objects derived from Num.
Num<double> *generator()
{
  switch(rand() % 2 ) {
    case 0: return new Square<double> (rand() % 100);
    case 1: return new Sqr_root<double> (rand() % 100);
  }
  return NULL;
}

int main()
{
  Num<double> ob1(10), *p1;
  Square<double> ob2(100.0);
  Sqr_root<double> ob3(999.2);
  int i;

  cout << typeid(ob1).name() << endl;
  cout << typeid(ob2).name() << endl;
  cout << typeid(ob3).name() << endl;

  if(typeid(ob2) == typeid(Square<double>))
    cout << "is Square<double>\n";

  p1 = &ob2;

  if(typeid(*p1) != typeid(ob1))
    cout << "Value is: " << p1->get_val();
  cout << "\n\n";

  cout << "Now, generate some Objects.\n";
  for(i=0; i<10; i++) {
```

```
    p1 = generator(); // get next object

  if(typeid(*p1) == typeid(Square<double>))
    cout << "Square object: ";
  if(typeid(*p1) == typeid(Sqr_root<double>))
    cout << "Sqr_root object: ";

  cout << "Value is: " << p1->get_val();
  cout << endl;
}

  return 0;
}
```

The output from the program is shown here.

```
class Num<double>
class Square<double>
class Sqr_root<double>
is Square<double>
Value is: 10000

Now, generate some Objects.
Sqr_root object: Value is: 8.18535
Square object: Value is: 0
Sqr_root object: Value is: 4.89898
Square object: Value is: 3364
Square object: Value is: 4096
Sqr_root object: Value is: 6.7082
Sqr_root object: Value is: 5.19615
Sqr_root object: Value is: 9.53939
Sqr_root object: Value is: 6.48074
Sqr_root object: Value is: 6
```

EXERCISES

1. Why is RTTI a necessary feature of C++?

2. Try the experiment described in Example 1. What output do you see?

3. Is the following fragment correct?

```
cout << typeid(float).name();
```

4. Given this fragment, show how to determine whether **p** is pointing to a **D2** object.

```
class B {
  virtual void f() {}
};

class D1: public B {
  void f() {}
};

class D2: public B {
  void f() {}
};

int main()
{
  B *p;
```

5. Assuming the **Num** class from Example 5, is the following expression true or false?

```
typeid(Num<int>) == typeid(Num<double>)
```

6. On your own, experiment with RTTI. Although its use might seem a bit esoteric in the context of simple, sample programs, it is a powerful construct that allows you to manage objects at run time.

---

*U***SING** *d y n a m i c _ c a s t*

Although C++ still fully supports the traditional casting operator defined by C, C++ adds four new ones. They are **dynamic_cast**, **const_cast**, **reinterpret_cast**, and **static_cast.** We will examine **dynamic_cast** first because it relates to RTTI. The other casting operators are examined in the following section.

The **dynamic_cast** operator performs a run-time cast that verifies the validity of a cast. If, at the time **dynamic_cast** is executed, the cast is invalid, the cast fails. The general form of **dynamic_cast** is shown here:

dynamic_cast<*target-type*> (*expr*)

Here *target-type* specifies the target type of the cast and *expr* is the expression being cast into the new type. The target type must be a pointer or reference type, and the expression being cast must evaluate to a pointer or reference. Thus, **dynamic_cast** can be used to cast one type of pointer into another or one type of reference into another.

The purpose of **dynamic_cast** is to perform casts on polymorphic types. For example, given the two polymorphic classes **B** and **D**, with **D** derived from **B**, a **dynamic_cast** can always cast a **D*** pointer into a **B*** pointer. This is because a base pointer can always point to a derived object. But a **dynamic_cast** can cast a **B*** pointer into an **D*** pointer only if the object being pointed to actually is a **D** object. In general, **dynamic_cast** will succeed if the pointer (or reference) being cast is a pointer (or reference) to either an object of the target type or an object derived from the target type. Otherwise, the cast will fail. If the cast fails, **dynamic_cast** evaluates to null if the cast involves pointers. If a **dynamic_cast** on reference types fails, a **bad_cast** exception is thrown.

Here is a simple example. Assume that **Base** is a polymorphic class and that **Derived** is derived from **Base**.

```
Base *bp, b_ob;
Derived *dp, d_ob;

bp = &d_ob; // base pointer points to Derived object
dp = dynamic_cast<Derived *> (bp);
if(dp) cout << "Cast OK";
```

Here the cast from the base pointer **bp** to the derived pointer **dp** works because **bp** is actually pointing to a **Derived** object. Thus, this fragment displays **Cast OK**. But in the next fragment, the cast fails because **bp** is pointing to a **Base** object and it is illegal to cast a base object into a derived object.

```
bp = &b_ob; // base pointer points to Base object
dp = dynamic_cast<Derived *> (bp);
if(!dp) cout << "Cast Fails";
```

Because the cast fails, this fragment displays **Cast Fails**.

The **dynamic_cast** operator can sometimes be used instead of **typeid** in certain cases. For example, again assume that **Base** is a polymorphic base class for **Derived.** The following fragment will assign **dp** the address of the object pointed to by **bp** if and only if the object is really a **Derived** object.

```
Base *bp;
Derived *dp;
// ...
if(typeid(*bp) == typeid(Derived)) dp =(Derived *) bp;
```

In this case, a C-style cast is used to actually perform the cast. This is safe because the **if** statement checks the legality of the cast using **typeid** before the cast actually occurs. However, a better way to accomplish this is to replace the **typeid** operators and **if** statement with this **dynamic_cast**:

```
dp = dynamic_cast<Derived *> (bp);
```

Because **dynamic_cast** succeeds only if the object being cast is either already an object of the target type or an object derived from the target type, after this statement executes **dp** will contain either a null or a pointer to an object of type **Derived**. Since **dynamic_cast** succeeds only if the cast is legal, it can simplify the logic in certain situations.

EXAMPLES

1. The following program demonstrates **dynamic_cast**:

```
// Demonstrate dynamic_cast.
#include <iostream>
using namespace std;

class Base {
public:
  virtual void f() { cout << "Inside Base\n"; }
  // ...
};

class Derived : public Base {
public:
  void f() { cout << "Inside Derived\n"; }
};
```

```
int main()
{
  Base *bp, b_ob;
  Derived *dp, d_ob;

  dp = dynamic_cast<Derived *> (&d_ob);
  if(dp) {
    cout << "Cast from Derived * to Derived * OK.\n";
    dp->f();
  } else
    cout << "Error\n";

  cout << endl;

  bp = dynamic_cast<Base *> (&d_ob);
  if(bp) {
    cout << "Cast from Derived * to Base * OK.\n";
    bp->f();
  } else
    cout << "Error\n";

  cout << endl;

  bp = dynamic_cast<Base *> (&b_ob);
  if(bp) {
    cout << "Cast from Base * to Base * OK.\n";
    bp->f();
  } else
    cout << "Error\n";

  cout << endl;

  dp = dynamic_cast<Derived *> (&b_ob);
  if(dp)
    cout << "Error\n";
  else
    cout << "Cast from Base * to Derived * not OK.\n";

  cout << endl;

  bp = &d_ob; // bp points to Derived object
  dp = dynamic_cast<Derived *> (bp);
  if(dp) {
    cout << "Casting bp to a Derived * OK\n" <<
      "because bp is really pointing\n" <<
```

```
      "to a Derived object.\n";
    dp->f();
  } else
    cout << "Error\n";

  cout << endl;

  bp = &b_ob; // bp points to Base object
  dp = dynamic_cast<Derived *> (bp);
  if(dp)
    cout << "Error";
  else {
    cout << "Now casting bp to a Derived *\n" <<
      "is not OK because bp is really \n" <<
      "pointing to a Base object.\n";
  }

  cout << endl;

  dp = &d_ob; // dp points to Derived object
  bp = dynamic_cast<Base *> (dp);
  if(bp) {
    cout << "Casting dp to a Base * is OK.\n";
    bp->f();
  } else
    cout << "Error\n";

  return 0;
}
```

The program produces the following output.

```
Cast from Derived * to Derived * OK.
Inside Derived

Cast from Derived * to Base * OK.
Inside Derived

Cast from Base * to Base * OK.
Inside Base

Cast from Base * to Derived * not OK.

Casting bp to a Derived * OK
because bp is really pointing
```

```
to a Derived object.
Inside Derived

Now casting bp to a Derived *
is not OK because bp is really
pointing to a Base object.

Casting dp to a Base * is OK.
Inside Derived
```

2. The following example illustrates how a **dynamic_cast** can be used to replace **typeid**.

```
// Use dynamic_cast to replace typeid.
#include <iostream>
#include <typeinfo>
using namespace std;

class Base {
public:
  virtual void f() {}
};

class Derived : public Base {
public:
  void derivedOnly() {
    cout << "Is a Derived Object\n";
  }
};

int main()
{
  Base *bp, b_ob;
  Derived *dp, d_ob;

  // **********************************
  // use typeid
  // **********************************
  bp = &b_ob;
  if(typeid(*bp) == typeid(Derived)) {
    dp = (Derived *) bp;
    dp->derivedOnly();
  }
  else
    cout << "Cast from Base to Derived failed.\n";
```

```
bp = &d_ob;
if(typeid(*bp) == typeid(Derived)) {
  dp = (Derived *) bp;
  dp->derivedOnly();
}
else
  cout << "Error, cast should work!\n";

// **********************************
// use dynamic_cast
// **********************************
bp = &b_ob;
dp = dynamic_cast<Derived *> (bp);
if(dp) dp->derivedOnly();
else
  cout << "Cast from Base to Derived failed.\n";

bp = &d_ob;
dp = dynamic_cast<Derived *> (bp);
if(dp) dp->derivedOnly();
else
  cout << "Error, cast should work!\n";

return 0;
}
```

As you can see, the use of **dynamic_cast** simplifies the logic required to cast a base pointer into a derived pointer. The output from the program is shown here.

```
Cast from Base to Derived failed.
Is a Derived Object
Cast from Base to Derived failed.
Is a Derived Object
```

3. The **dynamic_cast** operator can also be used with template classes. For example, the following program reworks the template class from Example 5 in the preceding section so that it uses **dynamic_cast** to determine the type of object returned by the **generator( )** function.

```
// dynamic_cast can be used with templates, too.
#include <iostream>
#include <typeinfo>
#include <cmath>
#include <cstdlib>
```

```
using namespace std;

template <class T> class Num {
public:
  T x;
  Num(T i) { x = i; }
  virtual T get_val() { return x; };
};

template <class T>
class Square : public Num<T> {
public:
  Square(T i) : Num<T>(i) {}
  T get_val() { return x*x; }
};

template <class T>
class Sqr_root : public Num<T> {
public:
  Sqr_root(T i) : Num<T>(i) {}
  T get_val() { return sqrt((double) x); }
};

// A factory for objects derived from Num.
Num<double> *generator()
{
  switch(rand() % 2 ) {
    case 0: return new Square<double> (rand() % 100);
    case 1: return new Sqr_root<double> (rand() % 100);
  }
  return NULL;
}

int main()
{
  Num<double> ob1(10), *p1;
  Square<double> ob2(100.0), *p2;
  Sqr_root<double> ob3(999.2), *p3;
  int i;

  cout << "Generate some objects.\n";
  for(i=0; i<10; i++) {
    p1 = generator();

    p2 = dynamic_cast<Square<double> *> (p1);
```

```
     if(p2) cout << "Square object: ";
     p3 = dynamic_cast<Sqr_root<double> *> (p1);
     if(p3) cout << "Sqr_root object: ";

     cout << "Value is: " << p1->get_val();
     cout << endl;
   }

   return 0;
}
```

EXERCISES

1. In your own words, explain the purpose of **dynamic_cast**.

2. Given the following fragment and using **dynamic_cast**, show how you can assign **p** a pointer to some object **ob** if and only if **ob** is a **D2** object.

```
class B {
  virtual void f() {}
};

class D1: public B {
  void f() {}
};

class D2: public B {
  void f() {}
};

B *p;
```

3. Convert the **main( )** function in Section 12.1, Exercise 4, so that it uses **dynamic_cast** rather than **typeid** to prevent a **NullShape** object from being displayed.

4. Using the **Num** class hierarchy from Example 3 in this section, will the following work?

```
Num<int> *Bp;
Square<double> *Dp;
// ...
Dp = dynamic_cast<Num<int>> (Bp);
```

12.3   **U**SING *const_cast, reinterpret_cast, AND static_cast*

Although **dynamic_cast** is the most important of the new casting operators, the other three are also valuable to the programmer. Their general forms are shown here:

const_cast<*target-type*> (*expr*)

reinterpret_cast<*target-ype*> (*expr*)

static_cast<*target-type*> (*expr*)

Here *target-type* specifies the target type of the cast and *expr* is the expression being cast into the new type. In general, these casting operators provide a safer, more explicit means of performing certain type conversions than that provided by the C-style cast.

The **const_cast** operator is used to explicitly override **const** and/or **volatile** in a cast. The target type must be the same as the source type except for the alteration of its **const** or **volatile** attributes. The most common use of **const_cast** is to remove **const**-ness.

The **static_cast** operator performs a non-polymorphic cast. For example, it can be used to cast a base class pointer into a derived class pointer. It can also be used for any standard conversion. No run-time checks are performed.

The **reinterpret_cast** operator changes one pointer type into another, fundamentally different, pointer type. It can also change a pointer into an integer and an integer into a pointer. A **reinterpret_cast** should be used for casting inherently incompatible pointer types.

Only **const_cast** can cast away **const**-ness. That is, neither **dynamic_cast, static_cast,** nor **reinterpret_cast** can alter the **const**-ness of an object.

EXAMPLES

1. The following program demonstrates the use of **reinterpret_cast**.

```
// An example that uses reinterpret_cast.
#include <iostream>
```

```
using namespace std;

int main()
{
  int i;
  char *p = "This is a string";

  i = reinterpret_cast<int> (p); // cast pointer to integer

  cout << i;

  return 0;
}
```

Here **reinterpret_cast** converts the pointer **p** into an integer. This conversion represents a fundamental type change and is a good use of **reinterpret_cast**.

2. The following program demonstrates **const_cast**.

```
// Demonstrate const_cast.
#include <iostream>
using namespace std;

void f(const int *p)
{
  int *v;

  // cast away const-ness.
  v = const_cast<int *> (p);

  *v = 100; // now, modify object through v
}


int main()
{
  int x = 99;

  cout << "x before call: " << x << endl;
  f(&x);
  cout << "x after call: " << x << endl;

  return 0;
}
```

The output produced by this program is shown here.

```
x before call: 99
x after call: 100
```

As you can see, **x** was modified by **f( )** even though the parameter to **f( )** was specified as a **const** pointer.

It must be stressed that the use of **const_cast** to cast way **const**-ness is a potentially dangerous feature. Use it with care.

3. The **static_cast** operator is essentially a substitute for the original cast operator. It simply performs a non-polymorphic cast. For example, the following casts a **float** into an **int**.

```
// use static_cast
#include <iostream>
using namespace std;

int main()
{
  int i;
  float f;

  f = 199.22;

  i = static_cast<int> (f);

  cout << i;

  return 0;
}
```

EXERCISES

1. Explain the rationale for **const_cast**, **reinterpret_cast**, and **static_cast**.

2. The following program contains an error. Show how to fix it using a **const_cast**.

```
#include <iostream>
using namespace std;
```

```
void f(const double &i)
{
  i = 100; // Error -- fix using const_cast
}


int main()
{
  double x = 98.6;

  cout << x << endl;
  f(x);
  cout << x << endl;

  return 0;
}
```

3. Explain why **const_cast** should normally be reserved for special cases.

S*KILLS CHECK*

Mastery
Skills Check

At this point you should be able to perform the following exercises and answer the questions.

1. Describe the operation of **typeid**.

2. What header must you include in order to use **typeid**?

3. In addition to the standard cast, C++ defines four casting operators. What are they and what are they for?

4. Complete the following partial program so that it reports which type of object has been selected by the user.

```
#include <iostream>
#include <typeinfo>
using namespace std;

class A {
  virtual void f() {}
};

class B : public A {
};

class C: public B {
};

int main()
{
  A *p, a_ob;
  B b_ob;
  C c_ob;
  int i;

  cout << "Enter 0 for A objects, ";
  cout << "1 for B objects or ";
  cout << "2 for C objects.\n";

  cin >> i;

  if(i==1) p = &b_ob;
  else if(i==2) p = &c_ob;
  else p = &a_ob;

  // report type of object selected by user

  return 0;
}
```

5. Explain how **dynamic_cast** can sometimes be an alternative to **typeid**.

6. What type of object is obtained by the **typeid** operator?

**Cumulative
Skills Check**

This section checks how well you have integrated material in this chapter with that from the preceding chapters.

1. Rework the program in Section 12.1, Example 4 so that it uses exception handling to watch for an allocation failure within the **generator( )** function.

2. Change the **generator( )** function from Question 1 so that it uses the **nothrow** version of **new**. Be sure to check for errors.

3. Special Challenge: On your own, create a class hierarchy that has at its top an abstract class called **DataStruct**. Create two concrete subclasses. Have one implement a stack, the other a queue. Create a function called **DataStructFactory( )** that has this prototype:

   DataStruct *DataStructFactory(char *what*);

   Have **DataStructFactory( )** create a stack if *what* is s and a queue if *what* is q. Return a pointer to the object created. Demonstrate that your factory function works.

13

*Namespaces,
Conversion Functions,
and Miscellaneous
Topics*

chapter objectives

13.1 Namespaces

13.2 Creating a conversion function

13.3 **static** class members

13.4 **const** member functions and **mutable**

13.5 A final look at constructors

13.6 Using linkage specifiers and the **asm** keyword

13.7 Array-based I/O

Tʜɪꜱ chapter discusses namespaces, conversion functions, static and const class members, and other specialized features of C++.

Review
Skills Check

Before proceeding, you should be able to correctly answer the following questions and do the exercises.

1. What are the casting operators and what do they do?

2. What is **type_info**?

3. What operator determines the type of an object?

4. Given this fragment, show how to determine whether **p** points to an object of **Base** or an object of **Derived**.

```
class Base {
  virtual void f() {}
};

class Derived : public Base {
};

int main()
{
  Base *p, b_ob;
  Derived d_ob;

  // ...
```

5. A **dynamic_cast** succeeds only if the object being cast is a pointer to either an object of the target type or an object _____ from the target type. (Fill in the blank.)

6. Can a **dynamic_cast** cast away **const**-ness?

13.1 **N**AMESPACES

Namespaces were briefly introduced in Chapter 1. Now it is time to look at them in detail. Namespaces are a relatively recent addition to C++. Their purpose is to localize the names of identifiers to avoid name collisions. In the C++ programming environment, there has been an explosion of variable, function, and class names. Prior to the invention of namespaces, all of these names competed for slots in the global namespace, and many conflicts arose. For example, if your program defined a function called **toupper( ),** it could (depending upon its parameter list) override the standard library function **toupper( )** because both names would be stored in the global namespace. Name collisions were compounded when two or more third-party libraries were used by the same program. In this case, it was possible—even likely—that a name defined by one library would conflict with the same name defined by another library.

The creation of the **namespace** keyword was a response to these problems. Because it localizes the visibility of names declared within it, a namespace allows the same name to be used in different contexts without giving rise to conflicts. Perhaps the most noticeable beneficiary of namespaces is the C++ standard library. In early versions of C++, the entire C++ library was defined within the global namespace (which was, of course, the only namespace). Now, however, the C++ library is defined within its own namespace, **std**, which reduces the chance of name collisions. You can also create your own namespaces within your program to localize the visibility of any names that you think might cause conflicts. This is especially important if you are creating class or function libraries.

The **namespace** keyword allows you to partition the global namespace by creating a declarative region. In essence, a namespace defines a scope. The general form of **namespace** is shown here:

```
namespace name {
  // declarations
}
```

Anything defined within a **namespace** statement is within the scope of that namespace.

Here is an example of a namespace:

```
namespace MyNameSpace {
  int i, k;
  void myfunc(int j) { cout << j; }

  class myclass {
   public:
     void seti(int x) { i = x; }
     int geti() { return i; }
  };
}
```

Here **i**, **k, myfunc( )**, and the class **myclass** are part of the scope defined by the **MyNameSpace** namespace.

Identifiers declared within a namespace can be referred to directly within that namespace. For example, in **MyNameSpace** the **return i** statement uses **i** directly. However, since **namespace** defines a scope, you need to use the scope resolution operator to refer to objects declared within a namespace from outside that namespace. For example, to assign the value 10 to **i** from code outside **MyNameSpace**, you must use this statement:

```
MyNameSpace::i = 10;
```

Or, to declare an object of type **myclass** from outside **MyNameSpace**, you use a statement like this:

```
MyNameSpace::myclass ob;
```

In general, to access a member of a namespace from outside its namespace, precede the member's name with the name of the namespace followed by the scope resolution operator.

As you can imagine, if your program includes frequent references to the members of a namespace, the need to specify the namespace and the scope resolution operator each time you need to refer to one quickly becomes a tedious chore. The **using** statement was invented to alleviate this problem. The **using** statement has these two general forms:

using namespace *name*;
using *name::member*;

In the first form, *name* specifies the name of the namespace you want to access. When you use this form, all of the members defined within the specified namespace are brought into the current namespace and can be used without qualification. If you use the second form, only a specific member of the namespace is made visible. For example, assuming **MyNameSpace** as shown above, the following **using** statements and assignments are valid:

```
using MyNameSpace::k; // only k is made visible
k = 10; // OK because k is visible

using namespace MyNameSpace; // all members are visible
i = 10; // OK because all members of MyNameSpace are visible
```

There can be more than one namespace declaration of the same name. This allows a namespace to be split over several files or even separated within the same file. Consider the following example:

```
namespace NS {
  int i;
}

// ...

namespace NS {
  int j;
}
```

Here **NS** is split into two pieces. However, the contents of each piece are still within the same namespace, **NS**.

A namespace must be declared outside of all other scopes, with one exception: a namespace can be nested within another. This means that you cannot declare namespaces that are localized to a function, for example.

There is a special type of namespace, called an *unnamed namespace*, that allows you to create identifiers that are unique within a file. It has this general form:

```
namespace {
  // declarations
}
```

Unnamed namespaces allow you to establish unique identifiers that are known only within the scope of a single file. That is, within the file that contains the unnamed namespace, the members of that namespace can be used directly, without qualification. But outside the file, the identifiers are unknown.

You will not usually need to create namespaces for most small- to medium-sized programs. However, if you will be creating libraries of reusable code or if you want to ensure the widest portability, consider wrapping your code within a namespace.

EXAMPLES

1. Here is an example that illustrates the attributes of a namespace.

```cpp
// Namespace Demo
#include <iostream>
using namespace std;

// define a namespace
namespace firstNS {
  class demo {
    int i;
  public:
    demo(int x) { i = x; }
    void seti(int x) { i = x; }
    int geti() { return i; }
  };

  char str[] = "Illustrating namespaces\n";
  int counter;
}

// define another namespace
namespace secondNS {
  int x, y;
}

int main()
{
  // use scope resolution
  firstNS::demo ob(10);
```

```
/* Once ob has been declared, its member functions
   can be used without namespace qualification. */
cout << "Value of ob is : " << ob.geti();
cout << endl;
ob.seti(99);
cout << "Value of ob is now : " << ob.geti();
cout << endl;

// bring str into current scope
using firstNS::str;
cout << str;

// bring all of firstNS into current scope
using namespace firstNS;
for(counter = 10; counter; counter--)
  cout << counter << " ";
cout << endl;

// use secondNS namespace
secondNS::x = 10;
secondNS::y = 20;

cout << "x, y: " << secondNS:: x;
cout << ", " << secondNS::y << endl;

// bring another namespace into view
using namespace secondNS;
demo xob(x), yob(y);

cout << "xob, yob: " << xob.geti() << ", ";
cout << yob.geti() << endl;

  return 0;
}
```

The output produced by this program is shown here.

```
Value of ob is : 10
Value of ob is now : 99
Illustrating namespaces
10 9 8 7 6 5 4 3 2 1
x, y: 10, 20
xob, yob: 10, 20
```

The program illustrates one important point: using one namespace does not override another. When you bring a namespace into view, it simply adds its names to whatever other namespaces are currently in effect. Thus, by the end of this program the **std**, **firstNS**, and **secondNS** namespaces have been added to the global namespace.

2. As mentioned, a namespace can be split between files or within a single file; its contents are additive. Consider this example:

```
// Namespaces are additive
#include <iostream>
using namespace std;

namespace Demo {
  int a; // In Demo namespace
}

int x; // this is in global namespace

namespace Demo {
  int b; // this is in Demo namespace, too
}

int main()
{
  using namespace Demo;

  a = b = x = 100;

  cout << a << " " << b << " " << x;

  return 0;
}
```

Here the **Demo** namespace contains both **a** and **b**, but not **x**.

3. As explained, Standard C++ defines its entire library in its own namespace, **std**. This is the reason that most of the programs in this book have included the following statement:

```
using namespace std;
```

This causes the **std** namespace to be brought into the current namespace, which gives you direct access to the names of the functions and classes defined within the library without having to qualify each one with **std::**.

Of course, you can explicitly qualify each name with **std::** if you like. For example, the following program does not bring the library into the global namespace.

```
// use explicit std:: qualification.
#include <iostream>

int main()
{
  double val;

  std::cout << "Enter a number: ";

  std::cin >> val;

  std::cout << "This is your number: ";
  std::cout << val;

  return 0;
}
```

Here **cout** and **cin** are both explicitly qualified by their namespace. That is, to write to standard output you must specify **std::cout**, and to read from standard input you must use **std::cin**.

You might not want to bring the Standard C++ library into the global namespace if your program will be making only limited use of it. However, if your program contains hundreds of references to library names, including **std** in the current namespace is far easier than qualifying each name individually.

4. If you are using only a few names from the standard library, it might make more sense to specify a **using** statement for each individually. The advantage to this approach is that you can still use those names without an **std::** qualification but you will not be bringing the entire standard library into the global namespace. Here's an example:

```
// Bring only a few names into the global namespace.
#include <iostream>

// gain access to cout and cin
```

```
using std::cout;
using std::cin;

int main()
{
  double val;

  cout << "Enter a number: ";

  cin >> val;
  cout << "This is your number: ";
  cout << val;

  return 0;
}
```

Here **cin** and **cout** can be used directly, but the rest of the **std** namespace has not been brought into view.

5. As explained, the original C++ library was defined in the global namespace. If you will be converting older C++ programs, you will need to either include a **using namespace std** statement or qualify each reference to a library member with **std::**. This is especially important if you are replacing old **.h** header files with the new-style headers. Remember, the old **.h** headers put their contents into the global namespace. The new-style headers put their contents into the **std** namespace.

6. In C, if you want to restrict the scope of a global name to the file in which it is declared, you declare that name as **static**. For example, consider the following two files that are part of the same program:

File One

```
static int counter;
void f1() {
  counter = 99; // OK
}
```

File Two

```
extern int counter;
void f2() {
  counter = 10; // error
}
```

Because **counter** is defined in File One, it can be used in File One. In File Two, even though **counter** is specified as **extern**, it is still unavailable, and any attempt to use it results in an error. By preceding **counter** with **static** in File One, the programmer has restricted its scope to that file.

Although the use of **static** global declarations is still allowed in C++, a better way to accomplish the same end is to use an unnamed namespace, as shown in this example:

File One	**File Two**

```
namespace {               extern int counter;
  int counter;            void f2() {
}                            counter = 10; // error
void f1() {               }
  counter = 99; // OK
}
```

Here **counter** is also restricted to File One. The use of the unnamed namespace rather than **static** is the method recommended by Standard C++.

EXERCISES

1. Convert the following program from Chapter 9 so that it does not use the **using namespace std** statement.

```
// Convert spaces to |s.
#include <iostream>
#include <fstream>
using namespace std;

int main(int argc, char *argv[])
{
  if(argc!=3) {
    cout << "Usage: CONVERT <input> <output>\n";
    return 1;
  }

  ifstream fin(argv[1]); // open input file
  ofstream fout(argv[2]);  // create output file

  if(!fout) {
    cout << "Cannot open output file.\n";
    return 1;
  }
  if(!fin) {
```

```
        cout << "Cannot open input file.\n";
        return 1;
    }

    char ch;

    fin.unsetf(ios::skipws);  // do not skip spaces
    while(!fin.eof()) {
        fin >> ch;
        if(ch==' ') ch = '|';
        if(!fin.eof()) fout << ch;
    }

    fin.close();
    fout.close();

    return 0;
}
```

2. Explain the operation of an unnamed namespace.

3. Explain the difference between the two forms of **using**.

4. Explain why most programs in this book contain a **using** statement. Describe one alternative.

5. Explain why you might want to put reusable code that you create into its own namespace.

13.2 *C*REATING A CONVERSION FUNCTION

Sometimes it is useful to convert an object of one type into an object of another. Although it is possible to use an overloaded operator function to accomplish such a conversion, there is often an easier (and better) way: using a conversion function. A *conversion function* converts an object into a value compatible with another type, which is often one of the built-in C++ types. In essence, a conversion function automatically converts an object into a value that is compatible with the type of the expression in which the object is used.

The general form of a conversion function is shown here:

operator *type*( ) { return *value*; }

Here *type* is the target type you will be converting to and *value* is the value of the object after the conversion has been performed. Conversion functions return a value of type *type*. No parameters can be specified, and a conversion function must be a member of the class for which it performs the conversion.

As the examples will illustrate, a conversion function generally provides a cleaner approach to converting an object's value into another type than any other method available in C++ because it allows an object to be included directly in an expression involving the target type.

EXAMPLES

1. In the following program, the **coord** class contains a conversion function that converts an object to an integer. In this case, the function returns the product of the two coordinates; however, any conversion appropriate to your specific application is allowed.

```
// A simple conversion function example.
#include <iostream>
using namespace std;

class coord {
  int x, y;
public:
  coord(int i, int j) { x = i; y = j; }
  operator int() { return x*y; } // conversion function
};

int main()
{
  coord o1(2, 3), o2(4, 3);
  int i;

  i = o1;  // automatically convert to integer
  cout << i << '\n';

  i = 100 + o2;  // convert o2 to integer
  cout << i << '\n';
```

```
    return 0;
}
```

This program displays 6 and 112.

In this example, notice that the conversion function is called when **o1** is assigned to an integer and when **o2** is used as part of a larger integer expression. As stated, by using a conversion function, you allow classes that you create to be integrated into "normal" C++ expressions without having to create a series of complex overloaded operator functions.

2. Following is another example of a conversion function. This one converts a string of type **strtype** into a character pointer to **str**.

```
#include <iostream>
#include <cstring>
using namespace std;

class strtype {
  char str[80];
  int len;
public:
  strtype(char *s) { strcpy(str, s); len = strlen(s); }
  operator char *() { return str; } // convert to char*
};

int main()
{
  strtype s("This is a test\n");
  char *p, s2[80];

  p = s; // convert to char *
  cout << "Here is string: " << p << '\n';

  // convert to char * in function call
  strcpy(s2, s);
  cout << "Here is copy of string: " << s2 << '\n';

  return 0;
}
```

This program displays the following:

```
Here is string: This is a test
Here is copy of string: This is a test
```

As you can see, not only is the conversion function invoked when object **s** is assigned to **p** (which is of type **char** *), but it is also called when **s** is used as a parameter to **strcpy( )**. Remember, **strcpy( )** has the following prototype:

```
char *strcpy(char *s1, const char *s2);
```

Because the prototype specifies that *s2* is of type **char** *, the conversion function to **char** * is automatically called. This illustrates how a conversion function can also help you seamlessly integrate your classes into C++'s standard library functions.

EXERCISES

1. Using the **strtype** class from Example 2, create a conversion that converts to type **int**. In this conversion, return the length of the string held in **str**. Illustrate that your conversion function works.

2. Given this class,

```
class pwr {
   int base;
   int exp;
public:
   pwr(int b, int e) { base = b; exp = e; }
   // create conversion to integer here
};
```

create a conversion function that converts an object of type **pwr** to type integer. Have the function return the result of **base**^{exp}.

13.3 STATIC CLASS MEMBERS

It is possible for a class member variable to be declared as **static**. By using **static** member variables, you can bypass a number of rather tricky problems. When you declare a member variable as **static**, you cause only one copy of that variable to exist—no matter how many objects of that class are created. Each object simply shares that one variable. Remember, for a normal member variable, each time an object is created, a new copy of that variable is created, and that copy is accessible only by that object. (That is, when normal variables are used, each object possesses its own copies.) However, there is only one copy of a **static** member variable, and all objects of its class share it. Also, the same **static** variable will be used by any classes derived from the class that contains the **static** member.

Although it might seem odd when you first think about it, a **static** member variable exists *before* any object of its class is created. In essence, a **static** class member is a global variable that simply has its scope restricted to the class in which it is declared. In fact, as you will see in one of the following examples, it is actually possible to access a **static** member variable independent of any object.

When you declare a **static** data member within a class, you are not defining it. Instead, you must provide a definition for it elsewhere, outside the class. To do this, you redeclare the **static** variable, using the scope resolution operator to identify which class it belongs to.

All **static** member variables are initialized to 0 by default. However, you can give a **static** class variable an initial value of your choosing, if you like.

Keep in mind that the principal reason **static** member variables are supported by C++ is to avoid the need for global variables. As you can surmise, classes that rely upon global variables almost always violate the encapsulation principle that is so fundamental to OOP and C++.

It is also possible for a member function to be declared as **static**, but this usage is not common. A member function declared as **static** can access only other **static** members of its class. (Of course, a **static** member function can access non-**static** global data and functions.) A **static** member function does not have a **this** pointer. Virtual **static** member functions are not allowed. Also, **static** member functions cannot be declared as **const** or **volatile**. A **static** member function can be invoked by an object of its class, or it can be called independent of any object, via the class name and the scope resolution operator.

1: Here is a simple example that uses a **static** member variable:

```
// A static member variable example.
#include <iostream>
using namespace std;

class myclass {
  static int i;
public:
  void seti(int n) { i = n; }
  int geti() { return i; }
};

// Definition of myclass::i. i is still private to myclass.
int myclass::i;

int main()
{
  myclass o1, o2;

  o1.seti(10);

  cout << "o1.i: " << o1.geti() << '\n'; // displays 10
  cout << "o2.i: " << o2.geti() << '\n'; // also displays 10

  return 0;
}
```

This program displays the following:

```
o1.i: 10
o2.i: 10
```

Looking at this program, you can see that only object **o1** actually sets the value of **static** member **i**. However, since **i** is shared by both **o1** and **o2** (and, indeed, by any object of type **myclass**), both calls to **geti( )** display the same result.

Notice how **i** is declared within **myclass** but defined outside of the class. This second step ensures that storage for **i** is defined. Technically, a class declaration is just that, only a declaration. No memory is actually set aside because of a declaration. Because a **static** data member *implies* that memory is allocated for that member, a separate definition is required that causes storage to be allocated.

2. Because a **static** member variable exists before any object of that class is created, it can be accessed within a program independent of any object. For example, the following variation of the preceding program sets the value of **i** to 100 without any reference to a specific object. Notice the use of the scope resolution operator and class name to access **i**.

```
// Use a static member variable independent of any object.
#include <iostream>
using namespace std;

class myclass {
public:
  static int i;
  void seti(int n) { i = n; }
  int geti() { return i; }
};

int myclass::i;

int main()
{
  myclass o1, o2;

  // set i directly
  myclass::i = 100; // no object is referenced.

  cout << "o1.i: " << o1.geti() << '\n'; // displays 100
  cout << "o2.i: " << o2.geti() << '\n'; // also displays 100
  return 0;
}
```

Because **i** is set to 100, the following output is displayed:

```
o1.i: 100
o2.i: 100
```

3. One very common use of a **static** class variable is to coordinate access to a shared resource, such as a disk file, printer, or network server. As you probably know from your previous programming experience, coordinating access to a shared

resource requires some means of sequencing events. To get an idea of how **static** member variables can be used to control access to a shared resource, examine the following program. It creates a class called **output**, which maintains a common output buffer called **outbuf** that is, itself, a **static** character array. This buffer is used to receive output sent by the **outbuf( )** member function. This function sends the contents of **str** one character at a time. It does so by first acquiring access to the buffer and then sending all the characters in **str**. It locks out access to the buffer by other objects until it is done outputting. You should be able to follow its operation by studying the code and reading the comments.

```cpp
// A shared resource example.
#include <iostream>
#include <cstring>
using namespace std;

class output {
  static char outbuf[255]; // this is the shared resource
  static int inuse; // buffer available if 0;
  static int oindex; // index of outbuf
  char str[80];
  int i; // index of next char in str
  int who; // identifies the object, must be > 0
public:
  output(int w, char *s) { strcpy(str, s); i = 0; who = w; }

  /* This function returns -1 if waiting for buffer,
     it returns 0 if it is done outputting, and
     it returns who if it is still using the buffer.
  */
  int putbuf()
  {
    if(!str[i]) { // done outputting
      inuse = 0; // release buffer
      return 0; // signal termination
    }
    if(!inuse) inuse = who; // get buffer
    if(inuse != who) return -1; // in use by someone else
    if(str[i]) { // still chars to output
      outbuf[oindex] = str[i];
      i++; oindex++;
```

```
        outbuf[oindex] = '\0';   // always keep null-terminated
        return 1;
      }
      return 0;
    }
    void show() { cout << outbuf << '\n'; }
};

char output::outbuf[255]; // this is the shared resource
int output::inuse = 0; // buffer available if 0
int output::oindex = 0; // index of outbuf

int main()
{
  output o1(1, "This is a test"), o2(2, " of statics");

  while(o1.putbuf() | o2.putbuf()) ; // output chars

  o1.show();

  return 0;
}
```

4. **static** member functions have limited applications, but one good use for them is to "preinitialize" private **static** data before any object is actually created. For example, this is a perfectly valid C++ program:

```
#include <iostream>
using namespace std;

class static_func_demo {
  static int i;
public:
  static void init(int x) {i = x;}
  void show() {cout << i;}
};

int static_func_demo::i; // define i

int main()
{
  // init static data before object creation
  static_func_demo::init(100);
```

```
static_func_demo x;
x.show(); // displays 100

return 0;
}
```

Here **i** is initialized by the call to **init( )** before an object of **static_func_demo** exists.

EXERCISES

1. Rework Example 3 so that it displays which object is currently outputting characters and which one or ones are blocked from outputting a character because the buffer is already in use by another.

2. One interesting use of a **static** member variable is to keep track of the number of objects of a class that are in existence at any given point in time. The way to do this is to increment a **static** member variable each time the class' constructor is called and decrement it each time the class' destructor is called. Implement such a scheme and demonstrate that it works.

13.4   ## *const MEMBER FUNCTIONS AND mutable*

Class member functions can be declared as **const**. When this is done, that function cannot modify the object that invokes it. Also, a **const** object cannot invoke a non-**const** member function. However, a **const** member function can be called by either **const** or non-**const** objects.

To specify a member function as **const,** use the form shown in the following example:

```
class X {
  int some_var;
public:
```

```
    int f1() const; // const member function
};
```

As you can see, the **const** follows the function's parameter declaration.

Sometimes there will be one or more members of a class that you want a **const** function to be able to modify even though you don't want the function to be able to modify any of its other members. You can accomplish this through the use of **mutable**, which overrides **const**-ness. That is, a **mutable** member can be modified by a **const** member function.

1. The purpose of declaring a member function as **const** is to prevent it from modifying the object that invokes it. For example, consider the following program.

```
/*
    Demonstrate const member functions.
    This program won't compile.
*/
#include <iostream>
using namespace std;

class Demo {
  int i;
public:
  int geti() const {
    return i; // ok
  }

  void seti(int x) const {
    i = x; // error!
  }
};

int main()
{
  Demo ob;

  ob.seti(1900);
  cout << ob.geti();
```

```
    return 0;
}
```

This program will not compile because **seti( )** is declared as **const**. This means that it is not allowed to modify the invoking object. Since it attempts to change **i**, the program is in error. In contrast, since **geti( )** does not attempt to modify **i**, it is perfectly acceptable.

2. To allow selected members to be modified by a **const** member function, specify them as **mutable**. Here's an example:

```
// Demonstrate mutable.
#include <iostream>
using namespace std;

class Demo {
  mutable int i;
  int j;
public:
  int geti() const {
    return i; // ok
  }

  void seti(int x) const {
    i = x; // now, OK.
  }

/* The following function won't compile.
  void setj(int x) const {
    j = x; // Still Wrong!
  }
*/
};

int main()
{
  Demo ob;

  ob.seti(1900);
  cout << ob.geti();

  return 0;
}
```

Here **i** is specified as **mutable**, so it can be changed by the **seti( )** function. However, **j** is not **mutable**, so **setj( )** is unable to modify its value.

EXERCISES

1. The following program attempts to create a simple countdown timer that rings a bell when the time period is over. You can specify the time period and increment when a **CountDown** object is created. Unfortunately, the program will not compile as shown here. Fix it.

```cpp
// This program contains an error.
#include <iostream>
using namespace std;

class CountDown {
  int incr;
  int target;
  int current;
public:
  CountDown(int delay, int i=1) {
    target = delay;
    incr = i;
    current = 0;
  }

  bool counting() const {
    current += incr;
    if(current >= target) {
      cout << "\a";
      return false;
    }
    cout << current << " ";
    return true;
  }
};

int main()
{
  CountDown ob(100, 2);

  while(ob.counting()) ;
```

```
      return 0;
   }
```

2. Can a **const** member function call a non-**const** function? Why not?

13.5 *A* FINAL LOOK AT CONSTRUCTORS

Although constructors were described early on in this book, there are still a few points that need to be made. Consider the following program:

```
#include <iostream>
using namespace std;

class myclass {
   int a;
public:
   myclass(int x) { a = x; }
   int geta() { return a; }
};

int main()
{
   myclass ob(4);

   cout << ob.geta();

   return 0;
}
```

Here the constructor for **myclass** takes one parameter. Pay special attention to how **ob** is declared in **main( )**. The value 4, specified in the parentheses following **ob**, is the argument that is passed to **myclass( )**'s parameter **x**, which is used to initialize **a**. This is the form of initialization that we have been using since the start of this book. However, there is an alternative. For example, the following statement also initializes **a** to 4:

```
myclass ob = 4; // automatically converts into myclass(4)
```

As the comment suggests, this form of initialization is automatically converted into a call to the **myclass** constructor with 4 as the argument. That is, the preceding statement is handled by the compiler as if it were written like this:

```
myclass ob(4);
```

In general, any time that you have a constructor that requires only one argument, you can use either *ob(x)* or *ob = x* to initialize an object. The reason for this is that whenever you create a constructor that takes one argument, you are also implicitly creating a conversion from the type of that argument to the type of the class.

If you do not want implicit conversions to be made, you can prevent them by using **explicit.** The **explicit** specifier applies only to constructors. A constructor specified as **explicit** will be used only when an initialization uses the normal constructor syntax. It will not perform any automatic conversion. For example, if the **myclass** constructor is declared as **explicit**, the automatic conversion will not be supplied. Here is **myclass( )** declared as **explicit**:

```
#include <iostream>
using namespace std;

class myclass {
  int a;
public:
  explicit myclass(int x) { a = x; }
  int geta() { return a; }
};
```

Now only constructors of the form

```
myclass ob(110);
```

will be allowed.

EXAMPLES

1. There can be more than one converting constructor in a class. For example, consider this variation on **myclass**:

```
#include <iostream>
#include <cstdlib>
using namespace std;
```

```
class myclass {
  int a;
public:
  myclass(int x) { a = x; }
  myclass(char *str) { a = atoi(str); }
  int geta() { return a; }
};

int main()
{
  myclass ob1 = 4;      // converts to myclass(4)
  myclass ob2 = "123"; // converts to myclass("123");

  cout << "ob1: " << ob1.geta() << endl;
  cout << "ob2: " << ob2.geta() << endl;

  return 0;
}
```

Since both constructors use different type arguments (as, of course, they must), each initialization statement is automatically converted into its equivalent constructor call.

2. The automatic conversion from the type of a constructor's first argument into a call to the constructor itself has interesting implications. For example, assuming **myclass** from Example 1, the following **main( )** function makes use of the conversions from **int** and **char *** to assign **ob1** and **ob2** new values.

```
int main()
{
  myclass ob1 = 4;      // converts to myclass(4)
  myclass ob2 = "123"; // converts to myclass("123");

  cout << "ob1: " << ob1.geta() << endl;
  cout << "ob2: " << ob2.geta() << endl;

  // use automatic conversions to assign new values
  ob1 = "1776"; // converts into ob1 = myclass("1776");
  ob2 = 2001;   // converts into ob2 = myclass(2001);

  cout << "ob1: " << ob1.geta() << endl;
  cout << "ob2: " << ob2.geta() << endl;
```

```
    return 0;
}
```

3. To prevent the conversions just shown, you could specify the constructors as **explicit**, as shown here:

```
#include <iostream>
#include <cstdlib>
using namespace std;

class myclass {
   int a;
public:
   explicit myclass(int x) { a = x; }
   explicit myclass(char *str) { a = atoi(str); }
   int geta() { return a; }
};
```

EXERCISES

1. In Example 3, if only **myclass(int)** is made explicit, will **myclass(char *)** still allow implicit conversions? (Hint: Try it.)

2. Will the following fragment work?

```
class Demo {
   double x
public:
   Demo(double i) { x = i; }
   // ...
};

// ...
Demo counter = 10;
```

3. Justify the inclusion of the **explicit** keyword. (In other words, explain why implicit constructor conversions might not be a desirable feature of C++ in some cases.)

13.6   *USING LINKAGE SPECIFIERS AND THE asm KEYWORD*

C++ provides two important mechanisms that make it easier to link C++ to other languages. One is the *linkage specifier,* which tells the compiler that one or more functions in your C++ program will be linked with another language that might have a different approach to naming, parameter passing, stack restoration, and the like. The second is the **asm** keyword, which allows you to embed assembly language instructions in your C++ source code. Both are examined here.

By default, all functions in a C++ program are compiled and linked as C++ functions. However, you can tell the C++ compiler to link a function so that it is compatible with another type of language. All C++ compilers allow functions to be linked as either C or C++ functions. Some also allow you to link functions with languages such as Pascal, Ada, or FORTRAN. To cause a function to be linked for a different language, use this general form of the linkage specification:

extern "*language*" *function-prototype*;

Here *language* is the name of the language with which you want the specified function to link. If you want to specify linkage for more than one function, use this form of the linkage specification:

extern "*language*" {
    function-prototypes
}

All linkage specifications must be global; they cannot be used inside a function.

The most common use of linkage specifications occurs when linking C++ programs to C code. By specifying "C" linkage you prevent the compiler from *mangling* (also known as *decorating*) the names of functions with embedded type information. Because of C++'s ability to overload functions and create member functions, the link-name of a function usually has type information added to it. Since C does not support overloading or member functions, it cannot recognize a mangled name. Using "C" linkage avoids this problem.

Although it is generally possible to link assembly language routines with a C++ program, there is often an easier way to use assembly language. C++ supports the special keyword **asm**, which allows you to embed assembly language instructions within a C++ function. These instructions are then compiled as is. The advantage of using an in-line assembler is that your entire program is completely defined as a C++ program and there is no need to link separate assembly language files. The general form of the **asm** keyword is shown here:

asm ("*op-code*");

where *op-code* is the assembly language instruction that will be embedded in your program.

It's important to note that several compilers accept these three slightly different forms of the **asm** statement:

asm *op-code*;

asm *op-code newline*

asm {
  instruction sequence
}

Here *op-code* is not enclosed in double quotes. Because embedded assembly language instruction tends to be implementation dependent, you will want to read your compiler's user manual on this issue.

*Microsoft Visual C++ uses _ _**asm** for embedding assembly code. It is otherwise similar to **asm**.*

EXAMPLES

1. This program links **func( )** as a C, rather than a C++, function:

```
// Illustrate linkage specifier.
#include <iostream>
using namespace std;

extern "C" int func(int x); // link as C function

// This function now links as a C function.
int func(int x)
```

```
{
  return x/3;
}
```

This function can now be linked with code compiled by
a C compiler.

2. The following fragment tells the compiler that **f1( )**, **f2( )**, and
   f3( ) should be linked as C functions:

```
extern "C" {
  void f1();
  int f2(int x);
  double f3(double x, int *p);
}
```

3. This fragment embeds several assembly language instructions
   into **func( )**:

```
// Don't try this function!
void func()
{
  asm("mov bp, sp");
  asm("push ax");
  asm("mov cl, 4");
  // ...
}
```

*You must be an accomplished assembly language
programmer in order to successfully use in-line assembly
language. Also, be sure to check your compiler's user
manual for details regarding assembly language usage.*

EXERCISE

1. On your own, study the sections in your compiler's user
   manual that refer to linkage specifications and assembly
   language interfacing.

13.7	# *A RRAY-BASED I/O*

In addition to console and file I/O, C++ supports a full set of functions that use character arrays as the input or output device. Although C++'s array-based I/O parallels, in concept, the array-based I/O found in C (specifically, C's **sscanf( )** and **sprintf( )** functions), C++'s array-based I/O is more flexible and useful because it allows user-defined types to be integrated into it. Although it is not possible to cover every aspect of array-based I/O here, the most important and commonly used features are examined.

It is important to understand from the outset that array-based I/O still operates through streams. Everything you learned about C++ I/O in Chapters 8 and 9 is applicable to array-based I/O. In fact, you need to learn to use just a few new functions to take full advantage of array-based I/O. These functions link a stream to a region of memory. Once this has been accomplished, all I/O takes place through the I/O functions you know already.

Before you can use array-based I/O, you must be sure to include the header **< strstream >** in your file. In this header are defined the classes **istrstream**, **ostrstream**, and **strstream**. These classes create array-based input, output, and input/output streams, respectively. These classes have as a base **ios**, so all the functions and manipulators included in **istream**, **ostream**, and **iostream** are also available in **istrstream**, **ostrstream**, and **strstream**.

To use a character array for output, use this general form of the **ostrstream** constructor:

ostrstream *ostr* (char **buf*, streamsize *size*, openmode *mode* = ios::out);

Here *ostr* will be the stream associated with the array *buf.* The size of the array is specified by *size.* Generally, *mode* is simply defaulted to output, but you can use any output mode flag defined by **ios** if you like. (Refer to Chapter 9 for details.)

Once an array has been opened for output, characters will be put into the array until it is full. The array will not be overrun. Any attempt to overfill the array will result in an I/O error. To find out how many characters have been written to the array, use the **pcount( )** member function, shown here:

streamsize pcount( );

You must call this function in conjunction with a stream, and it will return the number of characters written to the array, including any null terminator.

To open an array for input, use this form of the **istrstream** constructor:

istrstream *istr* (const char **buf*);

Here *buf* is a pointer to the array that will be used for input. The input stream will be called *istr*. When input is being read from an array, **eof( )** will return true when the end of the array has been reached.

To open an array for input/output operations, use this form of the **strstream** constructor:

strstream *iostr* (char **buf,* streamsize *size,* openmode *mode* = ios::in | ios::out);

Here *iostr* will be an input/output stream that uses the array pointed to by *buf,* which is *size* characters long.

The character-based streams are also referred to as *char * streams* in some C++ literature.

It is important to remember that all I/O functions described earlier operate with array-based I/O, including the binary I/O functions and the random-access functions.

The character-based stream classes have been deprecated by Standard C++. This means that they are still valid, but future versions of the C++ language might not support them. They are included in this book because they are still widely used. However, for new code you will probably want to use one of the containers described in Chapter 14.

EXAMPLES

1. Here is a short example that shows how to open an array for output and write data to it:

```
// A short example using array-based output.
#include <iostream>
#include <strstream>
using namespace std;

int main()
```

```
{
  char buf[255]; // output buffer

  ostrstream ostr(buf, sizeof buf); // open output array

  ostr << "Array-based I/O uses streams just like ";
  ostr << "'normal' I/O\n" << 100;
  ostr << ' ' << 123.23 << '\n';

  // you can use manipulators, too
  ostr << hex << 100 << ' ';
  // or format flags
  ostr.setf(ios::scientific);
  ostr << dec << 123.23;
  ostr << endl << ends;

  // show resultant string
  cout << buf;

  return 0;
}
```

This program displays

```
Array-based I/O uses streams just like 'normal' I/O
100 123.23
64 01.2323e+02
```

As you can see, the overloaded I/O operators, built-in I/O manipulators, member functions, and format flags are fully functional when you use array-based I/O. (This is also true of any manipulators or overloaded I/O operators you create relative to your own classes.)

This program manually null-terminates the output array by using the **ends** manipulator. Whether the array will be automatically null terminated or not is implementation dependent, so it is best to perform this manually if null termination is important to your application.

2. Here is an example of array-based input:

```
// An example using array-based input.
#include <iostream>
#include <strstream>
using namespace std;
```

```
int main()
{
  char buf[] = "Hello 100 123.125 a";

  istrstream istr(buf); // open input array

  int i;
  char str[80];
  float f;
  char c;

  istr >> str >> i >> f >> c;

  cout << str << ' ' << i << ' ' << f;
  cout << ' ' << c << '\n';
  return 0;
}
```

This program reads and then redisplays the values contained in the input array **buf**.

3. Keep in mind that an input array, once linked to a stream, will appear the same as a file. For example, this program uses **get( )** and the **eof( )** function to read the contents of **buf**:

```
// Demonstrate get() and eof() with array-based I/O.
#include <iostream>
#include <strstream>
using namespace std;

int main()
{
  char buf[] = "Hello 100 123.125 a";

  istrstream istr(buf);
  char c;

  while(!istr.eof()) {
    istr.get(c);
    if(!istr.eof()) cout << c;
  }

  return 0;
}
```

4. This program performs input and output on an array:

```cpp
// Demonstrate an input/output array.
#include <iostream>
#include <strstream>
using namespace std;

int main()
{
  char iobuf[255];

  strstream iostr(iobuf, sizeof iobuf);

  iostr << "This is a test\n";
  iostr << 100 << hex << ' ' << 100 << ends;

  char str[80];
  int i;

  iostr.getline(str, 79); // read string up to \n
  iostr >> dec >> i; // read 100

  cout << str << ' ' << i << ' ';

  iostr >> hex >> i;
  cout <<  hex << i;

  return 0;
}
```

The program first writes output to **iobuf**. It then reads it back. It first reads the entire line "This is a test" using the **getline( )** function. It then reads the decimal value 100 and the hexadecimal value 0x64.

EXERCISES

1. Modify Example 1 so it displays the number of characters written to **buf** prior to termination.

2. Write an application that uses array-based I/O to copy the contents of one array to another. (This is, of course, not the most efficient way to accomplish this task.)

3. Using array-based I/O, write a program that converts a string that contains a floating-point value into its internal representation.

*S**KILLS CHECK***

**Mastery
Skills Check**

At this point you should be able to perform the following exercises and answer the questions.

1. What makes a **static** member variable different from other member variables?

2. What header must be included in your program when you use array-based I/O?

3. Aside from the fact that array-based I/O uses memory as an input and/or output device, is there any difference between it and "normal" I/O in C++?

4. Given a function called **counter( )**, show the statement that causes the compiler to compile this function for C language linkage.

5. What does a conversion function do?

6. Explain the purpose of **explicit**.

7. What is the principal restriction placed on a **const** member function?

8. Explain **namespace**.

9. What does **mutable** do?

**Cumulative
Skills Check**

This section checks how well you have integrated material in this chapter with that from the preceding chapters.

1. Since a constructor that requires only one argument provides an automatic conversion of the type of that argument to its class type, is there a situation in which this feature eliminates the need to create an overloaded assignment operator?

2. Can a **const_cast** be used within a **const** member function to allow it to modify its invoking object?

3. Thought question: Since the original C++ library was contained in the global namespace and all old C++ programs have already dealt with this fact, what is the advantage to moving the library into the **std** namespace "after the fact," so to speak?

4. Look back at the examples in the first twelve chapters. Think about what member functions can be made **const** or **static**. Are there examples in which defining a namespace would be appropriate?

14

Introducing the Standard Template Library

ONGRATULATIONS! If you have worked your way through the preceding chapters of this book, you can definitely call yourself a C++ programmer. In this, the final chapter of the book, we will explore one of C++'s most exciting—and most advanced—features: the Standard Template Library. The inclusion of the Standard Template Library, or STL, was one of the major efforts that took place during the standardization of C++. The STL was not part of the original specification for C++ but was added during the standardization proceedings. The STL provides general-purpose, templatized classes and functions that implement many popular and commonly used algorithms and data structures. For example, it includes support for vectors, lists, queues, and stacks. It also defines various routines that access them. Because the STL is constructed from template classes, the algorithms and data structures can be applied to nearly any type of data.

It must be stated at the outset that the STL is a complex piece of software engineering that uses some of C++'s most sophisticated features. To understand and use the STL you must be comfortable with all of the material in the preceding chapters. Specifically, you must feel at home with templates. The template syntax that describes the STL can seem quite intimidating—although it looks more complicated than it actually is. While there is nothing in this chapter that is any more difficult than the material in the rest of this book, don't be surprised or dismayed if you find the STL confusing at first. Just be patient, study the examples, and don't let the unfamiliar syntax distract you from the STL's basic simplicity.

The STL is a large library, and not all of its features can be described in this chapter. In fact, a full description of the STL and all of its features, nuances, and programming techniques would fill a large book. The overview presented here is intended to familiarize you with its basic operation, design philosophy, and programming fundamentals. After working through this chapter, you will be able to easily explore the remainder of the STL on your own.

This chapter also describes one of C++'s most important new classes: **string**. The **string** class defines a string data type that allows you to work with character strings much as you do with other data types, using operators.

Before proceeding, you should be able to correctly answer the following questions and do the exercises.

1. Explain why **namespace** was added to C++.

2. How do you specify a **const** member function?

3. The **mutable** modifier allows a library function to be changed by the user of your program. True or false?

4. Given this class,

```
class X {
  int a, b;
public:
  X(int i, int j) { a = i, b = j; }
  // create conversion to int here.
};
```

   create an integer conversion function that returns the sum of **a** and **b**.

5. A **static** member variable can be used before an object of its class exists. True or false?

6. Given this class,

```
class Demo {
  int a;
public:
  explicit Demo(int i) { a = i; }
  int geta() { return a; }
};
```

   is the following declaration legal?

```
Demo o = 10;
```

AN OVERVIEW OF THE STANDARD TEMPLATE LIBRARY

Although the Standard Template Library is large and its syntax is, at times, rather intimidating, it is actually quite easy to use once you understand how it is constructed and what elements it employs. Therefore, before looking at any code examples, an overview of the STL is warranted.

At the core of the Standard Template Library are three foundational items: containers, algorithms, and iterators. These items work in conjunction with one another to provide off-the-shelf solutions to a variety of programming problems.

Containers are objects that hold other objects. There are several different types of containers. For example, the **vector** class defines a dynamic array, **queue** creates a queue, and **list** provides a linear list. In addition to the basic containers, the STL also defines *associative containers,* which allow efficient retrieval of values based on keys. For example, the **map** class defines a map that provides access to values with unique keys. Thus, a map stores a key/value pair and allows a value to be retrieved when its key is given.

Each container class defines a set of functions that can be applied to the container. For example, a list container includes functions that insert, delete, and merge elements. A stack includes functions that push and pop values.

Algorithms act on containers. Some of the services algorithms perform are initializing, sorting, searching, and transforming the contents of containers. Many algorithms operate on a *sequence,* which is a linear list of elements within a container.

Iterators are objects that are, more or less, pointers. They give you the ability to cycle through the contents of a container in much the same way that you would use a pointer to cycle through an array. The five types of iterators are described in the following table.

Iterator	Access Allowed
Random access	Stores and retrieves values. Elements can be accessed randomly.
Bidirectional	Stores and retrieves values. Forward and backward moving.
Forward	Stores and retrieves values. Forward moving only.

Iterator	Access Allowed
Input	Retrieves but does not store values. Forward moving only.
Output	Stores but does not retrieve values. Forward moving only.

In general, an iterator that has greater access capabilities can be used in place of one that has lesser capabilities. For example, a forward iterator can be used in place of an input iterator.

Iterators are handled just like pointers. You can increment and decrement them. You can apply the * operator to them. Iterators are declared using the **iterator** type defined by the various containers.

The STL also supports *reverse iterators*. Reverse iterators are either bidirectional or random-access iterators that move through a sequence in reverse direction. Thus, if a reverse iterator points to the end of a sequence, incrementing that iterator will cause it to point to one element before the end.

When referring to the various iterator types in template descriptions, this book will use the terms listed in the following table:

Term	Iterator Type
BiIter	Bidirectional iterator
ForIter	Forward iterator
InIter	Input iterator
OutIter	Output iterator
RandIter	Random-access iterator

In addition to containers, algorithms, and iterators, the STL relies upon several other standard components for support. Chief among these are allocators, predicates, and comparison functions.

Each container has an *allocator* defined for it. Allocators manage memory allocation for containers. The default allocator is an object of class **allocator**, but you can define your own allocators if you need them for specialized applications. For most uses, the default allocator is sufficient.

Several of the algorithms and containers use a special type of function called a *predicate*. There are two variations of predicates: unary and binary. A unary predicate takes one argument, and a binary predicate has two arguments. These functions return true or false; the precise conditions that make them return true or false are defined by the programmer. In this chapter, when a unary predicate function is used, it will be notated with the type **UnPred**. When a binary predicate is used, it will be of type **BinPred**. In a binary predicate, the arguments are always in the order of *first,second*. For both unary and binary predicates, the arguments will contain values of the same type as the objects being stored by the container.

Some algorithms and classes use a special type of binary predicate that compares two elements. Called a *comparison function,* this type of predicate returns true if its first argument is less than its second. Comparison functions will be notated by the type **Comp**.

In addition to the headers required by the various STL classes, the C++ standard library includes the **< utility >** and **< functional >** headers, which provide support for the STL. For example, **< utility >** contains the definition of the template class **pair,** which can hold a pair of values. We will make use of **pair** later in this chapter.

The templates in **< functional >** help you construct objects that define **operator( )**. These are called *function objects,* and they can be used in place of function pointers in many places. There are several predefined function objects declared within **< functional >**. Some are shown in the following table.

plus	minus	multiplies	divides	modulus
negate	equal_to	not_equal_to	greater	greater_equal
less	less_equal	logical_and	logical_or	logical_not

Perhaps the most widely used function object is **less,** which determines whether the value of one object is less than the value of another. Function objects can be used in place of actual function pointers in the STL algorithms described later. Using function objects rather than function pointers allows the STL to generate more efficient code. However, for the purposes of this chapter, function objects are not needed and we won't be using them directly. Although function objects are not difficult, a detailed discussion of function objects is quite lengthy and is beyond the scope of this book. They are something that you will need, however, to get maximum efficiency from the STL.

EXERCISES

1. As they relate to the STL, what are containers, algorithms, and iterators?

2. What are the two types of predicates?

3. What are the five types of iterators?

14.2   *T*HE CONTAINER CLASSES

As explained, containers are the STL objects that actually store data. The containers defined by the STL are shown in Table 14-1. Also shown are the headers you must include to use each container. The **string** class, which manages character strings, is also a container, but it is discussed later in this chapter.

Container	Description	Required Header
bitset	A set of bits	<bitset>
deque	A double-ended queue	<deque>
list	A linear list	<list>
map	Stores key/value pairs in which each key is associated with only one value	<map>
multimap	Stores key/value pairs in which one key can be associated with two or more values	<map>
multiset	A set in which each element is not necessarily unique	<set>
priority_queue	A priority queue	<queue>
queue	A queue	<queue>
set	A set in which each element is unique	<set>
stack	A stack	<stack>
vector	A dynamic array	<vector>

TABLE 14-1   *The Containers Defined by the STL* ▼

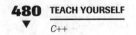
Because the names of the placeholder types in a template class declaration are arbitrary, the container classes declare **typedef**ed versions of these types. This makes the type names concrete. Some of the most common **typedef** names are shown in the following table.

typedef Name	Description
size_type	An integral type equivalent to **size_t**
reference	A reference to an element
const_reference	A **const** reference to an element
iterator	An iterator
const_iterator	A **const** iterator
reverse_iterator	A reverse iterator
const_reverse_iterator	A **const** reverse iterator
value_type	The type of a value stored in a container
allocator_type	The type of the allocator
key_type	The type of a key
key_compare	The type of a function that compares two keys
value_compare	The type of a function that compares two values

Although it is not possible to examine each container in this chapter, the next sections explore three representatives: **vector**, **list**, and **map**. Once you understand how these containers work, you will have no trouble using the others.

<table>
<tr><td>14.3</td><td></td></tr>
</table>

VECTORS

Perhaps the most general-purpose of the containers is the vector. The **vector** class supports a dynamic array. This is an array that can grow as needed. As you know, in C++ the size of an array is fixed at compile time. Although this is by far the most efficient way to implement arrays, it is also the most restrictive, because the size of the array cannot be adjusted at run time to accommodate changing program conditions. A vector solves this problem by allocating memory as needed. Although a vector is dynamic, you can still use the standard array subscript notation to access its elements.

The template specification for **vector** is shown here:

template <class T, class Allocator = allocator<T>> class vector

Here **T** is the type of data being stored and **Allocator** specifies the allocator, which defaults to the standard allocator. **vector** has the following constructors:

explicit vector(const Allocator &*a* = Allocator( ));

explicit vector(size_type *num*, const T &*val* = T (),
          const Allocator &*a* = Allocator( ));

vector(const vector<T, Allocator> &*ob*);

template <class InIter> vector(InIter *start*, InIter *end*,
          const Allocator &*a* = Allocator( ));

The first form constructs an empty vector. The second form constructs a vector that has *num* elements with the value *val*. The value of *val* can be allowed to default. The third form constructs a vector that contains the same elements as *ob*. The fourth form constructs a vector that contains the elements in the range specified by the iterators *start* and *end*.

Any object that will be stored in a vector must define a default constructor. It must also define the < and == operations. Some compilers might require that other comparison operators be defined. (Because implementations vary, consult your compiler's documentation for precise information.) All of the built-in types automatically satisfy these requirements.

Although the template syntax looks rather complex, there is nothing difficult about declaring a vector. Here are some examples:

```
vector<int> iv; // creates a zero-length int vector
vector<char> cv(5); // creates a 5-element char vector
vector<char> cv(5,  'x'); // initializes a 5-element char vector
vector<int> iv2(iv); // creates an int vector from an int vector
```

The following comparison operators are defined for **vector**:

==, <, <=, !=, >, >=

The subscripting operator **[ ]** is also defined for **vector**. This allows you to access the elements of a vector using standard array subscripting notation.

The member functions defined by **vector** are shown in Table 14-2. (Again, it is important not to be put off by the syntax.) Some of the most important member functions are **size( )**, **begin( )**, **end( )**, **push_back( )**, **insert( )**, and **erase( )**. The **size( )** function returns the current size of the vector. This function is quite useful because it allows you to determine the size of a vector at run time. Remember, vectors will increase in size as needed, so the size of a vector must be determined during execution, not during compilation.

The **begin( )** function returns an iterator to the start of the vector. The **end( )** function returns an iterator to the end of the vector. As explained, iterators are similar to pointers, and it is through the use of the **begin( )** and **end( )** functions that you obtain an iterator to the beginning and end of a vector.

Member Function	Description
template <class InIter> void assign(InIter _start_, InIter _end_);	Assigns the vector the sequence defined by _start_ and _end_.

template <class Size, class T>
    void assign(Size _num_,
                const T &_val_ = T());
	Assigns the vector _num_ elements of value _val_.

reference at(size_type _i_); const_reference at(size_type _i_) const;	Returns a reference to an element specified by _i_.
reference back(); const_reference back() const;	Returns a reference to the last element in the vector.
iterator begin(); const_iterator begin() const;	Returns an iterator to the first element in the vector.
size_type capacity() const;	Returns the current capacity of the vector. This is the number of elements it can hold before it will need to allocate more memory.
void clear();	Removes all elements from the vector.
bool empty() const;	Returns true if the invoking vector is empty and false otherwise.
iterator end(); const_iterator end() const;	Returns an iterator to the end of the vector.

TABLE 14-2   _The **vector** Member Functions_ ▼

Member Function	Description
iterator erase(iterator *i*);	Removes the element pointed to by *i*. Returns an iterator to the element after the one removed.
iterator erase(iterator *start*, iterator *end*);	Removes the elements in the range *start* to *end*. Returns an iterator to the element after the last element removed.
reference front(); const_reference front() const;	Returns a reference to the first element in the vector.
allocator_type get_allocator() const;	Returns the vector's allocator.
iterator insert(iterator *i*, const T &*val* = T());	Inserts *val* immediately before the element specified by *i*. An iterator to the element is returned.
void insert(iterator *i*, size_type *num*, const T &*val*)	Inserts *num* copies of *val* immediately before the element specified by *i*.

template <class InIter>
    void insert(iterator *i*, InIter *start*,
        InIter *end*);
	Inserts the sequence defined by *start* and *end* immediately before the element specified by *i*.

size_type max_size() const;	Returns the maximum number of elements that the vector can hold.
reference operator[ ](size_type *i*) const; const_reference operator[ ](size_type *i*) const;	Returns a reference to the element specified by *i*.
void pop_back();	Removes the last element in the vector.
void push_back(const T &*val*);	Adds an element with the value specified by *val* to the end of the vector.
reverse_iterator rbegin(); const_reverse_iterator rbegin() const;	Returns a reverse iterator to the end of the vector.
reverse_iterator rend(); const_reverse_iterator rend() const;	Returns a reverse iterator to the start of the vector.
void reserve(size_type *num*);	Sets the capacity of the vector so that it is equal to at least *num*.
void resize(size_type *num*, T *val* = T ());	Changes the size of the vector to that specified by *num*. If the vector must be lengthened, elements with the value specified by *val* are added to the end.
size_type size() const;	Returns the number of elements currently in the vector.
void swap(vector<T, Allocator> &*ob*)	Exchanges the elements stored in the invoking vector with those in *ob*.

TABLE 14-2 *The **vector** Member Functions* (continued) ▼

The **push_back( )** function puts a value onto the end of the vector. If necessary, the vector is increased in length to accommodate the new element. You can also add elements to the middle using **insert( )**. A vector can also be initialized. In any event, once a vector contains elements, you can use array subscripting to access or modify those elements. You can remove elements from a vector using **erase( )**.

EXAMPLES

1. Here is a short example that illustrates the basic operation of a vector.

```
// Vector basics.
#include <iostream>
#include <vector>
using namespace std;

int main()
{
  vector<int> v; // create zero-length vector
  int i;

  // display original size of v
  cout << "Size = " << v.size() << endl;

  /* put values onto end of vector --
     vector will grow as needed */
  for(i=0; i<10; i++) v.push_back(i);

  // display current size of v
  cout << "Size now = " << v.size() << endl;

  // display contents of vector
  cout << "Current contents:\n";
  for(i=0; i<v.size(); i++) cout << v[i] << " ";
  cout << endl;

  /* put more values onto end of vector --
     again, vector will grow as needed */
  for(i=0; i<10; i++) v.push_back(i+10);

  // display current size of v
  cout << "Size now = " << v.size() << endl;
```

```
  // display contents of vector
  cout << "Current contents:\n";
  for(i=0; i<v.size(); i++) cout << v[i] << " ";
  cout << endl;

  // change contents of vector
  for(i=0; i<v.size(); i++) v[i] = v[i] + v[i];

  // display contents of vector
  cout << "Contents doubled:\n";
  for(i=0; i<v.size(); i++) cout << v[i] << " ";
  cout << endl;

  return 0;
}
```

The output of this program is shown here:

```
Size = 0
Size now = 10
Current contents:
0 1 2 3 4 5 6 7 8 9
Size now = 20
Current contents:
0 1 2 3 4 5 6 7 8 9 10 11 12 13 14 15 16 17 18 19
Contents doubled:
0 2 4 6 8 10 12 14 16 18 20 22 24 26 28 30 32 34 36 38
```

Let's look at this program carefully. In **main( )**, an integer vector called **v** is created. Since no initialization is used, it is an empty vector with an initial capacity of zero. That is, it is a zero-length vector. The program confirms this by calling the **size( )** member function. Next, ten elements are added to the end of **v** with the member function **push_back( )**. This causes **v** to grow in order to accommodate the new elements. As the output shows, its size after these additions is 10. Next, the contents of **v** are displayed. Notice that the standard array subscripting notation is employed. Next, ten more elements are added and **v** is automatically increased in size to handle them. Finally, the values of **v**'s elements are altered using standard subscripting notation.

There is one other point of interest in this program. Notice that the loops that display the contents of **v** use as their target **v.size( )**. One of the advantages that vectors have over arrays is that it is possible to find the current size of a vector. As you can imagine, this is quite useful in a variety of situations.

2. As you know, arrays and pointers are tightly linked in C++. An array can be accessed either through subscripting or through a pointer. The parallel to this in the STL is the link between vectors and iterators. You can access the members of a vector by using subscripting or by using an iterator. The following example shows both of these approaches.

```cpp
// Access a vector using an iterator.
#include <iostream>
#include <vector>
using namespace std;

int main()
{
  vector<int> v; // create zero-length vector
  int i;

  // put values into a vector
  for(i=0; i<10; i++) v.push_back(i);

  // can access vector contents using subscripting
  for(i=0; i<10; i++) cout << v[i] << " ";
  cout << endl;

  // access via iterator
  vector<int>::iterator p = v.begin();
  while(p != v.end()) {
    cout << *p << " ";
    p++;
  }

  return 0;
}
```

The output from this program is:

```
0 1 2 3 4 5 6 7 8 9
0 1 2 3 4 5 6 7 8 9
```

In this program, the vector is initially created with zero length. The **push_back( )** member function puts values onto the end of the vector, expanding its size as needed.

Notice how the iterator **p** is declared. The type **iterator** is defined by the container classes. Thus, to obtain an iterator for a particular container, you will use a declaration similar to that shown in the example: simply qualify **iterator** with the name of the container. In the program, **p** is initialized to point to the start of the vector by using the **begin( )** member function. This function returns an iterator to the start of the vector. This iterator can then be used to access the vector an element at a time by incrementing it as needed. This process is directly parallel to the way a pointer can be used to access the elements of an array. To determine when the end of the vector has been reached, the **end( )** member function is employed. This function returns an iterator to the location that is one past the last element in the vector. Thus, when **p** equals **v.end( )**, the end of the vector has been reached.

3. In addition to putting new values on the end of a vector, you can insert elements into the middle using the **insert( )** function. You can also remove elements using **erase( )**. The following program demonstrates **insert( )** and **erase( )**.

```
// Demonstrate insert and erase.
#include <iostream>
#include <vector>
using namespace std;

int main()
{
  vector<int> v(5, 1); // create 5-element vector of 1s
  int i;

  // display original contents of vector
  cout << "Size = " << v.size() << endl;
  cout << "Original contents:\n";
  for(i=0; i<v.size(); i++) cout << v[i] << " ";
  cout << endl << endl;

  vector<int>::iterator p = v.begin();
  p += 2; // point to 3rd element

  // insert 10 elements with value 9
  v.insert(p, 10, 9);

  // display contents after insertion
```

```
cout << "Size after insert = " << v.size() << endl;
cout << "Contents after insert:\n";
for(i=0; i<v.size(); i++) cout << v[i] << " ";
cout << endl << endl;

// remove those elements
p = v.begin();
p += 2; // point to 3rd element
v.erase(p, p+10); // remove next 10 elements

// display contents after deletion
cout << "Size after erase = " << v.size() << endl;
cout << "Contents after erase:\n";
for(i=0; i<v.size(); i++) cout << v[i] << " ";
cout << endl;

return 0;
}
```

This program produces the following output.

```
Size = 5
Original contents:
1 1 1 1 1

Size after insert = 15
Contents after insert:
1 1 9 9 9 9 9 9 9 9 9 9 1 1 1

Size after erase = 5
Contents after erase:
1 1 1 1 1
```

4. Here is an example that uses a vector to store objects of a programmer-defined class. Notice that the class defines the default constructor and that overloaded versions of < and == are provided. Remember, depending upon how your compiler implements the STL, other comparison operators might need to be defined.

```
// Store a class object in a vector.
#include <iostream>
#include <vector>
using namespace std;
```

```
class Demo {
  double d;
public:
  Demo() { d = 0.0; }
  Demo(double x) { d = x; }

  Demo &operator=(double x) {
    d = x; return *this;
  }

  double getd() { return d; }
};

bool operator<(Demo a, Demo b)
{
  return a.getd() < b.getd();
}

bool operator==(Demo a, Demo b)
{
  return a.getd() == b.getd();
}

int main()
{
  vector<Demo> v;
  int i;

  for(i=0; i<10; i++)
    v.push_back(Demo(i/3.0));

  for(i=0; i<v.size(); i++)
    cout << v[i].getd() << " ";

  cout << endl;

  for(i=0; i<v.size(); i++)
    v[i] = v[i].getd() * 2.1;

  for(i=0; i<v.size(); i++)
    cout << v[i].getd() << " ";

  return 0;
}
```

The output from this program is shown here.

```
0 0.333333 0.666667 1 1.33333 1.66667 2 2.33333 2.66667 3
0 0.7 1.4 2.1 2.8 3.5 4.2 4.9 5.6 6.3
```

EXERCISES

1. Try the examples just shown, making small modifications and observing their effects.

2. In Example 4, both a default (i.e., parameterless) and a parameterized constructor were defined for **Demo**. Can you explain why this is important?

3. Here is a simple **Coord** class. Write a program that stores objects of type **Coord** in a vector. (Hint: Remember to define the **<** and **==** operators relative to **Coord**.)

```
class Coord {
public:
  int x, y;
  Coord() { x = y = 0; }
  Coord(int a, int b) { x = a; y = b; }
};
```

14.4 LISTS

The **list** class supports a bidirectional, linear list. Unlike a vector, which supports random access, a list can be accessed sequentially only. Because lists are bidirectional, they can be accessed front to back or back to front.

The **list** class has this template specification:

template <class T, class Allocator = allocator<T>> class list

Here **T** is the type of data stored in the list. The allocator is specified by **Allocator**, which defaults to the standard allocator. This class has the following constructors:

```
explicit list(const Allocator &a = Allocator( ) );

explicit list(size_type num, const T &val = T ( ),
              const Allocator &a = Allocator( ));

list(const list<T, Allocator> &ob);

template <class InIter> list(InIter start, InIter end,
              const Allocator &a = Allocator( ));
```

The first form constructs an empty list. The second form constructs a list that has *num* elements with the value *val*, which can be allowed to default. The third form constructs a list that contains the same elements as *ob*. The fourth form constructs a list that contains the elements in the range specified by the iterators *start* and *end*.

The following comparison operators are defined for **list**:

```
==, <, <=, !=, >, >=
```

The member functions defined for **list** are shown in Table 14-3. Like a vector, a list can have elements put into it with the **push_back( )** function. You can put elements on the front of the list by using **push_front( )**, and you can insert an element into the middle of a list by using **insert( )**. You can use **splice( )** to join two lists, and you can merge one list into another by using **merge( )**.

Any data type that will be held in a list must define a default constructor. It must also define the various comparison operators. At the time of this writing, the precise requirements for an object that will be stored in a list vary from compiler to compiler and are subject to change, so you will need to check your compiler's documentation.

Member Function	Description
template <class InIter> void assign(InIter *start*, InIter *end*);	Assigns the list the sequence defined by *start* and *end*.

template <class Size, class T>
    void assign(Size *num*,
        const T &*val* = T());
	Assigns the list *num* elements of value *val*.

reference back(); const_reference back() const;	Returns a reference to the last element in the list.
iterator begin(); const_iterator begin() const;	Returns an iterator to the first element in the list.
void clear();	Removes all elements from the list.
bool empty() const;	Returns true if the invoking list is empty and false otherwise.
iterator end(); const_iterator end() const;	Returns an iterator to the end of the list.
iterator erase(iterator *i*);	Removes the element pointed to by *i*. Returns an iterator to the element after the one removed.
iterator erase(iterator *start*, iterator *end*);	Removes the elements in the range *start* to *end*. Returns an iterator to the element after the last element removed.
reference front(); const_reference front() const;	Returns a reference to the first element in the list.
allocator_type get_allocator() const;	Returns the list's allocator.
iterator insert(iterator *i*, const T &*val* = T());	Inserts *val* immediately before the element specified by *i*. An iterator to the element is returned.
void insert(iterator *i*, size_type *num*, const T &*val*)	Inserts *num* copies of *val* immediately before the element specified by *i*.

template <class InIter>
    void insert(iterator *i*
        InIter *start*, InIter *end*);
	Inserts the sequence defined by *start* and *end* immediately before the element specified by *i*.

size_type max_size() const;	Returns the maximum number of elements that the list can hold.

TABLE 14-3   *The **list** Member Functions* ▼

Member Function	Description

void merge(list<T, Allocator> &*ob*);
template <class Comp>
   void merge(<list<T, Allocator> &*ob*,
        Comp *cmpfn*);
	Merges the ordered list contained in *ob* with the invoking ordered list. The result is ordered. After the merge, the list contained in *ob* is empty. In the second form, a comparison function can be specified to determine whether the value of one element is less than that of another.

void pop_back();	Removes the last element in the list.
void pop_front();	Removes the first element in the list.
void push_back(const T &*val*);	Adds an element with the value specified by *val* to the end of the list.
void push_front(const T &*val*);	Adds an element with the value specified by *val* to the front of the list.
reverse_iterator rbegin(); const_reverse_iterator rbegin() const;	Returns a reverse iterator to the end of the list.
void remove(const T &*val*);	Removes elements with the value *val* from the list.
template <class UnPred> void remove_if(UnPred *pr*);	Removes elements for which the unary predicate *pr* is true.
reverse_iterator rend(); const_reverse_iterator rend() const;	Returns a reverse iterator to the start of the list.
void resize(size_type *num*, T *val* = T ());	Changes the size of the list to that specified by *num*. If the list must be lengthened, elements with the value specified by *val* are added to the end.
void reverse();	Reverses the invoking list.
size_type size() const;	Returns the number of elements currently in the list.

void sort();
template <class Comp>
   void sort(Comp *cmpfn*);
	Sorts the list. The second form sorts the list using the comparison function *cmpfn* to determine whether the value of one element is less than that of another.

void splice(iterator *i*, list<T, Allocator> &*ob*);	Inserts the contents of *ob* into the invoking list at the location pointed to by *i*. After the operation, *ob* is empty.

TABLE 14-3 *The **list** Member Functions* (continued*)* ▼

Member Function	Description
void splice(iterator *i*, 　　　 list<T, Allocator> &*ob*, 　　　 iterator *el*);	Removes the element pointed to by *el* from the list *ob* and stores it in the invoking list at the location pointed to by *i*.
void splice(iterator *i*, 　　　 list<T, Allocator> &*ob*, 　　　 iterator *start*, iterator *end*);	Removes the range defined by *start* and *end* from *ob* and stores it in the invoking list beginning at the location pointed to by *i*.
void swap(list<T, Allocator> &*ob*)	Exchanges the elements stored in the invoking list with those in *ob*.

void unique();
template <class BinPred>
　 void unique(BinPred *pr*);
	Removes duplicate elements from the invoking list. The second form uses *pr* to determine uniqueness.

TABLE 14-3　*The **list** Member Functions (continued)* ▼

EXAMPLES

1. Here is a simple example of a list.

```cpp
// List basics.
#include <iostream>
#include <list>
using namespace std;

int main()
{
  list<char> lst; // create an empty list
  int i;

  for(i=0; i<10; i++) lst.push_back('A'+i);

  cout << "Size = " << lst.size() << endl;

  list<char>::iterator p;

  cout << "Contents: ";
  while(!lst.empty()) {
    p = lst.begin();
    cout << *p;
    lst.pop_front();
  }
```

```
   return 0;
}
```

The output produced by this program is shown here.

```
Size = 10
Contents: ABCDEFGHIJ
```

This program creates a list of characters. First, an empty **list** object is created. Next, ten characters, the letters A through J, are put into the list. This is accomplished with the **push_back( )** function, which puts each new value on the end of the existing list. Next, the size of the list is displayed. Then, the contents of the list are output by repeatedly obtaining, displaying, and then removing the first element in the list. This process stops when the list is empty.

2. In the previous example, the list was emptied as it was traversed. This is, of course, not necessary. For example, the loop that displays the list could be recoded as shown here.

```
list<char>::iterator p = lst.begin();

while(p != lst.end()) {
  cout << *p;
  p++;
}
```

Here the iterator **p** is initialized to point to the start of the list. Each time through the loop, **p** is incremented, causing it to point to the next element. The loop ends when **p** points to the end of the list.

3. Because lists are bidirectional, elements can be put on a list either at the front or at the back. For example, the following program creates two lists, with the first being the reverse of the second.

```
// Elements can be put on the front or end of a list.
#include <iostream>
#include <list>
using namespace std;

int main()
{
  list<char> lst;
```

```
       list<char> revlst;
       int i;

       for(i=0; i<10; i++) lst.push_back('A'+i);

       cout << "Size of lst = " << lst.size() << endl;
       cout << "Original contents: ";

       list<char>::iterator p;

       /* Remove elements from lst and put them
          into revlst in reverse order. */
       while(!lst.empty()) {
         p = lst.begin();
         cout << *p;
         lst.pop_front();
         revlst.push_front(*p);
       }
       cout << endl << endl;

       cout << "Size of revlst = ";
       cout << revlst.size() << endl;
       cout << "Reversed contents: ";
       p = revlst.begin();
       while(p != revlst.end()) {
         cout << *p;
         p++;
       }

       return 0;
     }
```

This program produces the following output.

```
Size of lst = 10
Original contents: ABCDEFGHIJ

Size of revlst = 10
Reversed contents: JIHGFEDCBA
```

In the program, the list is reversed by removing elements from the start of **lst** and pushing them onto the front of **revlst**. This causes the elements to be stored in reverse order in **revlst**.

4. You can sort a list by calling the **sort( )** member function. The following program creates a list of random characters and then puts the list into sorted order.

```cpp
// Sort a list.
#include <iostream>
#include <list>
#include <cstdlib>
using namespace std;

int main()
{
  list<char> lst;
  int i;

  // create a list of random characters
  for(i=0; i<10; i++)
    lst.push_back('A'+ (rand()%26));

  cout << "Original contents: ";
  list<char>::iterator p = lst.begin();
  while(p != lst.end()) {
    cout << *p;
    p++;
  }
  cout << endl << endl;

  // sort the list
  lst.sort();

  cout << "Sorted contents: ";
  p = lst.begin();
  while(p != lst.end()) {
    cout << *p;
    p++;
  }

  return 0;
}
```

Here is sample output produced by the program.

```
Original contents: PHQGHUMEAY
Sorted contents: AEGHHMPQUY
```

5. One ordered list can be merged with another. The result is an ordered list that contains the contents of the two original lists. The new list is left in the invoking list and the second list is left empty. This example merges two lists. The first contains the letters ACEGI and the second BDFHJ. These lists are then merged to produce the sequence ABCDEFGHIJ.

```cpp
// Merge two lists.
#include <iostream>
#include <list>
using namespace std;

int main()
{
  list<char> lst1, lst2;
  int i;

  for(i=0; i<10; i+=2) lst1.push_back('A'+i);
  for(i=1; i<11; i+=2) lst2.push_back('A'+i);

  cout << "Contents of lst1: ";
  list<char>::iterator p = lst1.begin();
  while(p != lst1.end()) {
    cout << *p;
    p++;
  }
  cout << endl << endl;

  cout << "Contents of lst2: ";
  p = lst2.begin();
  while(p != lst2.end()) {
    cout << *p;
    p++;
  }
  cout << endl << endl;

  // now, merge the two lists
  lst1.merge(lst2);
  if(lst2.empty())
    cout << "lst2 is now empty\n";

  cout << "Contents of lst1 after merge:\n";
  p = lst1.begin();
  while(p != lst1.end()) {
    cout << *p;
```

```
    p++;
  }

  return 0;
}
```

The output produced by this program is shown here.

```
Contents of lst1: ACEGI

Contents of lst2: BDFHJ

lst2 is now empty
Contents of lst1 after merge:
ABCDEFGHIJ
```

6. Here is an example that uses a list to store objects of type
   Project, which is a class that helps manage software projects.
   Notice that the < , > , != , and = = operators are overloaded for
   objects of type **Project**. These are the operators that were
   required by Microsoft's Visual C++ 5 (the compiler used to test
   the STL examples in this chapter). Other compilers might
   require you to overload additional operators. The STL uses
   these functions to determine the ordering and equality of
   objects in a container. Even though a list is not an ordered
   container, it still needs a way to compare elements when
   searching, sorting, or merging.

```cpp
#include <iostream>
#include <list>
#include <cstring>
using namespace std;

class Project {
public:
  char name[40];
  int days_to_completion;
  Project() {
    strcpy(name, "");
    days_to_completion = 0;
  }
  Project(char *n, int d) {
    strcpy(name, n);
    days_to_completion = d;
  }
```

```
  void add_days(int i) {
    days_to_completion += i;
  }

  void sub_days(int i) {
    days_to_completion -= i;
  }

  bool completed() { return !days_to_completion; }

  void report() {
    cout << name << ": ";
    cout << days_to_completion;
    cout << " days left.\n";
  }
};

bool operator<(const Project &a, const Project &b)
{
  return a.days_to_completion < b.days_to_completion;
}

bool operator>(const Project &a, const Project &b)
{
  return a.days_to_completion > b.days_to_completion;
}

bool operator==(const Project &a, const Project &b)
{
  return a.days_to_completion == b.days_to_completion;
}

bool operator!=(const Project &a, const Project &b)
{
  return a.days_to_completion != b.days_to_completion;
}

int main()
{
  list<Project> proj;

  proj.push_back(Project("Compiler", 35));
  proj.push_back(Project("Spreadsheet", 190));
  proj.push_back(Project("STL Implementation", 1000));
```

```
list<Project>::iterator p = proj.begin();

/* display projects */
while(p != proj.end()) {
  p->report();
  p++;
}

// add 10 days to 1st project
p = proj.begin();
p->add_days(10);

// move 1st project to completion
do {
  p->sub_days(5);
  p->report();
} while (!p->completed());

  return 0;
}
```

The output from this program is shown here.

```
Compiler: 35 days left.
Spreadsheet: 190 days left.
STL Implementation: 1000 days left.
Compiler: 40 days left.
Compiler: 35 days left.
Compiler: 30 days left.
Compiler: 25 days left.
Compiler: 20 days left.
Compiler: 15 days left.
Compiler: 10 days left.
Compiler: 5 days left.
Compiler: 0 days left.
```

EXERCISES

1. Experiment with the examples, trying minor variations.
2. In Example 1, the list was emptied in the process of displaying it. In Example 2, you saw another way to traverse a list that does

not destroy it. Can you think of another way to traverse a list without emptying it? Show that your solution works by substituting it into the program in Example 1.

3. Expand Example 6 by creating another list of projects that consists of the following:

Project	Days to Completion
Database	780
Mail merge	50
COM objects	300

Next, sort both lists and then merge them together. Display the final result.

<h2>14.5 MAPS</h2>

The **map** class supports an associative container in which unique keys are mapped with values. In essence, a key is simply a name that you give to a value. Once a value has been stored, you can retrieve it by using its key. Thus, in its most general sense a map is a list of key/value pairs. The power of a map is that you can look up a value given its key. For example, you could define a map that uses a person's name as its key and stores that person's telephone number as its value. Associative containers are becoming more popular in programming.

As mentioned, a map can hold only unique keys. Duplicate keys are not allowed. To create a map that allows nonunique keys, use **multimap**.

The **map** container has the following template specification:

```
template <class Key, class T, class Comp = less<Key>,
          class Allocator = allocator<T>> class map
```

Here **Key** is the data type of the keys, **T** is the data type of the values being stored (mapped), and **Comp** is a function that compares two keys. This defaults to the standard **less( )** utility function object. **Allocator** is the allocator (which defaults to **allocator**).

The **map** class has the following constructors:

```
explicit map(const Comp &cmpfn = Comp(),
        const Allocator &a = Allocator() );

map(const map<Key, T, Comp, Allocator> &ob);

template <class InIter> map(InIter start, InIter end,
        const Comp &cmpfn = Comp(), const Allocator &a = Allocator());
```

The first form constructs an empty map. The second form constructs a map that contains the same elements as *ob*. The third form constructs a map that contains the elements in the range specified by the iterators *start* and *end*. The function specified by *cmpfn*, if present, determines the ordering of the map.

In general, any object used as a key must define a default constructor and overload any necessary comparison operators.

The following comparison operators are defined for **map**.

```
==, <, <=, !=, >, >=
```

The member functions defined by **map** are shown in Table 14-4. In the descriptions, **key_type** is the type of the key and **value_type** represents **pair< Key, T >**.

Member Function	Description
iterator begin(); const_iterator begin() const;	Returns an iterator to the first element in the map.
void clear();	Removes all elements from the map.
size_type count(const key_type &k) const;	Returns the number of times *k* occurs in the map (1 or 0).
bool empty() const;	Returns true if the invoking map is empty and false otherwise.
iterator end(); const_iterator end() const;	Returns an iterator to the end of the map.

TABLE 14-4 *The **map** Member Functions* ▼

Member Function	Description

pair<iterator, iterator>
    equal_range(const key_type &*k*);
pair<const_iterator, const_iterator>
    equal_range(const key_type &*k*) const;
	Returns a pair of iterators that point to the first and last elements in the map that contain the specified key.

void erase(iterator *i*);	Removes the element pointed to by *i*.
void erase(iterator *start*, iterator *end*);	Removes the elements in the range *start* to *end*.
size_type erase(const key_type &*k*)	Removes elements that have keys with the value *k*.
iterator find(const key_type &*k*); const_iterator find(const key_type &*k*) const;	Returns an iterator to the specified key. If the key is not found, an iterator to the end of the map is returned.
allocator_type get_allocator( ) const;	Returns the map's allocator.
iterator insert(iterator *i*, const value_type &*val*);	Inserts *val* at or after the element specified by *i*. An iterator to the element is returned.
template <class InIter> void insert(InIter *start*, InIter *end*)	Inserts a range of elements.
pair<iterator, bool> insert(const value_type &*val*);	Inserts *val* into the invoking map. An iterator to the element is returned. The element is inserted only if it does not already exist. If the element was inserted, **pair<iterator, true>** is returned. Otherwise, **pair<iterator, false>** is returned.
key_compare key_comp( ) const;	Returns the function object that compares keys.

iterator lower_bound(const key_type &*k*);
const_iterator
    lower_bound(const key_type &*k*) const;
	Returns an iterator to the first element in the map with the key equal to or greater than *k*.

size_type max_size( ) const;	Returns the maximum number of elements that the map can hold.
reference operator[ ](const key_type &*i*)	Returns a reference to the element specified by *i*. If this element does not exist, it is inserted.
reverse_iterator rbegin( ); const_reverse_iterator rbegin( ) const;	Returns a reverse iterator to the end of the map.
reverse_iterator rend( ); const_reverse_iterator rend( ) const;	Returns a reverse iterator to the start of the map.

TABLE 14-4 *The **map** Member Functions (continued)* ▼

Member Function	Description
size_type size( ) const;	Returns the number of elements currently in the map.
void swap(map<Key, T, Comp, Allocator> &*ob*)	Exchanges the elements stored in the invoking map with those in *ob*.
iterator upper_bound(const key_type &*k*); const_iterator upper_bound(const key_type &*k*) const;	Returns an iterator to the first element in the map with the key greater than *k*.
value_compare value_comp( ) const;	Returns the function object that compares values.

TABLE 14-4   *The **map** Member Functions* (continued) ▼

Key/value pairs are stored in a map as objects of type **pair**, which has this template specification:

```
template <class Ktype, class Vtype> struct pair {
  typedef Ktype first_type; // type of key
  typedef Vtype second_type; // type of value
  Ktype first; // contains the key
  Vtype second; // contains the value

  // constructors
  pair();
  pair(const Ktype &k, const Vtype &v);
  template<class A, class B> pair(const<A, B> &ob);
}
```

As the comments suggest, the value in **first** contains the key and the value in **second** contains the value associated with that key.

You can construct a pair using either one of **pair**'s constructors or by using **make_pair( )**, which constructs a **pair** object based upon the types of the data used as parameters. **make_pair( )** is a generic function that has this prototype:

template <class *Ktype*, class *Vtype*>
    pair<*Ktype*, *Vtype*> make_pair(const *Ktype* &*k*, const *Vtype* &*v*);

As you can see, it returns a **pair** object consisting of values of the types specified by *Ktype* and *Vtype*. The advantage of **make_pair( )** is that it allows the types of the objects being stored to be determined automatically by the compiler rather than being explicitly specified by you.

EXAMPLES

1. The following program illustrates the basics of using a map. It stores ten key/value pairs. The key is a character and the value is an integer. The key/value pairs stored are

A	0
B	1
C	2

   and so on. Once the pairs have been stored, the user is prompted for a key (i.e., a letter from A through J), and the value associated with that key is displayed.

```cpp
// A simple map demonstration.
#include <iostream>
#include <map>
using namespace std;

int main()
{
  map<char, int> m;
  int i;

  // put pairs into map
  for(i=0; i<10; i++) {
    m.insert(pair<char, int>('A'+i, i));
  }

  char ch;
  cout << "Enter key: ";
  cin >> ch;

  map<char, int>::iterator p;

  // find value given key
```

```
p = m.find(ch);
if(p != m.end())
  cout << p->second;
else
  cout << "Key not in map.\n";

return 0;
}
```

Notice the use of the **pair** template class to construct the key/value pairs. The data types specified by **pair** must match those of the map into which the pairs are being inserted.

Once the map has been initialized with keys and values, you can search for a value given its key by using the **find( )** function. **find( )** returns an iterator to the matching element or to the end of the map if the key is not found. When a match is found, the value associated with the key is contained in the **second** member of **pair**.

2. In the preceding example, key/value pairs were constructed explicitly, using **pair < char, int >**. Although there is nothing wrong with this approach, it is often easier to use **make_pair( )**, which constructs a **pair** object based upon the types of the data used as parameters. For example, assuming the previous program, this line of code will also insert key/value pairs into **m**:

```
m.insert(make_pair((char)('A'+i), i));
```

Here the cast to **char** is needed to override the automatic conversion to **int** when **i** is added to 'A'. Otherwise, the type determination is automatic.

3. Like all of the containers, maps can be used to store objects of types that you create. For example, the program shown here creates a map of words with their opposites. To do this it creates two classes called **word** and **opposite**. Since a map maintains a sorted list of keys, the program also defines the < operator for objects of type **word**. In general, you must define the < operator for any classes that you will use as keys. (Some compilers might require that additional comparison operators be defined.)

```
// A map of opposites.
#include <iostream>
```

```
#include <map>
#include <cstring>
using namespace std;

class word {
  char str[20];
public:
  word() { strcpy(str, ""); }
  word(char *s) { strcpy(str, s); }
  char *get() { return str; }

};

// must define less than relative to word objects
bool operator<(word a, word b)
{
    return strcmp(a.get(), b.get()) < 0;
}

class opposite {
  char str[20];
public:
  opposite() { strcmp(str, ""); }
  opposite(char *s) { strcpy(str, s); }
  char *get() { return str; }
};


int main()
{
  map<word, opposite> m;

  // put words and opposites into map
  m.insert(pair<word,
    opposite>(word("yes"), opposite("no")));
  m.insert(pair<word,
    opposite>(word("good"), opposite("bad")));
  m.insert(pair<word,
    opposite>(word("left"), opposite("right")));
  m.insert(pair<word,
    opposite>(word("up"), opposite("down")));

  // given a word, find opposite
  char str[80];
  cout << "Enter word: ";
```

```
cin >> str;

map<word, opposite>::iterator p;

p = m.find(word(str));
if(p != m.end())
   cout << "Opposite: " <<  p->second.get();
else
   cout << "Word not in map.\n";

return 0;
}
```

In this example, each entry in the map is a character array that holds a null-terminated string. Later in this chapter, you will see an easier way to write this program that uses the standard **string** type.

EXERCISES

---

1. Experiment with the examples, trying small variations.

2. Create a map that contains names and telephone numbers. Allow names and numbers to be entered, and set up your program so that a number can be found when a name is given. (Hint: Use Example 3 as a model.)

3. Do you need to define the < operator for objects used as keys in a map?

14.6 ***A****LGORITHMS*

As explained, algorithms act on containers. Although each container provides support for its own basic operations, the standard algorithms provide more extended or complex actions. They also allow you to work with two different types of containers at the same time. To have access to the STL algorithms, you must include **< algorithm >** in your program.

The STL defines a large number of algorithms, which are summarized in Table 14-5. All of the algorithms are template functions. This means that they can be applied to any type of container. The examples that follow demonstrate a representative sample.

Algorithm	Purpose
adjacent_find	Searches for adjacent matching elements within a sequence and returns an iterator to the first match.
binary_search	Performs a binary search on an ordered sequence.
copy	Copies a sequence.
copy_backward	Same as **copy( )** except that it moves the elements from the end of the sequence first.
count	Returns the number of elements in the sequence.
count_if	Returns the number of elements in the sequence that satisfy some predicate.
equal	Determines whether two ranges are the same.
equal_range	Returns a range in which an element can be inserted into a sequence without disrupting the ordering of the sequence.
fill fill_n	Fills a range with the specified value.
find	Searches a range for a value and returns an iterator to the first occurrence of the element.
find_end	Searches a range for a subsequence. This function returns an iterator to the end of the subsequence within the range.
find_first_of	Finds the first element within a sequence that matches an element within a range.
find_if	Searches a range for an element for which a user-defined unary predicate returns true.
for_each	Applies a function to a range of elements.
generate generate_n	Assigns to elements in a range the values returned by a generator function.
includes	Determines whether one sequence includes all of the elements in another sequence.
inplace_merge	Merges a range with another range. Both ranges must be sorted in increasing order. The resulting sequence is sorted.

TABLE 14-5   *The STL Algorithms* ▼

Algorithm	Purpose
iter_swap	Exchanges the values pointed to by its two iterator arguments.
lexicographical_compare	Alphabetically compares one sequence with another.
lower_bound	Finds the first point in the sequence that is not less than a specified value.
make_heap	Constructs a heap from a sequence.
max	Returns the maximum of two values.
max_element	Returns an iterator to the maximum element within a range.
merge	Merges two ordered sequences, placing the result into a third sequence.
min	Returns the minimum of two values.
min_element	Returns an iterator to the minimum element within a range.
mismatch	Finds the first mismatch between the elements in two sequences. Iterators to the two elements are returned.
next_permutation	Constructs the next permutation of a sequence.
nth_element	Arranges a sequence such that all elements less than a specified element E come before that element and all elements greater than E come after it.
partial_sort	Sorts a range.
partial_sort_copy	Sorts a range and then copies as many elements as will fit into a result sequence.
partition	Arranges a sequence such that all elements for which a predicate returns true come before those for which the predicate returns false.
pop_heap	Exchanges the first and last-1 elements and then rebuilds the heap.
prev_permutation	Constructs the previous permutation of a sequence.
push_heap	Pushes an element onto the end of a heap.
random_shuffle	Randomizes a sequence.
remove remove_if remove_copy remove_copy_if	Removes elements from a specified range.
replace replace_copy replace_if replace_copy_if	Replaces elements within a range.

TABLE 14-5 *The STL Algorithms (continued)* ▼

Algorithm	Purpose
reverse reverse_copy	Reverses the order of a range.
rotate rotate_copy	Left-rotates the elements in a range.
search	Searches for a subsequence within a sequence.
search_n	Searches for a sequence of a specified number of similar elements.
set_difference	Produces a sequence that contains the difference between two ordered sets.
set_intersection	Produces a sequence that contains the intersection of two ordered sets.
set_symmetric_difference	Produces a sequence that contains the symmetric difference between two ordered sets.
set_union	Produces a sequence that contains the union of two ordered sets.
sort	Sorts a range.
sort_heap	Sorts a heap within a specified range.
stable_partition	Arranges a sequence such that all elements for which a predicate returns true come before those for which the predicate returns false. The partitioning is stable; the relative ordering of the sequence is preserved.
stable_sort	Sorts a range. The sort is stable; equal elements are not rearranged.
swap	Exchanges two values.
swap_ranges	Exchanges elements in a range.
transform	Applies a function to a range of elements and stores the outcome in a new sequence.
unique unique_copy	Eliminates duplicate elements from a range.
upper_bound	Finds the last point in a sequence that is not greater than some value.

TABLE 14-5   _The STL Algorithms (continued)_ ▼

EXAMPLES

1. Two of the simplest algorithms are **count( )** and **count_if( )**. Their general forms are shown here:

   template <class InIter, class T>
       size_t count(InIter *start*, InIter *end*, const T &*val*);

   template <class InIter, class T>
       size_t count(InIter *start*, InIter *end*, UnPred *pfn*);

   The **count( )** algorithm returns the number of elements in the sequence beginning at *start* and ending at *end* that match *val*. The **count_if( )** algorithm returns the number of elements in the sequence beginning at *start* and ending at *end* for which the unary predicate *pfn* returns true.

   The following program demonstrates **count( )** and **count_if( )**.

```
// Demonstrate count and count_if.
#include <iostream>
#include <vector>
#include <algorithm>
using namespace std;

/* This is a unary predicate that determines
   if a value is even. */
bool even(int x)
{
  return !(x%2);
}

int main()
{
  vector<int> v;
  int i;

  for(i=0; i<20; i++) {
    if(i%2) v.push_back(1);
    else v.push_back(2);
  }
```

```
cout << "Sequence: ";
for(i=0; i<v.size(); i++) cout << v[i] << " ";
cout << endl;

int n;
n = count(v.begin(), v.end(), 1);
cout << n << " elements are 1\n";

n = count_if(v.begin(), v.end(), even);
cout << n << " elements are even.\n";

return 0;
}
```

This program displays the following output:

```
Sequence: 2 1 2 1 2 1 2 1 2 1 2 1 2 1 2 1 2 1 2 1
10 elements are 1
10 elements are even.
```

The program begins by creating a 20-element vector that contains alternating 1s and 2s. Next, **count( )** is used to count the number of 1s. Then, **count_if( )** counts the number of elements that are even. Notice how the unary predicate **even( )** is coded. All unary predicates receive as a parameter an object that is of the same type as that stored in the container upon which the predicate is operating. The predicate must then return a true or false result based upon this object.

2. Sometimes it is useful to generate a new sequence that consists of only certain items from an original sequence. One algorithm that does this is **remove_copy( )**. Its general form is shown here:

template <class InIter, class OutIter, class T>
   OutIter remove_copy(InIter *start*, InIter *end*,
                      OutIter *result*, const T &*val*);

The **remove_copy( )** algorithm copies elements from the specified range that are equal to *val* and puts the result into the sequence pointed to by *result*. It returns an iterator to the end of the result. The output container must be large enough to hold the result.

The following program demonstrates **remove_copy( )**. It creates a sequence of 1s and 2s. It then removes all of the 1s from the sequence.

```
// Demonstrate remove_copy.
#include <iostream>
#include <vector>
#include <algorithm>
using namespace std;

int main()
{
  vector<int> v, v2(20);
  int i;

  for(i=0; i<20; i++) {
    if(i%2) v.push_back(1);
    else v.push_back(2);
  }

  cout << "Sequence: ";
  for(i=0; i<v.size(); i++) cout << v[i] << " ";
  cout << endl;

  // Remove 1s
  remove_copy(v.begin(), v.end(), v2.begin(), 1);
  cout << "Result: ";
  for(i=0; i<v2.size(); i++) cout << v2[i] << " ";
  cout << endl << endl;

  return 0;
}
```

The output produced by this program is shown here.

```
Sequence: 2 1 2 1 2 1 2 1 2 1 2 1 2 1 2 1 2 1 2 1
Result: 2 2 2 2 2 2 2 2 2 0 0 0 0 0 0 0 0 0 0 0
```

3. An often useful algorithm is **reverse( )**, which reverses a sequence. Its general form is

template <class BiIter> void reverse(BiIter *start*, BiIter *end*);

The **reverse( )** algorithm reverses the order of the range specified by *start* and *end*.

The following program demonstrates **reverse( )**:

```
// Demonstrate reverse.
#include <iostream>
#include <vector>
#include <algorithm>
using namespace std;

int main()
{
  vector<int> v;
  int i;

  for(i=0; i<10; i++) v.push_back(i);

  cout << "Initial: ";
  for(i=0; i<v.size(); i++) cout << v[i] << " ";
  cout << endl;

  reverse(v.begin(), v.end());

  cout << "Reversed: ";
  for(i=0; i<v.size(); i++) cout << v[i] << " ";

  return 0;
}
```

The output from this program is shown here.

```
Initial: 0 1 2 3 4 5 6 7 8 9
Reversed: 9 8 7 6 5 4 3 2 1 0
```

4. One of the more interesting algorithms is **transform( )**, which modifies each element in a range according to a function that you provide. The **transform( )** algorithm has these two general forms:

template <class InIter, class OutIter, class Func)
    OutIter transform(InIter *start*, InIter *end*, OutIter *result*, Func *unaryfunc*);

template <class InIter1, class InIter2, class OutIter, class Func)
    OutIter transform(InIter1 *start1*, InIter1 *end1*, InIter2 *start2*,
                OutIter *result*, Func *binaryfunc*);

The **transform( )** algorithm applies a function to a range of elements and stores the outcome in *result*. In the first form, the range is specified by *start* and *end*. The function to be applied is specified by *unaryfunc*. This function receives the value of an element in its parameter, and it must return the element's transformation. In the second form, the transformation is applied using a binary operator function that receives the value of an element from the sequence to be transformed in its first parameter and an element from a second sequence as its second parameter. Both versions return an iterator to the end of the resulting sequence.

The following program uses a simple transformation function called **xform( )** to square the contents of a list. Notice that the resulting sequence is stored in the same list that provided the original sequence.

```cpp
// An example of the transform algorithm.
#include <iostream>
#include <list>
#include <algorithm>
using namespace std;

// A simple transformation function.
int xform(int i) {
  return i * i; // square original value
}

int main()
{
  list<int> xl;
  int i;

  // put values into list
  for(i=0; i<10; i++) xl.push_back(i);

  cout << "Original contents of xl: ";
  list<int>::iterator p = xl.begin();
  while(p != xl.end()) {
    cout << *p << " ";
    p++;
  }

  cout << endl;
```

```
// transform xl
p = transform(xl.begin(), xl.end(), xl.begin(), xform);

cout << "Transformed contents of xl: ";
p = xl.begin();
while(p != xl.end()) {
  cout << *p << " ";
  p++;
}

return 0;
}
```

The output produced by the program is shown here:

```
Original contents of xl: 0 1 2 3 4 5 6 7 8 9
Transformed contents of xl: 0 1 4 9 16 25 36 49 64 81
```

As you can see, each element in the **xl** list has been squared.

EXERCISES

---

1. The **sort( )** algorithm has these forms:

   template <class RandIter> void sort(RandIter *start*, RandIter *end*);
   template <class RandIter, class Comp>
       void sort(RandIter *start*, RandIter *end*, Comp *cmpfn*);

   It sorts the range specified by *start* and *end*. The second form allows you to specify a comparison function that determines whether one element is less than another. Write a program that demonstrates **sort( )**. (Use either form you like.)

2. The **merge( )** algorithm merges two ordered sequences and places the result into a third. One of its general forms is shown here:

   template <class InIter1, class InIter2, class OutIter>
       OutIter merge(InIter1 *start1*, InIter1 *end1*, InIter2 *start2*, InIter2 *end2*,
                 OutIter *result*);

The sequences to be merged are defined by *start1, end1* and *start2, end2*. The result is put into the sequence pointed to by *result*. An iterator to the end of the resulting sequence is returned. Demonstrate this algorithm.

14.7   *T**HE STRING CLASS*

As you know, C++ does not support a built-in string type, per se. It does, however, provide two ways to handle strings. First, you can use the traditional, null-terminated character array with which you are already familiar. This is sometimes referred to as a *C string*. The second method is to use a class object of type **string**. This is the approach that is examined here.

Actually, the **string** class is a specialization of a more general template class called **basic_string**. In fact, there are two specializations of **basic_string**: **string**, which supports 8-bit character strings, and **wstring**, which supports wide character strings. Since 8-bit characters are by far the most commonly used characters in normal programming, **string** is the version of **basic_string** examined here.

Before you look at the **string** class, it is important that you understand why it is part of the C++ library. Standard classes have not been casually added to C++. In fact, a significant amount of thought and debate has accompanied each new addition. Given that C++ already contains some support for strings as null-terminated character arrays, it might at first seem that the inclusion of the **string** class is an exception to this rule. However, this is actually far from the truth. Here is why: Null-terminated strings cannot be manipulated by any of the standard C++ operators, nor can they take part in normal C++ expressions. For example, consider this fragment:

```
char s1[80], s2[80], s3[80];

s1 = "one"; // can't do
s2 = "two"; // can't do
s3 = s1 + s2; // error, not allowed
```

As the comments show, in C++ it is not possible to use the assignment operator to give a character array a new value (except during initialization), nor is it possible to use the **+** operator to concatenate two strings. These operations must be written using library functions. as shown here:

```
strcpy(s1, "one");
strcpy(s2, "two");
strcpy(s3, s1);
strcat(s3, s2);
```

Since null-terminated character arrays are not technically data types in their own right, the C++ operators cannot be applied to them. This makes even the most rudimentary string operations clumsy. More than anything else, it is the inability to operate on null-terminated strings using the standard C++ operators that has driven the development of a standard **string** class. Remember, when you define a class in C++, you are defining a new data type that can be fully integrated into the C++ environment. This, of course, means that the operators can be overloaded relative to the new class. Therefore, with the addition of a standard **string** class, it becomes possible to manage strings in the same way that any other type of data is managed: through the use of operators.

There is, however, one other reason for the standard **string** class: safety. An inexperienced or careless programmer can very easily overrun the end of an array that holds a null-terminated string. For example, consider the standard string copy function **strcpy( )**. This function contains no provision for checking the boundary of the target array. If the source array contains more characters than the target array can hold, a program error or system crash is possible (likely). As you will see, the standard **string** class prevents such errors.

In the final analysis, there are three reasons for the inclusion of the standard **string** class: consistency (a string now defines a data type), convenience (you can use the standard C++ operators), and safety (array boundaries will not be overrun). Keep in mind that there is no reason that you should abandon normal, null-terminated strings altogether. They are still the most efficient way in which to implement strings. However, when speed is not an overriding concern, the new **string** class gives you access to a safe and fully integrated way to manage strings.

Although not traditionally thought of as part of the STL, **string** is another container class defined by C++. This means that it supports the algorithms described in the previous section. However, strings have additional capabilities. To have access to the **string** class you must include **< string >** in your program.

The **string** class is very large, with many constructors and member functions. Also, many member functions have multiple overloaded forms. For this reason, it is not possible to look at the entire contents of **string** in this chapter. Instead, we will examine several of its most commonly used features. Once you have a general understanding of how **string** works, you will be able to easily explore the rest of it on your own.

The **string** class supports several constructors. The prototypes for three of its most commonly used constructors are shown here.

```
string( );
string(const char *str);
string(const string &str);
```

The first form creates an empty **string** object. The second creates a **string** object from the null-terminated string pointed to by *str*. This form provides a conversion from null-terminated strings to **string** objects. The third form creates a **string** object from another **string** object.

A number of operators that apply to strings are defined for **string** objects, including those listed in the following table:

Operator	Meaning
=	Assignment
+	Concatenation
+=	Concatenation assignment
==	Equality
!=	Inequality
<	Less than
<=	Less than or equal
>	Greater than
>=	Greater than or equal
[ ]	Subscripting

Operator	Meaning
<<	Output
>>	Input

These operators allow the use of **string** objects in normal expressions and eliminate the need for calls to functions such as **strcpy( )** or **strcat( )**, for example. In general, you can mix **string** objects with normal, null-terminated strings in expressions. For example, a **string** object can be assigned a null-terminated string.

The **+** operator can be used to concatenate a **string** object with another **string** object or a **string** object with a C-style string. That is, the following variations are supported:

```
string + string
string + C-string
C-string + string
```

The **+** operator can also be used to concatenate a character onto the end of a string.

The **string** class defines the constant **npos**, which is usually –1. This constant represents the length of the longest possible string.

Although most simple string operations can be accomplished with the string operators, more complex or subtle ones are accomplished with **string** class member functions. Although there are far too many to discuss in this chapter, we will examine several of the most common ones. To assign one string to another, use the **assign( )** function. Two of its forms are shown here:

string &assign(const string &*strob*, size_type *start*, size_type *num*);

string &assign(const char **str*, size_type *num*);

In the first form, *num* characters from *strob* beginning at the index specified by *start* will be assigned to the invoking object. In the second form, the first *num* characters of the null-terminated string *str* are assigned to the invoking object. In each case, a reference to the invoking object is returned. Of course, it is much easier to use the **=** operator to assign one entire string to another. You will need to use the **assign( )** function only when assigning a partial string.

You can append part of one string to another using the **append( )** member function. Two of its forms are shown here:

```
string &append(const string &strob, size_type start, size_type num);
```

```
string &append(const char *str, size_type num);
```

In the first form, *num* characters from *strob,* beginning at the index specified by *start,* will be appended to the invoking object. In the second form, the first *num* characters of the null-terminated string *str* are appended to the invoking object. In each case, a reference to the invoking object is returned. Of course, it is much easier to use the + operator to append one entire string to another. You will need to use the **append( )** function only when appending a partial string.

You can insert or replace characters within a string using **insert( )** and **replace( )**. The prototypes for their most common forms are shown here:

```
string &insert(size_type start, const string &strob);
```

```
string &insert(size_type start, const string &strob,
               size_type insStart, size_type num);
```

```
string &replace(size_type start, size_type num, const string &strob);
```

```
string &replace(size_type start, size_type orgNum, const string &strob,
                size_type replaceStart, size_type replaceNum);
```

The first form of **insert( )** inserts *strob* into the invoking string at the index specified by *start*. The second form of **insert( )** inserts *num* characters from *strob* beginning at *insStart* into the invoking string at the index specified by *start*.

Beginning at *start*, the first form of **replace( )** replaces *num* characters from the invoking string with *strob*. The second form replaces *orgNum* characters, beginning at s*tart* in the invoking string, with *replaceNum* characters from the string specified by *strob* beginning at *replaceStart*. In both cases, a reference to the invoking object is returned.

You can remove characters from a string using **erase( )**. One of its forms is shown here:

```
string &erase(size_type start = 0, size_type num = npos);
```

It removes *num* characters from the invoking string beginning at *start*. A reference to the invoking string is returned.

The **string** class provides several member functions, including **find( )** and **rfind( )**, that search a string. Here are the prototypes for the most common versions of these two functions:

size_type find(const string &_strob_, size_type _start_=0) const;

size_type rfind(const string &_strob_, size_type _start_=npos) const;

Beginning at _start_, **find( )** searches the invoking string for the first occurrence of the string contained in _strob_. If the search string is found, **find( )** returns the index at which the match occurs within the invoking string. If no match is found, **npos** is returned. **rfind( )** is the opposite of **find( )**. Beginning at _start_, it searches the invoking string in the reverse direction for the first occurrence of the string contained in _strob_. (I.e, it finds the last occurrence of _strob_ within the invoking string.) If the search string is found, **rfind( )** returns the index at which the match occurs within the invoking string. If no match is found, **npos** is returned.

To compare the entire contents of one string object to those of another, you will normally use the overloaded relational operators described earlier. However, if you want to compare a portion of one string to another, you will need to use the **compare( )** member function, shown here:

int compare(size_type _start_, size_type _num_, const string &_strob_) const;

Here _num_ characters in _strob_, beginning at _start_, will be compared against the invoking string. If the invoking string is less than _strob_, **compare( )** will return less than 0. If the invoking string is greater than _strob_, it will return greater than 0. If _strob_ is equal to the invoking string, **compare( )** will return 0.

Although **string** objects are useful in their own right, there will be times when you will need to obtain a null-terminated character array version of the string. For example, you might use a **string** object to construct a file name. However, when opening a file, you will need to specify a pointer to a standard, null-terminated string. To solve this problem, the member function **c_str( )** is provided. Its prototype is shown here:

const char *c_str( ) const;

This function returns a pointer to a null-terminated version of the string contained in the invoking **string** object. The null-terminated string must not be altered. It is also not guaranteed to be valid after any other operations have taken place on the **string** object.

Because it is a container, **string** supports the **begin( )** and **end( )** functions that return an iterator to the start and end of a string, respectively. Also included is the **size( )** function, which returns the number of characters currently in a string.

EXAMPLES

1. Although the traditional, C-style strings have always been simple to use, the C++ **string** class makes string handling extraordinarily easy. For example, with **string** objects you can use the assignment operator to assign a quoted string to a **string**, the **+** operator to concatenate strings, and the comparison operators to compare strings. The following program illustrates these operations.

```
// A short string demonstration.
#include <iostream>
#include <string>
using namespace std;

int main()
{
  string str1("Demonstrating Strings");
  string str2("String Two");
  string str3;

  // assign a string
  str3 = str1;
  cout << str1 << "\n" << str3 << "\n";

  // concatenate two strings
  str3 = str1 + str2;
  cout << str3 << "\n";

  // compare strings
  if(str3 > str1) cout << "str3 > str1\n";
  if(str3 == str1+str2)
    cout << "str3 == str1+str2\n";
```

```
/* A string object can also be
   assigned a normal string. */
str1 = "This is a normal string.\n";
cout << str1;

// create a string object using another string object
string str4(str1);
cout << str4;

// input a string
cout << "Enter a string: ";
cin >> str4;
cout << str4;

return 0;
}
```

This program produces the following output:

```
Demonstrating Strings
Demonstrating Strings
Demonstrating StringsString Two
str3 > str1
str3 == str1+str2
This is a normal string.
This is a normal string.
Enter a string: Hello
Hello
```

As you can see, objects of type **string** can be manipulated with techniques similar to those used to work with C++'s built-in data types. In fact, this is the main advantage to the string class.

Notice the ease with which the string handling is accomplished. For example, the **+** is used to concatenate strings and the **>** is use to compare two strings. To accomplish these operations using C-style, null-terminated strings, you must use the less convenient calls to the **strcat( )** and **strcmp( )** functions. Because C++ **string** objects can be freely mixed with C-style, null-terminated strings, there is no disadvantage to using them in your program—and there are considerable benefits to be gained.

There is one other thing to notice in the preceding program: the sizes of the strings are not specified. A **string** object is automatically sized to hold the string that it is given. Thus, when you are assigning or concatenating strings, the target string will grow as needed to accommodate the size of the new string. It is not possible to overrun the end of the string. This dynamic aspect of **string** objects is one of the reasons that they are considered better than standard null-terminated strings (which *are* subject to boundary overruns).

2. The following program demonstrates the **insert( )**, **erase( )**, and **replace( )** functions.

```
// Demonstrate insert(), erase(), and replace().
#include <iostream>
#include <string>
using namespace std;

int main()
{
  string str1("This is a test");
  string str2("ABCDEFG");

  cout << "Initial strings:\n";
  cout << "str1: " << str1 << endl;
  cout << "str2: " << str2 << "\n\n";

  // demonstrate insert()
  cout << "Insert str2 into str1:\n";
  str1.insert(5, str2);
  cout << str1 << "\n\n";

  // demonstrate erase()
  cout << "Remove 7 characters from str1:\n";
  str1.erase(5, 7);
  cout << str1 <<"\n\n";

  // demonstrate replace
  cout << "Replace 2 characters in str1 with str2:\n";
  str1.replace(5, 2, str2);
  cout << str1 << endl;

  return 0;
}
```

The output produced by this program is shown here:

```
Initial strings:
str1: This is a test
```

```
str2: ABCDEFG

Insert str2 into str1:
This ABCDEFGis a test

Remove 7 characters from str1:
This is a test

Replace 2 characters in str1 with str2:
This ABCDEFG a test
```

3. Since **string** defines a data type, it is possible to create containers that hold objects of type **string**. For example, here is a better way to write the word/opposite program shown in Example 3 of section 14.5.

```cpp
// A map of word opposites, using strings.
#include <iostream>
#include <map>
#include <string>
using namespace std;

int main()
{
  map<string, string> m;
  int i;

  m.insert(pair<string, string>("yes", "no"));
  m.insert(pair<string, string>("up", "down"));
  m.insert(pair<string, string>("left", "right"));
  m.insert(pair<string, string>("good", "bad"));

  string s;
  cout << "Enter word: ";
  cin >> s;

  map<string, string>::iterator p;

  p = m.find(s);
  if(p != m.end())
    cout << "Opposite: " << p->second;
  else
    cout << "Word not in map.\n";

  return 0;
}
```

1. Using objects of type **string**, store the following strings in a **list**.

one	two	three	four	five
six	seven	eight	nine	ten

Next, sort the list. Finally, display the sorted list.

2. Since **string** is a container, it can be used with the standard algorithms. Create a program that inputs a string from the user. Then, using **count( )**, report how many e's are in the string.

3. Modify your answer to Exercise 2 so that it reports the number of characters that are lowercase. (Hint: use **count_if( )**.)

4. The **string** class is a specialization of what template class?

S*KILLS CHECK*

Mastery
Skills Check

At this point you should be able to perform the following exercises and answer the questions.

1. How does the STL make it easier for you to create more reliable programs?

2. Define a container, an iterator, and an algorithm as they relate to the STL.

3. Write a program that creates a ten-element vector that contains the numbers 1 through 10. Next, copy only the even elements from this vector into a list.

4. Give one advantage of using the **string** data type. Give one disadvantage.

5. What is a predicate?

6. On your own, recode your answer to Exercise 2 in Section 14.5 so that it uses **string**.

7. Begin exploring the STL function objects. To get started, examine the two standard classes **unary_function** and **binary_function**, which aid in the construction of function objects.

8. Study the STL documentation that comes with your compiler. You will find several interesting features and techniques.

Cumulative Skills Check

This section checks how well you have integrated material in this chapter with that from the preceding chapters.

1. You have come a long way since Chapter 1. Take some time to skim through the book again. As you do so, think about ways you can improve the examples (especially those in the first six chapters) so that they take advantage of all the features of C++ you have learned.

2. Programming is learned best by doing. Write many C++ programs. Try to exercise those features of C++ that are unique to it.

3. Continue to explore the STL. In the future, many programming tasks will be framed in terms of the STL because often a program can be reduced to manipulations of containers by algorithms.

4. Finally, remember: C++ gives you unprecedented power. It is important that you learn to use this power wisely. Because of this power, C++ lets you push the limits of your programming ability. However, if this power is misused, you can also create programs that are hard to understand, nearly impossible to follow, and extremely difficult to maintain. C++ is a powerful tool. But, like any other tool, it is only as good as the person using it.

A

*A Few More
Differences Between
C and C++*

F OR the most part, C++ is a superset of ANSI-standard C, and virtually all C programs are also C++ programs. However, a few differences do exist, several of which were mentioned in Chapter 1. Here are a few more that you should be aware of:

▼ A small but potentially important difference between C and C++ is that in C, a character constant is automatically elevated to an integer, whereas in C++, it is not.

▼ In C, it is not an error to declare a global variable several times, even though it is bad programming practice. In C++, this is an error.

▼ In C, an identifier will have at least 31 significant characters. In C++, all characters are considered significant. However, from a practical point of view, extremely long identifiers are unwieldy and are seldom needed.

▼ In C, you can call **main( )** from within a program, although this would be unusual. In C++, this is not allowed.

▼ In C, you cannot take the address of a **register** variable. In C++, you can.

▼ In C, the type **wchar_t** is defined with a **typedef**. In C++, **wchar_t** is a keyword.

B

Answers

EXERCISES

1.
```cpp
#include <iostream>
using namespace std;

int main()
{
  double hours, wage;

  cout << "Enter hours worked: ";
  cin >> hours;

  cout << "Enter wage per hour: ";
  cin >> wage;

  cout << "Pay is: $" << wage * hours;

  return 0;
}
```

2.
```cpp
#include <iostream>
using namespace std;

int main()
{
  double feet;

  do {
    cout << "Enter feet (0 to quit): ";
    cin >> feet;

    cout << feet * 12 << " inches\n";
  } while (feet != 0.0);

  return 0;
}
```

3.
```cpp
/*
   This program computes the lowest
   common denominator.
*/
#include <iostream>
using namespace std;

int main()
```

```
{
  int a, b, d, min;

  cout << "Enter two numbers: ";
  cin >> a >> b;

  min = a > b ? b : a;

  for(d = 2; d<min; d++)
    if(((a%d)==0) && ((b%d)==0)) break;
  if(d==min) {
    cout << "No common denominators\n";
    return 0;
  }
  cout << "The lowest common denominator is " << d << ".\n";

  return 0;
}
```

1.4 ▮ **E**XERCISES

1. The comment, although strange, is valid.

1.5 ▮ **E**XERCISES

2.
```cpp
#include <iostream>
#include <cstring>
using namespace std;

class card {
  char title[80]; // book title
  char author[40]; // author
  int number; // number in library
public:
  void store(char *t, char *name, int num);
  void show();
};

void card::store(char *t, char *name, int num)
{
  strcpy(title, t);
  strcpy(author, name);
  number = num;
```

```
}

void card::show()
{
  cout << "Title: " << title << "\n";
  cout << "Author: " << author << "\n";
  cout << "Number on hand: " << number << "\n";
}

int main()
{
  card book1, book2, book3;

  book1.store("Dune", "Frank Herbert", 2);
  book2.store("The Foundation Trilogy", "Isaac Asimov", 2);
  book3.store("The Rainbow", "D. H. Lawrence", 1);

  book1.show();
  book2.show();
  book3.show();

  return 0;
}
```

3.
```
#include <iostream>
using namespace std;

#define SIZE 100

class q_type {
  int queue[SIZE]; // holds the queue
  int head, tail; // indices of head and tail
public:
  void init(); // initialize
  void q(int num); // store
  int deq();  // retrieve
};

// Initialize
void q_type::init()
{
  head = tail = 0;
}

// Put value on a queue.
```

```
void q_type::q(int num)
{
  if(tail+1==head || (tail+1==SIZE && !head)) {
    cout << "Queue is full\n";
    return;
  }
  tail++;
  if(tail==SIZE) tail = 0; // cycle around
  queue[tail] = num;
}

// Remove a value from a queue.
int q_type::deq()
{
  if(head == tail) {
    cout << "Queue is empty\n";
    return 0;  // or some other error indicator
  }
  head++;
  if(head==SIZE) head = 0; // cycle around
  return queue[head];
}

int main()
{
  q_type q1, q2;
  int i;

  q1.init();
  q2.init();

  for(i=1; i<=10; i++) {
    q1.q(i);
    q2.q(i*i);
  }

  for(i=1; i<=10; i++) {
    cout << "Dequeue 1: " << q1.deq() << "\n";
    cout << "Dequeue 2: " << q2.deq() << "\n";
  }

  return 0;
}
```

1.6 **E**XERCISES

1. The function **f( )** is not prototyped.

1.7 **E**XERCISES

1.
```cpp
#include <iostream>
#include <cmath>
using namespace std;

// Overload sroot() for integers, longs, and doubles.

int sroot(int i);
long sroot(long i);
double sroot(double i);

int main()
{
  cout << "Square root of 90.34 is : " << sroot(90.34);
  cout << "\n";
  cout << "Square root of 90L is : " << sroot(90L);
  cout << "\n";
  cout << "Square root of 90 is : " << sroot(90);

  return 0;
}

// Return square root of integer.
int sroot(int i)
{
  cout << "computing integer root\n";
  return (int) sqrt((double) i);
}

// Return square root of long.
long sroot(long i)
{
  cout << "computing long root\n";
  return (long) sqrt((double) i);
}

// Retur square root of double.
double sroot(double i)
```

```
{
  cout << "computing double root\n";
  return sqrt(i);
}
```

2. The functions **atof( )**, **atoi( )**, and **atol( )** cannot be overloaded because they differ only in the type of data they return. Function overloading requires that either the type or the number of arguments differs.

3.
```
// Overload the min() function.

#include <iostream>
#include <cctype>
using namespace std;

char min(char a, char b);
int min(int a, int b);
double min(double a, double b);

int main()
{
  cout << "Min is: " << min('x', 'a') << "\n";
  cout << "Min is: " << min(10, 20) << "\n";
  cout << "Min is: " << min(0.2234, 99.2) << "\n";

  return 0;
}

// min() for chars
char min(char a, char b)
{
  return tolower(a)<tolower(b) ? a : b;
}

// min() for ints
int min(int a, int b)
{
  return a<b ? a : b;
}

// min() for doubles
double min(double a, double b)
{
```

```
    return a<b ? a : b;
}
```

4.
```cpp
#include <iostream>
using namespace std;

// Overload sleep to accept integer or char * argument
void sleep(int n);
void sleep(char *n);

// Change this value to fit your processor speed.
#define DELAY 100000

int main()
{
  cout << '.';
  sleep(3);
  cout << '.';
  sleep("2");
  cout << '.';

  return 0;
}

// Sleep() with integer argument.
void sleep(int n)
{
  long i;

  for( ; n; n--)
    for(i=0; i<DELAY; i++) ;
}

// Sleep() with char * argument.
void sleep(char *n)
{
  long i;
  int j;

  j = atoi(n);

  for( ; j; j--)
    for(i=0; i<DELAY; i++) ;
}
```

MASTERY SKILLS CHECK: *Chapter 1*

1. Polymorphism is the mechanism by which one general interface can be used to access many specific implementations. Encapsulation provides a protected linkage between code and its related data. Access to encapsulated routines can be tightly controlled, thus preventing unwanted tampering. Inheritance is the process by which one object can acquire the traits of another. Inheritance is used to support a system of hierarchical classification.

2. You can include comments in a C++ program by using either the normal C-style comments or the C++-specific single-line comments.

3.
```cpp
#include <iostream>
using namespace std;

int main()
{
  int b, e, r;
  cout << "Enter base: ";
  cin >> b;
  cout << "Enter exponent: ";
  cin >> e;

  r = 1;
  for( ; e; e--) r = r * b;

  cout << "Result: " << r;

  return 0;
}
```

4.
```cpp
#include <iostream>
#include <cstring>
using namespace std;

// Overload string reversal function.
void rev_str(char *s); // reverse string in place
void rev_str(char *in, char *out); // put reversal into out

int main()
{
  char s1[80], s2[80];
```

```
    strcpy(s1, "This is a test");

    rev_str(s1, s2);
    cout << s2 << "\n";

    rev_str(s1);
    cout << s1 << "\n";

    return 0;
}

// Reverse string, put result in s.
void rev_str(char *s)
{
  char temp[80];
  int i, j;

  for(i=strlen(s)-1, j=0; i>=0; i--, j++)
    temp[j] = s[i];

  temp[j] = '\0'; // null-terminate result

  strcpy(s, temp);
}

// Reverse string, put result into out.
void rev_str(char *in, char *out)
{
  int i, j;

  for(i=strlen(in)-1, j=0; i>=0; i--, j++)
    out[j] = in[i];

  out[j] = '\0'; // null-terminate result
}
```

5. ```
#include <iostream.h>

int f(int a);

int main()
{
  cout << f(10);

  return 0;
```
```

```
   }

   int f(int a)
   {
     return a * 3.1416;
   }
```

6. The **bool** data type stores Boolean values. The only values an object of type **bool** can have are **true** and **false**.

REVIEW SKILLS CHECK: Chapter 2

1.
```
#include <iostream>
#include <cstring>
using namespace std;

int main()
{
  char s[80];

  cout << "Enter a string: ";
  cin >> s;

  cout << "Length: " << strlen(s) << "\n";

  return 0;
}
```

2.
```
#include <iostream>
#include <cstring>
using namespace std;

class addr {
  char name[40];
  char street[40];
  char city[30];
  char state[3];
  char zip[10];
public:
  void store(char *n, char *s, char *c, char *t,
             char *z);
  void display();
};
```

```
      void addr::store(char *n, char *s, char *c, char *t,
                       char *z)
      {
        strcpy(name, n);
        strcpy(street, s);
        strcpy(city, c);
        strcpy(state, t);
        strcpy(zip, z);
      }

      void addr::display()
      {
        cout << name << "\n";
        cout << street << "\n";
        cout << city << "\n";
        cout << state << "\n";
        cout << zip << "\n\n";
      }

      int main()
      {
        addr a;

        a.store("C. B. Turkle", "11 Pinetree Lane", "Wausau",
                "In", "46576");

        a.display();

        return 0;
      }

3. #include <iostream>
   using namespace std;

   int rotate(int i);
   long rotate(long i);

   int main()
   {
     int a;
     long b;

     a = 0x8000;
     b = 8;
```

```
      cout  << rotate(a);
      cout << "\n";
      cout << rotate(b);

      return 0;
    }

    int rotate(int i)
    {
      int x;

      if(i & 0x8000) x = 1;
      else x = 0;

      i = i << 1;
      i += x;

      return i;
    }

    long rotate(long i)
    {
      int x;

      if(i & 0x80000000) x = 1;
      else x = 0;

      i = i << 1;
      i += x;

      return i;
    }
```

4. The integer **i** is private to **myclass** and cannot be accessed inside **main( )**.

2.1 *EXERCISES*

```
1. #include <iostream>
   using namespace std;

   #define SIZE 100

   class q_type {
```

```
  int queue[SIZE]; // holds the queue
  int head, tail; // indices of head and tail
public:
  q_type(); // constructor
  void q(int num); // store
  int deq();   // retrieve
};

// Constructor
q_type::q_type()
{
  head = tail = 0;
}

// Put value on queue.
void q_type::q(int num)
{
  if(tail+1==head || (tail+1==SIZE && !head)) {
    cout << "Queue is full\n";
    return;
  }
  tail++;
  if(tail==SIZE) tail = 0; // cycle around
  queue[tail] = num;
}

// Remove value from queue.
int q_type::deq()
{
  if(head == tail) {
    cout << "Queue is empty\n";
    return 0;  // or some other error indicator
  }
  head++;
  if(head==SIZE) head = 0; // cycle around
  return queue[head];
}

int main()
{
  q_type q1, q2;
  int i;

  for(i=1; i<=10; i++) {
    q1.q(i);
```

```
      q2.q(i*i);
    }

    for(i=1; i<=10; i++) {
      cout << "Dequeue 1: " << q1.deq() << "\n";
      cout << "Dequeue 2: " << q2.deq() << "\n";
    }

    return 0;
  }
```

2.
```
// Stopwatch emulator
#include <iostream>
#include <ctime>
using namespace std;

class stopwatch {
  double begin, end;
public:
  stopwatch();
  ~stopwatch();
  void start();
  void stop();
  void show();
};

stopwatch::stopwatch()
{
  begin = end = 0.0;
}

stopwatch::~stopwatch()
{
  cout << "Stopwatch object being destroyed...";
  show();
}

void stopwatch::start()
{
  begin = (double) clock() / CLOCKS_PER_SEC;
}

void stopwatch::stop()
{
  end = (double) clock() / CLOCKS_PER_SEC;
```

```
   }

   void stopwatch::show()
   {
     cout << "Elapsed time: " << end - begin;
     cout << "\n";
   }

   int main()
   {
     stopwatch watch;
     long i;

     watch.start();
     for(i=0; i<320000; i++) ; // time a for loop
     watch.stop();

     watch.show();

     return 0;
   }
```

3. A constructor cannot have a return type.

2.2 **EXERCISES**

```
1. // Dynamically allocated stack.
   #include <iostream>
   #include <cstdlib>
   using namespace std;

   // Declare a stack class for characters
   class stack {
     char *stck; // holds the stack
     int tos; // index of top of stack
     int size; // size of stack
   public:
     stack(int s); // constructor
     ~stack(); // destructor
     void push(char ch); // push character on stack
     char pop(); // pop character from stack
   };

   // Initialize the stack
```

```
stack::stack(int s)
{
  cout << "Constructing a stack\n";
  tos = 0;
  stck = (char *) malloc(s);
  if(!stck) {
    cout << "Allocation error\n";
    exit(1);
  }
  size = s;
}

stack::~stack()
{
  free(stck);
}

// Push a character.
void stack::push(char ch)
{
  if(tos==size) {
    cout << "Stack is full\n";
    return;
  }
  stck[tos] = ch;
  tos++;
}

// Pop a character.
char stack::pop()
{
  if(tos==0) {
    cout << "Stack is empty\n";
    return 0; // return null on empty stack
  }
  tos--;
  return stck[tos];
}

int main()
{
  // Create two stacks that are automatically initialized.
  stack s1(10), s2(10);
  int i;
```

```
        s1.push('a');
        s2.push('x');
        s1.push('b');
        s2.push('y');
        s1.push('c');
        s2.push('z');

        for(i=0; i<3; i++) cout << "Pop s1: " << s1.pop() << "\n";
        for(i=0; i<3; i++) cout << "Pop s2: " << s2.pop() << "\n";

        return 0;
      }

2.  #include <iostream>
    #include <ctime>
    using namespace std;

    class t_and_d {
      time_t systime;
    public:
      t_and_d(time_t t); // constructor
      void show();
    };

    t_and_d::t_and_d(time_t t)
    {
      systime = t;
    }

    void t_and_d::show()
    {
      cout << ctime(&systime);
    }

    int main()
    {
      time_t x;

      x = time(NULL);

      t_and_d ob(x);

      ob.show();
```

```
      return 0;
    }

3. #include <iostream>
   using namespace std;

   class box {
     double l, w, h;
     double volume;
   public:
     box(double a, double b, double c);
     void vol();
   };

   box::box(double a, double b, double c)
   {
     l = a;
     w = b;
     h = c;

     volume = l * w * h;
   }

   void box::vol()
   {
     cout << "Volume is: " << volume << "\n";
   }

   int main()
   {
     box x(2.2, 3.97, 8.09), y(1.0, 2.0, 3.0);

     x.vol();
     y.vol();
     return 0;
   }
```

2.3 EXERCISE

```
1. #include <iostream>
   using namespace std;

   class area_cl {
   public:
```

```
  double height;
  double width;
};

class rectangle : public area_cl {
public:
  rectangle(double h, double w);
  double area();
};

class isosceles : public area_cl {
public:
  isosceles(double h, double w);
  double area();
};

rectangle::rectangle(double h, double w)
{
  height = h;
  width = w;
}

isosceles::isosceles(double h, double w)
{
  height = h;
  width = w;
}

double rectangle::area()
{
  return width * height;
}

double isosceles::area()
{
  return 0.5 * width * height;
}

int main()
{
  rectangle b(10.0, 5.0);
  isosceles i(4.0, 6.0);
```

```
cout << "Rectangle: " << b.area() << "\n";
cout << "Triangle: " << i.area() << "\n";

return 0;
}
```

2.5 *E*XERCISES

1.
```
// Stack class using a structure.
#include <iostream>
using namespace std;

#define SIZE 10

// Declare a stack class for characters using a structure.
struct stack {
  stack(); // constructor
  void push(char ch); // push character on stack
  char pop(); // pop character from stack
private:
  char stck[SIZE]; // holds the stack
  int tos; // index of top of stack
};

// Initialize the stack.
stack::stack()
{
  cout << "Constructing a stack\n";
  tos = 0;
}

// Push a character.
void stack::push(char ch)
{
  if(tos==SIZE) {
    cout << "Stack is full\n";
    return;
  }
  stck[tos] = ch;
  tos++;
}
```

```
// Pop a character.
char stack::pop()
{
  if(tos==0) {
    cout << "Stack is empty\n";
    return 0; // return null on empty stack
  }
  tos--;
  return stck[tos];
}

int main()
{
  // Create two stacks that are automatically initialized.
  stack s1, s2;
  int i;

  s1.push('a');
  s2.push('x');
  s1.push('b');
  s2.push('y');
  s1.push('c');
  s2.push('z');

  for(i=0; i<3; i++) cout << "Pop s1: " << s1.pop() << "\n";
  for(i=0; i<3; i++) cout << "Pop s2: " << s2.pop() << "\n";

  return 0;
}
```

2.
```
#include <iostream>
using namespace std;

union swapbytes {
  unsigned char c[2];
  unsigned i;
  swapbytes(unsigned x);
  void swp();
};

swapbytes::swapbytes(unsigned x)
{
  i = x;
}
```

```
void swapbytes::swp()
{
  unsigned char temp;

  temp = c[0];
  c[0] = c[1];
  c[1] = temp;
}

int main()
{
  swapbytes ob(1);

  ob.swp();
  cout << ob.i;

  return 0;
}
```

3. An anonymous union is the syntactic mechanism that allows
   two variables to share the same memory space. The members of
   an anonymous union are accessed directly, without reference to
   an object. They are at the same scope level as the union itself.

2.6 **EXERCISES**

```
1. #include <iostream>
   using namespace std;

   // Overload abs() three ways:

   // abs() for ints
   inline int abs(int n)
   {
     cout << "In integer abs()\n";
     return n<0 ? -n : n;
   }

   // abs() for longs
   inline long abs(long n)
   {
     cout << "In long abs()\n";
     return n<0 ? -n : n;
```

```
}

// abs() for doubles
inline double abs(double n)
{
  cout << "In double abs()\n";
  return n<0 ? -n : n;
}

int main()
{
  cout << "Absolute value of -10: " << abs(-10) << "\n";
  cout << "Absolute value of -10L: " << abs(-10L) << "\n";
  cout << "Absolute value of -10.01: " << abs(-10.01) << "\n";

  return 0;
}
```

2. The function might not be able to be in-lined because it contains a **for** loop. Some compilers will not in-line functions containing loops.

2.7 EXERCISES

1.
```
#include <iostream>
using namespace std;

#define SIZE 10

// Declare a stack class for characters.
class stack {
  char stck[SIZE]; // holds the stack
  int tos; // index of top of stack
public:
  stack() { tos = 0; }
  void push(char ch)
  {
    if(tos==SIZE) {
      cout << "Stack is full\n";
      return;
    }
    stck[tos] = ch;
    tos++;
  }
```

```cpp
    char pop()
    {
      if(tos==0) {
        cout << "Stack is empty\n";
        return 0; // return null on empty stack
      }
      tos--;
      return stck[tos];
    }
};

int main()
{
  // Create two stacks that are automatically initialized.
  stack s1, s2;
  int i;

  s1.push('a');
  s2.push('x');
  s1.push('b');
  s2.push('y');
  s1.push('c');
  s2.push('z');

  for(i=0; i<3; i++) cout << "Pop s1: " << s1.pop() << "\n";
  for(i=0; i<3; i++) cout << "Pop s2: " << s2.pop() << "\n";

  return 0;
}
```

2.
```cpp
#include <iostream>
#include <cstring>
#include <cstdlib>
using namespace std;

class strtype {
  char *p;
  int len;
public:
  strtype(char *ptr)
  {
    len = strlen(ptr);
    p = (char *) malloc(len+1);
    if(!p) {
```

```
        cout << "Allocation error\n";
        exit(1);
      }
      strcpy(p, ptr);
    }
    ~strtype() { cout << "Freeing p\n"; free(p); }

    void show()
    {
      cout << p << " - length: " << len;
      cout << "\n";
    }
};

int main()
{
  strtype s1("This is a test."), s2("I like C++.");

  s1.show();
  s2.show();

  return 0;
}
```

*M*ASTERY SKILLS CHECK: *Chapter 2*

1. A constructor is the function that is called when an object is created. A destructor is the function that is called when an object is destroyed.

2.
```
#include <iostream>
using namespace std;

class line {
  int len;
public:
  line(int l);
};

line::line(int l)
{
  len = l;

  int i;
```

```
      for(i=0; i<len; i++) cout << '*';
    }

    int main()
    {
      line l(10);

      return 0;
    }
```

3. 10 1000000 -0.0009

4.
```
#include <iostream>
using namespace std;

class area_cl {
public:
  double height;
  double width;
};

class rectangle : public area_cl {
public:
  rectangle(double h, double w) { height = h; width = w; }
  double area() { return height * width; }
};

class isosceles : public area_cl {
public:
  isosceles(double h, double w) { height = h; width = w; }
  double area() { return 0.5 * width * height; }};

class cylinder : public area_cl {
public:
  cylinder(double h, double w) { height = h; width = w; }
  double area()
  {
    return (2 * 3.1416 * (width/2) * (width/2)) +
           (3.1416 * width * height);
  }
};

int main()
{
  rectangle b(10.0, 5.0);
```

```
   isosceles i(4.0, 6.0);
   cylinder c(3.0, 4.0);

   cout << "Rectangle: " << b.area() << "\n";
   cout << "Triangle: " << i.area() << "\n";
   cout << "Cylinder: " << c.area() << "\n";

   return 0;
}
```

5. An in-line function's code is expanded in line. This means that the function is not actually called. This avoids the overhead associated with the function call and return mechanism. Its advantage is that it increases the execution speed. Its disadvantage is that it can increase the size of the program.

6. ```
#include <iostream>
using namespace std;

class myclass {
  int i, j;
public:
  myclass(int x, int y) { i = x; j = y; }
  void show() { cout << i << " " << j; }
};

int main()
{
  myclass count(2, 3);

  count.show();

  return 0;
}
```

7. In a class, members are private by default. In a structure, members are public by default.

8. Yes. It defines an anonymous union.

---

# CUMULATIVE SKILLS CHECK: Chapter 2

1. ```
#include <iostream>
using namespace std;
```

```
class prompt {
  int count;
public:
  prompt(char *s) { cout << s; cin >> count; };
  ~prompt();
};

prompt::~prompt() {
  int i, j;

  for(i=0; i<count; i++) {
    cout << '\a';
    for(j=0; j<32000; j++) ; // delay
  }
}

int main()
{
  prompt ob("Enter a number: ");

  return 0;
}
```

2.
```
#include <iostream>
using namespace std;

class ftoi {
  double feet;
  double inches;
public:
  ftoi(double f);
};

ftoi::ftoi(double f)
{
  feet = f;
  inches = feet * 12;
  cout << feet << " is " << inches << " inches.\n";
}

int main()
{
  ftoi a(12.0), b(99.0);
```

```
      return 0;
    }
```

3.
```
    #include <iostream>
    #include <cstdlib>
    using namespace std;

    class dice {
      int val;
    public:
      void roll();
    };

    void dice::roll()
    {
      val = (rand() % 6) + 1; // generate 1 through 6
      cout << val << "\n";
    }

    int main()
    {
      dice one, two;

      one.roll();
      two.roll();
      one.roll();
      two.roll();
      one.roll();
      two.roll();

      return 0;
    }
```

*R*EVIEW SKILLS CHECK: *Chapter 3*

1. The constructor is called **widgit( )** and the destructor is called **~widgit( )**.

2. The constructor function is called when an object is created (that is, when an object comes into existence). The destructor is called when an object is destroyed.

3.
```
    class Mars : public planet {
      // ...
    };
```

4. You can expand a function in line either by preceding its definition with the **inline** specifier or by including its definition within a class declaration.

5. An in-line function must be defined before it is first used. Other common restrictions include the following: It cannot contain any loops. It must not be recursive. It cannot contain a **goto** or a **switch** statement. It cannot contain any **static** variables.

6. ```
sample ob(100, 'X');
```

---

**3.1** **E**XERCISES

1. The assignment statement **x = y** is wrong because **cl1** and **cl2** are two different types of classes, and objects of differing class types cannot be assigned.

2. ```cpp
#include <iostream>
using namespace std;

#define SIZE 100

class q_type {
  int queue[SIZE]; // holds the queue
  int head, tail; // indices of head and tail
public:
  q_type(); // constructor
  void q(int num); // store
  int deq();  // retrieve
};

// Constructor
q_type::q_type()
{
  head = tail = 0;
}

// Put value on queue.
void q_type::q(int num)
{
  if(tail+1==head || (tail+1==SIZE && !head)) {
    cout << "Queue is full\n";
    return;
  }
```

```
    tail++;
    if(tail==SIZE) tail = 0; // cycle around
    queue[tail] = num;
}

// Remove value from queue.
int q_type::deq()
{
  if(head == tail) {
    cout << "Queue is empty\n";
    return 0;  // or some other error indicator
  }
  head++;
  if(head==SIZE) head = 0; // cycle around
  return queue[head];
}

int main()
{
  q_type q1, q2;
  int i;

  for(i=1; i<=10; i++) {
    q1.q(i);
  }

  // assign one queue to another
  q2 = q1;

  // show that both have the same contents
  for(i=1; i<=10; i++)
    cout << "Dequeue 1: " << q1.deq() << "\n";

  for(i=1; i<=10; i++)
    cout << "Dequeue 2: " << q2.deq() << "\n";

  return 0;
}
```

3. If memory to hold a queue is dynamically allocated, assigning
   one queue to another causes the dynamic memory allocated to
   the queue on the left side of the assignment statement to be lost
   and the memory allocated to the queue on the right side to be
   freed twice when the objects are destroyed. Either of these two
   conditions is an unacceptable error.

*E*XERCISES

1.
```cpp
#include <iostream>
using namespace std;

#define SIZE 10

// Declare a stack class for characters.
class stack {
  char stck[SIZE]; // holds the stack
  int tos; // index of top of stack
public:
  stack(); // constructor
  void push(char ch); // push character on stack
  char pop(); // pop character from stack
};

// Initialize the stack.
stack::stack()
{
  cout << "Constructing a stack\n";
  tos = 0;
}

// Push a character.
void stack::push(char ch)
{
  if(tos==SIZE) {
    cout << "Stack is full\n";
    return;
  }
  stck[tos] = ch;
  tos++;
}

// Pop a character.
char stack::pop()
{
  if(tos==0) {
    cout << "Stack is empty\n";
    return 0; // return null on empty stack
  }
  tos--;
  return stck[tos];
}
```

```
   void showstack(stack o);

int main()
{
   stack s1;
   int i;

   s1.push('a');
   s1.push('b');
   s1.push('c');

   showstack(s1);

   // s1 in main is still existent
   cout << "s1 stack still contains this: \n";
   for(i=0; i<3; i++) cout << s1.pop() << "\n";

   return 0;
}

// Display the contents of a stack.
void showstack(stack o)
{
   char c;

   // when this statement ends, the o stack is empty
   while(c=o.pop()) cout << c << "\n";
   cout << "\n";
}
```

This program displays the following:

```
Constructing a stack
c
b
a
Stack is empty
s1 stack still contains this:
c
b
a
```

2. The memory used to hold the integer pointed to by **p** in object **o** that is used to call **neg( )** is freed when the copy of **o** is destroyed when **neg( )** terminates, even though this memory is still needed by **o** inside **main( )**.

3.3 *E**XERCISES*

1.
```
#include <iostream>
using namespace std;

class who {
  char name;
public:
  who(char c) {
     name = c;
     cout << "Constructing who #";
     cout << name << "\n";
  }
  ~who() { cout << "Destructing who #" << name << "\n"; }
};

who makewho()
{
  who temp('B');
  return temp;
}

int main()
{
  who ob('A');

  makewho();

  return 0;
}
```

2. There are several situations in which it would be improper to return an object. Here is one: if an object opens a disk file when it is created and closes that file when it is destroyed, if that object is returned from a function, the file will be closed when the temporary object is destroyed.

3.4 *E**XERCISE*

1.
```
#include <iostream>
using namespace std;
```

```cpp
class pr2;  // forward declaration

class pr1 {
  int printing;
  // ...
public:
  pr1() { printing = 0; }
  void set_print(int status) { printing = status; }
  // ...
  friend int inuse(pr1 o1, pr2 o2);
};

class pr2 {
  int printing;
  // ...
public:
  pr2() { printing = 0; }
  void set_print(int status) { printing = status; }
  // ...
  friend int inuse(pr1 o1, pr2 o2);
};

// Return true if printer is in use.
int inuse(pr1 o1, pr2 o2)
{
  if(o1.printing || o2.printing) return 1;
  else return 0;
}

int main()
{
  pr1 p1;
  pr2 p2;

  if(!inuse(p1, p2)) cout << "Printer idle\n";

  cout << "Setting p1 to printing...\n";
  p1.set_print(1);
  if(inuse(p1, p2)) cout << "Now, printer in use.\n";

  cout << "Turn off p1...\n";
  p1.set_print(0);
  if(!inuse(p1, p2)) cout << "Printer idle\n";

  cout << "Turn on p2...\n";
```

```
    p2.set_print(1);
    if(inuse(p1, p2)) cout << "Now, printer in use.\n";

    return 0;
}
```

*M*ASTERY SKILLS CHECK: Chapter 3

1. For one object to be assigned to another, both must be of the same class type.

2. The trouble with the assignment of **ob1** to **ob2** is that the memory pointed to by **ob2**'s initial value of **p** is now lost because this value is overwritten by the assignment. This memory thus becomes impossible to free, and the memory pointed to by **ob1**'s **p** is freed twice when it is destroyed—possibly causing damage to the dynamic allocation system.

3.
```
int light(planet p)
{
    return p.get_miles() / 186000;
}
```

4. Yes.

5.
```
// Load a stack with the alphabet.
#include <iostream>
using namespace std;

#define SIZE 27

// Declare a stack class for characters.
class stack {
    char stck[SIZE]; // holds the stack
    int tos; // index of top of stack
public:
    stack(); // constructor
    void push(char ch); // push character on stack
    char pop(); // pop character from stack
};

// Initialize the stack.
stack::stack()
{
```

```
    cout << "Constructing a stack\n";
    tos = 0;
  }

  // Push a character.
  void stack::push(char ch)
  {
    if(tos==SIZE) {
      cout << "Stack is full\n";
      return;
    }
    stck[tos] = ch;
    tos++;
  }

  // Pop a character.
  char stack::pop()
  {
    if(tos==0) {
      cout << "Stack is empty\n";
      return 0; // return null on empty stack
    }
    tos--;
    return stck[tos];
  }

  void showstack(stack o);
  stack loadstack();

  int main()
  {
    stack s1;

    s1 = loadstack();
    showstack(s1);

    return 0;
  }

  // Display the contents of a stack.
  void showstack(stack o)

  {
    char c;
```

```
  // when this statement ends, the o stack is empty
  while(c=o.pop()) cout << c << "\n";
  cout << "\n";
}

// Load a stack with the letters of the alphabet.
stack loadstack()
{
  stack t;
  char c;
  for(c = 'a'; c <= 'z'; c++) t.push(c);
  return t;
}
```

6. When passing an object to a function or returning an object from a function, temporary copies of the object are created that will be destroyed when the function terminates. When a temporary copy of an object is destroyed, the destructor function might destroy something that is needed elsewhere in the program.

7. A friend is a nonmember function that is granted access to the private members of the class for which it is a friend.

CUMULATIVE SKILLS CHECK: Chapter 3

```
1. // Load a stack with the alphabet.
   #include <iostream>
   #include <cctype>
   using namespace std;

   #define SIZE 27

   // Declare a stack class for characters.
   class stack {
     char stck[SIZE]; // holds the stack
     int tos; // index of top of stack
   public:
     stack(); // constructor
     void push(char ch); // push character on stack
     char pop(); // pop character from stack
   };

   // Initialize the stack.
```

```cpp
stack::stack()
{
  cout << "Constructing a stack\n";
  tos = 0;
}

// Push a character.
void stack::push(char ch)
{
  if(tos==SIZE) {
    cout << "Stack is full\n";
    return;
  }
  stck[tos] = ch;
  tos++;
}

// Pop a character.
char stack::pop()
{
  if(tos==0) {
    cout << "Stack is empty\n";
    return 0; // return null on empty stack
  }
  tos--;
  return stck[tos];
}

void showstack(stack o);
stack loadstack();
stack loadstack(int upper);

int main()
{
  stack s1, s2, s3;

  s1 = loadstack();
  showstack(s1);

  // get uppercase letters
  s2 = loadstack(1);
  showstack(s2);

  // use lowercase letters
  s3 = loadstack(0);
```

```
  showstack(s3);

  return 0;
}

// Display the contents of a stack.
void showstack(stack o)
{
  char c;

  // when this statement ends, the o stack is empty
  while(c=o.pop()) cout << c << "\n";
  cout << "\n";
}

// Load a stack with the letters of the alphabet.
stack loadstack()
{
  stack t;
  char c;

  for(c = 'a'; c<='z'; c++) t.push(c);
  return t;
}

/* Load a stack with the letters of the alphabet. Uppercase
   letters if upper is 1; lowercase otherwise. */
stack loadstack(int upper)
{
  stack t;
  char c;

  if(upper) c = 'A';
  else c = 'a';

  for(; toupper(c)<='Z'; c++) t.push(c);
  return t;
}
```

```
2. #include <iostream>
   #include <cstring>
   #include <cstdlib>
   using namespace std;
```

```
class strtype {
  char *p;
  int len;
public:
  strtype(char *ptr);
  ~strtype();
  void show();
  friend char *get_string(strtype *ob);
};

strtype::strtype(char *ptr)
{
  len = strlen(ptr);
  p = (char *) malloc(len+1);
  if(!p) {
    cout << "Allocation error\n";
    exit(1);
  }
  strcpy(p, ptr);
}

strtype::~strtype()
{
  cout << "Freeing p\n";
  free(p);
}

void strtype::show()
{
  cout << p << " - length: " << len;
  cout << "\n";
}

char *get_string(strtype *ob)
{
  return ob->p;
}

int main()
{
  strtype s1("This is a test.");

  char *s;
```

```
    s1.show();

    // get pointer to string
    s = get_string(&s1);
    cout << "Here is string contained in s1: ";
    cout << s << "\n";

    return 0;
}
```

3. The outcome of the experiment is as follows: Yes, data from the base class is also copied when an object of a derived class is assigned to another object of the same derived class. Here is a program that demonstrates this fact:

```
#include <iostream>
using namespace std;

class base {
  int a;
public:
  void load_a(int n) { a = n; }
  int get_a() { return a; }
};

class derived : public base {
  int b;
public:
  void load_b(int n) { b = n; }
  int get_b() { return b; }
};

int main()
{
  derived ob1, ob2;

  ob1.load_a(5);
  ob1.load_b(10);

  // assign ob1 to ob2
  ob2 = ob1;

  cout << "Here is ob1's a and b: ";
  cout << ob1.get_a() << ' ' << ob1.get_b() << "\n";
```

```
    cout << "Here is ob2's a and b: ";
    cout << ob2.get_a() << ' ' << ob2.get_b() << "\n";

    /* As you can probably guess, the output is the same for
       each object. */

    return 0;
}
```

REVIEW SKILLS CHECK: Chapter 4

1. When one object is assigned to another of the same type, the current values of all data members of the object on the right are assigned to the corresponding data members on the left.

2. Trouble can occur when one object is assigned to another if that assignment overwrites important data already existing in the target object. For example, a pointer to dynamic memory or to an open file can be overwritten and, therefore, lost.

3. When an object is passed to a function, a copy is made. However, the copy's constructor function is not called. The copy's destructor is called when the object is destroyed by the termination of the function.

4. The violation of the separation between an argument and its copy when passed to a parameter can be caused by several situations. For example, if dynamic memory is freed by a destructor, that memory will also be lost to the argument. In general, if the destructor function destroys anything that the original argument requires, damage to the argument will occur.

5.
```
#include <iostream>
using namespace std;

class summation {
  int num;
  long sum; // summation of num
public:
  void set_sum(int n);
  void show_sum() {
    cout << num << " summed is " << sum << "\n";
  }
};
```

```
void summation::set_sum(int n)
{
  int i;

  num = n;

  sum = 0;
  for(i=1; i<=n; i++)
    sum += i;
}

summation make_sum()
{
  int i;
  summation temp;

  cout << "Enter number: ";
  cin >> i;

  temp.set_sum(i);

  return temp;
}

int main()
{
  summation s;

  s = make_sum();

  s.show_sum();

  return 0;
}
```

6. For some compilers, in-line functions cannot contain loops.

7.
```
#include <iostream>
using namespace std;

class myclass {
  int num;
public:
  myclass(int x) { num = x; }
  friend int isneg(myclass ob);
```

```
};

int isneg(myclass ob)
{
  return (ob.num < 0) ? 1 : 0;
}

int main()
{
  myclass a(-1), b(2);

  cout << isneg(a) << ' ' << isneg(b);
  cout << "\n";

  return 0;
}
```

8. Yes, a friend function can be friends with more than one class.

4.1 # EXERCISES

1.
```
#include <iostream>
using namespace std;

class letters {
  char ch;
public:
  letters(char c) { ch = c; }
  char get_ch() { return ch; }
};

int main()
{
  letters ob[10] = { 'a', 'b', 'c','d', 'e', 'f',
                     'g', 'h', 'i', 'j' };

  int i;

  for(i=0; i<10; i++)
    cout << ob[i].get_ch() << ' ';

  cout << "\n";
```

```
      return 0;
    }

2. #include <iostream>
   using namespace std;

   class squares {
     int num, sqr;
   public:
     squares(int a, int b) { num = a; sqr = b; }
     void show() {cout << num << ' ' << sqr << "\n"; }
   };

   int main()
   {
     squares ob[10] = {
       squares(1, 1),
       squares(2, 4),
       squares(3, 9),
       squares(4, 16),
       squares(5, 25),
       squares(6, 36),
       squares(7, 49),
       squares(8, 64),
       squares(9, 81),
       squares(10, 100)
     };
     int i;

     for(i=0; i<10; i++) ob[i].show();

     return 0;
   }

3. #include <iostream>
   using namespace std;

   class letters {
     char ch;
   public:
     letters(char c) { ch = c; }
     char get_ch() { return ch; }
   };

   int main()
```

```
{
  letters ob[10] = {
    letters('a'),
    letters('b'),
    letters('c'),
    letters('d'),
    letters('e'),
    letters('f'),
    letters('g'),
    letters('h'),
    letters('i'),
    letters('j')
  };

  int i;

  for(i=0; i<10; i++)
    cout << ob[i].get_ch() << ' ';

  cout << "\n";

  return 0;
}
```

4.2 EXERCISES

```
1. // Display in reverse order.
   #include <iostream>
   using namespace std;

   class samp {
     int a, b;
   public:
     samp(int n, int m) { a = n; b = m; }
     int get_a() { return a; }
     int get_b() { return b; }
   };

   int main()
   {
     samp ob[4] = {
       samp(1, 2),
       samp(3, 4),
       samp(5, 6),
```

```
      samp(7, 8)
    };
    int i;

    samp *p;

    p = &ob[3]; // get address of last element

    for(i=0; i<4; i++) {
      cout << p->get_a() << ' ';
      cout << p->get_b() << "\n";
      p--;  // advance to previous object
    }

    cout << "\n";

    return 0;
  }
```

2.
```
/* Create a two-dimensional array of objects.
    Access via a pointer. */
#include <iostream>
using namespace std;

class samp {
  int a;
public:
  samp(int n) { a = n; }
  int get_a() { return a; }
};

int main()
{
  samp ob[4][2] = {
    1, 2,
    3, 4,
    5, 6,
    7, 8
  };
  int i;

  samp *p;

  p = (samp *) ob;
```

```
  for(i=0; i<4; i++) {
    cout << p->get_a() << ' ';
    p++;
    cout << p->get_a() << "\n";
    p++;
  }

  cout << "\n";

  return 0;
}
```

<table>
<tr><td>**4.3**</td><td>**E** **XERCISE**</td></tr>
</table>

1.
```
// Use this pointer.
#include <iostream>
using namespace std;

class myclass {
  int a, b;
public:
  myclass(int n, int m) { this->a = n; this->b = m; }
  int add() { return this->a + this->b; }
  void show();
};

void myclass::show()
{
  int t;

  t = this->add(); // call member function
  cout << t << "\n";
}

int main()
{
  myclass ob(10, 14);

  ob.show();

  return 0;
}
```

4.4 **E**XERCISES

```cpp
1. #include <iostream>
   using namespace std;

   int main()
   {
     float *f;
     long *l;
     char *c;

     f = new float;
     l = new long;
     c = new char;

     if(!f || !l || !c) {
       cout << "Allocation error.";
       return 1;
     }

     *f = 10.102;
     *l = 100000;
     *c = 'A';

     cout << *f << ' ' << *l << ' ' << *c;
     cout << '\n';

     delete f; delete l; delete c;

     return 0;
   }

2. #include <iostream>
   #include <cstring>
   using namespace std;

   class phone {
     char name[40];
     char number[14];
   public:
     void store(char *n, char *num);
     void show();
   };
```

```
void phone::store(char *n, char *num)
{
  strcpy(name, n);
  strcpy(number, num);
}

void phone::show()
{
  cout << name << ": " << number;
  cout << "\n";
}

int main()
{
  phone *p;

  p = new phone;

  if(!p) {
    cout << "Allocation error.";
    return 1;
  }

  p->store("Isaac Newton", "111 555-2323");

  p->show();

  delete p;

  return 0;
}
```

3. On failure, **new** will either return a null pointer or generate an exception. You must check your compiler's documentation to determine which approach is used. In Standard C++, **new** generates an exception by default.

4.5 EXERCISES

1. ```
   char *p;

   p = new char [100];
   ```
   ```

```
// ...
strcpy(p, "This is a test");
```

2.
```
#include <iostream>
using namespace std;

int main()
{
  double *p;

  p = new double (-123.0987);

  cout << *p << '\n';

  return 0;
}
```

4.6 EXERCISES

1.
```
#include <iostream>
using namespace std;

void rneg(int &i); // reference version
void pneg(int *i); // pointer version

int main()
{
  int i = 10;
  int j = 20;

  rneg(i);
  pneg(&j);

  cout << i << ' ' << j << '\n';

  return 0;
}

// using a reference parameter
void rneg(int &i)
{
  i = -i;
}
```

```
// using a pointer parameter
void pneg(int *i)
{
  *i = - *i;
}
```

2. When **triple( )** is called, the address of **d** is explicitly obtained with the **&** operator. This is neither necessary nor legal. When a reference parameter is used, the argument is not preceded by the **&**.

3. The address of a reference parameter is automatically passed to the function. You need not obtain the address manually. Passing by reference is often faster than passing by value. No copy of the argument is generated. Therefore, there is no chance of a side effect occurring because the copy's destructor is called.

4.7 **E**XERCISE

1. In the original program, the object is passed to **show( )** by value. Thus, a copy is made. When **show( )** returns, the copy is destroyed and its destructor is called. This causes **p** to be released, but the memory pointed to it is still needed by the arguments to **show( )**. Here is a corrected version that uses a reference parameter to prevent a copy from being made when the function is called:

```
// This program is now fixed.
#include <iostream>
#include <cstring>
#include <cstdlib>
using namespace std;

class strtype {
  char *p;
public:
  strtype(char *s);
  ~strtype() { delete [] p; }
  char *get() { return p; }
};

strtype::strtype(char *s)
{
```

```
      int l;

      l = strlen(s)+1;

      p = new char [l];
      if(!p) {
        cout << "Allocation error\n";
        exit(1);
      }

      strcpy(p, s);
    }

    // Fix by using a reference parameter.
    void show(strtype &x)
    {
      char *s;

      s = x.get();
      cout << s << "\n";
    }

    int main()
    {
      strtype a("Hello"), b("There");

      show(a);
      show(b);

      return 0;
    }
```

| 4.8 | ***EXERCISES*** |

```
1. // A simple bounded two-dimensional array example.
   #include <iostream>
   #include <cstdlib>
   using namespace std;

   class array {
     int isize, jsize;
     int *p;
   public:
     array(int i, int j);
```

```
  int &put(int i, int j);
  int get(int i, int j);
};

array::array(int i, int j)
{
  p = new int [i*j];
  if(!p) {
    cout << "Allocation error\n";
    exit(1);
  }
  isize = i;
  jsize = j;
}

// Put something into the array.
int &array::put(int i, int j)
{
  if(i<0 || i>=isize || j<0 || j>=jsize) {
    cout << "Bounds error!!!\n";
    exit(1);
  }
  return p[i*jsize + j];   // return reference to p[i]
}

// Get something from the array.
int array::get(int i, int j)
{
  if(i<0 || i>=isize || j<0 || j>=jsize) {
    cout << "Bounds error!!!\n";
    exit(1);
  }
  return p[i*jsize +j]; // return character
}

int main()
{
  array a(2, 3);
  int i, j;

  for(i=0; i<2; i++)
    for(j=0; j<3; j++)
      a.put(i, j) = i+j;

  for(i=0; i<2; i++)
```

```
      for(j=0; j<3; j++)
        cout << a.get(i, j) << ' ';

    // generate out of bounds
    a.put(10, 10);

    return 0;
  }
```

2. No. A reference returned by a function cannot be assigned to a pointer.

ASTERY SKILLS CHECK: CHAPTER 4

```
1. #include <iostream>
   using namespace std;

   class a_type {
     double a, b;
   public:
     a_type(double x, double y) {
       a = x;
       b = y;
     }
     void show() { cout << a << ' ' << b << '\n'; }
   };

   int main()
   {
     a_type ob[2][5] = {
       a_type(1, 1), a_type(2, 2),
       a_type(3, 3), a_type(4, 4),
       a_type(5, 5), a_type(6, 6),
       a_type(7, 7), a_type(8, 8),
       a_type(9, 9), a_type(10, 10)
     };

     int i, j;

     for(i=0; i<2; i++)
       for(j=0; j<5; j++)
         ob[i][j].show();
```

```
    cout << '\n';

    return 0;
  }

2. #include <iostream>
   using namespace std;

   class a_type {
     double a, b;
   public:
     a_type(double x, double y) {
       a = x;
       b = y;
     }
     void show() { cout << a << ' ' << b << '\n'; }
   };

   int main()
   {
     a_type ob[2][5] = {
       a_type(1, 1), a_type(2, 2),
       a_type(3, 3), a_type(4, 4),
       a_type(5, 5), a_type(6, 6),
       a_type(7, 7), a_type(8, 8),
       a_type(9, 9), a_type(10, 10)
     };

     a_type *p;

     p = (a_type *) ob;

     int i, j;

     for(i=0; i<2; i++)
       for(j=0; j<5; j++) {
         p->show();
         p++;
       }

     cout << '\n';

     return 0;
   }
```

3. The **this** pointer is a pointer that is automatically passed to a member function and that points to the object that generated the call.

4. The general forms of **new** and **delete** are

   p-var = new *type*;
   delete *p-var*;

   When using **new**, you don't need to use a type cast. The size of the object is automatically determined; you don't need to use **sizeof**. Also, you don't need to include < **cstdlib** > in your program.

5. A reference is essentially an implicit pointer constant that is effectively a different name for another variable or argument. One advantage of using a reference parameter is that no copy of the argument is made.

6. ```cpp
#include <iostream>
using namespace std;

void recip(double &d);

int main()
{
  double x = 100.0;

  cout << "x is " << x << '\n';

  recip(x);

  cout << "Reciprocal is " << x << '\n';

  return 0;
}

void recip(double &d)
{
  d = 1/d;
}
```
```

1. To access a member of an object by using a pointer, use the arrow (->) operator.

2.
```cpp
#include <iostream>
#include <cstring>
#include <cstdlib>
using namespace std;

class strtype {
  char *p;
  int len;
public:
  strtype(char *ptr);
  ~strtype();
  void show();
};

strtype::strtype(char *ptr)
{
  len = strlen(ptr);
  p = new char [len+1];
  if(!p) {
    cout << "Allocation error\n";
    exit(1);
  }
  strcpy(p, ptr);
}

strtype::~strtype()
{
  cout << "Freeing p\n";
  delete [] p;
}

void strtype::show()
{
  cout << p << " - length: " << len;
  cout << "\n";
}

int main()
{
```

```
strtype s1("This is a test."), s2("I like C++.");

s1.show();
s2.show();

return 0;
}
```

*R*EVIEW SKILLS CHECK: *Chapter 5*

1. A reference is a special type of pointer that is automatically dereferenced and that can be used interchangeably with the object it is pointing to. There are three types of references: parameter references, independent references, and references that are returned by functions.

2.
```
#include <iostream>
using namespace std;

int main()
{
  float *f;
  int *i;

  f = new float;
  i = new int;

  if(!f || !i) {
    cout << "Allocation error\n";
    return 1;
  }

  *f = 10.101;
  *i = 100;

  cout << *f << ' ' << *i << '\n';

  delete f;
  delete i;

  return 0;
}
```

3. The general form of **new** that includes an initializer is shown here:

p-var = new *type* (*initializer*);

For example, this allocates an integer and gives it the value 10:

```
int *p;

p = new int (10);
```

4.
```
#include <iostream>
using namespace std;

class samp {
    int x;
public:
    samp(int n) { x = n; }
    int getx() { return x; }
};

int main()
{
    samp A[10] = { 1, 2, 3, 4, 5, 6, 7, 8, 9, 10 };
    int i;

    for(i=0; i<10; i++) cout << A[i].getx() << ' ';

    cout << "\n";

    return 0;
}
```

5. Advantages: A reference parameter does not cause a copy of the object used in the call to be made. A reference is often faster to pass than a value. The reference parameter streamlines the call-by-reference syntax and procedure, reducing the chance for errors.

Disadvantages: Changes to a reference parameter alter the variable used in the call. A reference parameter opens the possibility of side effects in the calling routine.

6. No.

7.
```cpp
#include <iostream>
using namespace std;

void mag(long &num, long order);

int main()
{
  long n = 4;
  long o = 2;

  cout << "4 raised to the 2nd order of magnitude is ";
  mag(n, o);
  cout << n << '\n';

  return 0;
}

void mag(long &num, long order)
{
  for( ; order; order--) num = num * 10;
}
```

5.1 EXERCISES

1.
```cpp
#include <iostream>
#include <cstring>
#include <cstdlib>
using namespace std;

class strtype {
  char *p;
  int len;
public:
  strtype();
  strtype(char *s, int l);
  char *getstring() { return p; }
  int getlength() { return len; }
};

strtype::strtype()
{
  p = new char [255];
  if(!p) {
    cout << "Allocation error\n";
```

```
      exit(1);
    }
    *p = '\0'; // null string
    len = 255;
  }

strtype::strtype(char *s, int l)
{
  if(strlen(s) >= l) {
    cout << "Allocating too little memory!\n";
    exit(1);
  }

  p = new char [l];
  if(!p) {
    cout << "Allocation error\n";
    exit(1);
  }
  strcpy(p, s);
  len = l;
}

int main()
{
  strtype s1;
  strtype s2("This is a test", 100);

  cout << "s1: " << s1.getstring() << " - Length: ";
  cout << s1.getlength() << '\n';

  cout << "s2: " << s2.getstring() << " - Length: ";
  cout << s2.getlength() << '\n';

  return 0;
}
```

2.
```
// Stopwatch emulator
#include <iostream>
#include <ctime>
using namespace std;

class stopwatch {
  double begin, end;
public:
  stopwatch();
```

```
   stopwatch(clock_t t);
   ~stopwatch();
   void start();
   void stop();
   void show();
};

stopwatch::stopwatch()
{
  begin = end = 0.0;
}

stopwatch::stopwatch(clock_t t)
{
  begin = (double) t / CLOCKS_PER_SEC;
  end = 0.0;
}

stopwatch::~stopwatch()
{
  cout << "Stopwatch object being destroyed...";
  show();
}

void stopwatch::start()
{
  begin = (double) clock() / CLOCKS_PER_SEC;
}

void stopwatch::stop()
{
  end = (double) clock() / CLOCKS_PER_SEC;
}

void stopwatch::show()
{
  cout << "Elapsed time: " << end - begin;
  cout << "\n";
}

int main()
{
  stopwatch watch;
  long i;
```

```
watch.start();
for(i=0; i<320000; i++) ; // time a for loop
watch.stop();
watch.show();

// create object using initial value
stopwatch s2(clock());
for(i=0; i<250000; i++) ; // time a for loop
s2.stop();
s2.show();

return 0;
}
```

5.2   EXERCISES

1. The **obj** and **temp** objects are constructed normally. However, when **temp** is returned by **f( )**, a temporary object is made, and it is this temporary object that generates the call to the copy constructor.

2. As the program is written, when an object is passed to **getval( )**, a bitwise copy is made. When **getval( )** returns and that copy is destroyed, the memory allocated to that object (which is pointed to by **p**) is released. However, this is the same memory still required by the object used in the call to **getval( )**. The correct version of the program is shown here. It uses a copy constructor to avoid this problem.

```
// This program is now fixed.
#include <iostream>
#include <cstdlib>
using namespace std;

class myclass {
  int *p;
public:
  myclass(int i);
  myclass(const myclass &o); // copy constructor
  ~myclass() { delete p; }
  friend int getval(myclass o);
};
```

```cpp
myclass::myclass(int i)
{
  p = new int;

  if(!p) {
    cout << "Allocation error\n";
    exit(1);
  }
  *p = i;
}

// Copy constructor
myclass::myclass(const myclass &o)
{
  p = new int; // allocate copy's own memory

  if(!p) {
    cout << "Allocation error\n";
    exit(1);
  }
  *p = *o.p;
}

int getval(myclass o)
{
  return *o.p; // get value
}

int main()
{
  myclass a(1), b(2);

  cout << getval(a) << " " << getval(b);
  cout << "\n";
  cout << getval(a) << " " << getval(b);

  return 0;
}
```

3. A copy constructor is invoked when one object is used to initialize another. A normal constructor is called when an object is created.

5.4 EXERCISES

1.
```cpp
#include <iostream>
#include <cstdlib>
using namespace std;

long mystrtol(const char *s, char **end, int base = 10)
{
  return strtol(s, end, base);
}

int main()
{
  long x;
  char *s1 = "100234";
  char *p;

  x = mystrtol(s1, &p, 16);
  cout << "Base 16: " << x << '\n';

  x = mystrtol(s1, &p, 10);
  cout << "Base 10: " << x << '\n';

  x = mystrtol(s1, &p); // use default base of 10
  cout << "Base 10 by default: " << x << '\n';

  return 0;
}
```

2. All parameters taking default arguments must appear to the right of those that do not. That is, once you begin giving parameters defaults, all subsequent parameters must also have defaults. In the question, **q** is not given a default.

3. Since cursor positioning functions differ from compiler to compiler and environment to environment, only one possible solution is shown. The following program works for Borland C++ under a command-prompt environment.

```cpp
// Note: This program is Borland C++-specific.
#include <iostream>
#include <conio.h>
using namespace std;
```

```cpp
void myclreol(int len = -1);

int main()
{
  int i;

  gotoxy(1, 1);
  for(i=0; i<24; i++)
    cout << "abcdefghijklmnopqrstuvwxyz1234567890\n";

  gotoxy(1, 2);
  myclreol();
  gotoxy(1, 4);
  myclreol(20);

  return 0;
}
// Clear to end of line unless len parameter is specified.
void myclreol(int len)
{
  int x, y;

  x = wherex();  // get x position
  y = wherey();  // get y position

  if(len == -1) len = 80-x;

  int i = x;

  for( ; i<=len; i++) cout << ' ';

  gotoxy(x, y); // reset the cursor
}
```

4. A default argument cannot be another parameter or a local variable.

5.6	**E**XERCISE

```cpp
1. #include <iostream>
   using namespace std;

   int dif(int a, int b)
```

```
{
  return a-b;
}

float dif(float a, float b)
{
  return a-b;
}

int main()
{
  int (*p1)(int, int);
  float (*p2)(float, float);

  p1 = dif; // address of dif(int, int)
  p2 = dif; // address of dif(float, float);

  cout << p1(10, 5) << ' ';
  cout << p2(10.5, 8.9) << '\n';

  return 0;
}
```

■■■■■*M*ASTERY SKILLS CHECK: Chapter 5

```
1. // Overload date() for time_t.
   #include <iostream>
   #include <cstdio> // included for sscanf()
   #include <ctime>
   using namespace std;

   class date {
     int day, month, year;
   public:
     date(char *str);
     date(int m, int d, int y) {
       day = d;
       month = m;
       year = y;
     }
     // overload for parameter of type time_t
     date(time_t t);
     void show() {
       cout << month << '/' << day << '/';
```

```
      cout << year << '\n';
  }
};

date::date(char *str)
{
  sscanf(str, "%d%*c%d%*c%d", &month, &day, &year);
}

date::date(time_t t)
{
  struct tm *p;

  p = localtime(&t); // convert to broken down time
  day = p->tm_mday;
  month = p->tm_mon;
  year = p->tm_year;
}

int main()
{
  // construct date object using string
  date sdate("12/31/99");

  // construct date object using integers
  date idate(12, 31, 99);

  /* construct date object using time_t - this
     creates an object using the system date */
  date tdate(time(NULL));

  sdate.show();
  idate.show();
  tdate.show();

  return 0;
}
```

2. The class **samp** defines only one constructor, and this constructor requires an initializer. Therefore, it is improper to declare an object of type **samp** without one. (That is, **samp x** is an invalid declaration.)

3. One reason to overload a constructor is to provide flexibility, allowing you to choose the most appropriate constructor in the specific instance. Another is to allow both initialized and uninitialized objects to be declared. You might want to overload a constructor so that dynamic arrays can be allocated.

4. The most common general form of a copy constructor is shown here:

   classname (const *classname* &*obj*) {
       // *body of constructor*
   }

5. A copy constructor is called when an initialization takes place—specifically, when one object is explicitly used to initialize another, when an object is passed as a parameter to a function, and when a temporary object is created when an object is returned by a function.

6. The **overload** keyword is obsolete. In early versions of C++ it was used to tell the compiler that a function will be overloaded. It is not supported by modern compilers.

7. A default argument is a value that is given to a function parameter when no corresponding argument appears when the function is called.

8.
```cpp
#include <iostream>
#include <cstring>
using namespace std;

void reverse(char *str, int count = 0);

int main()
{
  char *s1 = "This is a test.";
  char *s2 = "I like C++.";

  reverse(s1); // reverse entire string
  reverse(s2, 7);  // reverse first 7 chars

  cout << s1 << '\n';
  cout << s2 << '\n';

  return 0;
```

```
  }

  void reverse(char *str, int count)
  {
    int i, j;
    char temp;

    if(!count) count = strlen(str)-1;

    for(i=0, j=count; i<j; i++, j--) {
      temp = str[i];
      str[i] = str[j];
      str[j] = temp;
    }
  }
```

9. All parameters receiving default arguments must appear to the right of those that do not.

10. Ambiguity can be introduced by default type conversions, reference parameters, and default arguments.

11. It is ambiguous because the compiler cannot know which version of **compute( )** to call. Is it the first version, with **divisor** defaulting? Or is it the second version, which takes only one parameter?

12. When you are obtaining the address of an overloaded function, it is the type specification of the pointer that determines which function is used.

*C*UMULATIVE SKILLS CHECK: *Chapter 5*

1.
```
#include <iostream>
using namespace std;

void order(int &a, int &b)
{
  int t;

  if(a<b) return;
  else { // swap a and b
    t = a;
    a = b;
    b = t;
```

```
    }
  }

  int main()
  {
    int x=10, y=5;

    cout << "x: " << x << ", y: " << y << "\n";

    order(x, y);
    cout << "x: " << x << ", y: " << y << "\n";

    return 0;
  }
```

2. The syntax for calling a function that takes a reference parameter is identical to the syntax for calling a function that takes a value parameter.

3. A default argument is essentially a shorthand approach to function overloading because the net result is the same. For example,

```
int f(int a, int b = 0);
```

is functionally equivalent to these two overloaded functions:

```
int f(int a);
```

```
int f(int a, int b);
```

4. ```
#include <iostream>
using namespace std;

class samp {
  int a;
public:
  samp() { a = 0; }
  samp(int n) { a = n; }
  int get_a() { return a; }
};

int main()
{
  samp ob(88);
```
```

```
    samp obarray[10];

    // ...
}
```

5. Copy constructors are needed when you, the programmer, must control precisely how a copy of an object is made. This is important only when the default bitwise copy creates undesired side effects.

REVIEW SKILLS CHECK: Chapter 6

```
1. class myclass {
     int x, y;
   public:
     myclass(int i, int j) { x=i; y=j; }
     myclass() { x=0; y=0; }
   };
```

```
2. class myclass {
     int x, y;
   public:
     myclass(int i=0, int j=0) { x=i; y=j; }
   };
```

3. Once default arguments have begun, a nondefaulting parameter cannot occur.

4. A function cannot be overloaded when the only difference is that one version takes a value parameter and the other takes a reference parameter. (The compiler cannot tell them apart.)

5. It is appropriate to use default arguments when there are one or more values that will occur frequently. It is inappropriate when there is no value or values that have a greater likelihood of occurring.

6. No, because there is no way to initialize a dynamic array. This class has only one constructor, and it requires initializers.

7. A copy constructor is a special constructor that is called when one object initializes another. This circumstance can occur in any of the following three ways: When one object is explicitly used to initialize another, when an object is passed to a function, or when a temporary object is created as a function return value.

| 6.2 | **E**XERCISES |

```cpp
1. // Overload the * and / relative to coord class.
   #include <iostream>
   using namespace std;

   class coord {
     int x, y; // coordinate values
   public:
     coord() { x=0; y=0; }
     coord(int i, int j) { x=i; y=j; }
     void get_xy(int &i, int &j) { i=x; j=y; }
     coord operator*(coord ob2);
     coord operator/(coord ob2);
   };

   // Overload * relative to coord class.
   coord coord::operator*(coord ob2)
   {
     coord temp;

     temp.x = x * ob2.x;
     temp.y = y * ob2.y;

     return temp;
   }

   // Overload / relative to coord class.
   coord coord::operator/(coord ob2)
   {
     coord temp;

     temp.x = x / ob2.x;
     temp.y = y / ob2.y;

     return temp;
   }

   int main()
   {
     coord o1(10, 10), o2(5, 3), o3;
     int x, y;

     o3 = o1 * o2;
```

```
    o3.get_xy(x, y);
    cout << "(o1*o2) X: " << x << ", Y: " << y << "\n";

    o3 = o1 / o2;
    o3.get_xy(x, y);
    cout << "(o1/o2) X: " << x << ", Y: " << y << "\n";

    return 0;
}
```

2. The overloading of the **%** operator is inappropriate because its operation is unrelated to the traditional use.

6.3 *E*XERCISE

```
1. // Overload the < and > relative to coord class.
   #include <iostream>
   using namespace std;

   class coord {
     int x, y; // coordinate values
   public:
     coord() { x=0; y=0; }
     coord(int i, int j) { x=i; y=j; }
     void get_xy(int &i, int &j) { i=x; j=y; }
     int operator<(coord ob2);
     int operator>(coord ob2);
   };

   // Overload the < operator for coord.
   int coord::operator<(coord ob2)
   {
     return x<ob2.x && y<ob2.y;
   }

   // Overload the > operator for coord.
   int coord::operator>(coord ob2)
   {
     return x>ob2.x && y>ob2.y;
   }

   int main()
   {
```

```
      coord o1(10, 10), o2(5, 3);

      if(o1>o2) cout << "o1 > o2\n";
      else cout << "o1 <= o2 \n";

      if(o1<o2) cout << "o1 < o2\n";
      else cout << "o1 >= o2\n";

      return 0;
}
```

6.4	***E****XERCISES*

```
1. // Overload the -- relative to coord class.
   #include <iostream>
   using namespace std;

   class coord {
     int x, y; // coordinate values
   public:
     coord() { x=0; y=0; }
     coord(int i, int j) { x=i; y=j; }
     void get_xy(int &i, int &j) { i=x; j=y; }
     coord operator--(); // prefix
     coord operator--(int notused); // postfix
   };

   // Overload prefix -- for coord class.
   coord coord::operator--()
   {
     x--;
     y--;
     return *this;
   }

   // Overload postfix -- for coord class.
   coord coord::operator--(int notused)
   {
     x--;
     y--;
     return *this;
   }

   int main()
```

```
{
  coord o1(10, 10);
  int x, y;

  o1--; // decrement an object
  o1.get_xy(x, y);
  cout << "(o1--) X: " << x << ", Y: " << y << "\n";

  --o1; // decrement an object
  o1.get_xy(x, y);
  cout << "(--o1) X: " << x << ", Y: " << y << "\n";
  return 0;
}
```

2.
```
// Overload the + relative to coord class.
#include <iostream>
using namespace std;

class coord {
  int x, y; // coordinate values
public:
  coord() { x=0; y=0; }
  coord(int i, int j) { x=i; y=j; }
  void get_xy(int &i, int &j) { i=x; j=y; }
  coord operator+(coord ob2); // binary plus
  coord operator+(); // unary plus
};

// Overload + relative to coord class.
coord coord::operator+(coord ob2)
{
  coord temp;

  temp.x = x + ob2.x;
  temp.y = y + ob2.y;

  return temp;
}

// Overload unary + for coord class.
coord coord::operator+()
{
  if(x<0) x = -x;
  if(y<0) y = -y;
```

```
    return *this;
}

int main()
{
  coord o1(10, 10), o2(-2, -2);
  int x, y;
  o1 = o1 + o2; // addition
  o1.get_xy(x, y);
  cout << "(o1+o2) X: " << x << ", Y: " << y << "\n";

  o2 = +o2; // absolute value
  o2.get_xy(x, y);
  cout << "(+o2) X: " << x << ", Y: " << y << "\n";

  return 0;
}
```

6.5 EXERCISES

1. ```
   /* Overload the - and / relative to coord class
      using friend functions. */
   #include <iostream>
   using namespace std;

   class coord {
     int x, y; // coordinate values
   public:
     coord() { x=0; y=0; }
     coord(int i, int j) { x=i; y=j; }
     void get_xy(int &i, int &j) { i=x; j=y; }
     friend coord operator-(coord ob1, coord ob2);
     friend coord operator/(coord ob1, coord ob2);
   };

   // Overload - relative to coord class using friend.
   coord operator-(coord ob1, coord ob2)
   {
     coord temp;

     temp.x = ob1.x - ob2.x;
     temp.y = ob1.y - ob2.y;

     return temp;
   ```
   ```

```
}

// Overload / relative to coord class using friend.
coord operator/(coord ob1, coord ob2)
{
  coord temp;

  temp.x = ob1.x / ob2.x;
  temp.y = ob1.y / ob2.y;

  return temp;
}

int main()
{
  coord o1(10, 10), o2(5, 3), o3;
  int x, y;

  o3 = o1 - o2;
  o3.get_xy(x, y);
  cout << "(o1-o2) X: " << x << ", Y: " << y << "\n";

  o3 = o1 / o2;
  o3.get_xy(x, y);
  cout << "(o1/o2) X: " << x << ", Y: " << y << "\n";

  return 0;
}
```

2.
```
// Overload the * for ob*int and int*ob.
#include <iostream>
using namespace std;

class coord {
  int x, y; // coordinate values
public:
  coord() { x=0; y=0; }
  coord(int i, int j) { x=i; y=j; }
  void get_xy(int &i, int &j) { i=x; j=y; }
  friend coord operator*(coord ob1, int i);
  friend coord operator*(int i, coord ob2);
};

// Overload * one way.
coord operator*(coord ob1, int i)
```

```
{
  coord temp;

  temp.x = ob1.x * i;
  temp.y = ob1.y * i;

  return temp;
}

// Overload * another way.
coord operator*(int i, coord ob2)
{
  coord temp;

  temp.x = ob2.x * i;
  temp.y = ob2.y * i;

  return temp;
}

int main()
{
  coord o1(10, 10), o2;
  int x, y;

  o2 = o1 * 2;  // ob * int
  o2.get_xy(x, y);
  cout << "(o1*2) X: " << x << ", Y: " << y << "\n";

  o2 = 3 * o1; // int * ob
  o2.get_xy(x, y);
  cout << "(3*o1) X: " << x << ", Y: " << y << "\n";

  return 0;
}
```

3. By using friend functions, you make it possible to have a built-in
   type as the left operand. When member functions are used, the
   left operand must be an object of the class for which the
   operator is defined.

4. ```
   // Overload the -- relative to coord class using a friend.
   #include <iostream>
   using namespace std;
   ```
   ```

```
class coord {
  int x, y; // coordinate values
public:
  coord() { x=0; y=0; }
  coord(int i, int j) { x=i; y=j; }
  void get_xy(int &i, int &j) { i=x; j=y; }
  friend coord operator--(coord &ob); // prefix
  friend coord operator--(coord &ob, int notused); // postfix
};

// Overload -- (prefix) for coord class using a friend.
coord operator--(coord &ob)
{
  ob.x--;
  ob.y--;
  return ob;
}

// Overload -- (postfix) for coord class using a friend.
coord operator--(coord &ob, int notused)
{
  ob.x--;
  ob.y--;
  return ob;
}

int main()
{
  coord o1(10, 10);
  int x, y;

  --o1; // decrement an object
  o1.get_xy(x, y);
  cout << "(--o1) X: " << x << ", Y: " << y << "\n";

  o1--; // decrement an object
  o1.get_xy(x, y);
  cout << "(o1--) X: " << x << ", Y: " << y << "\n";

  return 0;
}
```

6.6 **E**XERCISE

```cpp
1. #include <iostream>
   #include <cstdlib>
   using namespace std;

   class dynarray {
     int *p;
     int size;
   public:
     dynarray(int s);
     int &put(int i);
     int get(int i);
     dynarray &operator=(dynarray &ob);
   };

   // Constructor
   dynarray::dynarray(int s)
   {
     p = new int [s];
     if(!p) {
       cout << "Allocation error\n";
       exit(1);
     }

     size = s;
   }

   // Store an element.
   int &dynarray::put(int i)
   {
     if(i<0 || i>=size) {
       cout << "Bounds error!\n";
       exit(1);
     }

     return p[i];
   }

   // Get an element.
   int dynarray::get(int i)
   {
```

```
    if(i<0 || i>=size) {
      cout << "Bounds error!\n";
      exit(1);
    }

    return p[i];
}

// Overload = for dynarray.
dynarray &dynarray::operator=(dynarray &ob)
{
  int i;

  if(size!=ob.size) {
    cout << "Cannot copy arrays of differing sizes!\n";
    exit(1);
  }

  for(i = 0; i<size; i++) p[i] = ob.p[i];
  return *this;
}

int main()
{
  int i;

  dynarray ob1(10), ob2(10), ob3(100);

  ob1.put(3) = 10;
  i = ob1.get(3);
  cout << i << "\n";

  ob2 = ob1;

  i = ob2.get(3);
  cout << i << "\n";

  // generates an error
  ob1 = ob3; //  !!!
  return 0;
}
```

6.7 **E**XERCISES

```cpp
1. #include <iostream>
   #include <cstring>
   #include <cstdlib>
   using namespace std;

   class strtype {
     char *p;
     int len;
   public:
     strtype(char *s);
     ~strtype() {
       cout << "Freeing " << (unsigned) p << '\n';
       delete [] p;
     }
     char *get() { return p; }
     strtype &operator=(strtype &ob);
     char &operator[](int i);
   };

   strtype::strtype(char *s)
   {
     int l;

     l = strlen(s)+1;

     p = new char [l];
     if(!p) {
       cout << "Allocation error\n";
       exit(1);
     }

     len = l;
     strcpy(p, s);
   }

   // Assign an object.
   strtype &strtype::operator=(strtype &ob)
   {
     // see if more memory is needed
     if(len < ob.len) { // need to allocate more memory
       delete [] p;
```

```
    p = new char [ob.len];
    if(!p) {
      cout << "Allocation error\n";
      exit(1);
    }
  }
  len = ob.len;
  strcpy(p, ob.p);
  return *this;
}

// Index characters in string.
char &strtype::operator[](int i)
{
  if(i<0 || i>len-1) {
    cout << "\nIndex value of ";
    cout << i << " is out-of-bounds.\n";
    exit(1);
  }

  return p[i];
}

int main()
{
  strtype a("Hello"), b("There");

  cout << a.get() << '\n';
  cout << b.get() << '\n';

  a = b; // now p is not overwritten

  cout << a.get() << '\n';
  cout << b.get() << '\n';

  // access characters using array indexing
  cout << a[0] << a[1] << a[2] << "\n";

  // assign characters using array indexing
  a[0] = 'X';
  a[1] = 'Y';
  a[2] = 'Z';

  cout << a.get() << "\n";
```

```
      return 0;
    }

2. #include <iostream>
   #include <cstdlib>
   using namespace std;

   class dynarray {
     int *p;
     int size;
   public:
     dynarray(int s);
     dynarray &operator=(dynarray &ob);
     int &operator[](int i);
   };

   // Constructor
   dynarray::dynarray(int s)
   {
     p = new int [s];
     if(!p) {
       cout << "Allocation error\n";
       exit(1);
     }

     size = s;
   }

   // Overload = for dynarray.
   dynarray &dynarray::operator=(dynarray &ob)
   {
     int i;

     if(size!=ob.size) {
       cout << "Cannot copy arrays of differing sizes!\n";
       exit(1);
     }

     for(i = 0; i<size; i++) p[i] = ob.p[i];
     return *this;
   }

   // Overload []
   int &dynarray::operator[](int i)
   {
```

```
  if(i<0 || i>size) {
    cout << "\nIndex value of ";
    cout << i << " is out-of-bounds.\n";
    exit(1);
  }
  return p[i];
}

int main()
{
  int i;

  dynarray ob1(10), ob2(10), ob3(100);

  ob1[3] = 10;
  i = ob1[3];
  cout << i << "\n";

  ob2 = ob1;

  i = ob2[3];
  cout << i << "\n";

  // generates an error
  ob1 = ob3; //  arrays differ sizes
  return 0;
}
```

MASTERY SKILLS CHECK: Chapter 6

```
1. // Overload << and >>.
   #include <iostream>
   using namespace std;

   class coord {
     int x, y; // coordinate values
   public:
     coord() { x=0; y=0; }
     coord(int i, int j) { x=i; y=j; }
     void get_xy(int &i, int &j) { i=x; j=y; }
     coord operator<<(int i);
     coord operator>>(int i);
   };
```

```
// Overload <<.
coord coord::operator<<(int i)
{
  coord temp;

  temp.x = x << i;
  temp.y = y << i;

  return temp;
}

// Overload >>.
coord coord::operator>>(int i)
{
  coord temp;

  temp.x = x >> i;
  temp.y = y >> i;

  return temp;
}

int main()
{
  coord o1(4, 4), o2;
  int x, y;

  o2 = o1 << 2;  // ob << int
  o2.get_xy(x, y);
  cout << "(o1<<2) X: " << x << ", Y: " << y << "\n";

  o2 = o1 >> 2; // ob >> int
  o2.get_xy(x, y);
  cout << "(o1>>2) X: " << x << ", Y: " << y << "\n";

  return 0;
}
```

2.
```
#include <iostream>
using namespace std;

class three_d {
  int x, y, z;
public:
  three_d(int i, int j, int k)
```

```
      {
        x = i; y = j; z = k;
      }
      three_d() { x=0; y=0; z=0; }
      void get(int &i, int &j, int &k)
      {
        i = x; j = y; k = z;
      }
      three_d operator+(three_d ob2);
      three_d operator-(three_d ob2);
      three_d operator++();
      three_d operator--();
    };

three_d three_d::operator+(three_d ob2)
{
  three_d temp;
  temp.x = x + ob2.x;
  temp.y = y + ob2.y;
  temp.z = z + ob2.z;

  return temp;
}

three_d three_d::operator-(three_d ob2)
{
  three_d temp;

  temp.x = x - ob2.x;
  temp.y = y - ob2.y;
  temp.z = z - ob2.z;

  return temp;
}

three_d three_d::operator++()
{
  x++;
  y++;
  z++;

  return *this;
}

three_d three_d::operator--()
```

```
{
  x--;
  y--;
  z--;

  return *this;
}

int main()
{
  three_d o1(10, 10, 10), o2(2, 3, 4), o3;
  int x, y, z;

  o3 = o1 + o2;
  o3.get(x, y, z);
  cout << "X: " << x << ", Y: " << y;
  cout << ", Z: " << z << "\n";

  o3 = o1 - o2;
  o3.get(x, y, z);
  cout << "X: " << x << ", Y: " << y;
  cout << ", Z: " << z << "\n";

  ++o1;
  o1.get(x, y, z);
  cout << "X: " << x << ", Y: " << y;
  cout << ", Z: " << z << "\n";

  --o1;
  o1.get(x, y, z);
  cout << "X: " << x << ", Y: " << y;
  cout << ", Z: " << z << "\n";

  return 0;
}
```

3.
```
#include <iostream>
using namespace std;

class three_d {
  int x, y, z;
public:
  three_d(int i, int j, int k)
  {
    x = i; y = j; z = k;
```

```
  }
  three_d() { x=0; y=0; z=0; }
  void get(int &i, int &j, int &k)
  {
     i = x; j = y; k = z;
  }
  three_d operator+(three_d &ob2);
  three_d operator-(three_d &ob2);
  friend three_d operator++(three_d &ob);
  friend three_d operator--(three_d &ob);
 };

three_d three_d::operator+(three_d &ob2)
{
  three_d temp;

  temp.x = x + ob2.x;
  temp.y = y + ob2.y;
  temp.z = z + ob2.z;

  return temp;
}

three_d three_d::operator-(three_d &ob2)
{
  three_d temp;

  temp.x = x - ob2.x;
  temp.y = y - ob2.y;
  temp.z = z - ob2.z;

  return temp;
}

three_d operator++(three_d &ob)
{
  ob.x++;
  ob.y++;
  ob.z++;

  return ob;
}

three_d operator--(three_d &ob)
{
```

```
    ob.x--;
    ob.y--;
    ob.z--;

    return ob;
}

int main()
{
  three_d o1(10, 10, 10), o2(2, 3, 4), o3;
  int x, y, z;

  o3 = o1 + o2;
  o3.get(x, y, z);
  cout << "X: " << x << ", Y: " << y;
  cout << ", Z: " << z << "\n";

  o3 = o1 - o2;
  o3.get(x, y, z);
  cout << "X: " << x << ", Y: " << y;
  cout << ", Z: " << z << "\n";

  ++o1;
  o1.get(x, y, z);
  cout << "X: " << x << ", Y: " << y;
  cout << ", Z: " << z << "\n";

  --o1;
  o1.get(x, y, z);
  cout << "X: " << x << ", Y: " << y;
  cout << ", Z: " << z << "\n";

  return 0;
}
```

4. A binary member operator function is passed the left operand implicitly via the **this** pointer. A binary friend operator function is passed both operands explicitly. Unary member operator functions have no explicit parameters. A friend unary operator function has one parameter.

5. You will need to overload the = operator when the default bitwise copy is insufficient. For example, you might have a situation in which you want only parts of the data in one object to be assigned to another object.

6. No.

7.
```cpp
#include <iostream>
using namespace std;

class three_d {
  int x, y, z;
public:
  three_d(int i, int j, int k)
  {
    x = i; y = j; z = k;
  }
  three_d() { x=0; y=0; z=0; }
  void get(int &i, int &j, int &k)
  {
    i = x; j = y; k = z;
  }
  friend three_d operator+(three_d ob, int i);
  friend three_d operator+(int i, three_d ob);
};

three_d operator+(three_d ob, int i)
{
  three_d temp;
  temp.x = ob.x + i;
  temp.y = ob.y + i;
  temp.z = ob.z + i;

  return temp;
}

three_d operator+(int i, three_d ob)
{
  three_d temp;

  temp.x = ob.x + i;
  temp.y = ob.y + i;
  temp.z = ob.z + i;

  return temp;
}

int main()
{
  three_d o1(10, 10, 10);
```

```
     int x, y, z;

     o1 = o1 + 10;
     o1.get(x, y, z);
     cout << "X: " << x << ", Y: " << y;
     cout << ", Z: " << z << "\n";

     o1 = -20 + o1;
     o1.get(x, y, z);
     cout << "X: " << x << ", Y: " << y;
     cout << ", Z: " << z << "\n";

     return 0;
   }
```

8.
```
   #include <iostream>
   using namespace std;

   class three_d {
     int x, y, z;
   public:
     three_d(int i, int j, int k)
     {
       x = i; y = j; z = k;
     }
     three_d() { x=0; y=0; z=0; }
     void get(int &i, int &j, int &k)
     {
       i = x; j = y; k = z;
     }
     int operator==(three_d ob2);
     int operator!=(three_d ob2);
     int operator||(three_d ob2);
   };

   int three_d::operator==(three_d ob2)
   {
     return x==ob2.x && y==ob2.y && z==ob2.z;
   }

   int three_d::operator!=(three_d ob2)
   {
     return x!=ob2.x && y!=ob2.y && z!=ob2.z;
   }
```

```
int three_d::operator||(three_d ob2)
{
  return x||ob2.x && y||ob2.y && z||ob2.z;
}

int main()
{
  three_d o1(10, 10, 10), o2(2, 3, 4), o3(0, 0, 0);

  if(o1==o1) cout << "o1 == o1\n";

  if(o1!=o2) cout << "o1 != o2\n";

  if(o3 || o1) cout << "o1 or o3 is true\n";

  return 0;
}
```

9. The **[ ]** is usually overloaded to allow an array encapsulated within a class to be indexed with the normal array indexing syntax.

*C*UMULATIVE SKILLS CHECK: *Chapter 6*

1. ```
   /*
       For clarity, no error checking has been used. However
       you should add some if using this code for a real
       application.
   */
   #include <iostream>
   #include <cstring>
   using namespace std;

   class strtype {
     char s[80];
   public:
     strtype() { *s = '\0'; }
     strtype(char *p) { strcpy(s, p); }
     char *get() { return s; }
     strtype operator+(strtype s2);
     strtype operator=(strtype s2);
     int operator<(strtype s2);
     int operator>(strtype s2);
     int operator==(strtype s2);
   ```
   ```

```cpp
};

strtype strtype::operator+(strtype s2)
{
  strtype temp;

  strcpy(temp.s, s);
  strcat(temp.s, s2.s);

  return temp;
}

strtype strtype::operator=(strtype s2)
{
  strcpy(s, s2.s);

  return *this;
}

int strtype::operator<(strtype s2)
{
  return strcmp(s, s2.s) < 0;
}

int strtype::operator>(strtype s2)
{
  return strcmp(s, s2.s) > 0;
}

int strtype::operator==(strtype s2)
{
  return strcmp(s, s2.s) == 0;
}

int main()
{
  strtype o1("Hello"), o2(" There"), o3;

  o3 = o1 + o2;
  cout << o3.get() << "\n";

  o3 = o1;
  if(o1==o3) cout << "o1 equals o3\n";
```

```
if(o1>o2) cout << "o1 > o2\n";

  if(o1<o2) cout << "o1 < o2\n";

  return 0;
}
```

REVIEW SKILLS CHECK: Chapter 7

1. No. Overloading an operator simply expands the data types upon which it can operate, but no preexisting operations are affected.

2. Yes. You cannot overload an operator relative to one of C++'s built-in types.

3. No, the precedence cannot be changed. No, the number of operands cannot be altered.

4.
```
#include <iostream>
using namespace std;

class array {
  int nums[10];
public:
  array();
  void set(int n[10]);
  void show();
  array operator+(array ob2);
  array operator-(array ob2);
  int operator==(array ob2);
};

array::array()
{
  int i;
  for(i=0; i<10; i++) nums[i] = 0;
}

void array::set(int *n)
{
  int i;
```

```
    for(i=0; i<10; i++) nums[i] = n[i];
}

void array::show()
{
  int i;

  for(i=0; i<10; i++)
    cout << nums[i] << ' ';

  cout << "\n";
}

array array::operator+(array ob2)
{
  int i;
  array temp;

  for(i=0; i<10; i++)
    temp.nums[i] = nums[i] + ob2.nums[i];

  return temp;
}

array array::operator-(array ob2)
{
  int i;
  array temp;

  for(i=0; i<10; i++)
    temp.nums[i] = nums[i] - ob2.nums[i];

  return temp;
}

int array::operator==(array ob2)
{
  int i;

  for(i=0; i<10; i++)
    if(nums[i]!=ob2.nums[i]) return 0;
```

```
      return 1;
    }

    int main()
    {
      array o1, o2, o3;

      int i[10] = { 1, 2, 3, 4, 5, 6, 7, 8, 9, 10 };

      o1.set(i);
      o2.set(i);

      o3 = o1 + o2;
      o3.show();

      o3 = o1 - o3;
      o3.show();

      if(o1==o2) cout << "o1 equals o2\n";
      else cout << "o1 does not equal o2\n";

      if(o1==o3) cout << "o1 equals o3\n";
      else cout << "o1 does not equal o3\n";

      return 0;
    }
```

5. ```
   #include <iostream>
   using namespace std;

   class array {
     int nums[10];
   public:
     array();
     void set(int n[10]);
     void show();
     friend array operator+(array ob1, array ob2);
     friend array operator-(array ob1, array ob2);
     friend int operator==(array ob1, array ob2);
   };

   array::array()
   {
     int i;
     for(i=0; i<10; i++) nums[i] = 0;
   ```
   ```

```
}

void array::set(int *n)
{
  int i;

  for(i=0; i<10; i++) nums[i] = n[i];
}

void array::show()
{
  int i;

  for(i=0; i<10; i++)
    cout << nums[i] << ' ';

  cout << "\n";
}

array operator+(array ob1, array ob2)
{
  int i;
  array temp;

  for(i=0; i<10; i++)
    temp.nums[i] = ob1.nums[i] + ob2.nums[i];

  return temp;
}

array operator-(array ob1, array ob2)
{
  int i;
  array temp;

  for(i=0; i<10; i++)
    temp.nums[i] = ob1.nums[i] - ob2.nums[i];

  return temp;
}

int operator==(array ob1, array ob2)
```

```
{
  int i;

  for(i=0; i<10; i++)
    if(ob1.nums[i]!=ob2.nums[i]) return 0;

  return 1;
}

int main()
{
  array o1, o2, o3;

  int i[10] = { 1, 2, 3, 4, 5, 6, 7, 8, 9, 10 };

  o1.set(i);
  o2.set(i);

  o3 = o1 + o2;
  o3.show();

  o3 = o1 - o3;
  o3.show();

  if(o1==o2) cout << "o1 equals o2\n";
  else cout << "o1 does not equal o2\n";

  if(o1==o3) cout << "o1 equals o3\n";
  else cout << "o1 does not equal o3\n";

  return 0;
}
```

6.
```
#include <iostream>
using namespace std;

class array {
  int nums[10];
public:
  array();
  void set(int n[10]);
  void show();
  array operator++();
```

```
  friend array operator--(array &ob);
};

array::array()
{
  int i;

  for(i=0; i<10; i++) nums[i] = 0;
}

void array::set(int *n)
{
  int i;

  for(i=0; i<10; i++) nums[i] = n[i];
}

void array::show()
{
  int i;

  for(i=0; i<10; i++)
    cout << nums[i] << ' ';

  cout << "\n";
}

// Overload unary op using member function.
array array::operator++()
{
  int i;

  for(i=0; i<10; i++)
    nums[i]++;

  return *this;
}

// Use a friend.
array operator--(array &ob)
{
  int i;

  for(i=0; i<10; i++)
```

```
      ob.nums[i]--;

    return ob;
  }

  int main()
  {
    array o1, o2, o3;

    int i[10] = { 1, 2, 3, 4, 5, 6, 7, 8, 9, 10 };

    o1.set(i);
    o2.set(i);

    o3 = ++o1;
    o3.show();

    o3 = --o1;
    o3.show();

    return 0;
  }
```

7. No. To overload the assignment operator you must use a member function.

7.1 ■ **E**XERCISES

1. A and C are legal statements.

2. A public member of a base becomes a public member of a derived class when it is inherited as public. When a public member of a base is inherited as private, it becomes a private member of the derived class.

7.2 ■ **E**XERCISES

1. When a protected member of a base class is inherited as public, it becomes a protected member of the derived class. If it is inherited as private, it becomes a private member of the derived class. If it is inherited as protected, it becomes a protected member of the derived class.

2. The protected category is needed to allow a base class to keep certain members private while still allowing a derived class to have access to them.

3. No.

7.3 EXERCISES

1.
```cpp
#include <iostream>
#include <cstring>
using namespace std;

class mybase {
  char str[80];
public:
  mybase(char *s) { strcpy(str, s); }
  char *get() { return str; }
};

class myderived : public mybase {
  int len;
public:
  myderived(char *s) : mybase(s) {
    len = strlen(s);
  }
  int getlen() { return len; }
  void show() { cout << get() << '\n'; }
};

int main()
{
  myderived ob("hello");

  ob.show();
  cout << ob.getlen() << '\n';

  return 0;
}
```

2.
```cpp
#include <iostream>
using namespace std;

// A base class for various types of vehicles.
class vehicle {
```

```
    int num_wheels;
    int range;
public:
    vehicle(int w, int r)
    {
      num_wheels = w; range = r;
    }
    void showv()
    {
      cout << "Wheels: " << num_wheels << '\n';
      cout << "Range: " << range << '\n';
    }
};

class car : public vehicle {
    int passengers;
public:
    car(int p, int w, int r) : vehicle(w, r)
    {
      passengers = p;
    }
    void show()
    {
      showv();
      cout << "Passengers: " << passengers << '\n';
    }
};

class truck : public vehicle {
    int loadlimit;
public:
    truck(int l, int w, int r) : vehicle(w, r)
    {
      loadlimit = l;
    }
    void show()
    {
      showv();
      cout << "loadlimit " << loadlimit << '\n';
    }
};

int main()
{
  car c(5, 4, 500);
```

```
    truck t(30000, 12, 1200);

    cout << "Car: \n";
    c.show();
    cout << "\nTruck:\n";
    t.show();

    return 0;
}
```

EXERCISES

1. Constructing A
   Constructing B
   Constructing C
   Destructing C
   Destructing B
   Destructing A

2. ```
   #include <iostream>
   using namespace std;

   class A {
     int i;
   public:
     A(int a) { i = a; }
   };

   class B {
     int j;
   public:
     B(int a) { j = a; }
   };

   class C : public A, public B {
     int k;
   public:
     C(int c, int b, int a) : A(a), B(b) {
       k = c;
     }
   };
   ```
   ```

7.5	

*E*XERCISES

2. A virtual base class is needed when a derived class inherits two (or more) classes, both of which are derived from the same base class. Without virtual base classes, two (or more) copies of the common base class would exist in the final derived class. However, if the original base is virtual, only one copy is present in the final derived class.

*M*ASTERY SKILLS CHECK: *Chapter 7*

```cpp
1. #include <iostream>
   using namespace std;

   class building {
   protected:
     int floors;
     int rooms;
     double footage;
   };

   class house : public building {
     int bedrooms;
     int bathrooms;
   public:
     house(int f, int r, double ft, int br, int bth) {
       floors = f;  rooms = r;  footage = ft;
       bedrooms = br; bathrooms = bth;
     }
     void show() {
       cout << "floors: " << floors << '\n';
       cout << "rooms: " << rooms << '\n';
       cout << "square footage: " << footage << '\n';
       cout << "bedrooms: " << bedrooms << '\n';
       cout << "bathrooms: " << bathrooms << '\n';
     }
   };

   class office : public building {
     int phones;
```

```
      int extinguishers;
    public:
      office(int f, int r, double ft, int p, int ext) {
        floors = f;  rooms = r;  footage = ft;
        phones = p; extinguishers = ext;
      }
      void show() {
        cout << "floors: " << floors << '\n';
        cout << "rooms: " << rooms << '\n';
        cout << "square footage: " << footage << '\n';
        cout << "Telephones: " << phones << '\n';
        cout << "fire extinguishers: ";
        cout << extinguishers << '\n';
      }
    };

    int main()
    {
      house h_ob(2, 12, 5000, 6, 4);
      office o_ob(4, 25, 12000, 30, 8);

      cout << "House: \n";
      h_ob.show();

      cout << "\nOffice: \n";
      o_ob.show();

      return 0;
    }
```

2. When a base class is inherited as public, the public members of
   the base become public members of the derived class, and the
   base's private members remain private to the base. If the base is
   inherited as private, all members of the base become private
   members of the derived class.

3. Members declared as **protected** are private to the base class but
   can be inherited (and accessed) by any derived class. When
   used as an inheritance access specifier, **protected** causes all
   public and protected members of the base class to become
   protected members of the derived class.

4. Constructors are called in order of derivation. Destructors are
   called in reverse order.

5.
```cpp
#include <iostream>
using namespace std;

class planet {
protected:
  double distance; // miles from the sun
  int revolve;   // in days
public:
  planet(double d, int r) { distance = d; revolve = r; }
};

class earth : public planet {
  double circumference; // circumference or orbit
public:
  earth(double d, int r) : planet(d, r) {
    circumference = 2*distance*3.1416;
  }
  void show() {
    cout << "Distance from sun: " << distance << '\n';
    cout << "Days in orbit: " << revolve << '\n';
    cout << "Circumference of orbit: ";
    cout << circumference << '\n';
  }
};

int main()
{
  earth ob(93000000, 365);

  ob.show();

  return 0;
}
```

6. To fix the program, have **motorized** and **road_use** inherit **vehicle** as a virtual base class. Also, refer to Question 1 in the Cumulative Skills Check in this chapter.

*C*UMULATIVE SKILLS CHECK: *Chapter 7*

1. Some compilers will not allow you to use a **switch** in an in-line function. If this is the case with your compiler, the functions were automatically made into "regular" functions.

2. The assignment operator is the only operator that is not inherited. The reason for this is easy to understand. Since a derived class will contain members not found in the base **class**, the overloaded = relative to the base has no knowledge of the members added by the derived class and, as such, cannot properly copy those new members.

REVIEW SKILLS CHECK: Chapter 8

1.
```
#include <iostream>
using namespace std;

class airship {
protected:
  int passengers;
  double cargo;
};

class airplane : public airship {
  char engine; // p for propeller, j for jet
  double range;
public:
  airplane(int p, double c, char e, double r)
  {
    passengers = p;
    cargo = c;
    engine = e;
    range = r;
  }
  void show();
};

class balloon : public airship {
  char gas; // h for hydrogen, e for helium
  double altitude;
public:
  balloon(int p, double c, char g, double a)
  {
    passengers = p;
    cargo = c;
    gas = g;
    altitude = a;
  }
```

```
    void show();
};

void airplane::show()
{
  cout << "Passengers: " << passengers << '\n';
  cout << "Cargo capacity: " << cargo << '\n';
  cout << "Engine: ";
  if(engine=='p') cout << "Propeller\n";
  else cout << "Jet\n";
  cout << "Range: " << range << '\n';
}

void balloon::show()
{
  cout << "Passengers: " << passengers << '\n';
  cout << "Cargo capacity: " << cargo << '\n';
  cout << "Gas: ";
  if(gas=='h') cout << "Hydrogen\n";
  else cout << "Helium\n";
  cout << "Altitude: " << altitude << '\n';
}

int main()
{
  balloon b(2, 500.0, 'h', 12000.0);
  airplane b727(100, 40000.0, 'j', 40000.0);

  b.show();
  cout << '\n';
  b727.show();

  return 0;
}
```

2. The **protected** access specifier causes a class member to be private to its class but still accessible by any derived class.

3. The program displays the following output, which indicates when the constructors and destructors are called.

```
Constructing A
Constructing B
Constructing C
Destructing C
```

```
Destructing B
Destructing A
```

4. Constructors are called in the order ABC, destructors in the order CBA.

5.
```cpp
#include <iostream>
using namespace std;

class base {
  int i, j;
public:
  base(int x, int y) { i = x; j = y; }
  void showij() { cout << i << ' ' << j << '\n'; }
};

class derived : public base {
  int k;
public:
  derived(int a, int b, int c) : base(b, c) {
    k = a;
  }
  void show() { cout << k << ' '; showij(); }
};

int main()
{
  derived ob(1, 2, 3);

  ob.show();

  return 0;
}
```

6. The missing words are "general" and "specific."

8.2 **E**XERCISES

1.
```cpp
#include <iostream>
using namespace std;

int main()
{
```

```
        cout.setf(ios::showpos);

        cout << -10 << ' ' << 10 << '\n';

        return 0;
    }
```

2.
```
#include <iostream>
using namespace std;

int main()
{
    cout.setf(ios::showpoint | ios::uppercase |
              ios::scientific);

    cout << 100.0;

    return 0;
}
```

3.
```
#include <iostream>
using namespace std;

int main()
{
    ios::fmtflags f;

    f = cout.flags(); // store flags

    cout.unsetf(ios::dec);
    cout.setf(ios::showbase | ios::hex);
    cout << 100 << '\n';

    cout.flags(f); // reset flags

    return 0;
}
```

8.3 EXERCISES

1.
```
// Create a table of log10 and log from 2 through 100.
#include <iostream>
#include <cmath>
```

```cpp
using namespace std;

int main()
{
  double x;

  cout.precision(5);
  cout << "           x        log x        ln e\n\n";

  for(x = 2.0; x <= 100.0; x++) {
    cout.width(10);
    cout << x << "   ";
    cout.width(10);
    cout << log10(x) << "   ";
    cout.width(10);
    cout << log(x) << '\n';
  }

  return 0;
}
```

2.
```cpp
#include <iostream>
#include <cstring>
using namespace std;

void center(char *s);

int main()
{
  center("Hi there!");
  center("I like C++.");

  return 0;
}

void center(char *s)
{
  int len;

  len = 40+(strlen(s)/2);

  cout.width(len);
  cout << s << '\n';
}
```

1a.
```cpp
// Create a table of log10 and log from 2 to 100.
#include <iostream>
#include <iomanip>
#include <cmath>
using namespace std;

int main()
{
  double x;

  cout << setprecision(5);
  cout << "          x          log x          ln e\n\n";

  for(x = 2.0; x <= 100.0; x++) {
    cout << setw(10) << x << "  ";
    cout << setw(10) << log10(x) << "  ";
    cout << setw(10) << log(x) << '\n';
  }

  return 0;
}
```

1b.
```cpp
#include <iostream>
#include <iomanip>
#include <cstring>
using namespace std;

void center(char *s);

int main()
{
  center("Hi there!");
  center("I like C++.");

  return 0;
}

void center(char *s)
{
  int len;
```

```
  len = 40+(strlen(s)/2);

  cout << setw(len) << s << '\n';
}
```

2. `cout << setiosflags(ios::showbase | ios::hex) << 100;`

3. Setting the **boolalpha** flag on an output stream causes Boolean values to be displayed using the words *true* and *false*. Setting **boolalpha** on an input stream allows you to enter Boolean values using the words *true* and *false*.

8.5 EXERCISES

1.
```
#include <iostream>
#include <cstring>
#include <cstdlib>
using namespace std;

class strtype {
  char *p;
  int len;
public:
  strtype(char *ptr);
  ~strtype() {delete [] p;}
  friend ostream &operator<<(ostream &stream, strtype &ob);
};

strtype::strtype(char *ptr)
{
  len = strlen(ptr)+1;
  p = new char [len];
  if(!p) {
    cout << "Allocation error\n";
    exit(1);
  }
  strcpy(p, ptr);
}

ostream &operator<<(ostream &stream, strtype &ob)
{
  stream << ob.p;
```

```
    return stream;
  }

  int main()
  {
    strtype s1("This is a test."), s2("I like C++.");

    cout << s1;
    cout << endl << s2 << endl;

    return 0;
  }
```

2.
```
#include <iostream>
using namespace std;

class planet {
protected:
  double distance; // miles from the sun
  int revolve;     // in days
public:
  planet(double d, int r) { distance = d; revolve = r; }
};

class earth : public planet {
  double circumference; // circumference or orbit
public:
  earth(double d, int r) : planet(d, r) {
    circumference = 2*distance*3.1416;
  }

  friend ostream &operator<<(ostream &stream, earth ob);
};

ostream &operator<<(ostream &stream, earth ob)
{
  stream << "Distance from sun: " << ob.distance << '\n';
  stream << "Days in orbit: " << ob.revolve << '\n';
  stream << "Circumference of orbit: " << ob.circumference;
  stream << '\n';

  return stream;
}
```

```
int main()
{
  earth ob(93000000, 365);

  cout << ob;

  return 0;
}
```

3. An inserter cannot be a member function because the object that generates a call to the inserter is *not* an object of a user-defined class.

8.6   EXERCISES

1.
```
#include <iostream>
#include <cstring>
#include <cstdlib>
using namespace std;

class strtype {
  char *p;
  int len;
public:
  strtype(char *ptr);
  ~strtype() {delete [] p;}
  friend ostream &operator<<(ostream &stream, strtype &ob);
  friend istream &operator>>(istream &stream, strtype &ob);
};

strtype::strtype(char *ptr)
{
  len = strlen(ptr)+1;
  p = new char [len];
  if(!p) {
    cout << "Allocation error\n";
    exit(1);
  }
  strcpy(p, ptr);
}

ostream &operator<<(ostream &stream, strtype &ob)
{
```

```
    stream << ob.p;

    return stream;
}

istream &operator>>(istream &stream, strtype &ob)
{
  char temp[255];

  stream >> temp;

  if(strlen(temp) >= ob.len) {
    delete [] ob.p;
    ob.len = strlen(temp)+1;
    ob.p = new char [ob.len];
    if(!ob.p) {
      cout << "Allocation error\n";
      exit(1);
    }
  }
  strcpy(ob.p, temp);

  return stream;
}

int main()
{
  strtype s1("This is a test."), s2("I like C++.");

  cout << s1;
  cout << '\n' << s2;

  cout << "\nEnter a string: ";
  cin >> s1;
  cout << s1;

  return 0;
}
```

2.
```
#include <iostream>
using namespace std;

class factor {
  int num; // number
  int lfact; // lowest factor
public:
```

```
    factor(int i);
    friend ostream &operator<<(ostream &stream, factor ob);
    friend istream &operator>>(istream &stream, factor &ob);
};

factor::factor(int i)
{
  int n;

  num = i;

  for(n=2; n < (i/2); n++)
    if(!(i%n)) break;

  if(n<(i/2)) lfact = n;
  else lfact = 1;
}

istream &operator>>(istream &stream, factor &ob)
{
  stream >> ob.num;

  int n;

  for(n=2; n < (ob.num/2); n++)
    if(!(ob.num%n)) break;
  if(n<(ob.num/2)) ob.lfact = n;
  else ob.lfact = 1;

  return stream;
}

ostream &operator<<(ostream &stream, factor ob)
{
  stream << ob.lfact << " is lowest factor of ";
  stream << ob.num << '\n';

  return stream;
}

int main()
{
  factor o(32);
```

```
    cout << o;

    cin >> o;
    cout << o;

    return 0;
}
```

***M**ASTERY SKILLS CHECK: Chapter 8*

1.
```
#include <iostream>
using namespace std;

int main()
{
  cout << 100 << ' ';

  cout.unsetf(ios::dec); // clear dec flag
  cout.setf(ios::hex);
  cout << 100 << ' ';

  cout.unsetf(ios::hex); // clear hex flag
  cout.setf(ios::oct);
  cout << 100 << '\n';

  return 0;
}
```

2.
```
#include <iostream>
using namespace std;

int main()
{
  cout.setf(ios::left);
  cout.precision(2);
  cout.fill('*');
  cout.width(20);

  cout << 1000.5364 << '\n';

  return 0;
}
```

```
3a. #include <iostream>
    using namespace std;

    int main()
    {
      cout << 100 << ' ';

      cout << hex << 100 << ' ';

      cout << oct << 100 << '\n';

      return 0;
    }

3b. #include <iostream>
    #include <iomanip>
    using namespace std;

    int main()
    {
      cout << setiosflags(ios::left);
      cout << setprecision(2);
      cout << setfill('*');
      cout << setw(20);

      cout << 1000.5364 << '\n';

      return 0;
    }

 4. ios::fmtflags f;

    f = cout.flags();  // save

    // ...

    cout.flags(f); // restore

 5. #include <iostream>
    using namespace std;

    class pwr {
      int base;
      int exponent;
      double result; // base to the exponent power
```

```
public:
  pwr(int b, int e);
  friend ostream &operator<<(ostream &stream, pwr ob);
  friend istream &operator>>(istream &stream, pwr &ob);
};

pwr::pwr(int b, int e)
{
  base = b;
  exponent = e;

  result = 1;
  for( ; e; e--) result = result * base;
}

ostream &operator<<(ostream &stream, pwr ob)
{
  stream << ob.base << "^" << ob.exponent;
  stream << " is " << ob.result << '\n';

  return stream;
}

istream &operator>>(istream &stream, pwr &ob)
{
  int b, e;

  cout << "Enter base and exponent: ";
  stream >> b >> e;

  pwr temp(b, e); // create temporary

  ob = temp;

  return stream;
}

int main()
{
  pwr ob(10, 2);

  cout << ob;

  cin >> ob;
```

```
      cout << ob;

      return 0;
    }

6.  // This program draws boxes.
    #include <iostream>
    using namespace std;

    class box {
      int len;
    public:
      box(int l) { len = l; }
      friend ostream &operator<<(ostream &stream, box ob);
    };

    // Draw a box.
    ostream &operator<<(ostream &stream, box ob)
    {
      int i, j;

      for(i=0; i<ob.len; i++) stream << '*';
      stream << '\n';
      for(i=0; i<ob.len-2; i++) {
        stream << '*';
        for(j=0; j<ob.len-2; j++) stream << ' ';
        stream << "*\n";
      }
      for(i=0; i<ob.len; i++) stream << '*';
      stream << '\n';

      return stream;
    }

    int main()
    {
      box b1(4), b2(7);

      cout << b1 << endl << b2;

      return 0;
    }
```

CUMULATIVE SKILLS CHECK: Chapter 8

```cpp
1. #include <iostream>
   using namespace std;

   #define SIZE 10

   // Declare a stack class for characters
   class stack {
     char stck[SIZE]; // holds the stack
     int tos; // index of top of stack
   public:
     stack();
     void push(char ch); // push character on stack
     char pop(); // pop character from stack
     friend ostream &operator<<(ostream &stream, stack ob);
   };

   // Initialize the stack
   stack::stack()
   {
     tos = 0;
   }

   // Push a character.
   void stack::push(char ch)
   {
     if(tos==SIZE) {
       cout << "Stack is full\n";
       return;
     }
     stck[tos] = ch;
     tos++;
   }

   // Pop a character.
   char stack::pop()
   {
     if(tos==0) {
       cout << "Stack is empty\n";
       return 0; // return null on empty stack
     }
```

```
      tos--;
      return stck[tos];
    }

    ostream &operator<<(ostream &stream, stack ob)
    {
      char ch;

      while(ch=ob.pop()) stream << ch;
      stream << endl;

      return stream;
    }

    int main()
    {
      stack s;

      s.push('a');
      s.push('b');
      s.push('c');

      cout << s;
      cout << s;

      return 0;
    }
```

2. ```
   #include <iostream>
   #include <ctime>
   using namespace std;

   class watch {
     time_t t;
   public:
     watch() { t = time(NULL); }
     friend ostream &operator<<(ostream &stream, watch ob);
   };

   ostream &operator<<(ostream &stream, watch ob)
   {
     struct tm *localt;

     localt = localtime(&ob.t);
     stream << asctime(localt) << endl;
   ```
   ```

```
    return stream;
  }

  int main()
  {
    watch w;

    cout << w;

    return 0;
  }

3. #include <iostream>
   using namespace std;

   class ft_to_inches {
     double feet;
     double inches;
   public:
     void set(double f) {
       feet = f;
       inches = f * 12;
     }
     friend istream &operator>>(istream &stream,
                                ft_to_inches &ob);
     friend ostream &operator<<(ostream &stream,
                                ft_to_inches ob);
   };

   istream &operator>>(istream &stream, ft_to_inches &ob)
   {
     double f;

     cout << "Enter feet: ";
     stream >> f;
     ob.set(f);

     return stream;
   }

   ostream &operator<<(ostream &stream, ft_to_inches ob)
   {
     stream << ob.feet << " feet is " << ob.inches;
     stream << " inches\n";
```

```
    return stream;
}

int main()
{
  ft_to_inches x;

  cin >> x;
  cout << x;

  return 0;
}
```

REVIEW SKILLS CHECK: Chapter 9

1.
```
#include <iostream>
using namespace std;

int main()
{
  cout.width(40);
  cout.fill(':');

  cout << "C++ is fun" << '\n';

  return 0;
}
```

2.
```
#include <iostream>
using namespace std;

int main()
{
  cout.precision(4);
  cout << 10.0/3.0 << '\n';

  return 0;
}
```

3.
```
#include <iostream>
#include <iomanip>
using namespace std;

int main()
```

```
{
  cout << setprecision(4) << 10.0/3.0 << '\n';

  return 0;
}
```

4. An inserter is an overloaded **operator << ( )** function that outputs a class's data to an output stream. An extractor is an overloaded **operator >> ( )** function that inputs a class's data from an input stream.

5.
```
#include <iostream>
using namespace std;

class date {
  char d[9]; // store date as string: mm/dd/yy
public:
  friend ostream &operator<<(ostream &stream, date ob);
  friend istream &operator>>(istream &stream, date &ob);
};

ostream &operator<<(ostream &stream, date ob)
{
  stream << ob.d << '\n';

  return stream;
}

istream &operator>>(istream &stream, date &ob)
{
  cout << "Enter date (mm/dd/yy): ";
  stream >> ob.d;

  return stream;
}

int main()
{
  date ob;

  cin >> ob;
  cout << ob;

  return 0;
}
```

6. To use a parameterized manipulator, you must include **< iomanip >** in your program.

7. The predefined streams are **cin**, **cout**, **cerr**, and **clog**.

9.1

EXERCISES

1.
```cpp
// Show time and date.
#include <iostream>
#include <ctime>
using namespace std;

// A time and date output manipulator.
ostream &td(ostream &stream)
{
  struct tm *localt;
  time_t t;

  t = time(NULL);
  localt = localtime(&t);
  stream << asctime(localt) << endl;

  return stream;
}

int main()
{
  cout << td << '\n';

  return 0;
}
```

2.
```cpp
#include <iostream>
using namespace std;

// Turn on hex output with uppercase X.
ostream &sethex(ostream &stream)
{
  stream.unsetf(ios::dec | ios::oct);
  stream.setf(ios::hex | ios::uppercase |
              ios::showbase);
```

```
    return stream;
}

// Reset flags.
ostream &reset(ostream &stream)
{
  stream.unsetf(ios::hex | ios::uppercase |
                ios::showbase);
  stream.setf(ios::dec);
  return stream;
}

int main()
{
  cout << sethex << 100 << '\n';
  cout << reset << 100 << '\n';

  return 0;
}
```

3. ```
   #include <iostream>
   using namespace std;

   // Skip 10 characters.
   istream &skipchar(istream &stream)
   {
     int i;
     char c;

     for(i=0; i<10; i++) stream >> c;

     return stream;
   }

   int main()
   {
     char str[80];

     cout << "Enter some characters: ";
     cin >> skipchar >> str;

     cout << str << '\n';

     return 0;
   }
   ```
   ```

Exercises

1.
```cpp
// Copy a text file and display number of chars copied.
#include <iostream>
#include <fstream>
using namespace std;

int main(int argc, char *argv[])
{
  if(argc!=3) {
    cout << "Usage: CPY <input> <output>\n";
    return 1;
  }

  ifstream fin(argv[1]); // open input file
  ofstream fout(argv[2]);  // create output file

  if(!fin) {
    cout << "Cannot open input file.\n";
    return 1;
  }

  if(!fout) {
    cout << "Cannot open output file.\n";
    return 1;
  }

  char ch;
  unsigned count=0;

  fin.unsetf(ios::skipws);  // do not skip spaces
  while(!fin.eof()) {
    fin >> ch;
    if(!fin.eof()) {
      fout << ch;
      count++;
    }
  }

  cout << "Number of bytes copied: " << count << '\n';

  fin.close();
  fout.close();
```

```
    return 0;
}
```

The reason this program might display a result different
from that shown when you list the directory is that some
character translations might be taking place. Specifically,
when a carriage-return/linefeed sequence is read, it is
converted into a newline. When output, newlines are counted
as one character but converted back into a carriage-return/
linefeed sequence again.

2.
```cpp
#include <iostream>
#include <fstream>
using namespace std;

int main()
{
  ofstream pout("phone");

  if(!pout) {
    cout << "Cannot open PHONE file.\n";
    return 1;
  }

  pout << "Isaac Newton   415 555-3423\n";
  pout << "Robert Goddard 213 555-2312\n";
  pout << "Enrico Fermi   202 555-1111\n";

  pout.close();

  return 0;
}
```

3.
```cpp
// Word count.
#include <iostream>
#include <fstream>
#include <cctype>
using namespace std;

int main(int argc, char *argv[])
{
  if(argc!=2) {
    cout << "Usage: COUNT <input>\n";
```

```
      return 1;
   }

   ifstream in(argv[1]);

   if(!in) {
     cout << "Cannot open input file.\n";
     return 1;
   }

   int count=0;
   char ch;

   in >> ch; // find first non-space char

   // after first non-space found, do not skip spaces
   in.unsetf(ios::skipws); // do not skip spaces

   while(!in.eof()) {
     in >> ch;
     if(isspace(ch)) {
       count++;
       while(isspace(ch) && !in.eof()) in >> ch;
     }
   }

   cout << "Word count: " << count << '\n';

   in.close();

   return 0;
}
```

4. The **is_open( )** function returns true if the invoking stream is linked to an open file.

9.3   EXERCISES

```
1a. // Copy a file and display number of chars copied.
    #include <iostream>
    #include <fstream>
    using namespace std;
```

```
int main(int argc, char *argv[])
{
  if(argc!=3) {
    cout << "Usage: CPY <input> <output>\n";
    return 1;
  }

  ifstream fin(argv[1], ios::in | ios::binary); // open input file
  ofstream fout(argv[2], ios::out | ios::binary); // create output file

  if(!fin) {
    cout << "Cannot open input file\n";
    return 1;
  }

  if(!fout) {
    cout << "Cannot open output file\n";
    return 1;
  }

  char ch;
  unsigned count=0;

  while(!fin.eof()) {
    fin.get(ch);
    if(!fin.eof()) {
      fout.put(ch);
      count++;
    }
  }

  cout << "Number of bytes copied: " << count << '\n';

  fin.close();
  fout.close();

  return 0;
}
```

1b.
```
// Word count.
#include <iostream>
#include <fstream>
#include <cctype>
using namespace std;
```

```
       int main(int argc, char *argv[])
       {
         if(argc!=2) {
           cout << "Usage: COUNT <input>\n";
           return 1;
         }

         ifstream in(argv[1], ios::in | ios::binary);

         if(!in) {
           cout << "Cannot open input file.\n";
           return 1;
         }

         int count=0;
         char ch;

         // find first non-space char
         do {
           in.get(ch);
         } while(isspace(ch));

         while(!in.eof()) {
           in.get(ch);
           if(isspace(ch)) {
             count++;
             while(isspace(ch) && !in.eof()) in.get(ch); // find next word
           }
         }

         cout << "Word count: " << count << '\n';

         in.close();

         return 0;
       }

    2. // Output account info to a file using an inserter.
       #include <iostream>
       #include <fstream>
       #include <cstring>
       using namespace std;

       class account {
         int custnum;
```

```
      char name[80];
      double balance;
    public:
      account(int c, char *n, double b)
      {
        custnum = c;
        strcpy(name, n);
        balance = b;
      }
      friend ostream &operator<<(ostream &stream, account ob);
    };

    ostream &operator<<(ostream &stream, account ob)
    {
      stream << ob.custnum << ' ';
      stream << ob.name << ' ' << ob.balance;
      stream << '\n';

      return stream;
    }

    int main()
    {
      account  Rex(1011, "Ralph Rex", 12323.34);
      ofstream out("accounts", ios::out | ios::binary);

      if(!out) {
        cout << "Cannot open output file.\n";
        return 1;
      }

      out << Rex;

      out.close();

      return 0;
    }
```

9.4 EXERCISES

1. ```
   // Use get() to read a string that contains spaces.
   #include <iostream>
   #include <fstream>
   ```
   ```

```
using namespace std;

int main()
{
  char str[80];

  cout << "Enter your name: ";
  cin.get(str, 79);

  cout << str << '\n';

  return 0;
}
```

The program functions the same whether it uses **get( )** or **getline( )**.

2.
```
// Use getline() to display a text file.
#include <iostream>
#include <fstream>
using namespace std;

int main(int argc, char *argv[])
{
  if(argc!=2) {
    cout << "usage: PR <filename>\n";
    return 1;
  }

  ifstream in(argv[1]);

  if(!in) {
    cout << "Cannot open input file.\n";
    return 1;
  }

  char str[255];

  while(!in.eof()) {
    in.getline(str, 254);
    cout << str << '\n';
  }

  in.close();
```

```
      return 0;
    }
```

9.5 — *E*XERCISES

1.
```
// Display a file backwards on the screen.
#include <iostream>
#include <fstream>
using namespace std;

int main(int argc, char *argv[])
{
  if(argc!=2) {
    cout << "usage: REVERSE <filename>\n";
    return 1;
  }

  ifstream in(argv[1], ios::in | ios::binary);

  if(!in) {
    cout << "Cannot open input file.\n";
    return 1;
  }

  char ch;
  long i;

  // go to end of file (less eof char)
  in.seekg(0, ios::end);
  i = (long) in.tellg(); // see how many bytes in file
  i -= 2; // backup before eof

  for( ;i>=0; i--) {
    in.seekg(i, ios::beg);
    in.get(ch);
    cout << ch;
  }

  in.close();

  return 0;
}
```

2.
```cpp
// Swap characters in a file.
#include <iostream>
#include <fstream>
using namespace std;

int main(int argc, char *argv[])
{
  if(argc!=2) {
    cout << "usage: SWAP <filename>\n";
    return 1;
  }

  // open file for input/output
  fstream io(argv[1], ios::in | ios::out | ios::binary);
  if(!io) {
    cout << "Cannot open file.\n";
    return 1;
  }

  char ch1, ch2;
  long i;

  for(i=0 ; !io.eof(); i+=2) {
    io.seekg(i, ios::beg);
    io.get(ch1);
    if(io.eof()) continue;
    io.get(ch2);
    if(io.eof()) continue;
    io.seekg(i, ios::beg);
    io.put(ch2);
    io.put(ch1);
  }

  io.close();

  return 0;
}
```

![9.6] **E**XERCISE

1a.
```cpp
/* Display a file backwards on the screen,
   plus error checking. */
#include <iostream>
#include <fstream>
```

```
using namespace std;

int main(int argc, char *argv[])
{
  if(argc!=2) {
    cout << "usage: REVERSE <filename>\n";
    return 1;
  }

  ifstream in(argv[1], ios::in | ios::binary);

  if(!in) {
    cout << "Cannot open input file\n";
    return 1;
  }

  char ch;
  long i;

  // go to end of file (less eof char)
  in.seekg(0, ios::end);
  if(!in.good()) return 1;
  i = (long) in.tellg(); // see how many bytes in file
  if(!in.good()) return 1;
  i -= 2; // backup before eof

  for( ;i>=0; i--) {
    in.seekg(i, ios::beg);
    if(!in.good()) return 1;
    in.get(ch);
    if(!in.good()) return 1;
    cout << ch;
  }

  in.close();
  if(!in.good()) return 1;

  return 0;
}
```

1b.
```
// Swap characters in a file with error checking.
#include <iostream>
#include <fstream>
using namespace std;
```

```cpp
int main(int argc, char *argv[])
{
  if(argc!=2) {
    cout << "usage: SWAP <filename>\n";
    return 1;
  }

  // open file for input/output
  fstream io(argv[1], ios::in | ios::out | ios::binary);

  if(!io) {
    cout << "Cannot open file.\n";
    return 1;
  }

  char ch1, ch2;
  long i;

  for(i=0 ;!io.eof(); i+=2) {
    io.seekg(i, ios::beg);
    if(!io.good()) return 1;
    io.get(ch1);
    if(io.eof()) continue;
    io.get(ch2);
    if(!io.good()) return 1;
    if(io.eof()) continue;
    io.seekg(i, ios::beg);
    if(!io.good()) return 1;
    io.put(ch2);
    if(!io.good()) return 1;
    io.put(ch1);
    if(!io.good()) return 1;
  }

  io.close();
  if(!io.good()) return 1;

  return 0;
}
```

░ **M**ASTERY SKILLS CHECK: Chapter 9

1.
```cpp
#include <iostream>
using namespace std;

ostream &tabs(ostream &stream)
{
  stream << '\t' << '\t' << '\t' ;
  stream.width(20);

  return stream;
}

int main()
{
  cout << tabs << "Testing\n";

  return 0;
}
```

2.
```cpp
#include <iostream>
#include <cctype>
using namespace std;

istream &findalpha(istream &stream)
{
  char ch;

  do {
    stream.get(ch);
  } while(!isalpha(ch));
  return stream;
}

int main()
{
  char str[80];

  cin >> findalpha >> str;
  cout << str << '\n';

  return 0;
}
```

3.
```cpp
// Copy a file and reverse case of letters.
#include <iostream>
#include <fstream>
#include <cctype>
using namespace std;

int main(int argc, char *argv[])
{
  char ch;

  if(argc!=3) {
    cout << "Usage: COPYREV <source> <target>\n";
    return 1;
  }

  ifstream in(argv[1]);

  if(!in) {
    cout << "Cannot open input file.\n";
    return 1;
  }

  ofstream out(argv[2]);

  if(!out) {
    cout << "Cannot open output file.\n";
    return 1;
  }

  while(!in.eof()) {
    ch = in.get();
    if(!in.eof()) {
      if(islower(ch)) ch = toupper(ch);
      else ch = tolower(ch);
      out.put(ch);
    }
  };

  in.close();
  out.close();

  return 0;
}
```

```
4. // Count letters.
   #include <iostream>
   #include <fstream>
   #include <cctype>
   using namespace std;

   int alpha[26];

   int main(int argc, char *argv[])
   {
     char ch;

     if(argc!=2) {
       cout << "Usage: COUNT <source>\n";
       return 1;
     }

     ifstream in(argv[1]);

     if(!in) {
       cout << "Cannot open input file.\n";
       return 1;
     }

     // init alpha[]
     int i;
     for(i=0; i<26; i++) alpha[i] = 0;

     while(!in.eof()) {
       ch = in.get();
       if(isalpha(ch)) { // if letter found, count it
         ch = toupper(ch); // normalize
         alpha[ch-'A']++; // 'A'-'A' == 0, 'B'-'A' == 1, etc.
       }
     };

     // display count
     for(i=0; i<26; i++) {
       cout << (char) ('A'+ i) << ": " << alpha[i] << '\n';
     }

     in.close();

     return 0;
   }
```

5a.
```cpp
/* Copy a file and reverse case of letters
     with error checking. */
#include <iostream>
#include <fstream>
#include <cctype>
using namespace std;

int main(int argc, char *argv[])
{
  char ch;

  if(argc!=3) {
    cout << "Usage: COPYREV <source> <target>\n";
    return 1;
  }

  ifstream in(argv[1]);

  if(!in) {
    cout << "Cannot open input file.\n";
    return 1;
  }

  ofstream out(argv[2]);

  if(!out) {
    cout << "Cannot open output file";
    return 1;
  }

  while(!in.eof()) {
    ch = in.get();
    if(!in.good() && !in.eof()) return 1;
    if(!in.eof()) {
      if(islower(ch)) ch = toupper(ch);
      else ch = tolower(ch);
      out.put(ch);
      if(!out.good()) return 1;
    }
  };

  in.close();
  out.close();
  if(!in.good() && !out.good()) return 1;
```

```
    return 0;
  }
```

5b.
```
// Count letters with error checking.
#include <iostream>
#include <fstream>
#include <cctype>
using namespace std;

int alpha[26];

int main(int argc, char *argv[])
{
  char ch;

  if(argc!=2) {
    cout << "Usage: COUNT <source>\n";
    return 1;
  }

  ifstream in(argv[1]);

  if(!in) {
    cout << "Cannot open input file.\n";
    return 1;
  }

  // init alpha[]
  int i;
  for(i=0; i<26; i++) alpha[i] = 0;

  while(!in.eof()) {
    ch = in.get();
    if(!in.good() && !in.eof()) return 1;
    if(isalpha(ch)) { // if letter found, count it
      ch = toupper(ch); // normalize
      alpha[ch-'A']++; // 'A'-'A' == 0, 'B'-'A' == 1, etc.
    }
  };

  // display count
  for(i=0; i<26; i++) {
    cout << (char) ('A'+ i) << ": " << alpha[i] << '\n';
  }
```

```
      in.close();
      if(!in.good()) return 1;

      return 0;
    }
```

6. To set the **get** pointer, use **seekg( )**. To set the **put** pointer, use **seekp( )**.

*C*UMULATIVE SKILLS CHECK: *Chapter 9*

```
1. #include <iostream>
   #include <fstream>
   #include <cstring>
   using namespace std;

   #define SIZE 40

   class inventory {
     char item[SIZE]; // name of item
     int onhand; // number on hand
     double cost;  // cost of item
   public:
     inventory(char *i, int o, double c)
     {
       strcpy(item, i);
       onhand = o;
       cost = c;
     }
     void store(fstream &stream);
     void retrieve(fstream &stream);
     friend ostream &operator<<(ostream &stream, inventory ob);
     friend istream &operator>>(istream &stream, inventory &ob);
   };

   ostream &operator<<(ostream &stream, inventory ob)
   {
     stream << ob.item << ": " << ob.onhand;
     stream << " on hand at $" << ob.cost << '\n';

     return stream;
   }

   istream &operator>>(istream &stream, inventory &ob)
```

```
{
  cout << "Enter item name: ";
  stream >> ob.item;
  cout << "Enter number on hand: ";
  stream >> ob.onhand;
  cout << "Enter cost: ";
  stream >> ob.cost;

  return stream;
}

void inventory::store(fstream &stream)
{
  stream.write(item, SIZE);
  stream.write((char *) &onhand, sizeof(int));
  stream.write((char *) &cost, sizeof(double));
}

void inventory::retrieve(fstream &stream)
{
  stream.read(item, SIZE);
  stream.read((char *) &onhand, sizeof(int));
  stream.read((char *) &cost, sizeof(double));
}

int main()
{

  fstream inv("inv", ios::out | ios::binary);
  int i;

  inventory pliers("pliers", 12, 4.95);
  inventory hammers("hammers", 5, 9.45);
  inventory wrenches("wrenches", 22, 13.90);
  inventory temp("", 0, 0.0);

  if(!inv) {
    cout << "Cannot open file for output.\n";
    return 1;
  }
  // write to file
  pliers.store(inv);
  hammers.store(inv);
  wrenches.store(inv);
```

```
      inv.close();

      // open for input
      inv.open("inv", ios::in | ios::binary);

      if(!inv) {
        cout << "Cannot open file for input.\n";
        return 1;
      }

      do {
        cout << "Record # (-1 to quit): ";
        cin >> i;
        if(i == -1) break;
        inv.seekg(i*(SIZE+sizeof(int)+sizeof(double)), ios::beg);
        temp.retrieve(inv);
        cout << temp;
      } while(inv.good());

      inv.close();

      return 0;
    }
```

REVIEW SKILLS CHECK: Chapter 10

```
1. #include <iostream>
   using namespace std;

   ostream &setsci(ostream &stream)
   {
     stream.setf(ios::scientific | ios::uppercase);

     return stream;
   }

   int main()
   {
     double f = 123.23;

     cout << setsci << f;
     cout << '\n';
```

```
      return 0;
    }

2.  // Copy and convert tabs to spaces.
    #include <iostream>
    #include <fstream>
    using namespace std;

    int main(int argc, char *argv[])
    {
      if(argc!=3) {
        cout << "Usage: CPY <in> <out>\n";
        return 1;
      }

      ifstream in(argv[1]);
      if(!in) {
        cout << "Cannot open input file.\n";
        return 1;
      }

      ofstream out(argv[2]);
      if(!out) {
        cout << "Cannot open output file.\n";
        return 1;
      }

      char ch;
      int i = 8;

      while(!in.eof()) {
        in.get(ch);
        if(ch=='\t') for( ; i>0; i--) out.put(' ');
        else out.put(ch);
        if(i == -1 || ch=='\n') i = 8;
        i--;
      }

      in.close();
      out.close();

      return 0;
    }
```

3.
```cpp
// Search file.
#include <iostream>
#include <fstream>
#include <cstring>
using namespace std;

int main(int argc, char *argv[])
{
  if(argc!=3) {
    cout << "Usage: SEARCH <file> <word>\n";
    return 1;
  }

  ifstream in(argv[1]);
  if(!in) {
    cout << "Cannot open input file.\n";
    return 1;
  }

  char str[255];
  int count=0;

  while(!in.eof()) {
    in >> str;
    if(!strcmp(str, argv[2])) count++;
  }

  cout << argv[2] << " found " << count;
  cout << " number of times.\n";

  in.close();

  return 0;
}
```

4. The statement is

```cpp
out.seekp(234, ios::beg);
```

5. The functions are **rdstate( )**, **good( )**, **eof( )**, **fail( )**, and **bad( )**.

6. The C++ I/O system can be customized to operate on classes that you create.

10.2   EXERCISES

1.
```cpp
#include <iostream>
using namespace std;

class num {
public:
  int i;
  num(int x) { i = x; }
  virtual void shownum() { cout << i << '\n'; }
};

class outhex : public num {
public:
  outhex(int n) : num(n) {}
  void shownum() { cout << hex << i << '\n'; }
};

class outoct : public num {
public:
  outoct(int n) : num(n) {}
  void shownum() { cout << oct << i << '\n'; }
};

int main()
{
  outoct o(10);
  outhex h(20);

  o.shownum();
  h.shownum();

  return 0;
}
```

2.
```cpp
#include <iostream>
using namespace std;

class dist {
public:
  double d;
  dist(double f) { d = f; }
  virtual void trav_time()
  {
```

```
        cout << "Travel time at 60 mph: ";
        cout << d / 60 << '\n';
      }
};

class metric : public dist {
public:
  metric(double f) : dist(f) {}
  void trav_time()
  {
    cout << "Travel time at 100 kph: ";
    cout << d / 100 << '\n';
  }
};

int main()
{
  dist *p, mph(88.0);
  metric kph(88);

  p = &mph;
  p->trav_time();

  p = &kph;
  p->trav_time();

  return 0;
}
```

10.3   EXERCISES

2. By definition, an abstract class contains at least one pure virtual
   function. This means that no body for that function exists
   relative to that class. Thus, there is no way that an object can be
   created because the class definition is not complete.

3. When **func( )** is called relative to **derived1**, it is the **func( )**
   inside **base** that is used. The reason this works is that virtual
   functions are hierarchical.

1.
```cpp
// Demonstrate virtual functions.
#include <iostream>
#include <cstdlib>
using namespace std;

class list {
public:
  list *head;  // pointer to start of list
  list *tail;  // pointer to end of list
  list *next;  // pointer to next item
  int num; // value to be stored

  list() { head = tail = next = NULL; }
  virtual void store(int i) = 0;
  virtual int retrieve() = 0;
};

// Create a queue-type list.
class queue : public list {
public:
  void store(int i);
  int retrieve();
};

void queue::store(int i)
{
  list *item;

  item = new queue;
  if(!item) {
    cout << "Allocation error.\n";
    exit(1);
  }
  item->num = i;

  // put on end of list
  if(tail) tail->next = item;
  tail = item;
  item->next = NULL;
  if(!head) head = tail;
}
```

```
int queue::retrieve()
{
  int i;
  list *p;

  if(!head) {
    cout << "List empty.\n";
    return 0;
  }

  // remove from start of list
  i = head->num;
  p = head;
  head = head->next;
  delete p;

  return i;
}

// Create a stack-type list.
class stack : public list {
public:
  void store(int i);
  int retrieve();
};

void stack::store(int i)
{
  list *item;

  item = new stack;
  if(!item) {
    cout << "Allocation error.\n";
    exit(1);
  }
  item->num = i;

  // put on front of list for stack-like operation
  if(head) item->next = head;
  head = item;
  if(!tail) tail = head;
}

int stack::retrieve()
{
```

```
    int i;
    list *p;

    if(!head) {
      cout << "List empty.\n";
      return 0;
    }

    // remove from start of list
    i = head->num;
    p = head;
    head = head->next;
    delete p;

    return i;
}

// Create a sorted list.
class sorted : public list {
public:
  void store(int i);
  int retrieve();
};

void sorted::store(int i)
{
  list *item;
  list *p, *p2;

  item = new sorted;
  if(!item) {
    cout << "Allocation error.\n";
    exit(1);

  }
  item->num = i;

  // find where to put next item
  p = head;
  p2 = NULL;
  while(p) { // goes in middle
    if(p->num > i) {
      item->next = p;
      if(p2) p2->next = item;  // not 1st element
      if(p==head) head = item; // new 1st element
```

```
      break;
    }
    p2 = p;
    p = p->next;
  }
  if(!p) { // goes on end
    if(tail) tail->next = item;
    tail = item;
    item->next = NULL;
  }
  if(!head) // is first element
    head = item;
}

int sorted::retrieve()
{
  int i;
  list *p;

  if(!head) {
    cout << "List empty.\n";
    return 0;
  }

  // remove from start of list
  i = head->num;
  p = head;
  head = head->next;
  delete p;

  return i;
}

int main()
{
  list *p;

  // demonstrate queue
  queue q_ob;
  p = &q_ob; // point to queue

  p->store(1);
  p->store(2);
  p->store(3);
```

```
        cout << "Queue: ";
        cout << p->retrieve();
        cout << p->retrieve();
        cout << p->retrieve();

        cout << '\n';

        // demonstrate stack
        stack s_ob;
        p = &s_ob; // point to stack

        p->store(1);
        p->store(2);
        p->store(3);

        cout << "Stack: ";
        cout << p->retrieve();
        cout << p->retrieve();
        cout << p->retrieve();

        cout << '\n';

        // demonstrate sorted list
        sorted sorted_ob;
        p = &sorted_ob;

        p->store(4);
        p->store(1);
        p->store(3);
        p->store(9);
        p->store(5);

        cout << "Sorted: ";
        cout << p->retrieve();
        cout << p->retrieve();
        cout << p->retrieve();
        cout << p->retrieve();
        cout << p->retrieve();

        cout << '\n';


        return 0;
}
```

■■■■ **M**ASTERY SKILLS CHECK: Chapter 10

1. A virtual function is essentially a placeholder function that is declared in a base class and that is redefined by a class derived from that base. The process of redefinition is called overriding.

2. Nonmember functions and constructor functions cannot be made virtual.

3. A virtual function supports run-time polymorphism through the use of base class pointers. When a base class pointer points to an object of a derived class containing a virtual function, the specific function called is determined by the type of object being pointed to.

4. A pure virtual function is one that contains no definition relative to the base class.

5. An abstract class is a base class that contains at least one pure virtual function. A polymorphic class is one that contains at least one virtual function.

6. The fragment is incorrect because the redefinition of a virtual function must have the same return type and type and number of parameters as the original function. In this case, the redefinition of **f( )** differs in the number of its parameters.

7. Yes.

■■■■ **C**UMULATIVE SKILLS CHECK: Chapter 10

1.
```cpp
// Demonstrate virtual functions.
#include <iostream>
#include <cstdlib>
using namespace std;

class list {
public:
  list *head;  // pointer to start of list
  list *tail;  // pointer to end of list
  list *next;  // pointer to next item
  int num; // value to be stored

  list() { head = tail = next = NULL; }
  virtual void store(int i) = 0;
  virtual int retrieve() = 0;
```

```
};

// Create a queue-type list.
class queue : public list {
public:
  void store(int i);
  int retrieve();
  queue operator+(int i) { store(i); return *this; }
  int operator--(int unused) { return retrieve(); }
};

void queue::store(int i)
{
  list *item;

  item = new queue;
  if(!item) {
    cout << "Allocation error.\n";
    exit(1);
  }
  item->num = i;

  // put on end of list
  if(tail) tail->next = item;
  tail = item;
  item->next = NULL;
  if(!head) head = tail;
}

int queue::retrieve()
{
  int i;
  list *p;

  if(!head) {
    cout << "List empty.\n";
    return 0;
  }

  // remove from start of list
  i = head->num;
  p = head;
  head = head->next;
  delete p;
```

```
      return i;
}

// Create a stack-type list.
class stack : public list {
public:
  void store(int i);
  int retrieve();
  stack operator+(int i) { store(i); return *this; }
  int operator--(int unused) { return retrieve(); }
};

void stack::store(int i)
{
  list *item;

  item = new stack;
  if(!item) {
    cout << "Allocation error.\n";
    exit(1);
  }
  item->num = i;

  // put on front of list for stack-like operation
  if(head) item->next = head;
  head = item;
  if(!tail) tail = head;
}

int stack::retrieve()
{
  int i;
  list *p;

  if(!head) {
    cout << "List empty.\n";
    return 0;
  }

  // remove from start of list
  i = head->num;
  p = head;
  head = head->next;
  delete p;
```

```
      return i;
    }

    int main()
    {
      // demonstrate queue
      queue q_ob;

      q_ob + 1;
      q_ob + 2;
      q_ob + 3;

      cout << "Queue: ";
      cout << q_ob--;
      cout << q_ob--;
      cout << q_ob--;

      cout << '\n';

      // demonstrate stack
      stack s_ob;

      s_ob + 1;
      s_ob + 2;
      s_ob + 3;

      cout << "Stack: ";
      cout << s_ob--;
      cout << s_ob--;
      cout << s_ob--;

      cout << '\n';

      return 0;
    }
```

2. Virtual functions differ from overloaded functions in that overloaded functions *must* differ in either the number of parameters or the type of parameters. An overridden virtual function must have exactly the same prototype (that is, the same return type and the same type and number of parameters) as the original function.

■■■■ *R*EVIEW SKILLS CHECK: *Chapter 11*

1. A virtual function is a function that is declared as **virtual** by a base class and then overridden by a derived class.

2. A pure virtual function is one that has no body defined within the base class. This means that the function must be overridden by a derived class. A base class that contains at least one pure virtual function is called an abstract class.

3. The missing words are "virtual" and "base".

4. If a derived class does not override a non-pure virtual function, the derived class will use the base class's version of the virtual function.

5. The main advantage of run-time polymorphism is flexibility. The main disadvantage is loss of execution speed.

■■■ 11.1 *E*XERCISES

2.
```
#include <iostream>
using namespace std;

template <class X> X min(X a, X b)
{
  if(a<=b) return a;
  else return b;
}

int main()
{
  cout << min(12.2, 2.0);
  cout << endl;
  cout << min(3, 4);
  cout << endl;
  cout << min('c', 'a');
  return 0;
}
```

3.
```
#include <iostream>
#include <cstring>
using namespace std;

template <class X> int find(X object, X *list, int size)
```

```
{
  int i;

  for(i=0; i<size; i++)
    if(object == list[i]) return i;
  return -1;
}

int main()
{
  int a[] = {1, 2, 3, 4};
  char *c = "this is a test";
  double d[] = {1.1, 2.2, 3.3};

  cout << find(3, a, 4);
  cout << endl;
  cout << find('a', c, (int) strlen(c));
  cout << endl;
  cout << find(0.0, d, 3);

  return 0;
}
```

4. Generic functions are valuable because they allow you to define a general algorithm that can be applied to various types of data. (That is, specific versions of the algorithm need not be explicitly created by you.) Generic functions further help implement the concept of "one interface, multiple methods," which is a common theme in C++ programming.

11.2   *E*XERCISES

2.
```
// Create a generic queue.
#include <iostream>
using namespace std;

#define SIZE 100

template <class Qtype> class q_type {
  Qtype queue[SIZE]; // holds the queue
  int head, tail; // indices of head and tail
public:
  q_type() { head = tail = 0; }
```

```
  void q(Qtype num); // store
  Qtype deq();   // retrieve
};

// Put value on queue.
template <class Qtype> void q_type<Qtype>::q(Qtype num)
{
  if(tail+1==head || (tail+1==SIZE && !head)) {
    cout << "Queue is full.\n";
    return;
  }
  tail++;
  if(tail==SIZE) tail = 0; // cycle around
  queue[tail] = num;
}

// Remove value from queue.
template <class Qtype> Qtype q_type<Qtype>::deq()
{
  if(head == tail) {
    cout << "Queue is empty.\n";
    return 0;  // or some other error indicator
  }
  head++;
  if(head==SIZE) head = 0; // cycle around
  return queue[head];
}

int main()
{
  q_type<int> q1;
  q_type<char> q2;
  int i;

  for(i=1; i<=10; i++) {
    q1.q(i);
    q2.q(i-1+'A');
  }

  for(i=1; i<=10; i++) {
    cout << "Dequeue 1: " << q1.deq() << "\n";
    cout << "Dequeue 2: " << q2.deq() << "\n";
  }
```

```
    return 0;
  }
```

3.
```cpp
#include <iostream>
using namespace std;

template <class X> class input {
  X data;
public:
  input(char *s, X min, X max);
  // ...
};

template <class X>
input<X>::input(char *s, X min, X max)
{
  do {
    cout << s << ": ";
    cin >> data;
  } while( data < min || data > max);
}

int main()
{
  input<int> i("enter int", 0, 10);
  input<char> c("enter char", 'A', 'Z');

  return 0;
}
```

11.3 ___EXERCISES___

2. The **throw** is called before execution passes through a **try** block.

3. A character exception is thrown, but the **catch** statement will handle only a character pointer. (That is, there is no corresponding **catch** statement to handle the character exception.)

4. If an exception is thrown for which there is no corresponding **catch**, **terminate( )** is called and abnormal program termination might occur.

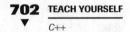

11.4 EXERCISES

2. There is no corresponding **catch** statement for the **throw**.

3. One way to fix the problem is to create a **catch(int)** handler. Another way to fix it is to catch all exceptions with a **catch(...)** handler.

4. **catch(...)** catches all exceptions.

5.
```cpp
#include <iostream>
#include <cstdlib>
using namespace std;

double divide(double a, double b)
{
  try {
    if(!b) throw(b);
  }
  catch(double) {
    cout << "Cannot divide by zero.\n";
    exit(1);
  }
  return a/b;
}

int main()
{
  cout << divide(10.0, 2.5) << endl;
  cout << divide(10.0, 0.0);

  return 0;
}
```

11.5 EXERCISES

1. By default, **new** throws an exception when an allocation error occurs. The **nothrow** version of **new** returns a null pointer if memory cannot be allocated.

2.
```cpp
p = new(nothrow) int;

if(!p) {
  cout << "Allocation error.\n";
  // ...
```

```
  }

  try {
    p = new int;
  } catch(bad_alloc ba) {
    cout << "Allocation error.\n";
    // ...
  }
```

M*ASTERY SKILLS CHECK: *Chapter 11

1.
```
#include <iostream>
#include <cstring>
using namespace std;

// A generic mode-finding function.
template <class X> X mode(X *data, int size)
{
  register int t, w;
  X md, oldmd;
  int count, oldcount;

  oldmd = 0;
  oldcount = 0;
  for(t=0; t<size; t++) {
    md = data[t];
    count = 1;
    for(w = t+1; w < size; w++)
      if(md==data[w]) count++;
    if(count > oldcount) {
      oldmd = md;
      oldcount = count;
    }
  }
  return oldmd;
}

int main()
{
  int i[] = { 1, 2, 3, 4, 2, 3, 2, 2, 1, 5};
  char *p = "this is a test";
```

```
      cout << "mode of i: " << mode(i, 10) << endl;
      cout << "mode of p: " << mode(p, (int) strlen(p));

      return 0;
    }
```

2.
```
   #include <iostream>
   using namespace std;

   template <class X> X sum(X *data, int size)
   {
     int i;
     X result = 0;

     for(i=0; i<size; i++) result += data[i];

     return result;
   }

   int main()
   {
     int i[] = {1, 2, 3, 4};
     double d[] = {1.1, 2.2, 3.3, 4.4};

     cout << sum(i, 4) << endl;
     cout << sum(d, 4) << endl;

     return 0;
   }
```

3.
```
   #include <iostream>
   using namespace std;

   // A generic bubble sort.
   template <class X> void bubble(X *data, int size)
   {
     register int a, b;
     X t;

     for(a=1; a < size; a++)
       for(b=size-1; b >= a; b--)
         if(data[b-1] > data[b]) {
           t = data[b-1];
           data[b-1] = data[b];
           data[b] = t;
```

```
        }
    }

    int main()
    {
      int i[] = {3, 2, 5, 6, 1, 8, 9, 3, 6, 9};
      double d[] = {1.2, 5.5, 2.2, 3.3};
      int j;

      bubble(i, 10); // sort ints
      bubble(d, 4);  // sort doubles

      for(j=0; j<10; j++) cout << i[j] << ' ';
      cout << endl;

      for(j=0; j<4; j++) cout << d[j] << ' ';
      cout << endl;

      return 0;
    }
```

4.
```
   /* This function demonstrates a generic stack that
       holds two values. */
   #include <iostream>
   using namespace std;

   #define SIZE 10

   // Create a generic stack class
   template <class StackType> class stack {
     StackType stck[SIZE][2]; // holds the stack
     int tos; // index of top of stack

   public:
     void init() { tos = 0; }
     void push(StackType ob, StackType ob2);
     StackType pop(StackType &ob2);
   };

   // Push objects.
   template <class StackType>
   void stack<StackType>::push(StackType ob, StackType ob2)
   {
     if(tos==SIZE) {
       cout << "Stack is full.\n";
```

```
      return;
    }
    stck[tos][0] = ob;
    stck[tos][1] = ob2;
    tos++;
}

// Pop objects.
template <class StackType>
StackType stack<StackType>::pop(StackType &ob2)
{
    if(tos==0) {
      cout << "Stack is empty.\n";
      return 0; // return null on empty stack
    }
    tos--;
    ob2 = stck[tos][1];
    return stck[tos][0];
}

int main()
{
    // Demonstrate character stacks.
    stack<char> s1, s2;  // create two stacks
    int i;
    char ch;

    // initialize the stacks
    s1.init();
    s2.init();

    s1.push('a', 'b');
    s2.push('x', 'z');
    s1.push('b', 'd');
    s2.push('y', 'e');
    s1.push('c', 'a');
    s2.push('z', 'x');

    for(i=0; i<3; i++) {
      cout << "Pop s1: " << s1.pop(ch);
      cout << ' ' << ch << "\n";
    }
    for(i=0; i<3; i++) {
      cout << "Pop s2: " << s2.pop(ch);
      cout << ' ' << ch << "\n";
```

```
    }

    // demonstrate double stacks
    stack<double> ds1, ds2;  // create two stacks
    double d;

    // initialize the stacks
    ds1.init();
    ds2.init();

    ds1.push(1.1, 2.0);
    ds2.push(2.2, 3.0);
    ds1.push(3.3, 4.0);
    ds2.push(4.4, 5.0);
    ds1.push(5.5, 6.0);
    ds2.push(6.6, 7.0);

    for(i=0; i<3; i++) {
      cout << "Pop ds1: " << ds1.pop(d);
      cout << ' '<< d << "\n";
    }

    for(i=0; i<3; i++) {
      cout << "Pop ds2: " << ds2.pop(d);
      cout << ' '<< d << "\n";
    }

    return 0;
  }
```

5. The general forms of **try**, **catch**, and **throw** are shown here:

```
try {
 // try block
 throw exp;
}
catch(type arg) {
 // ...
}
```

6.
```
/* This function demonstrates a generic stack
    that includes exception handling. */
#include <iostream>
```

```
using namespace std;

#define SIZE 10

// Create a generic stack class
template <class StackType> class stack {
  StackType stck[SIZE]; // holds the stack
  int tos; // index of top of stack

public:
  void init() { tos = 0; } // initialize stack
  void push(StackType ch); // push object on stack
  StackType pop(); // pop object from stack
};

// Push an object.
template <class StackType>
void stack<StackType>::push(StackType ob)
{
  try {
    if(tos==SIZE) throw SIZE;
  }
  catch(int) {
    cout << "Stack is full.\n";
    return;
  }
  stck[tos] = ob;
  tos++;
}

// Pop an object.
template <class StackType>
StackType stack<StackType>::pop()
{
  try {
    if(tos==0) throw 0;
  }
  catch(int) {
    cout << "Stack is empty.\n";
    return 0; // return null on empty stack
  }
  tos--;
  return stck[tos];
}
```

```
int main()
{
  // Demonstrate character stacks.
  stack<char> s1, s2;  // create two stacks
  int i;
  // initialize the stacks
  s1.init();
  s2.init();

  s1.push('a');
  s2.push('x');
  s1.push('b');
  s2.push('y');
  s1.push('c');
  s2.push('z');

  for(i=0; i<3; i++) cout << "Pop s1: " << s1.pop() << "\n";
  for(i=0; i<4; i++) cout << "Pop s2: " << s2.pop() << "\n";

  // demonstrate double stacks
  stack<double> ds1, ds2;  // create two stacks

  // initialize the stacks
  ds1.init();
  ds2.init();

  ds1.push(1.1);
  ds2.push(2.2);
  ds1.push(3.3);
  ds2.push(4.4);
  ds1.push(5.5);
  ds2.push(6.6);

  for(i=0; i<3; i++) cout << "Pop ds1: " << ds1.pop() << "\n";
  for(i=0; i<4; i++) cout << "Pop ds2: " << ds2.pop() << "\n";

  return 0;
}
```

8. If **new** throws an exception when an allocation error occurs,
   you can be sure that the error will be handled one way or
   another—even if only by abnormal program termination. In
   contrast, an allocation failure that is reported by **new**'s return of
   a null pointer can be overlooked if you forget to check for this

possibility. The trouble is that when your program attempts to use the null pointer, it might work for a while, then behave erratically, and finally crash in unpredictable (and unduplicatable) ways. This is a very difficult type of bug to diagnose.

REVIEW SKILLS CHECK: Chapter 12

1. In C++, a generic function defines a general set of operations that will be applied to various types of data. It is implemented with the keyword **template**. Its general form is shown here:

   template <class *Ttype*> *ret-type func-name(param-list)*
   {
       // ...
   }

2. In C++, a generic class defines all operations that relate to that class, but the actual data is specified as a parameter when an object of that class is created. Its general form is shown here:

   template <class *Ttype*> class *class-name*
   {
       // ...
   }

3.
```cpp
#include <iostream>
using namespace std;

// Return a to the b.
template <class X> X gexp(X a, X b)
{
    X i, result=1;

    for(i=0; i<b; i++) result *= a;

    return result;
}

int main()
{
    cout << gexp(2, 3) << endl;
```

```
    cout << gexp(10.0, 2.0);

    return 0;
  }
```

4.
```
#include <iostream>
#include <fstream>
using namespace std;

template <class CoordType> class coord {
  CoordType x, y;
public:
  coord(CoordType i, CoordType j) { x = i; y = j; }
  void show() { cout << x << ", " << y << endl; }
};

int main()
{
  coord<int> o1(1, 2), o2(3, 4);

  o1.show();
  o2.show();

  coord<double> o3(0.0, 0.23), o4(10.19, 3.098);

  o3.show();
  o4.show();

  return 0;
}
```

5. **try**, **catch**, and **throw** work together like this: Put all statements that you wish to monitor for exceptions within a **try** block. If an exception occurs, throw that exception using **throw** and handle it with a corresponding **catch** statement.

6. No.

7. **terminate( )** is called when an exception is thrown for which there is no corresponding **catch** statement. **unexpected( )** is called when an attempt is made to throw an exception out of a function that is not specified in the function's **throws** clause.

8. **catch(...)**

12.1	**E**XERCISES

1. RTTI is necessary to C++ because it is not always possible to know at compile time what type of object is being pointed to by a base class pointer or referenced by a base class reference.

2. Here is the output produced when **BaseClass** is no longer a polymorphic class.

```
Typeid of i is int
p is pointing to an object of type class BaseClass
p is pointing to an object of type class BaseClass
p is pointing to an object of type class BaseClass
```

3. Yes.

4. `if(typeid(*p) == typeid(D2)) ...`

5. False. Although the same template class is used, the type of data used by each version is different.

12.2	**E**XERCISES

1. The **dynamic_cast** operator determines the validity of a polymorphic cast.

2.
```
#include <iostream>
#include <typeinfo>
using namespace std;

class B {
  virtual void f() {}
};

class D1: public B {
  void f() {}
};

class D2: public B {
  void f() {}
};

int main()
{
  B *p;
```

```
        D2 ob;

        p = dynamic_cast<D2 *> (&ob);

        if(p) cout << "Cast OK";
        else cout << "Cast Fails";

        return 0;
    }
```

3. ```
   int main()
   {
       int i;
       Shape *p;

       for(i=0; i<10; i++) {
         p = generator(); // get next object

         cout << typeid(*p).name() << endl;

         // draw object only if it is not a NullShape
         if(!dynamic_cast<NullShape *> (p))
           p->example();
       }

       return 0;
   }
   ```

4. No. **Bp** and **Dp** are pointers to two fundamentally different types of objects.

12.3 *EXERCISES*

1. The new casting operators provide safer, more explicit ways to perform casts.

2. ```
   #include <iostream>
   using namespace std;

   void f(const double &i)
   {
     double &v = const_cast<double &> (i);

     v = 100.0;
   ```

```
}

int main()
{
  double x = 98.6;

  cout << x << endl;
  f(x);
  cout << x << endl;

  return 0;
}
```

3. Since **const_cast** overrides the **const** specifier, it allows unexpected modifications to objects.

*M*ASTERY SKILLS CHECK: *Chapter 12*

1. The **typeid** operator returns a reference to an object of the class **type_info** that contains type information.

2. You must include **< typeinfo >** in order to use **typeid**.

3. The new casting operators are shown here.

Operator	Purpose
dynamic_cast	Performs a polymorphic cast
reinterpret_cast	Converts one type of pointer into another
static_cast	Performs a "normal" cast
const_cast	Casts away **const**-ness

4.
```
#include <iostream>
#include <typeinfo>
using namespace std;

class A {
  virtual void f() {}
};

class B : public A {
};
```

```
class C: public B {
};

int main()
{
  A *p, a_ob;
  B b_ob;
  C c_ob;
  int i;

  cout << "Enter 0 for A objects, ";
  cout << "1 for B objects or ";
  cout << "2 for C objects.\n";

  cin >> i;

  if(i==1) p = &b_ob;
  else if(i==2) p = &c_ob;
  else p = &a_ob;

  if(typeid(*p) == typeid(A))
    cout << "A object";
  if(typeid(*p) == typeid(B))
    cout << "B object";
  if(typeid(*p) == typeid(C))
    cout << "C object";

  return 0;
}
```

5. The **dynamic_cast** operator can replace **typeid** in situations in which **typeid** is being used to determine the validity of a polymorphic cast.

6. The **typeid** operator returns a reference to a **type_info** object.

CUMULATIVE SKILLS CHECK: Chapter 12

1. Here is a version of **generator( )** that uses exception handling to check for an allocation failure.

```
// Use exception handling to check for allocation failure.
Shape *generator()
{
```

```
          try {
            switch(rand() % 4) {
              case 0:
                return new Line;
              case 1:
                return new Rectangle;
              case 2:
                return new Triangle;
              case 3:
                return new NullShape;
            }
          } catch (bad_alloc ba) {
            return NULL;
          }
          return NULL;
        }
```

2. Here is **generator( )** recoded to use **new(nothrow)**.

```
// Use new(nothrow).
Shape *generator()
{
  Shape *temp;

  switch(rand() % 4) {
    case 0:
      temp = new(nothrow) Line;
      break;
    case 1:
      temp = new(nothrow) Rectangle;
      break;
    case 2:
      temp = new(nothrow) Triangle;
      break;
    case 3:
      temp = new(nothrow) NullShape;
  }

  if(temp) return temp;
  else return NULL;
}
```

REVIEW SKILLS CHECK: Chapter 13

1. In addition to the C-like cast, the casting operators are

Operator	Purpose
dynamic_cast	Performs a polymorphic cast
reinterpret_cast	Converts one type of pointer into another
static_cast	Performs a "normal" cast
const_cast	Casts away **const**-ness

2. **type_info** is a class that encapsulates information about a data type. A reference to a **type_info** object is returned by the **typeid** operator.

3. **typeid**

4.
```
if(typeid(Derived) == typeid(*p))
   cout << "p points to derived object\n";
else
   cout << "p points to a Base object\n";
```

5. The missing word is "derived."

6. No.

13.1 **E**XERCISES

1.
```
/* Convert spaces to ls without the
     "using namespace std" statement. */
#include <iostream>
#include <fstream>

int main(int argc, char *argv[])
{
  if(argc!=3) {
    std::cout << "Usage: CONVERT <input> <output>\n";
    return 1;
  }

  std::ifstream fin(argv[1]); // open input file
  std::ofstream fout(argv[2]);  // create output file

  if(!fout) {
```

```
      std::cout << "Cannot open output file.\n";
      return 1;
    }
    if(!fin) {
      std::cout << "Cannot open input file.\n";
      return 1;
    }

    char ch;

    fin.unsetf(std::ios::skipws);  // do not skip spaces
    while(!fin.eof()) {
      fin >> ch;
      if(ch==' ') ch = '|';
      if(!fin.eof()) fout << ch;
    }

    fin.close();
    fout.close();

    return 0;
  }
```

2. A unnamed namespace restricts the scope of the identifiers declared within it to its file.

3. This form of **using**,

   using *name::member*;

   brings only the specified member into the current namespace. The form

   using namespace *name*;

   brings the entire namespace into view.

4. Since the entire C++ standard library, including the streams **cin** and **cout**, is declared within the **std** namespace, for convenience most programs have brought the **std** namespace into view. This allows the standard library names to be used directly without qualification by **std::**. For many programs, an alternative would be to simply qualify all references to the standard library with **std::**. Another alternative is to create **using** statements for only **std::cin** or **std::cout**.

5. By putting library code into its own namespace you reduce the possibility of name conflicts.

1.
```cpp
// Convert string type to integer.
#include <iostream>
#include <cstring>
using namespace std;

class strtype {
  char str[80];
  int len;
public:
  strtype(char *s) { strcpy(str, s); len = strlen(s); }
  operator char *() { return str; }
  operator int() { return len; }
};

int main()
{
  strtype s("Conversion functions are convenient.");
  char *p;
  int l;

  l = s; // convert s to integer - which is length of string
  p = s; // convert s to char * - which is pointer to string

  cout << "The string:\n";
  cout << p << "\nis " << l << " chars long.\n";

  return 0;
}
```

2.
```cpp
#include <iostream>
using namespace std;

int p(int base, int exp);

class pwr {
  int base;
  int exp;
public:
  pwr(int b, int e) { base = b; exp = e; }
```

```
  operator int() { return p(base, exp); }
};

// Return base to the exp power.
int p(int base, int exp)
{
  int temp;

  for(temp=1; exp; exp--) temp = temp * base;

  return temp;
}

 int main()
{
  pwr o1(2, 3), o2(3, 3);
  int result;

  result = o1;
  cout << result << '\n';

  result = o2;
  cout << result << '\n';

  // can use directly in a cout statement like this:
  cout << o1+100 << '\n';

  return 0;
}
```

13.3 EXERCISES

1.
```
// A shared resource example that traces output.
#include <iostream>
#include <cstring>
using namespace std;

class output {
  static char outbuf[255]; // this is the shared resource
  static int inuse; // buffer available if 0; in use otherwise
  static int oindex; // index of outbuf
  char str[80];
  int i; // index of next char in str
  int who; // identifies the object, must be > 0
```

```
public:
  output(int w, char *s) { strcpy(str, s); i = 0; who = w; }

  /* This function returns -1 if waiting for buffer,
     it returns 0 if it is done outputting, and
     it returns who if it is still using the buffer.
  */
  int putbuf()
  {
    if(!str[i]) { // done outputting
      inuse = 0; // release buffer
      return 0; // signal termination
    }
    if(!inuse) inuse = who; // get buffer
    if(inuse != who) {
      cout << "Process " << who << " Currently blocked\n";
      return -1; // in use by someone else
    }
    if(str[i]) { // still chars to output
      outbuf[oindex] = str[i];
      cout << "Process " << who << " sending char\n";
      i++; oindex++;
      outbuf[oindex] = '\0';  // always keep null-terminated
      return 1;
    }
    return 0;
  }
  void show() { cout << outbuf << '\n'; }
};

char output::outbuf[255]; // this is the shared resource
int output::inuse = 0; // buffer available if 0; in use otherwise
int output::oindex = 0; // index of outbuf

int main()
{
  output o1(1, "This is a test"), o2(2, " of statics");

  while(o1.putbuf() | o2.putbuf()) ; // output chars

  o1.show();

  return 0;
}
```

2.
```
#include <iostream>
#include <new>
using namespace std;

class test {
  static int count;
public:
  test() { count++; }
  ~test() { count--; }
  int getcount() { return count; }
};

int test::count = 0;

int main()
{
  test o1, o2, o3;

  cout << o1.getcount() << " objects in existence\n";

  test *p;

  /* Watch for allocation errors using both
     old-style and new-style error handling. */
  try {
    p = new test; // allocate an object
    if(!p) { // old-style
      cout << "Allocation error\n";
      return 1;
    }
  } catch(bad_alloc ba) { // new-style
      cout << "Allocation error\n";
      return 1;
  }

  cout << o1.getcount();
  cout << " objects in existence after allocation\n";

  // delete object
  delete p;

  cout << o1.getcount();
  cout << " objects in existence after deletion\n";
```

```
    return 0;
}
```

1. To fix the program, simply make **current** mutable so that it can be modified by **counting( )**, which is a **const** member function. The solution is shown here:

```cpp
// This program is now fixed.
#include <iostream>
using namespace std;

class CountDown {
  int incr;
  int target;
  mutable int current; // make current mutable
public:
  CountDown(int delay, int i=1) {
    target = delay;
    incr = i;
    current = 0;
  }

  bool counting() const {
    current += incr;
    if(current >= target) {
      cout << "\a";
      return false;
    }
    cout << current << " ";
    return true;
  }
};

int main()
{
  CountDown ob(100, 2);

  while(ob.counting()) ;

  return 0;
}
```

2. No. If it were possible for a **const** member function to call a non-**const** member function, the non-**const** function could be used to modify the invoking object.

![13.5] EXERCISES

1. Yes.

2. Yes, because C++ defines an automatic conversion from **int** to **double**.

3. One potential problem with implicit constructor conversions is that you might forget that such a conversion is taking place. For example, an implicit conversion that takes place in an assignment statement looks a lot like an overloaded assignment operator. However, their actions are not necessarily the same. When you are creating classes that others will be using, it might be wise to prevent implicit constructor conversions to avoid misconceptions on the part of the users of your classes.

![13.7] EXERCISES

1.
```
/* This version displays the number of chars
   written to buf.
*/
#include <iostream>
#include <strstream>
using namespace std;

int main()
{
  char buf[255];

  ostrstream ostr(buf, sizeof buf);

  ostr << "Array-based I/O uses streams just like ";
  ostr << "'normal' I/O\n" << 100;
  ostr << ' ' << 123.23 << '\n';

  // you can use manipulators, too
  ostr << hex << 100 << ' ';
  // or format flags
  ostr.setf(ios::scientific);
```

```
      ostr << dec << 123.23;
      ostr << endl << ends; // ensure that buffer is
                            //  null-terminated

      // show resultant string
      cout << buf;

      cout << ostr.pcount();

      return 0;
    }
```

2. ```
   /* Use array-based I/O to copy contents of one
        array into another.
   */
   #include <iostream>
   #include <strstream>
   using namespace std;

   char inbuf[] = "This is a test of C++ array-based I/O";
   char outbuf[255];

   int main()
   {
     istrstream istr(inbuf);
     ostrstream ostr(outbuf, sizeof outbuf);

     char ch;

     while(!istr.eof()) {
       istr.get(ch);
       if(!istr.eof()) ostr.put(ch);
     }
     ostr.put('\0'); // null terminate

     cout << "Input: " << inbuf << '\n';
     cout << "Output: " << outbuf << '\n';

     return 0;
   }
   ```

3. ```
   // Convert string to float.
   #include <iostream>
   #include <strstream>
   ```

```
using namespace std;

int main()
{
  float f;
  char s[] = "1234.564";  // float represented as string

  istrstream istr(s);

  // Convert to internal representation the easy way!
  istr >> f;

  cout << "Converted form: " << f << '\n';

  return 0;
}
```

*M*ASTERY SKILLS CHECK: *Chapter 13*

1. Unlike a normal member variable, for which each object has its own copy, only one copy of a **static** member variable exists, and it is shared by all objects of that class.

2. To use array-based I/O, include **< strstream >**.

3. No.

4. `extern "C" int counter();`

5. A conversion function simply converts an object into a value compatible with another type. Conversion functions are typically used to convert objects into values compatible with the built-in data types.

6. The **explicit** keyword applies only to constructors. It prevents implicit constructor conversions.

7. A **const** member function cannot modify the object that invokes it.

8. A namespace, which is declared with the **namespace** keyword, defines a declarative region.

9. The keyword **mutable** allows a **const** member function to modify a data member of its class.

CUMULATIVE SKILLS CHECK: *Chapter 13*

1. Yes. In cases in which the implicit conversion performs the same action that would be performed by an overloaded assignment operator for the type of the constructor's parameter, there is no need to overload the assignment operator.

2. Yes.

3. New libraries can be contained within their own namespaces, thus preventing name conflicts with other code. This benefit applies even to old code that is being updated with new libraries.

REVIEW SKILLS CHECK: *Chapter 14*

1. Namespaces were added to C++ to localize identifier names in order to prevent name collisions. The problem of name collisions was becoming severe because of the growth of third-party class libraries.

2. To specify a member function as **const**, follow the function's parameter list with the keyword **const**. Here's an example:

```
int f(int a) const;
```

3. False. **mutable** allows a member variable to be changed by a **const** member function.

4.
```
class X {
  int a, b;
public:
  X(int i, int j) { a = i, b = j; }
  operator int() { return a+b; }
};
```

5. True.

6. No. The **explicit** specifier prevents the automatic conversion from **int** to **Demo**.

14.1 **E**XERCISES

1. A container is an object that holds other objects. An algorithm is a routine that acts upon the contents of containers. An iterator is similar to a pointer.

2. Binary and unary.

3. The five types of iterators are random access, bidirectional, forward, input, and output.

14.3 **E**XERCISES

2. Any object stored in a vector must provide a default constructor.

3.
```cpp
// Store Coord objects in a vector.
#include <iostream>
#include <vector>
using namespace std;

class Coord {
public:
  int x, y;
  Coord() { x = y = 0; }
  Coord(int a, int b) { x = a; y = b; }
};

bool operator<(Coord a, Coord b)
{
  return (a.x+a.y) < (b.x+b.y);
}

bool operator==(Coord a, Coord b)
{
  return (a.x+a.y) == (b.x+b.y);
}

int main()
{
  vector<Coord> v;
  int i;

  for(i=0; i<10; i++)
    v.push_back(Coord(i, i));
```

```
      for(i=0; i<v.size(); i++)
        cout << v[i].x << "," << v[i].y << " ";

      cout << endl;

      for(i=0; i<v.size(); i++)
        v[i].x = v[i].x * 2;

      for(i=0; i<v.size(); i++)
        cout << v[i].x << "," << v[i].y << " ";

      return 0;
    }
```

14.4   EXERCISES

```
2. // List basics.
   #include <iostream>
   #include <list>
   using namespace std;

   int main()
   {
     list<char> lst; // create an empty list
     int i;

     for(i=0; i<10; i++) lst.push_back('A'+i);

     cout << "Size = " << lst.size() << endl;

     list<char>::iterator p;

     cout << "Contents: ";
     for(i=0; i<lst.size(); i++) {
       p = lst.begin();
       cout << *p;
       lst.pop_front();
       lst.push_back(*p); // put element on end of list
     }

     cout << endl;

     if(!lst.empty())
```

```
      cout << "List is not empty.\n";

    return 0;
}
```

This program displays the following output.

```
Size = 10
Contents: ABCDEFGHIJ
List is not empty.
```

In this approach, elements are removed from the front but put on the back. Thus, the list is not emptied. The loop that displays the list is controlled by obtaining the size of the list using **size( )**.

3.
```
// Merge two projects lists.
#include <iostream>
#include <list>
#include <cstring>
using namespace std;

class Project {
public:
  char name[40];
  int days_to_completion;
  Project() {
    strcpy(name, "");
    days_to_completion = 0;
  }
  Project(char *n, int d) {
    strcpy(name, n);
    days_to_completion = d;
  }

  void add_days(int i) {
    days_to_completion += i;
  }

  void sub_days(int i) {
    days_to_completion -= i;
  }

  bool completed() { return !days_to_completion; }

  void report() {
    cout << name << ": ";
```

```
      cout << days_to_completion;
      cout << " days left.\n";
    }
};

bool operator<(const Project &a, const Project &b)
{
  return a.days_to_completion < b.days_to_completion;
}

bool operator>(const Project &a, const Project &b)
{
  return a.days_to_completion > b.days_to_completion;
}

bool operator==(const Project &a, const Project &b)
{
  return a.days_to_completion == b.days_to_completion;
}

bool operator!=(const Project &a, const Project &b)
{
  return a.days_to_completion != b.days_to_completion;
}

int main()
{
  list<Project> proj;
  list<Project> proj2;

  proj.push_back(Project("Compiler", 35));
  proj.push_back(Project("Spreadsheet", 190));
  proj.push_back(Project("STL Implementation", 1000));

  proj2.push_back(Project("Database", 780));
  proj2.push_back(Project("Mail Merge", 50));
  proj2.push_back(Project("COM Objects", 300));

  proj.sort();
  proj2.sort();

  proj.merge(proj2); // merge projects

  list<Project>::iterator p = proj.begin();
```

```
    /* display projects */
    while(p != proj.end()) {
      p->report();
      p++;
    }

    return 0;
}
```

EXERCISES

2.
```
// A map of names and phone numbers.
#include <iostream>
#include <map>
#include <cstring>
using namespace std;

class name {
  char str[20];
public:
  name() { strcpy(str, ""); }
  name(char *s) { strcpy(str, s); }
  char *get() { return str; }
};

// must define less than relative to name objects
bool operator<(name a, name b)
{
    return strcmp(a.get(), b.get()) < 0;
}

class phonenum {
  char str[20];
public:
  phonenum() { strcmp(str, ""); }
  phonenum(char *s) { strcpy(str, s); }
  char *get() { return str; }
};


int main()
{
  map<name, phonenum> m;
```

```
// put names and phone numbers into map
m.insert(pair<name,
  phonenum>(name("Joe"), phonenum("555-4323")));
m.insert(pair<name,
  phonenum>(name("Tom"), phonenum("555-9784")));
m.insert(pair<name,
  phonenum>(name("Larry"), phonenum("212 555-9372")));
m.insert(pair<name,
  phonenum>(name("Tod"), phonenum("01 11 232-4232")));

// given a name, find phone number
char str[80];
cout << "Enter name: ";
cin >> str;

map<name, phonenum>::iterator p;

p = m.find(name(str));
if(p != m.end())
  cout << "Phone Number: " <<  p->second.get();
else
  cout << "Name not in map.\n";

return 0;
}
```

3. Yes.

14.6 EXERCISES

```
1. // Sort a vector using the sort algorithm.
   #include <iostream>
   #include <vector>
   #include <cstdlib>
   #include <algorithm>
   using namespace std;

   int main()
   {
     vector<char> v;
     int i;

     // create a vector of random characters
     for(i=0; i<10; i++)
```

```
      v.push_back('A'+ (rand()%26));

    cout << "Original contents: ";
    for(i=0; i<v.size(); i++)
      cout << v[i] << " ";

    cout << endl << endl;

    // sort the vector
    sort(v.begin(), v.end());

    cout << "Sorted contents: ";
    for(i=0; i<v.size(); i++)
      cout << v[i] << " ";

    return 0;
  }
```

2.
```
   // Merge two lists using the merge algorithm.
   #include <iostream>
   #include <list>
   #include <algorithm>
   using namespace std;

   int main()
   {
     list<char> lst1, lst2, lst3(20);
     int i;

     for(i=0; i<10; i+=2) lst1.push_back('A'+i);
     for(i=1; i<11; i+=2) lst2.push_back('A'+i);

     cout << "Contents of lst1: ";
     list<char>::iterator p = lst1.begin();
     while(p != lst1.end()) {
       cout << *p;
       p++;
     }
     cout << endl << endl;

     cout << "Contents of lst2: ";
     p = lst2.begin();
     while(p != lst2.end()) {
       cout << *p;
       p++;
```

```
      }
      cout << endl << endl;

      // now, merge the two lists
      merge(lst1.begin(), lst1.end(),
            lst2.begin(), lst2.end(),
            lst3.begin());

      cout << "Merged list:\n";
      p = lst3.begin();
      while(p != lst3.end()) {
        cout << *p;
        p++;
      }

      return 0;
    }
```

14.7   EXERCISES

```
1. #include <iostream>
   #include <string>
   #include <list>
   using namespace std;

   int main()
   {
     list<string> str;

     str.push_back(string("one"));
     str.push_back(string("two"));
     str.push_back(string("three"));
     str.push_back(string("four"));
     str.push_back(string("five"));
     str.push_back(string("six"));
     str.push_back(string("seven"));
     str.push_back(string("eight"));
     str.push_back(string("nine"));
     str.push_back(string("ten"));

     str.sort(); // sort the vector

     list<string>::iterator p = str.begin();
     while(p != str.end()) {
```

```
      cout << *p << " ";
      p++;
    }

    return 0;
  }
```

2.
```
  #include <iostream>
  #include <string>
  #include <algorithm>
  using namespace std;

  int main()
  {
    string str;

    cout << "Enter a string: ";
    cin >> str;

    int i = count(str.begin(), str.end(), 'e');

    cout << i << " of them are e.\n";

    return 0;
  }
```

3.
```
  #include <iostream>
  #include <string>
  #include <algorithm>
  #include <cctype>
  using namespace std;

  int main()
  {
    string str;

    cout << "Enter a string: ";
    cin >> str;

    int i = count_if(str.begin(), str.end(), islower);

    cout << i << " of them are lowercase.\n";

    return 0;
  }
```

4. **string** is a specialization of **basic_string**.

*M*ASTERY SKILLS CHECK: Chapter 14

1. The STL provides off-the-shelf, debugged versions of many common data structures and algorithms. Because the STL classes are templatized, they can be used with any type of data.

2. A container is an object that holds other objects. An iterator is similar to a pointer. An algorithm acts on the contents of containers.

3.
```cpp
#include <iostream>
#include <vector>
#include <list>
using namespace std;

int main()
{
  vector<int> v(10);
  list<int> lst;
  int i;

  for(i=0; i<10; i++) v[i] = i;

  for(i=0; i<10; i++)
    if(!(v[i]%2)) lst.push_back(v[i]);

  list<int>::iterator p = lst.begin();
  while(p != lst.end()) {
    cout << *p << " ";
    p++;
  }

  return 0;
}
```

4. The **string** type allows strings to be manipulated with operators. However, working with **string** objects is not as efficient as working with null-terminated character arrays.

5. A predicate is a function that returns either true or false.

Index